Lecture Notes in Computer Scien

Edited by G. Goos, J. Hartmanis, and J. van L

Springer
Berlin
Heidelberg
New York
Barcelona
Hong Kong
London
Milan
Paris
Tokyo

Yahiko Kambayashi   Werner Winiwarter
Masatoshi Arikawa (Eds.)

Data Warehousing and Knowledge Discovery

4th International Conference, DaWaK 2002
Aix-en-Provence, France, September 4-6, 2002
Proceedings

Springer

Series Editors

Gerhard Goos, Karlsruhe University, Germany
Juris Hartmanis, Cornell University, NY, USA
Jan van Leeuwen, Utrecht University, The Netherlands

Volume Editors

Yahiko Kambayashi
Kyoto University, Graduate School of Informatics
Yoshida-Honmachi, Sakyo-ku, Kyoto 606-8501, Japan
E-mail: yahiko@i.kyoto-u.ac.jp

Werner Winiwarter
University of Vienna, Institute for Computer Science and Business Informatics
Liebiggasse 4, 1010 Vienna, Austria
E-mail: werner.winiwarter@univie.ac.at

Masatoshi Arikawa
University of Tokyo, Center for Spatial Information Science (CSIS)
4-6-1, Komaba, Meguro-ku, Tokyo 153-8904, Japan
E-Mail: arikawa@csis.u-tokyo.ac.jp

Cataloging-in-Publication Data applied for

Die Deutsche Bibliothek - CIP-Einheitsaufnahme

Data warehousing and knowledge discovery : 4th international conference ;
proceedings / DaWaK 2002, Aix-en-Provence, France, September 4 - 6, 2002.
Yahiko Kambayashi ... (ed.). - Berlin ; Heidelberg ; New York ; Barcelona ;
Hong Kong ; London ; Milan ; Paris ; Tokyo : Springer, 2002
  (Lecture notes in computer science ; Vol. 2454)
  ISBN 3-540-44123-9

CR Subject Classification (1998): H.2, H.3, C.2, H.4, H.5, J.1

ISSN 0302-9743
ISBN 3-540-44123-9 Springer-Verlag Berlin Heidelberg New York

Springer-Verlag Berlin Heidelberg New York,
a member of BertelsmannSpringer Science+Business Media GmbH

http://www.springer.de

© Springer-Verlag Berlin Heidelberg 2002
Printed in Germany

Typesetting: Camera-ready by author, data conversion by PTP-Berlin, Stefan Sossna e.K.
Printed on acid-free paper   SPIN: 10871144   06/3142   5 4 3 2 1 0

Preface

Within the last few years Data Warehousing and Knowledge Discovery technology has established itself as a key technology for enterprises that wish to improve the quality of the results obtained from data analysis, decision support, and the automatic extraction of knowledge from data.

The Fourth International Conference on Data Warehousing and Knowledge Discovery (DaWaK 2002) continues a series of successful conferences dedicated to this topic. Its main objective is to bring together researchers and practitioners to discuss research issues and experience in developing and deploying data warehousing and knowledge discovery systems, applications, and solutions.

The conference focuses on the logical and physical design of data warehousing and knowledge discovery systems. The scope of the papers covers the most recent and relevant topics in the areas of association rules, clustering, Web mining, security, data mining techniques, data cleansing, applications, data warehouse design and maintenance, and OLAP. These proceedings contain the technical papers selected for presentation at the conference.

We received more than 100 papers from over 20 countries, and the program committee finally selected 32 papers. The conference program included one invited talk: "Text Mining Applications of a Shallow Parser" by Walter Daelemans, University of Antwerp, Belgium.

We would like to thank the DEXA 2002 Workshop General Chair (Roland Wagner) and the organizing committee of the 13th International Conference on Database and Expert Systems Applications (DEXA 2002) for their support and their cooperation. Many thanks go to Gabriela Wagner for providing a great deal of assistance as well as to Andreas Dreiling for administrating the conference management software. We are very indebted to all program committee members and external reviewers who reviewed the papers very carefully and in a timely manner. We would also like to thank all the authors who submitted their papers to DaWaK 2002; they provided us with an excellent technical program.

September 2002

Yahiko Kambayashi
Werner Winiwarter
Masatoshi Arikawa

Program Committee

General Chair
Yahiko Kambayashi, Kyoto University, Japan

Program Chairs
Werner Winiwarter, University of Vienna, Austria
Masatoshi Arikawa, University of Tokyo, Japan

Program Committee
Tatsuya Akutsu, Kyoto University, Japan
Hiroki Arimura, Kyushu University, Japan
Mike Bain, The University of New South Wales, Australia
Elena Baralis, Politecnico di Torino, Italy
Stefan Berchtold, stb software technology beratung gmbh, Germany
Jorge Bernardino, Polytechnic of Coimbra, Portugal
Anjali Bhargava, TRW, USA
Bharat K. Bhargava, Purdue University, USA
Sourav S. Bhowmick, Nanyang Technological University, Singapore
Ulrich Bodenhofer, Software Competence Center Hagenberg, Austria
Christian Böhm, Ludwig-Maximilians-University of Munich, Germany
Luca Cabibbo, Università degli Studi Roma Tre, Italy
Murray Campbell, IBM TJ Watson Research Center, USA
Tiziana Catarci, Università degli Studi di Roma "La Sapienza", Italy
Peter Chamoni, Gerhard-Mercator-University Duisburg, Germany
Arbee L. P. Chen, National Dong Hwa University, Taiwan
Janet Chen, Philips Research East Asia, Taiwan
Ming-Syan Chen, National Taiwan University, Taiwan
Sunil Choenni, Nyenrode University/ University of Twente, The Netherlands
Vic Ciesielski, RMIT University, Australia
Walter Daelemans, University of Antwerp, Belgium
Vasant Dhar, New York University, USA
Luc De Raedt, Albert-Ludwigs-University of Freiburg, Germany
Gillian Dobbie, The University of Auckland, New Zealand
Guozhu Dong, Wright State University, USA
Saso Dzeroski, J. Stefan Institute, Slovenia
Wolfgang Essmayr, Software Competence Center Hagenberg, Austria
Martin Ester, Ludwig-Maximilians-University of Munich, Germany
Vladimir Estivill-Castro, The University of Newcastle, Australia
Wenfei Fan, Temple University, USA
Li Min Fu, University of Florida, USA
Jean-Gabriel Ganascia, Université Paris VI, France
Minos Garofalakis, Bell Laboratories, USA
Ashish Ghosh, Indian Statistical Institute, India
Ananth Grama, Purdue University, USA
Marko Grobelnik, J. Stefan Institute, Slovenia

External Reviewers

Table of Contents

OLAP

Data Warehouse Maintenance

A Comparison between Query Languages for the Extraction of Association Rules

Marco Botta[1], Jean-Francois Boulicaut[2], Cyrille Masson[2], and Rosa Meo[1]

[1] Universitá di Torino, Dipartimento di Informatica,
corso Svizzera 185, 10149, Torino, Italy
[2] Institut National des Sciences Appliquées de Lyon,
69621 Villeurbanne cedex, France

Abstract. Recently inductive databases (IDBs) have been proposed to afford the problem of knowledge discovery from huge databases. With an IDB the user/analyst performs a set of very different operations on data using a special-purpose language, powerful enough to perform all the required manipulations, such as data preprocessing, pattern discovery and pattern post-processing. In this paper we present a comparison between query languages (MSQL, DMQL and MINE RULE) that have been proposed for association rules extraction in the last years and discuss their common features and differences. We present them using a set of examples, taken from the real practice of data mining. This allows us to define the language design guidelines, with particular attention to the open issues on IDBs.

1 Introduction

Knowledge Discovery in Databases (KDD) is a complex process which involves many steps that must be done sequentially. When considering the whole KDD process, the proposed approaches and querying tools are still unsatisfactory. The relation among the various proposals is also sometimes unclear because, at the moment, a general understanding of the fundamental primitives and principles that are necessary to support the search of knowledge in databases is still lacking.

In the cInQ project[1] we want to develop a new generation of databases, called *"inductive databases"*, suggested in [2]. This kind of databases integrates *raw data* with *knowledge* extracted from *raw data*, materialized under the form of patterns into a common framework that supports the KDD process. In this way, the KDD process consists essentially in a querying process, enabled by an ad-hoc, powerful and universal query language that can deal both with raw data or patterns. A few query languages can be considered as candidates for inductive databases. Most of the proposals emphasize one of the different phases of the KDD process. This paper is a critical evaluation of three proposals in the light of the IDBs' requirements: `MSQL` [3,4], `DMQL` [6,7] and `MINE RULE` [8,9].

The paper is organized as follows. Section 2 summarizes the desired properties of a language for mining inside an inductive database. Section 3 introduces

---

[1] Project (IST 2000-26469) partially funded by the EC IST Programme - FET.

Y. Kambayashi, W. Winiwarter, M. Arikawa (Eds.): DaWaK 2002, LNCS 2454, pp. 1–10, 2002.

the main features of the analyzed languages, whereas in Section 4 some real examples of queries are discussed, so that the comparison between the languages is straightforward. Finally Section 5 draws some conclusions.

2 Desired Properties of a Data Mining Language

A *query language* for IDBs, is an extension of a database query language that includes primitives for supporting the steps of a KDD process, that are:

- The selection of data to be mined. The language must offer the possibility to select (e.g., via standard queries but also by means of sampling), to manipulate and to query data and views in the database. It must also provide support for multi-dimensional data manipulation.
  DMQL and MINE RULE allow the selection of data. None of them has primitives for sampling. All of them allow multi-dimensional data manipulation (because this is inherent to SQL).
- The specification of the type of patterns to be mined. Clearly, real-life KDD processes need for different kinds of patterns like various types of descriptive rules, clusters or predictive models.
  DMQL considers different patterns beyond association rules.
- The specification of the needed background knowledge (e.g., the definition of a concept hierarchy).
  Even though both MINE RULE and MSQL can treat hierarchies if the relationship 'is-a' is represented in a companion relation, DMQL allows its explicit definition and use during the pattern extraction.
- The definition of constraints that the extracted patterns must satisfy. This implies that the language allows the user to define constraints that specify the interesting patterns (e.g., using measures like frequency, generality, coverage, similarity, etc).
  All the three languages allow the specification of various kinds of constraints based on rule elements, rule cardinality and aggregate values. They allow the specification of support and confidence measures. DMQL allows some other measures like novelty.
- The satisfaction of the *closure property* (by storing the results in the database).
  All the three languages satisfy this property.
- The post-processing of results. The language must allow to browse the patterns, apply selection templates, *cross over* patterns and data, e.g., by selecting the data in which some patterns hold, or aggregating results.
  MSQL is richer than the other two languages in its offer of few post-processing primitives (it has a dedicated operator, SelectRules). DMQL allows some visualization options. However, the three languages are quite poor for rule post-processing.

3 Query Languages for Rule Mining

MSQL has been described in [4,5], and designed at the Rutgers University, New Jersey, USA. The main features of MSQL, as stated by the authors, are the following: (1) *Ability to nest SQL expressions* such as sorting and grouping in a `MSQL` statement and allowing nested SQL queries. (2) Satisfaction of the *closure* property and availability of operators to further manipulate results of previous `MSQL` queries. (3) *cross-over between data and rules* with operations allowing to identify subsets of data satisfying or violating a given set of rules. (4) *distinction between rule generation and rule querying.* Indeed, as the volume of generated rules might explode, rules might be extensively generated only at querying time, and not at generation time.

The language comprises five basic statements: `GetRules` that generates rules into a rule base; `SelectRules` that queries the rule base; `Create Encoding` that efficiently encodes discrete values into continuous valued attributes; `satisfies` and `violates` that allow to cross-over data and rules, and that can be used in a data selection statement.

DMQL has been presented in [6,7] and designed at the Simon Fraser University, Canada. The language consists of the specification of four major primitives in data mining that manage: (1) the set of *relevant data* w.r.t. a data mining process; (2) the *kind of knowledge* to be discovered; (3) the *background knowledge*; (4) the *justification of the interestingness* of the knowledge (i.e., thresholds).

(1) This primitive is specified as a relational conventional query.

(2) This primitive may include association rules, classification rules (rules that assign data to disjoint classes according to the value of a chosen classifying attribute), characteristica (descriptions that constitute a summarization of the common properties in a given set of data), comparisons (descriptions that allow to compare the total number of tuples belonging to a class with different, contrasting classes), generalized relations (obtained by generalizing a set of data corresponding to low level concepts with data corresponding to higher level concepts according to a specified concept hierarchy).

(3) This primitive manages a set of concept hierarchies or generalization operators that assist the generalization processes.

(4) This primitive is included as a set of different constraints depending on the kind of target rules. For association rules, e.g., besides the classical support and confidence thresholds, `DMQL` allows the specification of noise (the minimum percentage of tuples in the database that must satisfy a rule so that it is not discarded) and rule novelty, i.e., electing the more specific rule.

MINE RULE proposal can be found in [8] and [9]. This operator extracts a set of association rules from the database and stores them back in the database in a separate relation. This language is an extension of SQL. Its main features are the following. (1) *Selection of the relevant set of data* for a data mining process; (2) Definition of the *structure of the rules* to be mined and of constraints applied at different granularity levels; (3) Definition of the *grouping condition* that determines which data of the relation can take part to an association rule; (4) Definition of *rule evaluation measures* (i.e., support and confidence thresholds).

The selection above mentioned as the first feature of `MINE RULE` is applied at different granularity levels, that is at the row level (selection of a subset of the rows of a relation) or at the group level (*group condition*). The second feature defines unidimensional association rule (i.e., its elements are the different values of the same dimension or attribute), or multidimensional one (each rule element involves the value of more attributes). Furthermore, rules constraints belong to two categories: the former ones are applied at the rule level (*mining conditions*), while the second ones (*cluster conditions*), are applied at the *body* or *head* level (i.e., the sets of rule elements that compose each rule).

4   Comparative Examples

We describe here a classical basket analysis problem that will serve as a running example troughout the paper: we are considering information of Table 1 and we are looking for association rules between bought items and customer's age for payments with a credit cards. We are considering a complete KDD process. We will consider two manipulations at the pre-processing step (selection of the items bought by credit card and encoding of the `age` attribute), crossing-over between extracted rules and original data (selecting tuples of the source table that violate all the extracted rules of size 3), and two post-processing operations (selection of rules with 2 items in the body and selection of rules having a maximal body).

Table 1. Sales Transactional table used with MSQL

t_id	ski_pants	hiking_boots	col_shirts	brown_boots	jackets	customer_age	payment
t1	1	1	0	0	0	26	credit_card
t2	0	0	1	1	0	35	credit_card
t3	0	0	1	1	0	48	cash
t4	0	0	0	0	1	29	credit_card
t5	0	0	1	0	1	46	credit_card
t6	0	1	0	1	0	25	cash
t7	1	1	0	1	0	29	credit_card
t8	1	1	0	1	1	34	credit_card
t9	0	1	0	0	0	28	credit_card
t10	1	0	0	0	0	41	credit_card
t11	1	0	0	1	1	36	cash

4.1   MSQL

Table 1 corresponds to the source data encoded in the input format used by MSQL. There are as many boolean attributes as there are possible items.

Pre-processing step 1: selection of the subset of data to be mined.
We are interested only in clients paying with a credit card. MSQL requires that we make a selection of the subset of data to be mined, before the extraction task. The relation on which we will work is supposed to have been correctly selected from a pre-existing set of data, by means of a view, named **RSales**.

Pre-processing step 2: encoding age. MSQL provides methods to declare encodings on some attributes. It is important to note that MSQL is able to do discretization "on the fly", so that the intermediate encoded value will not appear in the final results. The following query will encode the **age** attribute:

```
CREATE ENCODING e_age ON RSales.customer_age AS
BEGIN
   (MIN, 9, 0), (10, 19, 1), (20, 29, 2), (30, 39, 3), (40, 49, 4),
   (50, 59, 5), (60, 69, 6), (70, MAX,7), 0
END;
```

Rules extraction. We want to extract rules associating a set of items to the customer's age and having a support over 25 % and a confidence over 50 %.

```
GETRULES(RSales) INTO RSalesRB
WHERE BODY has {(ski_pants=1) OR (hiking_boots=1) OR (col_shirts=1)
     OR (brown_boots=1) OR (jackets=1)} AND
     Consequent is {(Age = *)} AND support>=0.25 AND confidence>=0.5
USING e_age FOR customer_age
```

This example puts in evidence a limit of MSQL: if the number of items is high, the number of predicates in the WHERE clause increases correspondingly!

Crossing-over: looking for exceptions in the original data. Finally, we select tuples from **RSales** that violate all the extracted rules of size 3.

```
SELECT * FROM RSales
WHERE VIOLATES ALL (SELECTRULES(RSalesRB) WHERE length=3)
```

Post-processing step 1: manipulation of rules. We select rules with 2 items in the body. As MSQL is designed to extract rules with one item in the head and as it provides access only to the extracted rules (and not to the originating itemsets), we must specify that the total size of the rule is 3.

```
SelectRules(RSalesRB) where length=3
```

Post-processing step 2: extraction of rules with a maximal body. It is equivalent to require that there is no couple of rules with the same consequent, such that the body of one rule is included in the body of the other one.

```
SELECTRULES(RSalesRB) AS R1
WHERE NOT EXISTS (SELECTRULES(RSalesRB) AS R2
                WHERE R2.body has R1.body
                AND NOT (R2.body is R1.body)
                AND R2.consequent is R1.consequent )
```

Pros and cons of MSQL. Clearly, the main advantage of MSQL is that it is possible to query knowledge as well as data, by using **SelectRules** on rule-bases and **GetRules** on data (and it is possible to specify if we want rules to be materialized or not). Another good point is that MSQL has been designed to be an extension of classical SQL, making the language quite easy to understand. For example, it is quite simple to test rules against a dataset and to make crossing-over between the original data and query results, by using SATISFY and VIOLATES. To be considered as a good candidate language for inductive databases, it is clear that MSQL, which is essentially built around the extraction phase, should be extended, particularly with a better handling of pre- and post-processing steps. For instance, even if it provides some pre-processing operators like ENCODE for discretization of quantitative attributes, it does not provide any support for complex pre-processing operations, like sampling. Moreover, tuples on which the extraction task must be performed are supposed to have been selected in advance. Concerning the extraction phase, the user can specify some constraints on rules to be extracted (e.g., inclusion of an item in the body or in the head, rule's length, mutually exclusive items, etc) and the support and confidence thresholds. It would be useful however to have the possibility to specify more complex constraints and interest measures, for instance user defined ones.

4.2 MINE RULE

We include the same information of Table 1 into a normalized relation Sales over a schema (t_id, customer_age, item, payment).

Pre-processing step 1: selection of the subset of data to be mined. In contrast to MSQL, MINE RULE does not require to apply some pre-defined view on the original data. As it is designed as an extension to SQL, it perfectly nest SQL, and thus, it is possible to select the relevant subset of data to be mined by specifying it in the WHERE clause of the query.

Pre-processing step 2: encoding age. Since MINE RULE does not have an encoding operator for performing pre-processing tasks, we must encode by ourselves the interval values (2 represents an age in the interval [20-29], 3 represents an age in [30-39], and so on).

Rules extraction. In MINE RULE, we specify that we are looking for rules associating one or more items (rule's body) and customer's age (rule's head):

```
MINE RULE SalesRB AS
SELECT DISTINCT 1..n item AS BODY, 1..1 customer_age AS head,
        SUPPORT, CONFIDENCE
FROM Sales WHERE payment='credit_card'
GROUP BY t_id
EXTRACTING RULES WITH SUPPORT: 0.25, CONFIDENCE: 0.5
```

Extracted rules are stored into the table SalesRB(r_id, b_id, h_id, sup, conf) where r_id, b_id, h_id are respectively the identifiers assigned to rules, body itemsets and head itemsets. The body and head itemsets are stored resp. in tables SalesRB_B(b_id, <bodySchema>) and SalesRB_H(h_id, <headSchema>).

Crossing-over: looking for exceptions in the original data. We want to find tuples of the original relation violating all rules with 2 items in the body. As rules' components (bodies and heads) are stored in relational tables, we use an SQL query to manipulate itemsets. The correspondent query is reported here:

```
SELECT * FROM Sales AS S1 WHERE NOT EXISTS
      (SELECT * FROM SalesRB AS R1
       WHERE (SELECT customer_age FROM SalesRB_H
                WHERE h_id=R1.h_id)=S1.customer_age
        AND (SELECT COUNT(*) FROM SalesRB_B
             WHERE R1.b_id=SalesRB_B.b_id)=2
        AND NOT EXISTS (SELECT * FROM SalesRB_B AS I1
                         WHERE I1.b_id=R1.b_id AND NOT EXISTS
                         (SELECT * FROM Sales AS S2
                         WHERE S2.t_id=S1.t_id
                         AND S2.item=I1.item )));
```

This query is hard to write and to understand. It aims at selecting tuples of the original table such that there are no rules of size 3 that hold in it. To check that, we verify that the consequent of the rule occurs in a tuple associated to a transaction and that there are no items of the rule's body that do not occur in the same transaction.

Post-processing step 1: manipulation of rules. Once again, as itemsets corresponding to rule's components are stored in tables (SalesRB_B,SalesRB_H), we can select rules having two items in the body with a simple SQL query.

```
SELECT * FROM SalesRB AS R1 WHERE 2=
    (SELECT COUNT(*) FROM SalesRB_B R2 WHERE R1.b_id=R2.b_id);
```

Post-processing step 2: selection of rules with a maximal body. We select rules with a maximal body for a given consequent. As rules' components are stored in relational tables, we use again a SQL query to perform such a task.

```
SELECT * FROM SalesRB AS R1             # We select the rules in R1
WHERE NOT EXISTS                        # such that there are no
 (SELECT * FROM SalesRB AS R2           # other rules (in R2) with
  WHERE R2.h_id=R1.h_id                 # the same head, a different
    AND NOT R2.b_id=R1.b_id             # body such that it has no
    AND NOT EXISTS (SELECT *            # items that do not occur in
       FROM SalesRB_B AS B1             # the body of the R1 rule
      WHERE R1.b_id=B1.b_id AND NOT EXISTS (SELECT *
           FROM SalesRB_B AS B2
           WHERE B2.b_id=R2.b_id AND B2.item=B1.item)))
```

This rather complex query aims at selecting rules such that there are no rules with the same consequent and a body that strictly includes the body of the former rule. The two inner sub-queries are used to check that rule body in R1 is a superset of the rule body in R2. These queries probably could result simpler if SQL-3 standard for the ouput of the rules were adopted.

Pros and cons of MINE RULE. The first advantage of MINE RULE is that it has been designed as an extension to SQL. Moreover, as it perfectly nests SQL, it is possible to use classical statements to pre-process the data, and, for instance, select the subset of data to be mined. Like MSQL, data pre-processing is limited to operations that can be expressed in SQL: it is not possible to sample data before extraction, and the discretization must be done by the user. Notice however, that, by using the CLUSTER BY keyword, we can specify on which subgroups of a group association rules must be found. Like MSQL, MINE RULE allows the user to specify some constraints on rules to be extracted (on items belonging to head or body, on their cardinality as well as more complex constraints based on the use of a taxonomy). The interested reader is invited to read [8,9] to have illustration of these latter capabilities. Like MSQL, MINE RULE is essentially designed around the extraction step, and it does not provide much support for the other KDD steps (e.g., post-processing tasks must be done with SQL queries). Finally, according to our knowledge, MINE RULE is one of the few languages that have a well defined semantics [9] for each of its operations. Indeed, it is clear that a clean theoretical background is a key issue to allow the generation of efficient compilers.

4.3   DMQL

DMQL can work with traditional databases, so let's consider that we have encoded information of Table 1 into a **sales_db** database which is made of the relations **Sales**(customer_id, item) and **Customer_info**(customer_id, age, payment).

Pre-processing step 1: selection of the subset of data to be mined. Like MINE RULE, DMQL nests SQL for relational manipulations. So the selection of the relevant subset of data (i.e. clients buying products with their credit card) will be done via the use of the WHERE statement of the extraction query.

Pre-processing step 2: encoding age. DMQL does not provide primitives to encode data like MSQL. However, it allows us to define a hierarchy to specify ranges of values for customer's age, as follows:

```
define hierarchy age_hierarchy for customer_info on sales as
level1:min...9<level0:all
level1:10...19<level0:all
...
level1:60...69<level0:all
level1:70...max<level0:all
```

Rules extraction. DMQL allows the user to specify templates of rules to be discovered, called *metapatterns*, by using the **matching** keyword. These metapatterns can be used to impose strong syntactic constraints on rules to be discovered. So we can specify that we are looking for rule's bodies relative to bought items and rule's heads relative to customer's age. Moreover, we can specify that we desire to use the predefined hierarchy for the age attribute.

use database sales_db
use hierarchy age_hierarchy **for** customer_info.age
mine association as SalesRB
matching with $sales^+(X, \{I\}) \Rightarrow customer\_info(X, A)$
from sales, customer_info
where sales.customer_id=customer_info.customer_id

AND customer_info.payment='credit_card'
with support threshold=25% **with confidence** threshold=50%

Crossing-over and post-processing operations. Like MINE RULE, DMQL does not provide support for post-processing operations and performings them requires writing SQL queries or using *ad hoc* tools provided externally.

Pros and cons of DMQL. Like MINE RULE, one of the main advantages of DQML is that it completely nests classical SQL, and so it is quite easy for a new user to learn and use the language. Moreover, DMQL is designed to work with traditional databases and datacubes. Concerning the extraction step, DMQL allows to impose strong syntactic contraints on patterns to be extracted, by means of metapatterns allowing the user to specify the form of extracted rules. Another advantage of DMQL is that we can include some background knowledge in the process, by defining hierarchies on items occurring in the database and mining rules across different levels of hierarchies. Once rules are extracted, we can perform roll-up and drill-down manipulations on extracted rules. Clearly, analogously to the other languages studied so far, the main drawback of DMQL is that the language capabilities are essentially centered around the extraction phase, and the language relies on SQL or additional tools to perform pre- and post-processing operations. Finally, we can notice that, beyond association rules, DMQL can perform many mining operations, like mining characteristic descriptions, discriminant descriptions, or classification rules.

5   Conclusions

In this paper, we have considered various features of three languages, MSQL, DMQL and MINE RULE, that extract association rules from a relational database and support the "closure property", a crucial property for inductive databases. Then, we have compared them with the desired properties of an ideal query language for inductive databases. Next, we have presented a set of queries taken from data mining practice and have discussed the suitability of these languages for querying inductive databases. The outcome is that no language presents all the desired properties: MSQL seems the one that offers the larger number of primitives tailored for post-processing and an on-the-fly encoding, specifically designed for efficiency; DMQL allows the extraction of the most large set of different data patterns and the definition and use of hierarchies and of some visualization primitives during the rule extraction; MINE RULE is the only one that allows to dynamically partition the source relation into groups from which the rules will be extracted; a second level of grouping, the clusters, from which more sophisticated rule constraints can be applied, is also possible. Furthermore, at our knowledge, it looks as the only one with an algebraic semantics, what could become an important positive factor when query optimization issues will be addressed.

However, one of the main limits of all the three languages is the insufficient support of post-processing issues. Whatever the language is, the user must use one of the predefined built-in options. This problem becomes crucial when considering user-defined post-processing operations involving something else than rule's component, support and confidence. Instead, in our view, a good candidate language for inductive databases must be flexible enough in its grammar to let the user specify its own constraints and different post-processing operations. Another important issue is the simplicity of the language and its ease of use. Indeed, we think that a good candidate language for data mining must be flexible enough to specify a lot of different mining tasks in a declarative fashion. However the powerful declarative semantics must not affect the simplicity of use. At our knowledge, these languages tackle this problem by being embedded in a data mining tool, which provides a front end to the grammar.

Another crucial issue relative to query languages for data mining is the optimization problem. When designing a language compiler, we must pay attention to optimizations issues; for instance, trying to make profit of previously generated results, or to analyze the equivalence between queries. In these terms, at our knowledge, a lot of work must still be done. Furthermore, it could reveal as very important the ability to manipulate intermediate representation like condensed representations of frequent patterns (see, e.g., [1]). A challenge tightly linked to such a functionality would be to find ways to characterize constraints defined in an operation of rule extraction in terms such that they could eventually be exploited during the mining process.

This study allows us to conclude that the path to reach the maturity in inductive database technology is still far to be reached. However, the limits and the merits of the current query languages to give support to the knowledge discovery process have been already identified.

References

1. Boulicaut J-F., Jeudy B.: Mining free-sets under constraints. Proc. of Database Engineering & Applications Symposium, IDEAS'01, Grenoble, France (2001).
2. Imielinski, T., Mannila, H.: A Database Perspective on Knowledge Discovery. Communications of the ACM. **3:4** (1996) 58–64.
3. Imielinski, T., Virmani, A., Abdulghani, A.: DataMine: Application Programming Interface and Query Language for Database Mining. Proc. of the 2nd Int. Conf. on Knowledge Discovery and Data Mining, KDD'96. 3 (1996) 256–261.
4. Imielinski, T., Virmani, A.: MSQL: A Query Language for Database Mining. Data Mining and Knowledge Discovery. 3 (1999) 373–408.
5. Virmani, A.: Second Generation Data Mining. PhD Thesis, Rutgers Univ. (1998).
6. Han, J., Fu, Y., Wang, W., Koperski, K., Zaiane, O.: DMQL: A Data Mining Query Language for Relational Databases.
7. Han, J., Kamber, M.: Data Mining – Concepts and Techniques. Morgan Kaufmann Publishers (2001).
8. Meo, R., Psaila, G., Ceri, S.: A New SQL-like Operator for Mining Association Rules. Proc. of the 22nd Int. Conf. of Very Large Data Bases. Bombay, India (1996).
9. Meo, R., Psaila, G., Ceri, S.: An Extension to SQL for Mining Association Rules. Data Mining and Knowledge Discovery. **9:4** (1997).

Learning from Dissociations*

Choh Man Teng

Institute for Human and Machine Cognition
University of West Florida, Pensacola FL 32501, USA
cmteng@ai.uwf.edu

Abstract. Standard association rules encapsulate the *positive* relationship between two sets of items: the presence of X is a good predictor for the simultaneous presence of Y. We argue that the absence of an association rule conveys valuable information as well. Dissociation rules are rules that capture the *negative* relationship between two sets of items: the presence of X *and* z is *not* a good predictor for the presence of Y. We developed a representation for augmenting standard association rules with dissociation information, and presented some experimental results suggesting that such augmented rules can improve the quality of the associations obtained, both in terms of rule accuracy and in terms of using these rules as a guide to making decisions.

1 Introduction

An association rule [1] is meant to denote a positive relationship between two sets of items. For example, the rule

$$\text{potato chips } \Rightarrow \text{ coke} \qquad (^*1)$$

says that people who buy potato chips also tend to buy coke. While this rule provides us with useful information, in many cases it may be beneficial to, in addition, take into account possible exceptions to the association rules we have discovered. For example, we might note that the rule

$$\text{potato chips and pepsi } \Rightarrow \text{ coke} \qquad (^*2)$$

is *not* an acceptable association rule. What are the implications of the absence of this rule? Loosely speaking, rule (^{*1}) is concerned with people, or more specifically transactions of people, who buy potato chips in general, and rule (^{*2}) is concerned with a special subsection of this population, namely people who buy pepsi in addition to potato chips. These two groups of people have different buying behaviors with respect to coke: the former group often buy coke, the latter often do not.

Let us denote the absence of rule (^{*2}) by

$$\text{potato chips and pepsi } \not\Rightarrow \text{ coke.} \qquad (^*3)$$

---

* This work was supported by NASA NCC2-1239.

Y. Kambayashi, W. Winiwarter, M. Arikawa (Eds.): DaWaK 2002, LNCS 2454, pp. 11–20, 2002.

Such rules indicate a *negative* relationship between two sets of attributes. We will use the term "dissociations" for this relationship, in contrast to *positive* "associations". We will give a more formal definition of dissociations in Section 2.

Our motivation is closely related to that discussed in [2]. Our approaches differ, however, in that the formulation in the present paper does not rely on the existence of a strict taxonomy, which may be difficult to construct. We make use of the information contained in the "parent" rule in a more general way.

1.1   Subclass Dissociations

Dissociations by themselves can be quite arbitrary:

$$\text{potato chips} \not\Rightarrow \text{cotton swabs};$$
$$\text{light bulbs} \not\Rightarrow \text{wine openers.}$$

We focus here on a case of particular interest, namely, when a subclass exhibits a dissociation that contradicts an association in the original class. Symbolically, this can be represented as

$$X \Rightarrow Y;$$
$$XZ \not\Rightarrow Y. \qquad (^*4)$$

Rules (*1) and (*3) above are an example of such a situation. The products coke and pepsi are competitors, and people who buy one kind may be disinclined to buy the other kind at the same time.

Subclass dissociations can also indicate a special niche in the market. Consider the two rules

$$\text{yeast} \Rightarrow \text{flour};$$
$$\text{yeast and hops} \not\Rightarrow \text{flour.} \qquad (^*5)$$

In general people who get yeast also get flour, to bake sumptuous cakes, but if they in addition also get hops, they are more likely to be making beer and have no use for flour. Here the beer-brewers constitutes a niche with a buying pattern that is different from that of the general population.

We can make this even more explicit by eliciting rules such as

$$\text{yeast} \Rightarrow \text{flour};$$
$$\text{(yeast and) brewer's yeast} \not\Rightarrow \text{flour.} \qquad (^*6)$$

Here there is a strict set-inclusion relationship between yeast and brewer's yeast. Again, brewer's yeast picks out a special subclass of people who are not very interested in flour.

Taxonomically speaking, in the first case (with rules (*1) and (*3)), the two items represented by Y (coke) and Z (pepsi) in the pair of rules in (*4) are comparable subclasses of the same superclass "cola". In the rules in (*6), Z is a strict subclass of X. In the rules in (*5), it is intended that "yeast and hops" picks out the same subclass as "brewer's yeast", although the taxonomic relationship between the items are only implicit and approximate.

2   Constructing Associations and Dissociations

First we will define the basic terminology that will be used in this paper. Let $A = \{a_1, \ldots, a_m\}$ be a set of m binary attributes. Let Δ be a data set of transactions, each transaction being a subset of A. In other words, a transaction is represented by the set of attributes in A that are present in that transaction. For a set of attributes $X \subseteq A$, let $\#(X)$ denote the number of transactions containing X in the data set, that is, $\#(X) = |S|$, where $S = \{\delta \in \Delta : X \subseteq \delta\}$. Similarly, for $Y \subseteq A$ and $z \in A$, let $\#(XY)$ denote $\#(X \cup Y)$ and $\#(Xz)$ denote $\#(X \cup \{z\})$.

2.1   Associations

An *association rule* is a rule of the form

$$X \Rightarrow Y,$$

where $X, Y \subseteq A$ and $X \cap Y = \emptyset$. We call X the *antecedent* and Y the *consequent* of the rule. The *support* of an association rule $X \Rightarrow Y$ is given by $\frac{\#(XY)}{|\Delta|}$, and its *confidence* is given by $\frac{\#(XY)}{\#(X)}$.

Typically rule mining is focused on enumerating association rules whose support and confidence are above certain thresholds, namely,

1. $\frac{\#(XY)}{|\Delta|} \geq s_{\min}$ (support threshold);
2. $\frac{\#(XY)}{\#(X)} \geq c_{\min}$ (confidence threshold).   **[Associations]**

2.2   Dissociations $\neq$ Non-associations

We will, in addition to associations, also report dissociations found in the data set. One might think that we do not need to formulate dissociations. We may infer dissociations by the mere absence of the corresponding association rules. However, this is not a very desirable solution. First of all, observe that the sequence of rules almost always follow the following pattern.

$$X_1 \Rightarrow Y$$
$$X_1 X_2 \Rightarrow Y$$
$$\vdots$$
$$X_1 X_2 \ldots X_i \overset{?}{\Rightarrow} Y$$

We start out with an acceptable association rule $X_1 \Rightarrow Y$. As the rule becomes progressively specialized, it is almost always the case that sooner or later we will come to a point where for some i the rule $X_1 X_2 \ldots X_i \Rightarrow Y$ is considered unacceptable as an association rule.

We need to differentiate between the two reasons why a prospective rule $X \Rightarrow Y$ can fail to be an acceptable association rule, as per the criteria given in Section 2.1.

1. $\frac{\#(XY)}{|\Delta|} < s_{\min}$ (below threshold support);
2. $\frac{\#(XY)}{\#(X)} < c_{\min}$ (below threshold confidence).

In the first case, the low support indicates there is not enough evidence (occurrences of XY in the data set) available to make any conclusive association. In the second case, the low confidence indicates that the Y's do not occur often enough among the X's.

In other words, in the first case, the rule $X \Rightarrow Y$ fails, through no fault of its own, because of the sparseness of the data, while in the second case, the rule fails because a genuine dissociation exists between X and Y. This latter case is what we will concentrate on.

2.3   Dissociation Rules

A *dissociation rule* is a rule of the form

$$X \not\Rightarrow Y,$$

following the notation in Section 2.1. The support and confidence of a dissociation rule are defined in the same way as for standard association rules. In the most general sense, this rule represents that the available evidence indicates it is not the case that $X \Rightarrow Y$. In our construction, we will denote by $X \not\Rightarrow Y$ the following conditions.

1. $\frac{\#(XY)}{|\Delta|} \geq s_{\min}$ (support threshold);
2. $\frac{\#(XY)}{\#(X)} < d_{\max}$ (dissociation threshold).   **[Dissociations]**

A dissociation rule is a rule with low confidence even though its support is high. The dissociation threshold $d_{\max}$ indicates how low this confidence has to be. When $d_{\max} = 0$, no dissociation rules will be reported, and the system reduces to that of the standard association rule formulation. When $d_{\max} = c_{\min}$, the confidence threshold, all rules of high support but not high enough confidence will be reported as dissociations.

Note that having $X \not\Rightarrow Y$ does *not* necessarily mean we have $X \Rightarrow \bar{Y}$ ($\bar{Y}$ stands for the negation of Y). This may be the interpretation at times, for example, we may say that people who buy potato chips and pepsi often do not buy coke at the same time. However, in general $X \not\Rightarrow Y$ merely indicates that there is enough negative evidence to disqualify the association $X \Rightarrow Y$. We will then say that we do not know whether people who buy X's also buy Y's. They may very well do (but then again they may not), but our evidence is not strong enough for us to make a conclusive statement.

The strength of the implication derived from a dissociation rule depends on, among other factors, the dissociation threshold $d_{\max}$. The lower the value of $d_{\max}$, the closer $X \not\Rightarrow Y$ approximates $X \Rightarrow \bar{Y}$.

3   Representation

The syntactic structure of the rules, both associations and dissociations, places only very loose constraints on their support and confidence levels. We know that given $X \Rightarrow Y$ or $X \not\Rightarrow Y$, any shorter rule involving only attributes contained in XY will have an above threshold support. Beyond this, little can be said about the relationship between similar looking rules. It is possible to have, for instance, alternating associations and dissociations.

$$X_1 \Rightarrow Y$$
$$X_1 X_2 \not\Rightarrow Y$$
$$X_1 X_2 X_3 \Rightarrow Y$$

In this section we will consider how these relationships can best be represented.

We may simply list independently all the association rules and dissociation rules found in a data set, as shown above. This lengthy approach is comprehensive, but the information concerning a set of attributes is scattered over potentially many rules, which makes the overall structure hard to grasp.

Alternatively, for the above three rules, we could have some form of summary to the effect that

"if X_1 then Y, but not if X_2 unless also X_3."

Instead of very many short rules, we now have relatively few very long rules. There is a tradeoff between accuracy and intelligibility. By simplifying the information retained, we can construct rules that are easier to understand and manage.

3.1   Augmenting Standard Association Rules

Let us consider the case where $d_{\max} = c_{\min}$. Given a rule $X \Rightarrow Y$ or $X \not\Rightarrow Y$, any shorter rule involving only attributes from the set XY is both above support threshold and either above confidence threshold ($\geq c_{\min}$) or below dissociation threshold ($< d_{\max}$). Thus, any such shorter rule is either an acceptable association rule or an acceptable dissociation rule, according to the criteria specified in Sections 2.1 and 2.3 respectively.

We will augment standard association rules with selected dissociation information. An *augmented association rule* is a rule of the form

$$X \,\|\, Z \Rightarrow Y.$$

Given this rule, the following two conditions hold.

1. $X \Rightarrow Y$; and
2. $\forall z \in Z : Xz \not\Rightarrow Y.$ [Augmented Associations]

We can think of this as starting off with an acceptable association rule $X \Rightarrow Y$. This rule is augmented with a set Z of attributes, each of which, when added individually to the antecedent X of the original association rule, gives rise to an acceptable dissociation rule .

The support and confidence of a rule $X \,\|\, Z \Rightarrow Y$ is defined as follows.

support $\min\limits_{z \in Z} \{\frac{\#(XY\bar{z})}{|\Delta|}\}$;

confidence $\min\limits_{z \in Z} \{\frac{\#(XY\bar{z})}{\#(X\bar{z})}\}$.

In other words, the support and confidence of an augmented rule are respectively the lowest corresponding values among the dissociation rules represented.

3.2   Where Are the "Longer" Dissociation Rules?

Note that we choose to only include dissociations whose rule antecedents are each one element "longer" (or larger, in the set-theoretic sense) than that of the association rule under consideration. Why do we not in addition annotate the rule with the longer dissociations?

One reason is obviously complexity considerations. Our formulation is much simpler and easier to understand than a full-blown augmentation, and it arguably captures the portion of dissociation information that generates the most interest. Compare the two findings:

- "people who get yeast also get flour, but not if they also get hops";
- "people who get yeast also get flour, but not if they also get hops and glass bottles and malt".

The first rule is likely to see more use, since it involves less complicated conditions and is applicable to a wider range of situations.

Another basis for our choice of formulation is that the longer rules are already implicitly represented in our dissociation component. Suppose we have the following two rules.

$$r_1 : X \Rightarrow Y; \qquad r_2 : Xz_1z_2 \not\Rightarrow Y.$$

According to our scheme of representation, we will not augment rule r_1 directly with the dissociation information contained in rule r_2. However, as we will see in the following analysis, this dissociation information nonetheless does get (at least partially) relayed to r_1 through the "intermediate" rules.

Recall that since we have r_2 and $d_{\max} = c_{\min}$, every shorter rule involving only X, z_1, z_2, and Y is above support threshold and satisfies the criteria for either association (Section 2.1) or dissociation (Section 2.3). There can be four cases regarding the status of the two intermediate rules.

1. Both rules are associations.
   $$r_3 : Xz_1 \Rightarrow Y; \qquad r_4 : Xz_2 \Rightarrow Y.$$
   In this case r_2 is used to augment both r_3 and r_4, and we have
   $$r_1 : X \qquad\quad \Rightarrow Y;$$
   $$r_3' : Xz_1 \,\|\, z_2 \Rightarrow Y;$$
   $$r_4' : Xz_2 \,\|\, z_1 \Rightarrow Y.$$

2. The first rule is an association, and the second a dissociation.
   $$r_3 : Xz_1 \Rightarrow Y; \qquad r_4 : Xz_2 \not\Rightarrow Y.$$

In this case r_2 goes into annotating r_3, while r_4 goes into annotating r_1. This reduces to two augmented association rules.

$$r'_1 : X \quad \| z_2 \Rightarrow Y;$$
$$r'_3 : X z_1 \| z_2 \Rightarrow Y.$$

3. The first rule is a dissociation, and the second an association.

$$r_3 : X z_1 \not\Rightarrow Y; \qquad r_4 : X z_2 \Rightarrow Y.$$

This is the mirror image of the previous case. We have

$$r'_1 : X \quad \| z_1 \Rightarrow Y;$$
$$r'_4 : X z_2 \| z_1 \Rightarrow Y.$$

4. Both rules are dissociations.

$$r_3 : X z_1 \not\Rightarrow Y; \qquad r_4 : X z_2 \not\Rightarrow Y.$$

In this case r_1 is the only association rule. We will augment it as follows.

$$r'_1 : X \| z_1 z_2 \Rightarrow Y.$$

Note that in this last case the augmentation of r_1 is *not* with respect to r_2, but rather is a direct consequence of the two intermediate dissociation rules r_3 and r_4. However, in all but the first case, the dissociation represented by the longer rule r_2 is indirectly, albeit sometimes partially, propagated to r_1 through the two shorter rules. In the first case, the effect of r_2 is contained in the two intermediate association rules.

4   Experiments

We modified a standard association rule algorithm Apriori [3] to generate augmented association rules. To obtain dissociation information, we check the confidence of a potential rule against the dissociation threshold. This produces the set of acceptable dissociation rules straightforwardly. To combine the associations and dissociations into augmented association rules, we simply need to take note of the association rules produced in the previous iteration of large itemsets, and modify their dissociation components accordingly.

We carried out a set of illustrative experiments designed to bring into focus the motivation and utility of dissociations. In addition we also tested the algorithm on some larger scale synthetic data.

4.1   Comparing the Rule Confidence

Consider a data set of 10000 transactions, generated according to the following parameters.

$$\Pr(x) = 0.5; \quad \Pr(y \mid x) = 0.7; \quad \Pr(y \mid xz); \quad \Pr(z \mid x). \qquad (*7)$$

Our goal here is to investigate the effects of different distributions of the three attributes x, y, and z on rule confidence. The three rules of interest are

$$r_1 : x \quad \Rightarrow y;$$
$$r_2 : xz \quad \Rightarrow y \quad \text{(the ``inverse'' of } xz \not\Rightarrow y);$$
$$r_3 : x \| z \Rightarrow y.$$

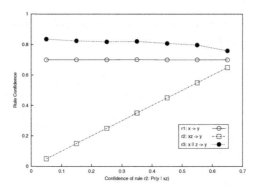

Fig. 1. Rule confidence. The confidence of r_1 was held at 0.7. The confidence of r_2 took on values from 0.05 to 0.65 in steps of 0.1. We required the confidence of r_2 to be less than that of r_1; otherwise r_3 would not have been generated. The augmented association rule r_3 had a higher confidence than the un-augmented rule r_1. As the confidence of r_2 approached that of r_1, so did the confidence of r_3 from the other side.

The parameters $\Pr(y \mid x)$ and $\Pr(y \mid xz)$ correspond to the confidence of the two rules r_1 and r_2 respectively. By manipulating these and other parameters specified in (*7), we can compare the confidence of the rules under various conditions.

For the purposes of our experiments, we fixed the values of the first two parameters $\Pr(x)$ and $\Pr(y \mid x)$ and let the other two vary. Note that it makes sense to generate the augmented association rule r_3 only when the confidence of r_2 is lower than that of r_1. We thus required $\Pr(y \mid xz) < \Pr(y \mid x)$. The value of $\Pr(z \mid x)$ (fixed for each run) was chosen randomly from a uniform distribution within acceptable bounds.[1] The support threshold was set at 0.5% and no rule was ruled out by low support.

The confidence levels of the three rules, averaged over 1000 runs, are plotted in Figure 1. The confidence of rule r_1 was held at a constant 0.7, while the confidence of rule r_2 was varied between 0.05 and 0.65, in steps of 0.1. The augmented rule r_3 had a higher confidence than the un-augmented rule r_1 in all cases. As the confidence of r_2 was increased, the confidence of r_3 decreased gradually. We can expect the confidence of all three rules to converge to the same value (0.7 in this case).

4.2   Profiting from the Rules

Next we simulated a situation in which we would utilize the rules to choose between two courses of action. For instance, suppose we have a choice of two actions, a_1 and a_2, which cost c_1 and c_2 units respectively to execute. If according to the information we have, it is likely that the next case is a "y" (coke-buying

---

[1] We have $0 < \Pr(z \mid x) \le \min[\frac{\Pr(y|x)}{\Pr(y|xz)}, \frac{1-\Pr(y|x)}{1-\Pr(y|xz)}]$. The confidence of rule r_3 depends on, among other factors, the proportion of z's among x's. The higher this proportion, the more profound the effect of the parameter $\Pr(y \mid xz)$. We randomized $\Pr(z \mid x)$ to get a general idea of the confidence of r_3 across different values of this proportion.

Table 1. Payoffs of various combinations of actions and outcomes.

Action	Cost	Return		Net Profit	
		y	$\bar{y}$	y	$\bar{y}$
a_1	c_1	p_1	0	$p_1 - c_1$	$-c_1$
a_2	c_2	0	p_2	$-c_2$	$p_2 - c_2$

customer), we carry out a_1 (send a buy-1-get-1 free coupon for coke); otherwise we carry out a_2 (send a trade-in-your-pepsi-for-two-cokes coupon). We earn p_1 units if we correctly chose action a_1, and p_2 units if we correctly chose action a_2. If we miss we earn nothing. The payoffs of various combinations of actions and outcomes are summarized in Table 1.

We compared the performance of the two rules

$$r_1 : x \quad \Rightarrow y,$$
$$r_3 : x \,\|\, z \Rightarrow y,$$

in the same setting as in Section 4.1. In our experiments, the parameters were fixed as follows: $c_1 = c_2 = 1$; $p_1 = p_2 = 1000$. Using r_1 as our guide of action, action a_1 was performed on all x's. Using r_3 as our guide of action, we performed action a_1 on all x's which were not also z's, and performed a_2 on the xz's.

The net returns per customer (a total of 10000 customers in each run), averaged over 1000 runs, are shown in Figure 2. Again the confidence of r_1 was held at 0.7 while the confidence of r_2 was varied from 0.05 to 0.65. When rule r_2 had a confidence below 0.5, the recommendations of rule r_3 gave rise to higher profit earnings than those of rule r_1. This situation was reversed as the confidence of r_2 rose above 0.5.

These results suggest that by incorporating dissociation information, our policy can be more profitable in a number of cases. However, the profit decreased as the confidence of rule r_2 increased, and thus it may be desirable to cap the dissociation threshold at, for instance, 0.5 to maximize the net return. We would then have a mixed policy that adheres to the recommendations of rule r_3 where applicable, and reverts to those of rule r_1 when r_3 does not satisfy the dissociation threshold and thus is not available.

Note that these results were obtained with respect to the payoff structure in Table 1. In another scenario, with analytically different costs and consequences associated with different actions, the relative performance of the two rules may very well differ.

4.3   Larger Scale Data

We experimented with some synthetic data generated according to the method described in [3]. Here we just give a few examples of the augmented association rules found in a data set T10.I2.D100K. In this data set, approximately 100000 transactions (D) are generated, each containing an average of 10 items (T), and the average size of the maximal potentially large itemsets (I) is 2. In addition, there are 100000 distinct items (N) and 2000 maximal potentially large itemsets (L). Refer to [3] for the details of the structure of this data.

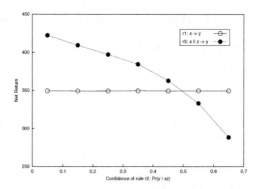

Fig. 2. Net returns per customer, using rules r_1 and r_3 as a policy guide respectively. The confidence of r_1 was held at 0.7. The confidence of r_2 took on values from 0.05 to 0.65 in steps of 0.1. We required the confidence of r_2 to be less than that of r_1; otherwise r_3 would not have been generated. Rule r_3 generated more profits than rule r_1 when r_2 had a relatively low confidence. As the confidence of r_2 was increased above 0.5, r_1 was more profitable than r_3.

Among the augmented and un-augmented association rules discovered, we have for example

$r_1 : x_{89595} \Rightarrow x_{86949}$ (support: 1.7%; confidence 56.9%);
$r_2 : x_{89595} \, \| \, x_{93250} \Rightarrow x_{86949}$ (support: 1.5%; confidence 96.4%).

By augmenting rule r_1 with dissociation information to form rule r_2, the confidence of the rule was improved 39.5%.

Other rules discovered include the same rule r_1 augmented with a different dissociation component:

$r_1 : x_{89595} \Rightarrow x_{86949}$ (support: 1.7%; confidence 56.9%);
$r_3 : x_{89595} \, \| \, x_{3552} \Rightarrow x_{86949}$ (support: 1.5%; confidence 71.2%);

and rules involving lengthier items:

$r_4 : x_{809} \, x_{177} \Rightarrow x_{682}$ (support: 2.7%; confidence 72.3%);
$r_5 : x_{809} \, x_{177} \, \| \, x_{431} \Rightarrow x_{682}$ (support: 2.5%; confidence 75.5%).

We utilized these rules as a policy guide of action in the same setting as in Section 4.2. With the un-augmented rules the net return was on average 61.25 units, versus 76.90 units with the augmented rules.

References

1. Agrawal, R., Imielinski, T., Swami, A.: Mining association rules between sets of items in large databases. In: Proceedings of the ACM SIGMOD Conference on the Management of Data. (1993) 207–216
2. Savasere, A., Omiecinski, E., Navathe, S.: Mining for strong negative associations in a large database of customer transactions. In: Proceedings of the Fourteenth International Conference on Data Engineering. (1998) 494–502
3. Agrawal, R., Srikant, R.: Fast algorithms for mining association rules. In: Proceedings of the 20th International Conference on Very Large Databases. (1994)

Mining Association Rules from XML Data

Daniele Braga[1], Alessandro Campi[1], Mika Klemettinen[2], and PierLuca Lanzi[3]

[1] Politecnico di Milano, Dipartimento di Elettronica e Informazione,
P.za L. da Vinci 32,I-20133 Milano, Italy
{braga,campi}@elet.polimi.it
[2] Nokia Research Center, P.O.Box 407, FIN-00045 Nokia Group, Finland
mika.klemettinen@nokia.com
[3] Artificial Intelligence and Robotic Laboratory
Politecnico di Milano, Dipartimento di Elettronica e Informazione
pierluca.lanzi@polimi.it

Abstract. The eXtensible Markup Language (XML) rapidly emerged as a standard for representing and exchanging information. The fast-growing amount of available XML data sets a pressing need for languages and tools to manage collections of XML documents, as well as to *mine interesting information* out of them. Although the data mining community has not yet rushed into the use of XML, there have been some proposals to exploit XML. However, in practice these proposals mainly rely on more or less traditional relational databases with an XML interface. In this paper, we introduce association rules from native XML documents and discuss the new challenges and opportunities that this topic sets to the data mining community. More specifically, we introduce an *extension of XQuery* for mining association rules. This extension is used throughout the paper to better define association rule mining within XML and to emphasize its implications in the XML context.

1 Introduction

Knowledge discovery in databases (KDD) deals with the extraction of *interesting* knowledge from large amounts of data usually stored in databases or data warehouses. This knowledge can be represented in many different ways such as clusters, decision trees, decision rules, etc. Among the others, association rules [4], proved effective in discovering interesting relations in massive amounts of data.

During the recent years, we have seen the dramatic development of the eXtensible Markup Language (XML) [19] as a standard for representing and exchanging information. Accordingly, there is a pressing need for languages and tools to manage collections of XML documents and to *extract interesting knowledge* from XML documents. At the moment, the use of XML within the data mining community is still quite limited. There are some proposals to exploit XML within the knowledge discovery tasks, but most of them still rely on the traditional relational framework with an XML interface. However, the pressure for data mining tools for native XML data is rapidly increasing.

Y. Kambayashi, W. Winiwarter, M. Arikawa (Eds.): DaWaK 2002, LNCS 2454, pp. 21–30, 2002.
© Springer-Verlag Berlin Heidelberg 2002

In this paper, we introduce association rules from *native* XML documents. This extension arises nontrivial problems, related to the hierarchical nature of the XML data model. Consequently, most of the common and well-known abstractions of the relational framework need to be adapted to and redefined in the specific XML context.

2   Association Rules

Association rules (ARs) were first introduced in [3] to analyze customer habits in retail databases; up-to-date definitions can be found in [8]. An association rule is an implication of the form $X \Rightarrow Y$, where the rule *body* X and *head* Y are subsets of the set $\mathcal{I}$ of *items* ($\mathcal{I} = \{I_1, \ldots, I_n\}$) within a set of *transactions* $\mathcal{D}$. A rule $X \Rightarrow Y$ states that the transactions T ($T \in \mathcal{D}$) that contain the items in X ($X \subset T$) are *likely* to contain also the items in Y ($Y \subset T$). ARs are usually characterized by two statistical measures: *support*, which measures the percentage of transactions that contain the items in both X and Y, and *confidence*, which measures the percentage of transactions that contain the items in X and also contain the items in Y. More formally, given the function $freq(X, \mathcal{D})$, denoting the percentage of transactions in $\mathcal{D}$ which contains X, we define:

$$support(X \Rightarrow Y) = freq(X \cup Y, \mathcal{D})$$

$$confidence(X \Rightarrow Y) = freq(X \cup Y, \mathcal{D})/freq(X, \mathcal{D})$$

Suppose there is an AR "*bread, butter* $\Rightarrow$ *milk*" with confidence 0.9 and support 0.05. The rule states that customers who buy *bread* and *butter*, also buy *milk* in 90% of the cases and that this holds in 5% of the transactions. The problem of mining ARs from a set of transactions $\mathcal{D}$ consists of generating all the ARs that have support and confidence greater than two user-defined thresholds: minimum support (*minsupp*) and minimum confidence (*minconf*).

To help the specification of complex AR mining tasks, a number of query languages have been proposed (see [8] for a review). In particular, [13] introduced the MINE RULE operator, an extension of SQL specifically designed for modeling the problem of mining ARs from relational databases. The MINE RULE operator captures the high-level semantics of AR mining tasks and allows the specification of complex mining tasks with an intuitive SQL-like syntax. For instance, consider the table in Figure 1, contains the purchase records from a clothing store. The transaction column (tr) contains an identifier of the transaction; the other columns correspond to the customer identifier, the type of purchased item, the date of the purchase, the unitary price, and the purchase quantity (qty). Suppose that we want to mine ARs with a minimum support of 0.1, a minimum confidence of 0.2, at most four items in the body, and exactly one item in the head. Using MINE RULE, this task is formalized by the following statement:

tr	customer	item	date	price	qty
1	$cust_1$	ski_pants	2001/12/17	140	1
1	$cust_1$	hiking_boots	2001/12/17	180	1
2	$cust_2$	col_shirts	2001/12/18	25	2
2	$cust_2$	brown_boots	2001/12/18	150	1
2	$cust_2$	jackets	2001/12/18	300	1
3	$cust_1$	jackets	2001/12/18	300	1
4	$cust_2$	col_shirts	2001/12/19	25	3
4	$cust_2$	jackets	2001/12/19	300	2

(a) **Purchase** table

HEAD	BODY	SUPPORT	CONFIDENCE
{ski_pants}	{hiking_boots}	0.25	1.00
{hiking_boots}	{ski_pants}	0.25	1.00
{col_shirts}	{brown_boots}	0.25	0.50
{col_shirts}	{jackets}	0.50	1.00
{brown_boots}	{brown_boots}	0.25	1.00
{brown_boots}	{jackets}	0.25	1.00
{jackets}	{col_shirts}	0.50	0.66
{jackets}	{brown_boots}	0.25	0.33
{col_shirts,brown_boots}	{jackets}	0.25	1.00
{col_shirts,jackets}	{brown_boots}	0.25	0.50
{brown_boots,jackets}	{col_shirts}	0.25	1.00

(b) `SimpleAssociation` table

Fig. 1. The `Purchase` table for a store and `SimpleAssociation` table.

```
MINE RULE SimpleAssociations AS
SELECT DISTINCT 1..4 item AS BODY, 1..1 item AS HEAD, SUPPORT, CONFIDENCE
FROM Purchase
GROUP BY tr
EXTRACTING RULES WITH SUPPORT: 0.1, CONFIDENCE: 0.2
```

The statement produces the table `SimpleAssociations` (see Figure 1) where each tuple corresponds to a discovered AR. The `SELECT` clause defines the structure of output table which collects the extracted rules: the rule `BODY` is defined as a set of at most four `items`, the `HEAD` as a set with one single `item`, and the `DISTINCT` keyword specifies that no replications are allowed in the rule head and body. The resulting table contains the `CONFIDENCE` and `SUPPORT` values for each AR. The `GROUP BY` clause specifies that the set of transactions ($\mathcal{D}$) is derived from the original table `Purchase` by grouping it with respect to the transaction identifier attribute (`tr`). Finally, the `EXTRACTING RULES WITH` clause specifies the minimum support and confidence.

 `MINE RULE` is particularly effective when the mining task is complex. Suppose that we want to find interesting intra-customer relations which associate past customer purchases with future ones. Note that in this case we are looking for *generalized* ARs, since there are no constraints on the number of items in the

head and in the body ("1..n" indicates that both the rule head and body contain
an arbitrary number of items). This task is formalized by the following statement:

```
MINE RULE OrderedSets AS
SELECT DISTINCT 1..n item AS BODY, 1..n item AS HEAD, SUPPORT, CONFIDENCE
FROM Purchase
WHERE date > 2001/12/17
GROUP BY customer
CLUSTER BY date HAVING BODY.date < HEAD.date
EXTRACTING RULES WITH SUPPORT: 0.1, CONFIDENCE: 0.2
```

The GROUP BY clause indicates that ARs will be extracted w.r.t. customers and
not the transaction identifiers, as in the previous case. In addition, the CLUSTER
BY clause specifies that the customer purchases should be further grouped by
date so that all the items in the rule body will have the same date and all
the items in the rule head will have same date. The HAVING clause specifies a
temporal constraint on the output rules: the items in the rule body should have
a purchase date previous to those in the rule head.

3   From Relational Data to XML Data

Any AR mining task can be brought down to four main steps: (i) *context identification*, which defines the *structure* of the set $\mathcal{D}$; (ii) *context selection*, which
defines constraints on set δ of *transactions in* $\mathcal{D}$ that are relevant to the problem;
(iii) *rule selection*, which defines a set of constraints on the *generated ARs*; (iv)
result construction, which specifies a *format* to represent the generated ARs.
For instance, if we consider the second MINE RULE example, (i) the structure of
the set of transactions $\mathcal{D}$ is derived from the table Purchase, first grouped by
the attribute customer and then by the attribute date through the CLUSTER
BY clause; (ii) only the purchases occurred after 2001/12/17 are considered for
the mining purposes; (iii) the items in the rule head must be purchased after
those in the rule body; (iv) the SELECT clause declares the columns of the output table which represents the result. Note that, steps (ii), (iii), and (iv) are
smoothly mapped into XML. In fact, both *context selection* and *rule selection*
phases involve the selection of parts of XML documents which define the source
data (i.e., $\mathcal{D}$) and the output ARs. These operations are easily expressed in
terms of XQuery statements [21], while the *result construction* phase is naturally expressed using the XML node construction statements. In contrast, the
context identification in XML documents is where the differences between the
"flat" relational data model and the hierarchical XML data model fully emerge.

4   Association Rules from XML Data

We now introduce association rules from *native* XML data. The problem we
address can be stated as follows. Given a *generic* XML document, we want to
extract a set of ARs (still represented in XML) that describe interesting relations among parts, i.e., fragments, of the source XML document. To accomplish

```
<Department>
  <People>
    <Employee>
      <PersonalInfo> <Name>...</Name> ... </PersonalInfo>
      <Education>
        <Higher>
          <MsC year="1996"> yes </MsC>
          <PhD year="1999"> yes </PhD>
        </Higher> ...
      </Education>
      <Publications>
        <Book year="2001" name="XML Query Languages">
          <Author>...</Author>
          <Publisher>...</Publisher>
          <Keyword>XML</Keyword>...<Keyword>XQuery</Keyword>
        </Book> ...
        <Journal year="2000" month="4" vol="4" name="DMKD"
                  publisher="Kluwer">
          <Author>...</Author>
          <Keyword>RDF</Keyword>...<Keyword>XML</Keyword>
        </Journal>
      </Publications>
      <Awards>
        <Award year="2001" Society="IEEE">This award ...</Award>
      </Awards>
    </Employee> ...
  </People> ...
</Department>
```

Fig. 2. An XML document http://www.cs.atlantis.com/staff.xml with various information about the personnel of a university department

this, we follow the approach of [13], and define an extension of the XML query language, XQuery [21], which captures the high-level semantics of the problem and allows the specification of complex mining tasks within an intuitive syntax, inspired to the XML world. We will refer to a sample XML document, depicted in Figure 2, which describes the personnel of a university department.

4.1 Simple Mining

As a first basic example, we wish to discover the associations among the research topics that have been investigated in recent years. For this purpose we extract rules which associate the keywords of the publications since 1990. More specifically, we are interested in ARs of the form "$XML \Rightarrow XQuery$ with support 0.1 and confidence 0.4" which state that researchers who published about XML also published something related to XQuery in 40% of the cases and that this rule applies to 10% of the personnel. We can formulate this as follows.

```
IN document("http://www.cs.atlantis.com/staff.xml")
MINE RULE
FOR ROOT IN /Department//Employee
LET BODY := ROOT/Publications//Keyword,
    HEAD := ROOT/Publications//Keyword
WHERE ROOT//@year > 1990
EXTRACTING RULES WITH SUPPORT = 0.1 AND CONFIDENCE = 0.4
RETURN <AssocRule support = { SUPPORT } confidence = { CONFIDENCE }
                  antecedent = { BODY } consequent = { HEAD } />
```

The IN clause specifies the source data. In this case we address *one* XML document (in Figure 2), but in general any XQuery statement to construct the data source might be used instead.

The FOR clause implements the *context identification* step. A special variable, ROOT, defines through an XPath [20] expression the set of XML fragments constituting the *context* in which the ARs will be extracted (this set corresponds to the set of transactions $\mathcal{D}$ in the relational framework). The ROOT variable is fundamental to the process since support and confidence values are computed w.r.t. the fragments in ROOT. In the above statement, the XPath expression /Department//Employee/Publications specifies that we are interested in rules that are extracted from the publications of *each* employee. Then two special variables, BODY and HEAD, identify the XML fragments which should appear in the rule body and head respectively. Note that both BODY and HEAD *have* to be defined w.r.t. the *context* (i.e., to the ROOT variable), since confidence and support values have meaning only w.r.t. the *context*. More specifically, both BODY and HEAD are defined as Keyword elements appearing in the Publications element of each employee. Since the Keyword element appears both in journals and in books, Keyword is specified as a subelement of Publications placed to an arbitrary level of depth (with the "//" XPath step).

The WHERE clause filters out some of the source fragments, thus expressing the conditions for the *context selection*. Our example requires that among all the subelements of Publications only those published after 1990 are considered.

The EXTRACTING clause specifies the minimum support and confidence values.

The final RETURN clause imposes the structure of the generated rules. An AR is defined by an AssocRule tag, with four attributes, support and confidence which specify the support and confidence values, antecedent and consequent, which specifies the items in the head and body respectively. A sketch of a possible result produced by the above statement follows.

```
<AssocRule support="0.25" confidence="0.45"
           antecedent="XML" consequent="XQuery" />
...
<AssocRule support="0.3" ...   consequent="RDF" />
```

4.2   Advanced Mining

We now move to a slightly more complex AR mining problem. Suppose we wish to find out any interesting dependency between the fact that employees have published books with particular publishers along their career, and the fact that they have later been awarded by a particular society. In addition, we require that the employee is actually an author, and not just an editor of the book, and that the employee has a PhD degree. This problem can be mapped into an AR mining task. Rules have a set of `Publisher` XML elements in the body and a set of `Society` elements in the head, and these elements must be descendants of *the same* `Employee` node. This task can be formulated as follows:

```
IN document("http://www.cs.atlantis.com/staff.xml")
MINE RULE
FOR ROOT IN /Department/Employee
LET BODY := ROOT/Publications/Book/Publisher,
    HEAD := ROOT//Award/@Society
WHERE count(ROOT//Education//PhD) > 0 AND
      contains(BODY//Author,ROOT/PersonalInfo/Name) AND
      BODY/../@year < HEAD/../@year
EXTRACTING RULES WITH count(BODY) = 1 AND count(HEAD) = 1 AND
                    SUPPORT = 0.1 AND CONFIDENCE = 0.2
```

The mining *context* (`ROOT`) is defined with the XPath expression `/Department/People/Employee` which retrieves the set of XML fragments which represent each employee. Then `BODY` is defined as the set of `Publisher` elements within the books published by an employee (referenced by `ROOT`), while `HEAD` is defined as the set of `Society` attributes of every award received by the *same* employee (still referenced by `ROOT`).

In the `WHERE` clause, "`count(ROOT//Education//PhD) > 0`" requires that only the employees with a PhD degree are considered; the clause "`contains(BODY//Author,ROOT/Personal/Name)`" requires that the employee's name appears among the authors of the book (`contains` is one of the core XQuery functions [21]); "`BODY/../@year < HEAD/../@year`" requires that the year of publication of the books precedes the year of the award in the rule head. In the final `EXTRACTING` clause, the "`count(...)=1`" clauses require that both the rule body and head contain exactly one XML fragment.

The `RETURN` clause is optional. If not included, the output is an XML document which contains a set of ARs expressed according to the Predictive Model Markup Language (PMML) standard [2] (a sketch of the produced result follows).

```
<PMML>
 <AssociationModel>
  <AssocItem id="307" value="IEEE" />
   ...
  <AssocItemset id="1" support="..." numberOfItems="1">
   <AssocItemRef itemRef="307" />
  </AssocItemset>
   ...
  <AssocRule support="0.2" confidence="1.0"
             antecedent="2" consequent="1" />
 </AssociationModel>
</PMML>
```

ARs are described by `AssocRule` elements connecting two sets of items, identified by two `AssocItemSet` elements. Each item set is in turn defined as a collection of items (`AssocItem` elements), identified by `ids`. It is easy to note that the PMML representation for ARs tends to be quite lengthy as the complexity of the mining problem increases. For this reason, we included the `RETURN` clause to allow the specification of (possibly) more compact formats for the output result.

5 Related Work

Association rules (ARs) have been first introduced in [4] upon retail databases. The famous Apriori algorithm for extracting ARs was independently published in [5] and in [12]. Although the first algorithms assumed that transactions were represented as sets of binary attributes, along the years many algorithms for the extraction of ARs from multivariate data have been proposed. This includes the use of quantitative attributes (e.g., [18,10]) as well as the integration of concept hierarchies to support the mining of ARs from different levels of abstractions (e.g., [7,17]). Association rules and *episode rules* (a modification of the concept of ARs introduced in [11]) have been applied to the mining of plain text (e.g., [6,15]), or to semi-structured data [16]. However, as far as we know, ARs within the context of *native* XML documents have never been proposed. To assist association rule mining, a number of query languages have been proposed. The `MINE RULE` operator, used in this paper, was first introduced in [13] and extended in [14]. Separately, [9] introduced MSQL, an SQL extension which implements various operations over association rules (e.g., generation, selection, and pruning). [8] introduced DMSQL, a general purpose query language to specify data mining tasks.

Data Mining and XML. A number of proposals to exploit XML within Data Mining have been proposed. These proposals regard both the use of XML as a format to represent the knowledge extracted from the data *and* the development of techniques and tools for *mining* XML documents. The Predictive Model Markup Language (PMML) [2] is an XML standard which can be used to represent most of the types of patterns which can be extracted from the data, e.g., association rules, decision trees, decision rules, etc. PMML does not represent the data themselves but it only allows the description of the data.

6 Conclusions

We have introduced association rules (ARs) from native XML data, starting from their formal definition and the consolidated `MINE RULE` operator [13], a declarative operator that formulates ARs mining tasks on relational data by means of statements that recall SQL. In the same spirit, we defined ARs on native XML data using an XQuery-like operator which allowed us to demonstrate some semantic features of the AR mining from XML data.

Many issues remain open, and there are a number of future research directions; an interesting direction regards the possibility to simultaneously mine both the structure and the contents of XML documents. In fact, XML sets a smooth distinction between the data and their structure.

Another relevant open issue concerns the specification of the *context* for a giving mining problem. Dealing with many generic XML documents, their physical structure might limit the feasible contexts which can be used to extract association rules. This depends on the fact that we use plain XPath expressions to identify the mining context. Our choice is strongly motivated by the intuitiveness and diffusion of the XPath formalism, but if the information is not stored according to the correct mining criteria that suit the user needs, *context identification* becomes a hard task. In order to meet the user needs, a set of transformations might be required, which should simplify the specification of the right context for a specific mining tasks, even if the document schema does not match the given task. In fact, a more general question is how to consider and connect all available metadata, not only the XML DTD or schema information as above, for a specific mining task in a specific domain. As more and more data will be encoded in XML, also an increasing amount of background knowledge will be available in, e.g., RDF metadata or DAML+OIL format ontologies. This additional metadata provides enhanced possibilities to constrain the mining queries both automatically and manually, but it also increases the complexity and thus poses new requirements upon the data mining query language.

Finally, association rules from XML data could be extended to the case of *episode rules*. These are a modification of association rules that take into special account the temporal relations among the different times at which the investigated items are generated. A suitable extension of our proposal could address this specific domain, that proved to be interesting in some telecommunications fields (to mine the log files of nodes in networks for interesting time series that precede several kinds of network faults).

Acknowledgements. The authors have been supported by the *consortium on discovering knowledge with Inductive Queries (cInQ)* [1], a project funded by the Future and Emerging Technologies arm of the IST Programme (Contr. no. IST-2000-26469). Daniele Braga and Alessandro Campi are supported by Microsoft Research. The authors wish to thank Stefano Ceri for the inspiration and discussions that made this work possible.

References

1. consortium on discovering knowledge with INductive Queries (*cInQ*). http://www.cinq-project.org.
2. PMML 2.0 Predictive Model Markup Language. http://www.dmg.org, August 2001.
3. Rakesh Agrawal, Tomasz Imielinski, and Arun Swami. Mining association rules between sets of items in large databases. In P. Buneman and S. Jajodia, editors, *SIGMOD93*, pages 207 – 216, Washington, D.C., USA, May 1993.

4. Rakesh Agrawal, Tomasz Imielinski, and Arun N. Swami. Mining association rules between sets of items in large databases. In Peter Buneman and Sushil Jajodia, editors, *Proceedings of the 1993 ACM SIGMOD International Conference on Management of Data*, pages 207–216, Washington, D.C., 26–28 1993.
5. Rakesh Agrawal and Ramakrishnan Srikant. Mining sequential patterns. In Philip S. Yu and Arbee L. P. Chen, editors, *Proc. 11th Int. Conf. Data Engineering, ICDE*, pages 3–14. IEEE Press, 6–10 1995.
6. Helena Ahonen, Oskari Heinonen, Mika Klemettinen, and A. Inkeri Verkamo. Mining in the phrasal frontier. In *Principles of Data Mining and Knowledge Discovery*, pages 343–350, 1997.
7. J. Han and Y. Fu. Discovery of multiple-level association rules from large databases. In *Proc. of 1995 Int'l Conf. on Very Large Data Bases (VLDB'95), Zürich, Switzerland, September 1995*, pages 420–431, 1995.
8. Jiawei Han and Micheline Kamber. *Data Mining Concepts and Techniques*. Morgan Kaufmann, San Francisco (CA).
9. Tomasz Imielinski and Aashu Virmani. MSQL: A query language for database mining, 1999.
10. Brian Lent, Arun N. Swami, and Jennifer Widom. Clustering association rules. In *ICDE*, pages 220–231, 1997.
11. Heikki Mannila, Hannu Toivonen, and et al. Discovering frequent episodes in sequences (extended abstract), August 1995.
12. Heikki Mannila, Hannu Toivonen, and A. Inkeri Verkamo. Efficient algorithms for discovering association rules. In Usama M. Fayyad and Ramasamy Uthurusamy, editors, *AAAI Workshop on Knowledge Discovery in Databases (KDD-94)*, pages 181–192, Seattle, Washington, 1994. AAAI Press.
13. Rosa Meo, Giuseppe Psaila, and Stefano Ceri. A new sql-like operator for mining association rules. In *VLDB'96, September 3-6, 1996, Mumbai (Bombay), India*, pages 122–133.
14. Rosa Meo, Giuseppe Psaila, and Stefano Ceri. A tightly-coupled architecture for data mining. In *ICDE*, pages 316–323, Orlando, Florida, USA, February 1998.
15. M. Rajman and R. Besanon. Text mining: Natural language techniques and text mining applications, 1997.
16. Lisa Singh, Peter Scheuermann, and Bin Chen. Generating association rules from semi-structured documents using an extended concept hierarchy. In *CIKM*, pages 193–200, 1997.
17. Ramakrishnan Srikant and Rakesh Agrawal. Mining generalized association rules. In *The VLDB Journal*, pages 407–419, 1995.
18. Ramakrishnan Srikant and Rakesh Agrawal. Mining quantitative association rules in large relational tables. In H. V. Jagadish and Inderpal Singh Mumick, editors, *Proceedings of the 1996 ACM SIGMOD International Conference on Management of Data*, pages 1–12, Montreal, Quebec, Canada, 4–6 1996.
19. World Wide Web Consortium. Extensible Markup Language (XML) Version 1.0 W3C Recommendation. http://www.w3c.org/xml/, February 1998.
20. World Wide Web Consortium. XML Path Language (XPath) Version 1.0, W3C Recommendation. http://www.w3c.org/tr/xpath/, November 1999.
21. World Wide Web Consortium. XQuery 1.0: An XML Query Language W3C Working Draft. http://www.w3.org/TR/2001/WD-xquery-20010607, June 2001.

Estimating Joint Probabilities from Marginal Ones*

Tao Li, Shenghuo Zhu, Mitsunori Ogihara, and Yinhe Cheng

Computer Science Department
University of Rochester
Rochester, New York 14627-0226
{taoli,zsh,ogihara,cheng}@cs.rochester.edu

Abstract. Estimating joint probabilities plays an important role in many data mining and machine learning tasks. In this paper we introduce two methods, $minAB$ and $prodAB$, to estimate joint probabilities. Both methods are based on a light-weight structure, *partition support*. The core idea is to maintain the partition support of itemsets over logically disjoint partitions and then use it to estimate joint probabilities of itemsets of higher cardinalitiess. We present extensive mathematical analyses on both methods and compare their performances on synthetic datasets. We also demonstrate a case study of using the estimation methods in *Apriori* algorithm for fast association mining. Moreover, we explore the usefulness of the estimation methods in other mining/learning tasks [9]. Experimental results show the effectiveness of the estimation methods.

Keywords: *Joint Probability, Estimation, Association Mining*

1 Introduction

Estimating the joint probabilities in a collection of N observations on M events is the problem of estimating the joint probabilities of events, given the probabilities of single events. Generally the collection of N observations on M events is represented by a $N \times M$ binary table D where $D_{ij} = 1$ denotes that the i-th event occurs in the j-th observation and $D_{ij} = 0$ otherwise. Let $\{\mathcal{I}_j\}$, $j = 1, \cdots, M$, represent the events. $P(\mathcal{I}_j)$ can be estimated by computing its occurrence frequency in the table. Thus given $P(\mathcal{I}_j)$, $j = 1, \cdots, M$, the goal is to estimate the joint probability $P(\mathcal{I}_{j_1}, \cdots, \mathcal{I}_{j_l})$, $l \geq 2, 1 \leq j_1, \cdots, j_l \leq M$.

A simple way to estimate joint probabilities is, like we approximate the probabilities of a single event, to just count the co-occurrences of the events in the table D (i.e., via combinatory counting). Although in many cases this simple method does provide satisfactory solutions, there are cases in which the time

---

* The project is supported in part by NIH Grants 5-P41-RR09283, RO1-AG18231, and P30-AG18254 and by NSF Grants EIA-0080124, NSF CCR-9701911, and DUE-9980943. We would also like to thank Dr. Meng Xiang Tang and Xianghui Liu for their helpful discussions.

Y. Kambayashi, W. Winiwarter, M. Arikawa (Eds.): DaWaK 2002, LNCS 2454, pp. 31–41, 2002.
© Springer-Verlag Berlin Heidelberg 2002

or space complexity of combinatory counting is very large even unacceptable. For example, in a large dataset which cannot fit in the main memory, combinatory counting would incur considerable overheads. Even in cases in which the complexity of combinatory counting is manageable, there can also be reasons to consider the estimation methods. First, the given dataset can be viewed as a sample of some source distribution. So, even the exact counting just provides an approximation to the source distribution. On the other hand, in many application domains, the goals are finding the interesting patterns which satisfies some given thresholds to support the decision processes. Most of those thresholds are given by estimations or specified manually. Hence, the combinatory counting may not be worth the computation cost in these cases.

Since $P(\mathcal{A}|\mathcal{B}) = \frac{P(\mathcal{A},\mathcal{B})}{P(\mathcal{B})}$, knowing the joint probabilities is useful to infer the intrinsic relations between events such as associations [1], correlations [3], causalities [10] and multidimensional patterns [7]. Hence, it plays an important role in many data mining tasks. For example, frequent itemset mining in the discovery of association rules [1,4] can be thought as finding the set of items whose joint probabilities satisfy the given parameters. In the rest of the paper, we use D to denote the given $N \times M$ dataset, and $I = \mathcal{I}_1, \mathcal{I}_2, ..., \mathcal{I}_M$ be a set of events[1]. Each row, R_i, in the dataset, D, is referred as an observation (a record). An itemset with k items is called k-itemset.

In this paper we present two methods, $minAB$ and $prodAB$, to estimate the joint probabilities without combinatory counting and explores their applications in data mining. Both methods are based on a structure called *partition support*. The main idea is to maintain the partition support information of items (or itemsets) over each logically disjoint partition and then use it to carry out the estimation. The rest of the paper is organized as follows: Section 2 introduces the basic concepts of *partition support*. Section 3 describes the $minAB$ estimation methods and analyzes its properties. Section 4 presents $prodAB$ estimation methods. Section 5 shows the performances of the two estimation methods on synthetic datasets. Section 6 gives a case study on using the estimation methods for fast association mining. Section 7 concludes and proposes our future work.

2   Partition Support

Definition 1. *The* **support count** $\lambda(S, D)$ *of itemset* S *in dataset* D *is the number of records in* D *containing* S. *If we logically divided the datasets* D *into disjoint partition* $D_1, ..., D_n, n \geq 1$, *the* **partition support** $PS(S, D, n)$ *of an itemset* S *over* D *is a n-tuple* $(\lambda(S, D_1), \lambda(S, D_2), ..., \lambda(S, D_n))$.

The support count of itemset S in D, $|\lambda(S, D)|$, is the sum of all the elements in $PS(S, D, n)$. The partition support $PS(S, D, n)$ is a structure consisting of the support counts of S in each partition. Figure 2 shows an example of the dataset. It has five items (A, B, C, E, F) and six records $(1, 2, 3, 4, 5, 6)$. Clearly,

---

[1] items or attributes.

	A	B	C	E	F
1	0	1	1	1	1
2	1	0	0	1	1
3	1	1	0	1	1
4	0	1	1	1	1
5	1	1	1	0	0
6	0	1	1	0	1

$$PS(\{A\}, D, 3) = (\lambda(\{A\}, D1), \lambda(\{A\}, D2), \lambda(\{A\}, D3)) = (1, 1, 1),$$
$$PS(\{B\}, D, 3) = (\lambda(\{B\}, D1), \lambda(\{B\}, D2), \lambda(\{B\}, D3)) = (1, 2, 2),$$
$$PS(\{A, B\}, D, 3) = (\lambda(\{A, B\}, D1), \lambda(\{A, B\}, D2), \lambda(\{A, B\}, D3))$$
$$= (0, 1, 1),$$
$$|\lambda(\{A, B\}, D)| = 2;$$
$$PS(\{B, C\}, D, 3) = (1, 2, 2), \quad |\lambda(\{A, B, C\}, D)| = 2.$$

Fig. 1. An Example Dataset

Fig. 2. The Partition Support

$\lambda(\{A\}, D) = 3, \lambda(\{B\}, D) = 5, \lambda(\{A, B\}, D) = 2$. If we divide D into $D_1 = \{1, 2\}, D_2 = \{3, 4\}, D_3 = \{5, 6\}$, then the partition support is given in Fig. 2.

3   *minAB* Estimation

3.1   Method Description

Note that in the above example,

$$|\lambda(\{A, B, C\}, D)| \leq \sum_{i=1}^{3} \min\{\lambda(\{A\}, D_i), \lambda(\{B\}, D_i), \lambda(\{C\}, D_i)\} = 3, \quad (1)$$

where $min(x, y)$ returns the smaller value of x and y. In general, given the partition support $PS(\{\mathcal{I}_i\}, D)$ of any singleton itemset $\{\mathcal{I}_i\}$, $i = 1, \cdots, M$, we can get an upper estimation of the support count of any itemset $S = \{\mathcal{I}_{i1}, \mathcal{I}_{i2}, \cdots, \mathcal{I}_{ik}\}$ since $\lambda(S, D) \leq \sum_i \min\{\lambda(\{\mathcal{I}_{i1}\}, D_i), \cdots, \lambda(\{\mathcal{I}_{ik}\}, D_i)\}$. In other words, knowing the approximate distribution of each singleton item over the partitions, we can estimate the joint probabilities. Clearly we can also maintain the partition support of size k, $k \geq 1$, itemsets and use it to get an upper estimation of the support counts of itemsets with higher cardinalities. For example, if we have the support count of any 2-itemset, we can use it to obtain a tighter upper bound of the itemset $S : \sum_i \min\{\lambda(S_1^{(2)}, D_i), \cdots \lambda(S_t^{(2)}, D_i)\}$, where $S_j^{(2)}$, $j = 1, \cdots, t$, are all the 2-subsets of S. For previous example, using the partition support of singleton sets, we have Eq. (1). We get a tighter estimate Eq. (2) by using the partition support of 2-sets.

$$|\lambda(\{A, B, C\}, D)| \leq \sum_{i=1}^{3} \min\{\lambda(\{A, B\}, D_i), \lambda(\{A, C\}, D_i), \lambda(\{B, C\}, D_i)\} = 2.$$
$$(2)$$

The *minAB* estimation method can be described as follows: divide the dataset into logical partitions, maintain the partition support of itemsets and then use summation of the minimums of the partition support of itemsets to estimate the joint probability of itemsets with higher cardinalities. Note that the space complexity for partition support is increased exponentially with respect to the size of the itemsets (and the time complexity is increased too). Hence in most applications, we only maintain the partition support for singleton sets.

3.2   Method Analysis

In this section, we analyze the relationship between the number of partitions and the accuracy of the estimate and try to come up with the methods to determine the approximate number of partitions k. We model their relationship in two different ways. One is to establish the expression of the probability of correct estimate in terms of number of partitions and the other is to establish the relationship between the estimation error and the number of partitions.

Probability of Correct Estimation. We first analyze the case of using the partition support of singleton sets to estimate the joint probability of 2-sets. The problem can be described as follows: given the dataset D with N records, consider two boolean attributes a and b, i.e., a and b are either 0 or 1. Let the number of records in D such that $a = 1$ be $\lambda(\{a\}, D) = A$, i.e., $P(a = 1) \approx \frac{A}{N}$, the number of records with $b = 1$ be $\lambda(\{b\}, D) = B$, i.e., $P(b = 1) \approx \frac{B}{N}$, then we use $min(A, B)$ to estimate $\lambda(\{a, b\}, D)$, the number of records with both $a = 1$ and $b = 1$. In other words, we use $min(A, B)$ to estimate $P(a = 1, b = 1) \leq \frac{min(A,B)}{N}$. The following lemma (proved in [9]) gives the probability of correct estimate.

Lemma 1. *Suppose that A, B subject to the binomial probability $Binomial(N, p_a)$ and $Binomial(N, p_b)$, respectively, and $P(a = 1, b = 1) = q$. Let P_N be the probability of the correct estimation, i.e., $min(A, B) = \lambda(\{a, b\}, D))$. We have,*

$$P_N \equiv P(min(A, B) = \lambda(\{a, b\}, D)|N) \tag{3}$$
$$= (1 + q - p_a)^N + (1 + q - p_b)^N - (1 + 2q - p_a - p_b)^N.$$

In particular, $P_1 = 1$. Observe that the above lemma can be easily extend to more attributes. If we divide the dataset into two disjoint partitions and assume the partitions are independent, then the probability of correct estimation is $P_{N/2} \times P_{N/2}$.

Lemma 2. $P_{N/2} \times P_{N/2} > P_N$.

If we divide the database into k partitions and assume the independence among the partitions, the probability of the correct estimation of the $minAB$ method is $P_{N/k}^k$. In general, we have

Proposition 1. $P_{N/(k+1)}^{k+1} > P_{N/k}^k, k \geq 1$.

The above proposition (proved in [9]) illustrates that the more the number of partitions, the more accurate the estimation. In particular, if $k = N$, i.e., if we view each record as a partition, then we always get the correct estimation. However, it would cost more time and space for larger k. Hence, from practical perspective, we need choose the proper k to reduce the computation cost while ensure the enough accuracy. Figure 3(a) and 3(b) depict the probabilities of correct estimate for $N = 10000, p_a = p_b = 0.005, q = 0.0045$, and $N = 100000, p_a = p_b = 0.001, q = 0.0009$, respectively, on different partitions.

So given two itemsets S_1 and S_2, suppose that $\lambda(S_1, D)$ and $\lambda(S_2, D)$ satisfy the conditions of Lemma 1, then when we use the partition support of S_1 and S_2 to estimate the actual support count of $S_1 \cup S_2$, the probability of correct estimation is $P^k_{N/k}$. Therefore we can choose the number of partitions based on the probability of the correct estimation: given a pre-defined parameter σ, we want the probability of correct estimation to be no less than σ, i.e., $P^k_{N/k} \geq \sigma$. To compute $P^k_{N/k}$, we use Lemma 1. p_a and p_b can be approximated by the number of occurrences of the respective attributes, and let q be some given parameter (say, the minimum support of the association rules in Section 6). Hence the above inequality gives us a principle to choose k.

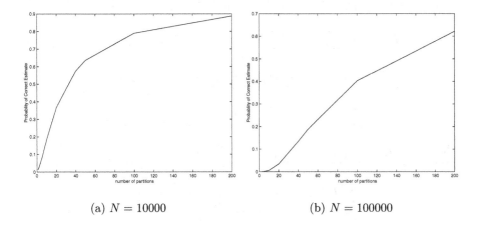

(a) $N = 10000$ (b) $N = 100000$

Fig. 3. Probability of the Correct Estimation

Estimation Error. Another way to model the relation between the number of partitions and the estimate is to compute the expectation of the estimation error between $min(A, B)$ and $\lambda(\{a, b\}, D)$. It's not difficult to get the distribution function for $min(A, B)$, where A is $Binomial(N, p_a)$, B is $Binomial(N, p_b)$, $P(a = 1, b = 1) = q$. Denote $X = min(A, B)$, then X assumes discrete value $0, 1, ..., N$. We could directly calculate the probability of $P(X = t)$, where $t = 0, 1, ..., N$. More details of the computation can be found in [9]. The expectation of $min(A, B)$ is $E(min(A, B)) = \sum_{t=0}^{N} t P(X = t)$ and the expectation of the number of transactions with both $a = 1$ and $b = 1$ is $E_{ab} = Nq$. Hence we get the mean value of the estimate error $e(N) = |E(min(A, B)) - E_{ab}|$. If we divide the database into two partitions, the estimation error is then $2 \times e(N/2)$. In general the estimation error of the $minAB$ method is $k \times e(\frac{N}{k})$ if we have $k \geq 1$ partitions. The estimation error also gives us another heuristic to pick the number of database partitions: given a pre-defined error bound γ, we want the estimation error to be smaller than γ. We can also derive the *probability error* of the $minAB$ estimation method by $\frac{k \times e(\frac{N}{k})}{N}$.

4   *prodAB* Estimation

The *prodAB* estimation is also based on partition support. Suppose there are N data points, which are randomly divided into k partitions and each partition contains $n = N/k$ points. Let $X_{ij} = 1$ be the event that the attribute a of the j-th point in i-th partition is active, $X_{ij} = 0$ otherwise. Let $Y_{ij} = 1$ be the event that the attribute b of the j-th point in i-th partition is active, $Y_{ij} = 0$ otherwise. X_{ij}'s are i.i.d.(independent identically distributed) and obey zero-one distribution with probability p_a. Y_{ij}'s are i.i.d. and obey zero-one distribution with p_b. X_{ij} and $Y_{i'j'}$ are independent if $(i,j) \neq (i',j')$. $P(X_{ij} = 1, Y_{ij} = 1) = q$. Of course, $q \leq p_a$ and $q \leq p_b$. Knowing $A_i = \sum_{j=1}^{n} X_{ij}$ and $B_i = \sum_{j=1}^{n} Y_{ij}$, which is just the *partition support* of $\{a\}$ and $\{b\}$, the goal is to estimate q.

$$EA_i = E\sum_j X_{ij} = \sum_j EX_{ij} = np_a, \quad EB_i = np_b \tag{4}$$

$$EA_iB_i = E(\sum_j X_{ij} \sum_j Y_{ij}) = E(\sum_j X_{ij}Y_{ij} + \sum_{j \neq j'} X_{ij}Y_{ij'})$$
$$= \sum_j EX_{ij}Y_{ij} + \sum_{j \neq j'} EX_{ij}EY_{ij'} = nq + n(n-1)p_ap_b \tag{5}$$

$$E(\sum_i A_i \sum_i B_i) = E(\sum_{ij} X_{ij} \sum_{ij} Y_{ij}) = E(\sum_{ij} X_{ij}Y_{ij} + \sum_{(i,j) \neq (i',j')} X_{ij}Y_{i'j'})$$
$$= \sum_{ij} E(X_{ij}Y_{ij}) + \sum_{(i,j) \neq (i',j')} EX_{ij}EY_{i'j'} = nkq + nk(nk-1)p_ap_b \tag{6}$$

Inserting Eq. (4) into Eq. (5), Eq. (7) can be derived.

$$q = \frac{nEA_iB_i - (n-1)EA_iEB_i}{n^2} \tag{7}$$

If we estimate $E(A_iB_i)$ with $\frac{1}{k}\sum_i A_iB_i$, EA_i with $\frac{1}{k}\sum_i A_i$ and EB_i with $\frac{1}{k}\sum_i B_i$, we can estimate q by

$$\hat{q} = \frac{nk\sum_i A_iB_i - (n-1)\sum_i A_i \sum_i B_i}{n^2k^2} \tag{8}$$

In the case $n = 1$, $\hat{q} = \frac{1}{k}\sum_i A_iB_i$ is the exact rate of the points whose attributes $\mathcal{A}$ and $\mathcal{B}$ are active. In the case $k = 1$, $\hat{q} = \frac{1}{n^2}A_iB_i$ is the rate of the points whose attribute $\mathcal{A}$ is active times the rate of the points whose attribute $\mathcal{B}$ is active, i.e., it is the estimation by assuming attributes $\mathcal{A}$ and attribute $\mathcal{B}$ are independent.

Unfortunately, Eq. (8) is a biased estimation, i.e., $E\hat{q} \neq q$. Now, replacing p_ap_b in Eq. (5) with the one in Eq. (6), we have

$$q = \frac{k(nk-1)E(A_iB_i) - (n-1)E(\sum_i A_i \sum_i B_i)}{n^2k(k-1)} \tag{9}$$

If we estimate $E(A_iB_i)$ with $\frac{1}{k}\sum_i A_iB_i$ and $E(\sum_i A_i \sum_i B_i)$ with $\sum_i A_i \sum_i B_i$, we estimate q by

$$\hat{q} = \frac{(nk-1)\sum_i A_iB_i - (n-1)\sum_i A_i \sum_i B_i}{n^2k(k-1)} \tag{10}$$

This estimation Eq. (10) is referred as $prodAB$ estimation and it is an unbiased estimation because

$$E\hat{q} = \frac{(nk-1)\sum_i E(A_iB_i) - (n-1)E(\sum_i A_i \sum_i B_i)}{n^2k(k-1)} = q \tag{11}$$

The *probability error* of $prodAB$ method can be estimated by Eq. (12)(proof in [9]). The error goes to zeros as the number of partitions, k, goes to infinite.

$$E(\hat{q}-q)^2 = \frac{(nk-1)(n-1)}{n^2k(k-1)}[(q-p_ap_b)^2 - p_ap_b(p_a+p_b)] + \frac{1}{nk}q - \frac{1}{n^2k(k-1)}q^2 \tag{12}$$

Moreover, $minAB$ can be used to improve the accuracy of $prodAB$ by restricting the estimation with the upper bound provided by $minAB$.

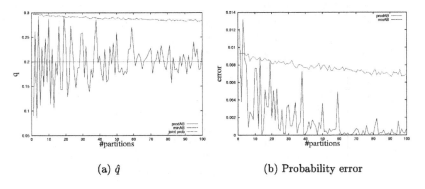

(a) $\hat{q}$ (b) Probability error

Fig. 4. Experimental results of $prodAB$ and $minAB$, $p_a = p_b = 0.3, q = 0.2$

5   Experimental Results of Two Estimation Methods

In this section, we present the experimental results of two estimation methods: $prodAB$ and $minAB$. We generate synthetic data sets with attributes a and b according to the known probabilities p_a, p_b and q. Each data set has $N = 100000$ data points. Fig.4 and Fig.5 illustrate the result of the experiments. It is clear that the *probability error* of the estimations decreases as the number of partitions increases. Also, we find that when a and b are strongly correlated, i.e., $q \sim min(p_a, p_b)$ (e.g., Fig.5), the $minAB$ method produces more stable results than the $prodAB$ method. Otherwise, (e.g., Fig.4), the $prodAB$ method provides more accurate estimations.

6   A Case Study for Fast Association Mining

In this section, we demonstrate a case study of using estimation methods for fast association mining. More applications of using estimation methods for rule pruning, online and distributed mining can be found in [9].

Table 1. Comparison of $MPSE1$ and $Apriori$

Setting	Size of Itemsets	Number of Candidates Eliminated	Number of Candidates Remained	Total Number of of Candidates	Number of Frequent Itemsets
D_1	2	955	72581	73536	1245
with	3	1602	1352	2954	145
$k = 10$	4	17	62	79	62
	5	6	14	20	14
	6	0	1	1	1
D_1	2	10998	62538	73536	1245
with	3	2788	166	2954	145
$k = 100$	4	17	62	79	62
	5	6	14	20	14
	6	0	1	1	1
D_2	2	919	72617	73536	1164
with	3	1714	997	2711	63
$k = 50$	4	3	25	28	25
	5	1	7	8	7
	6	0	0	0	0
D_3	2	899	72264	73153	1143
with	3	1702	971	2673	75
$k = 100$	4	19	20	39	20
	5	0	5	5	5
	6	0	0	0	0

6.1   Background on Association Mining

The association mining task, first introduced in [1] can be broken into two steps: The first step is to identify all frequent itemsets and the second step is to generate association rules with high confidence. There is a vast literature on this topic (for a survey, see [6]). Among the existing algorithms, $Apriori$ [2] is a standard one and is used as the basis for many other existing algorithms. $Apriori$ effectively uses the fact that the collection of frequent itemsets is a set lattice. To discover all frequent itemsets, $Apriori$ goes by the size k of the itemsets that are examined. For $k = 1, 2, ...$, one finds all frequent itemsets having cardinality exactly k, and then, based on the lattice property, generates the candidate for the next value of k. The search is entirely terminated when no frequent itemsets are discovered at any value of k, when, by the lattice property, one can guarantee that there is no frequent itemset of a larger size. Our estimation methods can be used in the *Apriori* algorithm for fast association mining. In [8], a novel structure *segment support map (SSM)* is proposed to improve the performance of frequent-set mining algorithms. An SSM is a structure consisting of the support counts for all singleton itemsets in each segment of the transaction database. The authors also show how to use SSM in *Carma* [5] for efficient on-line mining. In this paper we extend the concept of SSM to partition support count and explore how to use the partition support to estimate the joint probabilities. We will show how to use the partition support estimate in *Apriori* for fast association mining.

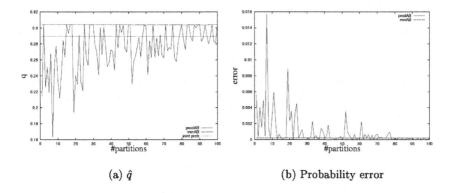

(a) $\hat{q}$ (b) Probability error

Fig. 5. Experimental results of *prodAB* and *minAB*, $p_a = 0.7, p_b = 0.3, q = 0.29$

6.2   Use Estimates for Fast Mining

Partition support based estimate methods can be used in *Apriori* to reduce the size of candidate itemsets or reduce the scans of the databases. The algorithm $MPSE1$ (Mining with Partition Support Estimate 1) uses the $minAB$ estimation method to prune the candidate itemsets. The underlying framework of $MPSE1$ is the same as that of *Apriori* except that a process of partition support estimating is inserted between the candidate generation phase and the counting phase[2]. In general, $MPSE1$ can maintain the partition support of frequent i-itemsets for some $i \geq 1$. However, as described in Section 3.1, in our implementation we only maintain the partition support for singleton sets with the consideration of space and time complexity.

The estimation methods can be used more aggressively to reduce the number of scans. Algorithm $MPSE2$ uses *Apriori* as the basis, but it scans the database only twice, at the beginning and the end. First, $MPSE2$ scans the database to compute all frequent 1-itemsets and the partition support of all singleton sets. Then it executes *Apriori* for itemsets of size greater than one, but database scan is postponed. Instead, $MPSE2$ estimates the support of each candidate

---

[2] Since the $minAB$ estimate is an upper bound, so we will not eliminate any valid frequent itemsets.

itemset using $minAB$ method. Eventually, $MPSE2$ checks for each candidate that remained after pruning whether it is frequent or not.[3]

6.3   Experimental Result and Analysis

Test Organization. We evaluated the algorithms using synthetic datasets as well as real database. We used three synthetic datasets $T10.I5.D10k$, $T10.I5.D50k$, and $T10.I5.D100k$ with 500 items as described in [2]. We denote them by D_1, D_2, D_3. These database model supermarket basket data and have been used as benchmarks for association rule algorithms. We also tested our algorithms on a real database, called the Perinatal Database(PD)[4]. After preprocessing, the database has information of 16304 different birth records with 197 binary attributes. Unlike the sales market database, associations in the Perinatal Database are relatively large. The size of the maximal frequent itemset is twelve with the minimum support of 15%. All the experiments are performed on a Sun $U5/333$ machine with 128 MB memory, running on Sun OS 5.7.

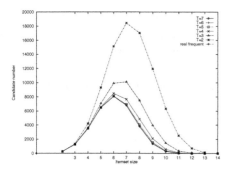

Database	$Apriori$	$MPSE2$
D_2	36.258	28.621
D_3	67.245	44.879

Fig. 7. Comparison of Running Time of $MPSE2$ and $Apriori$ on D_2 and D_3 with $k = 10$

Fig. 6. Candidate Number Generated by $MPSE2$ on PD

Candidate Reducing using $MPSE1$. Table 1 shows the results on D_1 when the database is divided into ten parts (i.e., $k = 10$) and one hundred parts (i.e., $k = 100$), and the results on D_2 with $k = 50$ and D_3 with $k = 100$. The columns are the setting, the size of itemsets, the number of candidates eliminated by $MPSE1$, the number of candidates that remained in C after the pruning phase of $MPSE2$, the total number of candidates before pruning, and the number of frequent itemsets, respectively. There is a significant amount of reduction in the number of candidates for 2-itemsets and 3-itemsets.

---

[3] $MPSE2$ can be modified so that it takes as parameter T and switch from $Apriori$ to $MPSE2$ at level T. By default $T = 2$.

[4] This database contains information of newborns in the Great Rochester area in the calendar year of 1998.

Candidate Reducing using $MPSE2$. Figure 6 shows the results of running $MPSE2$ on PD with the minimum support of 15%, $k = 100$, for various values of T. We observe that with $T > 4$, the candidate set gets very close to the actual collection of frequent itemsets. This is very effective, given that the size of the maximal large itemsets is 12. Figure 7 shows the running time (in seconds) of $MPSE2$ on D_2, D_3 with $k = 10$ and minimum support of 0.1% comparing with $Apriori$.

7   Conclusion

In this paper we present two methods of estimating joint probabilities and discuss their applications in data mining. We are currently implementing the idea of using the estimation methods for distributed and online mining.

References

1. R. Agrawal, T. Imielinski, and A. Swami. Mining associations between sets of items in massive databases. In *Proc. of ACM SIGMOD*, 1993.
2. R. Agrawal and R. Srikant. Fast algorithms for mining association rules in large databases. In *VLDB*, 1994.
3. S. Brin, R. Motwani, and C. Silverstein. Beyond market baskets: generalizaing association rules to correlation. In *Proc. of ACM SIGMOD*, 1997.
4. Trevor Hastie, Robert Tibshirani, and Jerome Friedman. *The Elemetns of Statistical Learning: Data Mining, Inference, Prediction.* Springer, 2001.
5. C. Hidber. Online association rule mining. In *Proc. of ACM SIGMOD*, 1999.
6. J. Hipp, U. Güntzer, and G. Nakhaeizadeh. Algorithms for association rule mining: a general survey and comparison. *SIGKDD Explorations*, 2(1):58–63, 2000.
7. M. Kamber, J. Han, and J. Y. Chiang. Metarules-guided mining of multidimensional association rules using data cubes. In *Proc. of ACM SIGKDD*, 1997.
8. L. V. S. Lakshmanan, C. K. S. Leung, and R. T. Ng. The segment support map: Scalable mining of frequent itemsets. *SIGKDD Explorations*, 2(2), December 2000.
9. Tao Li, Shenghuo Zhu, Mitsunori Ogihara, and Yinhe Cheng. Estimating joint probabilities without combinatory counting. Technical Report TR-764, Computer Science Department,University of Rochester, 2002.
10. C. Silverstein, S. Brin, R. Motwani, and J. Ullman. Scalable techniques for mining causal structures. In *Proc. of VLDB*, 1998.

Self-Tuning Clustering: An Adaptive Clustering Method for Transaction Data

Ching-Huang Yun[1], Kun-Ta Chuang[2], and Ming-Syan Chen[1]

[1] Department of Electrical Engineering
National Taiwan University
Taipei, Taiwan, ROC
mschen@cc.ee.ntu.edu.tw, chyun@arbor.ee.ntu.edu.tw
[2] Graduate Institute of Communication Engineering
National Taiwan University
Taipei, Taiwan, ROC
doug@arbor.ee.ntu.edu.tw

Abstract. In this paper, we devise an efficient algorithm for clustering market-basket data items. Market-basket data analysis has been well addressed in mining association rules for discovering the set of large items which are the frequently purchased items among all transactions. In essence, clustering is meant to divide a set of data items into some proper groups in such a way that items in the same group are as similar to one another as possible. In view of the nature of clustering market basket data, we present a measurement, called the small-large (SL) ratio, which is in essence the ratio of the number of small items to that of large items. Clearly, the smaller the SL ratio of a cluster, the more similar to one another the items in the cluster are. Then, by utilizing a self-tuning technique for adaptively tuning the input and output SL ratio thresholds, we develop an efficient clustering algorithm, *algorithm STC* (standing for *Self-Tuning Clustering*), for clustering market-basket data. The objective of algorithm STC is *"Given a database of transactions, determine a clustering such that the average SL ratio is minimized."* We conduct several experiments on the real data and the synthetic workload for performance studies. It is shown by our experimental results that by utilizing the self-tuning technique to adaptively minimize the input and output SL ratio thresholds, algorithm STC performs very well. Specifically, algorithm STC not only incurs an execution time that is significantly smaller than that by prior works but also leads to the clustering results of very good quality.

Keywords: Data mining, clustering market-basket data, small-large ratios, adaptive self-tuning.

1 Introduction

Mining of databases has attracted a growing amount of attention in database communities due to its wide applicability to improving marketing strategies [3].

Y. Kambayashi, W. Winiwarter, M. Arikawa (Eds.): DaWaK 2002, LNCS 2454, pp. 42–51, 2002.

Among others, data clustering is an important technique for exploratory data analysis [6]. In essence, clustering is meant to divide a set of data items into some proper groups in such a way that items in the same group are as similar to one another as possible. Most clustering techniques utilize a pairwise similarity for measuring the distance of two data points. Recently, there has been a growing emphasis on clustering very large datasets to discover useful patterns and correlations among attributes [4] [10]. Note that clustering is a very service dependent issue and its potential applications call for their own specific requirements.

Itemset data, referred to as market-basket data, has been well studied in mining association rules for discovering the set of frequently purchased items [2]. Different from the traditional data, the features of market basket data are known to be high dimensionality, sparsity, and with massive outliers. It is noted that there are several clustering technologies which addressed the issue of clustering market-basket data [5][7][8][9]. ROCK [5] is an agglomerative hierarchical clustering algorithm by treating market-basket data as categorical data and using the links between the data points for clustering categorical data. The authors in [7] proposed an algorithm by using large items as the similarity measurement to divide the transactions into clusters such that similar transactions are in the same clusters. OAK [8] combines hierarchical and partitional clustering techniques. The work in [9] utilized a predetermined ratio for clustering market-basket data.

In view of the nature of clustering market-basket data, we present in [9] a measurement, called the *small-large (SL) ratio*, which is in essence the ratio of the number of small items to that of large items. With their formal definitions given in Section 2, a *large item* is basically an item with frequent occurrence in transactions whereas a *small item* is an item with infrequent occurrence in transactions. Clearly, the smaller the SL ratio of a cluster, the more similar to one another the items in the cluster are. Then, by utilizing a self-tuning technique for adaptively tuning the input and output SL ratio thresholds, we develop an efficient clustering algorithm, referred to as *algorithm STC* (standing for *Self-Tuning Clustering*), for clustering market-basket data. Algorithm STC consists of three phases, namely, *the pre-determination phase, the allocation phase,* and *the refinement phase*. In the pre-determination phase, the *minimum support S* and the *maximum ceiling E* are calculated according to a given parameter, called *SL distribution rate β*. In the allocation phase, algorithm STC uses the minimum support S to identify the large items and uses the maximum ceiling E to identify the small items. Explicitly, algorithm STC scans the database and allocates each transaction to a cluster for minimizing the SL ratio. In the refinement phase, each transaction will be evaluated for its status to minimize its SL ratio in the corresponding cluster. Algorithm STC utilizes two kinds of SL ratio thresholds, *output SL ratio threshold α^o* and *input SL ratio threshold α^i*, to evaluate the quality of the clustering. Explicitly, a transaction is moved from one cluster to the excess pool if its SL ratio is larger than α^o, and a transaction is moved from the excess pool to one cluster if the SL ratio is smaller than α^i. Detailed operations of STC will be described in Section 3 later. It is important to note that by utilizing $\alpha(U)$ to tune both α^i and α^o, STC is able to minimize the SL ratios of transactions in individual clusters, thereby improving the quality of clustering. As will be shown by our experimental results, algorithm STC devised in this paper significantly outperforms previous efforts [5][7] in the execution efficiency and also the clustering quality for both synthetic and real market-basket data.

This paper is organized as follows. Preliminaries are given in Section 2. In Section 3, algorithm STC is devised for clustering market-basket data. Experimental studies are conducted in Section 4. This paper concludes with Section 5.

2   Problem Description

In this paper, the market-basket data is represented by a set of transactions. A database of transactions is denoted by $D = \{t_1, t_2, ..., t_h\}$, where each transaction t_i is a set of items $\{i_1, i_2, ..., i_h\}$. Similarly to the definition taken by [7], a clustering $U = < C_1, C_2, ..., C_k >$ is a partition of transactions, where C_i is a cluster consisting of a set of transactions. Note that the minimum support S and the maximum ceiling E are determined according to the SL distribution rate β in the pre-determination phase. The details of the pre-determination phase will be shown later.

2.1   Large Items and Small Items

The support of an item i in a cluster C, called $Sup_C(i)$, is defined as the percentage of transactions which contain this item i in cluster C. An item i in a cluster C is called a *large item* if $Sup_C(i)$ is larger than the minimum support S. On the other hand, an item j in a cluster C is called a *small item* if $Sup_C(j)$ is less than the maximum ceiling E. In addition, an item is called a middle item if it is neither large nor small.

2.2   Small-Large (SL) Ratio

Note that there are three kinds of SL ratios, i.e., *SL ratio of a transaction*, *SL ratio of a clustering*, and *average SL ratio*, to be calculated in the data clustering procedure.

SL Ratio of a Transaction: For a transaction t in cluster C_i, the SL ratio of t in cluster C_i is defined as:

$$R_{SL}(C_i, t) = \frac{|S(C_i, t)|}{|L(C_i, t)|},$$

where $|L(C_i, t)|$ represents the number of the large items in t and $|S(C_i, t)|$ represents the number of the small items in t.

SL Ratio of a Clustering: For a clustering $U = < C_1, ..., C_p >$, the SL ratio of U is defined as:

$$R_{SL}(U) = \sum_{i=1}^{p} \sum_{j=1}^{N^T(C_i)} R_{SL}(C_i, t_j),$$

where $N^T(C_i)$ is the number of transactions and t_j is the jth transaction in cluster C_i.

Average SL Ratio: For a clustering $U =< C_1, ..., C_p >$, the average SL ratio is defined as:

$$\alpha(U) = \frac{R_{SL}(U)}{N^T(U)},$$

where $N^T(U)$ is the number of transactions in clustering U.

2.3   Objective of Clustering Market-Basket Data

The objective of clustering market-basket data is *"Given a database of transactions, determine a clustering U such that the average SL ratio $\alpha(U)$ is minimized."* For each cluster, the large items correspond to the products which are sold frequently. Such an information is usually useful for vendors to deal with market segmentation. Note that the clustering technique we devise aims to maximizing both the *intra-cluster similarity* and the *inter-cluster dissimilarity*.

Intra-Cluster Similarity: An item i is large if there are sufficient transactions containing i. These transactions are said to be similar to one another if they contain many common large items. On the other hand, an item j is small if there are relatively few transactions containing j. Thus, having fewer small items implies that these transactions are more similar to one another. To achieve the intra-cluster similarity of transactions, the number of large items is to be maximized whereas that of small items should be minimized in each cluster. The average SL ratio can hence be minimized.

Inter-Cluster Dissimilarity: To achieve the inter-cluster dissimilarity of transactions, a large item in one cluster is expected be a small item in another cluster. Explicitly, if an item i is large in cluster C_a, there should be relatively few transactions in another cluster C_b containing i. By maximizing the number of large items and minimizing the number of small items, dissimilar transactions will be allocated to the different clusters. By increasing the inter-cluster dissimilarity, the average SL ratio is reduced.

3   Algorithm STC for Adaptively Clustering Market-Basket Data

By utilizing the concept of SL ratios, we devise an algorithms, called algorithm STC, for clustering market-basket data with the self-tuning technique to adaptively tune both the input and output SL ratio thresholds for iteratively minimizing $\alpha(U)$. Algorithm STC has three phases: the pre-determination phase, the allocation phase, and the refinement phase. An algorithmic form of algorithm STC can be found in the Appendix A for interested readers. In the pre-determination phase, the minimum support S and the maximum ceiling E are obtained by calculating the supports of items and identifying the related items according to SL distribution rate β. The procedure of algorithm STC is shown in Figure 1. First, STC counts the supports of items by scanning the database and the items are sorted according to their supports. Let $Count(\beta)$ be $N^I \times \beta$, where N^I is the number of total items. Then, in the sorted items, the support of the item whose support is the $Count(\beta)$th largest one among all item supports is the minimum support S, and the support of the item whose support is the $Count(\beta)$th smallest one is the maximum ceiling E.

After obtaining the minimum support S and the maximum ceiling E in the pre-determination phase, STC determines the initial clustering U_0 for transactions in the allocation phase. Then, each transaction is read in sequence and assigned to an existing cluster or a new cluster created to accommodate that transaction with the objective of minimizing the SL ratio. Explicitly, STC reads each transaction t from database D. In this paper, N_C is defined as the number of clusters and μ is defined as the upper bound of the number of clusters. In the case of $N_C < \mu$, t is assigned to an existing cluster C_i if $R_{SL}(C_i, t)$ is the smallest and $R_{SL}(C_i, t)$ is smaller than one. Otherwise, t is assigned to a new cluster and N_C is increased by one. If $N_C = \mu$, t is assigned to an existing cluster C_i so that $R_{SL}(C_i, t)$ is the smallest. After all transactions are allocated to the clusters, STC obtains the initial clustering $U_0 = < C_1, C_2, ..., C_{N_C} >$.

The self-tuning technique devised in this paper is exhibited in the refinement phase. After obtaining the initial clustering U_0, STC adaptively tunes the input and output SL ratio thresholds for clustering market-basket data in the refinement phase. In the beginning of the refinement phase, algorithm STC will identify the large, middle, and small items in each cluster in accordance with their supports. In iteration 1, STC sets $\alpha_1^o = \alpha_1^i = \alpha(U_0)$. Then, STC moves the transactions, whose SL ratios are larger than α_1^o, from their clusters to the excess pool. The transactions in the excess pool are also called *excess transactions*. After all transactions with their SL ratios larger than α_1^o are moved from their clusters to the excess pool, STC obtains an intermediate clustering U_1'. For the intermediate clustering U_1', STC counts the supports of items again to identify the large, middle, and small items in each cluster. Then, for each excess transaction t, algorithm STC calculates its SL ratio in each cluster based on the large and small items in that cluster of the intermediate clustering U_1'. If the smallest SL ratio of t is in cluster C_j and is smaller than α_1^i, STC shall move t from the excess pool to cluster C_j.

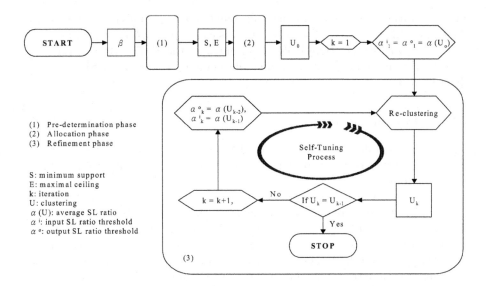

Fig. 1. The procedure of algorithm STC with the self-tuning process in the refinement phase.

After all excess transactions are evaluated in iteration 1, STC finishes the re-clustering and obtains the clustering U_1. In each subsequent iteration, STC starts with the clustering found in the previous iteration, adaptively tunes input and output SL ratio thresholds, and then re-clusters the transactions in the clustering and the excess pool. Explicitly, in iteration k, algorithm STC sets output SL ratio threshold α_k^o to be $\alpha(U_{k-2})$ and input SL ratio threshold α_k^i to be $\alpha(U_{k-1})$. Recall that α_k^o is the threshold for moving the transactions from their clusters to the excess pool. If the SL ratio of a transaction t in the clustering U_{k-1} is larger than α_k^o, t will be moved to the excess pool. On the other hand, if the SL ratio of a transaction t in the excess pool is smaller than α_k^i, t will be moved from the excess pool and become a member in the clustering U_k. The procedure continues until no further movement is required (i.e., the average SL ratio $\alpha(U)$ cannot be reduced any more). As will be validated by the experimental studies later, with the advantage of adaptive tuning, algorithm STC is able to efficiently attain the clustering results of very high quality.

4   Experimental Results

To assess the comparison among algorithms, we conducted several experiments. The details of data generation are described in Section 4.1. In Section 4.2, the quality and performance comparisons among algorithms are discussed. Without adaptively tuning the input and output SL ratio thresholds, algorithm SLR will cluster market-basket data with the fixed output SL ratio threshold α^o and fixed input SL ratio threshold α^i in the refinement phase. Explicitly, in iteration k, algorithm SLR sets $\alpha_k^o = \alpha_k^i = \alpha$, where α is called *fixed SL ratio threshold* and is given *apriori*. Rather than being determined by the SL distribution rate β as in STC, the minimum support S and the maximal ceiling E in SLR are also given *apriori*.

4.1   Data Generation

We take the real data sets of the United States Congressional Votes records in 1984 [1] for performance evaluation. The file of 1984 United States Congressional Votes contains 435 records, each of which includes 16 binary attributes corresponding to every congressman's vote on 16 key issues, e.g., the problem of the immigration, the duty of export, and the educational spending, and so on. There are 168 records for Republicans and 267 for Democrats. To provide more insight into this study, we use a well-known market-basket synthetic data generated by the IBM Quest Synthetic Data Generation Code [2], as the synthetic data for performance evaluation. This code will generate volumes of transaction data over a large range of data characteristics. These transactions mimic the transactions in the real world retailing environment. In addition, we take the real market-basket data from a large bookstore company for performance evaluation. In this real data set, there are $|D| = 98934$ transactions and $N^I = 58909$ items.

4.2   Performance Study

For the voting data, we conduct three experiments, from Experiment One to Experiment Three, for evaluating the clustering quality of algorithms. In algorithm STC, the SL distribution rate β is set to 30% and μ is set to 2. This algorithm in [7] will be referred to as algorithm Basic in our experimental studies. In algorithm Basic, the minimum support S is set to 60%, which is the same as the minimum support setting in [7] for comparison purposes. In algorithm ROCK, the threshold θ is set to 0.73, which is the same as the value setting in [5]. In algorithm SLR, we set the fixed SL ratio threshold $\alpha = 2.5$, $S = 60\%$, and $E = 60\%$. For the synthetic market-basket data, we conduct Experiment Four for evaluating the clustering performance of algorithms. For the experiment on synthetic data, we set $\beta = 30\%$ in algorithm STC, $S = 0.1\%$ in algorithm Basic, and $\theta = 0.73$ in algorithm ROCK. In addition, we set $\alpha = 2.5$, $S = 0.05$, and $E = 0.05$ in SLR. For the real market-basket data, we also conduct Experiments Five and Six to assess the performance of algorithms proposed.

Experiment One: Evaluating clustering quality for congressional voting data. In Table 1, the quality of the clustering algorithms is evaluated by *noise ratios* of the clustering [5], where the *noise ratio* can be obtained by dividing the number of obscure politics in the clustering by the total number in the clustering. For example, the democrats is the obscure politics in cluster 1 and therefore the noise ratio of algorithm Basic is $\frac{46}{171} = 26.9\%$. The smaller the

Table 1. Comparison on the clustering quality for congressional voting data.

Cluster 1	No. of Republicans	No. of Democrats	Total No.	Noise Ratio
Basic	125	46	171	0.269
ROCK	144	22	166	0.133
SLR	161	62	223	0.278
STC	132	13	145	0.090
Cluster 2	No. of Republicans	No. of Democrats	Total No.	Noise Ratio
Basic	43	221	264	0.163
ROCK	5	201	206	0.024
SLR	6	205	211	0.028
STC	3	187	190	0.016

noise ratio, the better quality this algorithm has. With self-tuning techniques, it shows that STC emerges as the one with the best clustering quality.

Experiment Two: Evaluating the clustering quality of issues for congressional voting data. For each issue in the Congressional Votes records, each congressman can vote for the issue (marked as 1) or vote against the issue (marked as 0). Each record represents a transaction. For each issue, voting for the issue (or voting against the issue) represents an item in the clusters. In our opinion, for Congressional Votes records, the better clustering quality also means that the issues in each cluster should be closer to 1 (which means that the members in the cluster vote for the issue) or closer to 0 (which means that the members in the cluster vote against the issue). By minimizing the SL ratios of records in cluster 1 and cluster 2, it is shown in Figure 2 that STC has the best clustering quality in most issues ($\frac{22}{32}$) among all schemes.

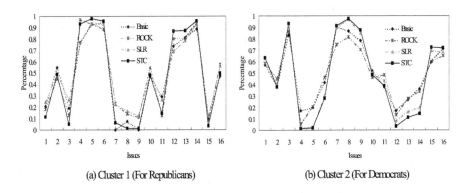

(a) Cluster 1 (For Republicans)   (b) Cluster 2 (For Democrats)

Fig. 2. The percentage of the issues in cluster 1 and cluster 2.

Experiment Three: Evaluating the scalability by synthetic workload.
Figure 3(a) shows the performance comparison between STC and Basic when
the number of transactions $|D|$ varies from 5000 to 20000. In this experiment, the
number of items, denoted by N^I, is set to 1000 and the size of the transaction is
picked from a Poisson distribution with mean $|T| = 5$. It shows that algorithm
STC in general outperforms algorithm Basic in clustering large market-basket
database. In addition, it is shown in Figure 3(b) that STC possesses very good
scalability, showing another advantage of the self-tuning mechanism. The curve
of SLR(k) is the result obtained by SLR with the setting of the fixed SL ratio
threshold α to be k.

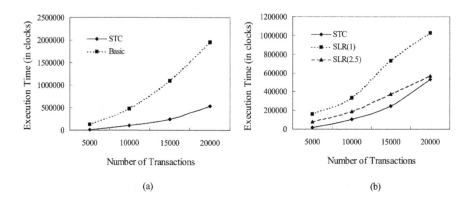

(a)   (b)

Fig. 3. Scale-up analysis of clustering algorithms.

Experiment Four: When β varies in real data. In this experiment for real
data, we set $|D| = 98934$ and $\mu = 5$. To examine the sensitivity of varying the
SL distribution rate β, Table 2 shows that STC increases the number of large
items in the refinement phase, where $I^L_{C_i,U_0}$ is the number of large items in the
initial clustering U_0 and $I^L_{C_i}$ is the number of large items in the final clustering.
It can be seen that STC puts similar transactions together by self-tuning SL
ratios iteratively.

5   Conclusion

In this paper, we designed algorithm STC for clustering market-basket data
items. By utilizing a self-tuning technique for adaptively tuning the input and
output SL ratio thresholds, algorithm STC is able to minimize the SL ratios of
transactions in the clusters efficiently. We conducted several experiments on the
real data and the synthetic workload for performance studies. It is shown by our
experimental results that by utilizing the self-tuning technique for adaptively

Table 2. Comparison between the initial clustering and the final clustering on the number of large items for real data when β varies.

Cluster ID	$\beta = 10\%$		$\beta = 20\%$		$\beta = 30\%$		$\beta = 40\%$	
	$I^L_{C_i,U_0}$	$I^L_{C_i}$	$I^L_{C_i,U_0}$	$I^L_{C_i}$	$I^L_{C_i,U_0}$	$I^L_{C_i}$	$I^L_{C_i,U_0}$	$I^L_{C_i}$
C_1	70	80	173	177	251	253	325	328
C_2	18	60	77	137	120	187	232	291
C_3	41	65	112	138	226	261	303	343
C_4	29	48	70	94	156	211	297	343
C_5	23	49	67	133	163	229	230	303
Average	36.2	60.4	99.8	135.8	183.2	228.2	277.4	321.6

minimizing the input and output SL ratio thresholds, algorithm STC performs very well in both synthetic and real data sets. Specifically, algorithm STC not only incurs an execution time that is significantly smaller than that by prior works but also leads to the clustering results of very good quality.

References

1. UCI Machine Learning Repository.
   http://www.ics.uci.edu/~mlearn/MLRepository.html.
2. R. Agrawal and R. Srikant. Fast Algorithms for Mining Association Rules in Large Databases. *Proceedings of the 20th International Conference on Very Large Data Bases*, pages 478–499, September 1994.
3. M.-S. Chen, J. Han, and P. S. Yu. Data Mining: An Overview from a Database Perspective. *IEEE Transactions on Knowledge and Data Engineering*, 8(6):866–833, 1996.
4. S. Guha, R. Rastogi, and K. Shim. CURE: An Efficient Clustering Algorithm for Large Databases. *ACM SIGMOD International Conference on Management of Data*, 27(2):73–84, June 1998.
5. S. Guha, R. Rastogi, and K. Shim. ROCK: A Robust Clustering Algorithm for Categorical Attributes. *Proceedings of the 15th International Conference on Data Engineering*, 1999.
6. A. K Jain, M. N. Murty, and P. J. Flynn. Data Clustering: A Review. *ACM Computer Surveys*, 31(3), Sept. 1999.
7. K. Wang, C. Xu, and B. Liu. Clustering Transactions Using Large Items. *Proceedings of ACM CIKM International Conference on Information and Knowledge Management*, 1999.
8. Y. Xiao and M. H. Dunham. Interactive Clustering for Transaction Data. *Proceedings of the 3rd International Conference on Data Warehousing and Knowledge Discovery (DaWaK 2001)*, Sept. 2001.
9. C.-H. Yun, K.-T. Chuang, and M.-S. Chen. An Efficient Clustering Algorithm for Market Basket Data Based on Small-Large Ratios. *Proceedings of the 25th International Computer Software and Applications Conference (COMPSAC 2001)*, October 2001.
10. T. Zhang, R. Ramakrishnan, and M. Livny. BIRCH: An Efficient Data Clustering Method for Very Large Databases. *ACM SIGMOD International Conference on Management of Data*, 25(2):103–114, June 1996.

CoFD: An Algorithm for Non-distance Based Clustering in High Dimensional Spaces*

Shenghuo Zhu, Tao Li, and Mitsuonri Ogihara

Department of Computer Science
University of Rochester
Rochester, NY 14620
{zsh,taoli, ogihara}@cs.rochester.edu

Abstract. The clustering problem, which aims at identifying the distribution of patterns and intrinsic correlations in large data sets by partitioning the data points into similarity clusters, has been widely studied. Traditional clustering algorithms use distance functions to measure similarity and are not suitable for high dimensional spaces. In this paper, we propose *CoFD* algorithm, which is a non-distance based clustering algorithm for high dimensional spaces. Based on the maximum likelihood principle, *CoFD* is to optimize parameters to maximize the likelihood between data points and the model generated by the parameters. Experimental results on both synthetic data sets and a real data set show the efficiency and effectiveness of *CoFD*.

1 Introduction

Clustering problems arise in many disciplines and have a wide range of applications. Intuitively, the clustering problem can be described as follows: let W be a set of n multi-dimensional data points, we want to find a partition of W into clusters such that the points within each cluster are "similar" to each other. Various distance functions have been widely used to define the measure of similarity. The problem of clustering has been studied extensively in the database [20,13], statistics [5,7] and machine learning communities [8,12] with different approaches and different focuses.

Most clustering algorithms do not work efficiently in high dimensional spaces due to the *curse of dimensionality*. It has been shown that in a high dimensional space, the distance between every pair of points is almost the same for a wide variety of data distributions and distance functions [6]. Many feature selection techniques have been applied to reduce the dimensionality of the space [17]. However, as demonstrated in [2], the correlations in the dimensions are often specific to data locality; in other words, some data points are correlated with a given set of features and others are correlated with respect to different features.

---

* The project is supported in part by NIH Grants 5-P41-RR09283, RO1-AG18231, and P30-AG18254 and by NSF Grants EIA-0080124, NSF CCR-9701911, and DUE-9980943.

Y. Kambayashi, W. Winiwarter, M. Arikawa (Eds.): DaWaK 2002, LNCS 2454, pp. 52–62, 2002.
© Springer-Verlag Berlin Heidelberg 2002

As pointed out in [15], all methods that overcome the dimensionality problems have an associated and often implicit or adaptive-metric for measuring neighborhoods.

In this paper, we present *CoFD*[1], a non-distance based algorithm for clustering in high dimensional spaces. The *CoFD* algorithm described here is an improvement over our previous method [22] and it contains several major extensions and revisions. The main idea of *CoFD* is as follows: Suppose that a data set W with feature set S needs to be clustered into K classes, $C_1, \ldots, C_K$ with the possibility of recognizing some data points to be outliers. The clustering of the data then is represented by two functions, the *data map* $D : W \rightarrow \{0, 1, \ldots, K\}$ and the *feature map* $F : S \rightarrow \{0, 1, \ldots, K\}$, where $1, \ldots, k$ correspond to the clusters and 0 corresponds to the set of outliers. Accuracy of such representation is measured using the log likelihood. Then, by the *Maximum Likelihood Principle*, the best clustering will be the representation that maximizes the likelihood. In *CoFD*, several approximation methods are used to optimize D and F iteratively. The *CoFD* algorithm can also be easily adapted to estimate the number of classes when the value K is not given as a part of the input. An added bonus of *CoFD* is that it produces interpretable descriptions of the resulting classes since it produces an explicit feature map. The rest of the paper is organized as follows: section 2 introduces the core idea and presents the details of *CoFD*; section 3 shows our experimental results on both the synthetic data sets and a real data set; section 4 surveys the related work; finally our conclusions and directions for future research are presented in section 5.

2   The *CoFD* Algorithm

This section describes *CoFD* and the core idea behind it. We first present the *CoFD* algorithm for binary data sets. Then we will show how to extend it to continuous or non-binary categorical data sets in Section 2.4.

2.1   The Model of *CoFD*

Suppose we wish to divide W into K classes with the possibility of declaring some data as outliers. Such clustering can be represented by a pair of functions, (F, D), where $F : S \rightarrow \{0, 1, \ldots, K\}$ is the *feature map* and $D : W \rightarrow \{0, 1, \ldots, K\}$ is the *data map*.

Given a representation (F, D) we wish to be able to evaluate how good the representation is. To accomplish this we use the concept of *positive features*. Intuitively, a positive feature is one that best describes the class it is associated with. Suppose that we are dealing with a data set of animals in a zoo, where the vast majority of the animals is the monkey and and the vast majority of the animals is the four-legged animal. Then, given an unidentified animal having four legs in the zoo, it is quite natural for one to guess that the animal is a monkey

---

[1] *CoFD* is the abbreviation of Co-training between Feature maps and Data maps.

because the conditional probability of that event is high. Therefore, we regard the feature "having four legs" as a *positive* (characteristic) feature of the class. In most practical cases, characteristic features of a class do not overlap with those of another class. Even if some overlaps exist, we can add the combinations of those features into the feature space.

Let N be the total number of data points and let d be the number of features. Since we are assuming that the features are binary, W can be represented as a 0-1 matrix, which we call the data-feature matrix. Let $1 \leq i \leq N$ and $1 \leq j \leq d$. We say that the jth feature is *active* in the ith point if and only if $W_{ij} = 1$. We also say that the ith data point *possesses* the ith feature if and only if $W_{ij} = 1$.

The key idea behind the *CoFD* algorithm is the use of the Maximum Likelihood Principle, which states that the best model is the one that has the highest likelihood of generating the observed data. We apply this principle by regarding the data-feature matrix as the observed data and the representation (D, F) as the model. Let the data map D and the feature map F be given. Consider the $N \times K$ matrix, $\hat{W}(D, F)$, defined as follows: for each i, $1 \leq i \leq N$, and each j, $1 \leq j \leq d$, the ij entry of the matrix is 1 if $1 \leq D(i) = F(j) \leq K$ and 0 otherwise. This is the model represented by F and D. interpreted as the consistence of $D(i)$ and $F(j)$. Note that $\hat{W}(D, F) = 0$ if $0 = D(i) = F(j)$. For all i, $1 \leq i \leq N$, j, $1 \leq j \leq d$, $b \in \{0, 1\}$, and $c \in \{0, 1\}$, we consider $P(W_{ij} = b \mid \hat{W}_{ij}(D, F) = c)$, the probability of the jth feature being active in the ith data point in the real data conditioned upon the jth feature being active in the ith data in the model represented by D and F. We assume that this conditional probability is dependent only on the values of b and c. Let $Q(b, c)$ denote the probability of an entry being observed as b while the entry in the model being equal to c. Also, let $p(b, c)$ denote the proportion of (i, j) such that $W_{ij} = b$ and $\hat{W}_{ij}(D, F) = c$. Then the likelihood of the model can be expressed as follows:

$$\log L(D, F) = \log \prod_{i,j} P(W_{ij} \mid \hat{W}_{i,j}(D, F)) = \log \prod_{b,c} Q(b, c)^{dN p(b,c)}$$

$$= dN \sum_{b,c} p(b, c) \log Q(b, c) \equiv -dN H(W \mid \hat{W}(D, F)) \qquad (1)$$

$$\hat{D}, \hat{F} = \arg \max_{D,F} \log L(D, F) \qquad (2)$$

We apply the hill-climbing method to maximize $\log L(D, F)$, *i.e.*, alternatively optimizing one of D and F by fixing the other. First, we try to optimize F by fixing D. The problem of optimizing F over all data-feature pairs can be approximately decomposed into subproblems of optimizing each $F(j)$ over all data-feature pairs of feature j, i.e., minimizing the conditional entropy $H(W_{.j} \mid \hat{W}_{.j}(D, F))$. If D and $F(j)$ are given, the entropies can be directly estimated. Therefore, $F(j)$ is assigned to the class in which the conditional entropy of $W_{.j}$ is the smallest. Optimizing D while fixing F is the dual. Hence, we only need to minimize $H(W_{i.} \mid \hat{W}_{i.}(D, F))$ for each i. A straightforward approximation method for minimizing $H(W_{.j} \mid \hat{W}_{.j}(D, F))$ is to assign $F(j)$ to $\arg \max_k \| \{i \mid W_{ij} = k\} \|$. This approximation method is also applicable to minimization of

$H(W_i. \mid \hat{W}_i.(D, F))$ where we assign $D(i)$ to $\arg\max_k \|\{j \mid W_{ij} = k\}\|$. A direct improvement of the approximation is possible by using the idea of entropy-constrained vector quantizer [10] and assigning $F(j)$ and $D(i)$ to $\arg\max_k (\|\{i \mid W_{ij} = k\}\| + \log(\frac{d(k)}{d}))$ and $\arg\max_k (\|\{j \mid W_{ij} = k\}\| + \log(\frac{N(k)}{N}))$, respectively, where $d(k)$ and $N(k)$ are the number of features and the number of points in class k.

There are two auxiliary procedures in the algorithm: EstimateFeatureMap estimates the feature map from the data map; EstimateDataMap estimates the data map from the feature map. Chi-square tests are used for deciding if a feature is an outlier or not. The main procedure, CoFD, attempts to find a best class by an iterative process similar to the EM algorithm. Here the algorithm iteratively estimates the data and feature maps based on the estimations made in the previous round, until no more changes occur in the feature map. The detailed pseudo-code of EstimateFeatureMap and EstimateDataMap can be found in [21]. It can be observed from the pseudo-code description in Fig 1 that the time complexities of both EstimateFeatureMap and EstimateDataMap are $O(K \times N \times d)$. The number of iterations in CoFD is not related to N or d.

Algorithm CoFD(data points: W, # of classes: K)
begin
    let $W1$ be the set of randomly chosen nK distinct data points from W;
    assign each n of them to one class, say the map be $D1$;
    assign EstimateFeatureMap($W1,D1$) to F;
    repeat
        assign F to $F1$;
        assign EstimateDataMap(W,F) to D;
        assign EstimateFeatureMap(W,D) to F;
    until conditional entropy $H(F|F1)$ is zeros;
    return D;
end

Fig. 1. Clustering algorithm

2.2 Refining

Clustering results are sensitive to initial seed points. Randomly chosen seed points may make the search trapped in local minima. We use a refining procedure, whose idea is to use conditional entropy to measure the similarity between a pair of clustering results. CoFD attempts to find a best clustering result having the smallest average conditional entropy against all others. The clustering results are sensitive to the initial seed points. Randomly chosen seed points may result trapping into local minima. We present a refining method (Figure 2). The idea is to use conditional entropy to measure the similarity between a pair of clustering results. CoFD is to find a best clustering result which has smallest average conditional entropy to all others.

Clustering a large data set may be time consuming. To speed up the algorithm, we focus on reducing the number of iterations. A small set of data points, for example, 1% of the entire data set, may be selected as the *bootstrap* data set. First, the clustering algorithm is executed on the bootstrap data set. Then, the clustering algorithm is run on the entire data set using the data map obtained from clustering on the bootstrap data set (instead of using randomly generated seed points).

Algorithm Refine(data points: W, the number of clusters: K)
begin
    do m times of CoFD(W,K) and
        assign the results to C_i for $i = 1, \cdots, m$;
    compute the average conditional entropies
        $T(C_i) = \frac{1}{m} \sum_{j=1}^{m} H(C_j|C_i)$ for $i = 1, \cdots, m$;
    return $\arg\min_{C_i} T(C_i)$;
end

Fig. 2. Clustering and refining algorithm

2.3   Informal Description

CoFD presents an effective method for finding clusters in high dimensional spaces without explicit distance functions. The clusters are defined as the group of points that have many features in common. *CoFD* iteratively selects features with high accuracy and assigns data points into clusters based on the selected features. A feature f with high accuracy means that there is a "large" subset V of data set W such that f is present in most data points of set V. In other words, feature f has a small variance on set V. A feature f with low accuracy means that there is no such a "large" subset V of data set W on which feature f has a small variance. That is, f spreads largely within data set W. Hence our algorithm repeatedly projects the data points to the subspaces defined by the selected features of each cluster, assigns them to the clusters based on the projection, recalculate the accuracies of the features, then selects the features. As the process moves on, the selected features tend to converge to the set of features which have small variances among all the features.

CoFD can be easily adapted to estimate the number of clusters instead of using K as an input parameter. We observed that the best number of clusters results the smallest average conditional entropy between clustering results obtained from different random seed point sets. Based on the observation, *CoFD* of guessing the number of clusters is described in Figure 3.

2.4   Extending to Non-binary Data Sets

In order to handle non-binary data sets, we first translate raw attribute values of data points into binary feature spaces. The translation scheme in [18] can be

Algorithm GuessK(data points: W) {L is the estimated maximum number of clusters;}
begin
    for K in $2 \cdots L$ **do**
        do m times of CoFD(W,K) and
            assign the results to C_{Ki} for $i = 1, \cdots, m$;
        compute the average conditional entropies
            $T(C_{Ki}) = \frac{1}{m} \sum_{j=1}^{m} H(C_{Kj}|C_{Ki})$ for $i = 1, \cdots, m$;
    end
    return $\arg \min_K \min_i T(C_{Ki})$;
end

Fig. 3. Algorithm of guessing the number of clusters

used to discretize categorical and continuous attributes. However, this type of translation is vulnerable to outliers that may drastically skew the range. In our algorithm, we use two other discretization methods. The first is combining *Equal Frequency Intervals* method with the idea of CMAC [4]. Given m instances, the method divides each dimension into k bins with each bin containing $\frac{m}{k} + \gamma$ adjacent values[2]. In other words, with the new method, each dimension is divided into several overlapped segments and the size of overlap is determined by γ. An attribute is then translated into a binary sequence having bit-length equal to the number of the overlapped segments, where each bit represents whether the attribute belongs to the corresponding segment. We can also use Gaussian mixture models to fit each attribute of the original data sets, since most of them are generated from Gaussian mixture models. The number of Gaussian distributions n can be obtained by maximizing the Bayesian information criterion of the mixture model. Then the value is translated into n feature values in the binary feature space. The jth feature value is 1 if the probability that the value of the data point is generated from the jth Gaussian distribution is the largest.

3   Experimental Results

There are many ways to measure how accurately *CoFD* performs. One is the *confusion matrix* which is described in [2]. Entry (o, i) of a confusion matrix is the number of data points assigned to output cluster o and generated from input cluster i.

For input map I, which maps data points to input clusters, the entropy $H(I)$ measures the information of the input map. The task of clustering is to find out an output map O which recover the information. Therefore, the condition entropy $H(I|O)$ is interpreted as the information of the input map given the output map O, i.e., the portion of information which is not recovered by the clustering algorithm. Therefore, the *recovering rate* of a clustering algorithm

---

[2] The parameter γ can be a constant for all bins or different constants for different bins depending on the distribution density of the dimension. In our experiment, we set $\gamma = \lfloor m/5k \rfloor$.

is defined as $1 - H(I|O)/H(I) = MI(I,O)/H(I)$, where $MI(I,O)$ is mutual information between I and O.

To test the performance of our algorithm, we did experiments on both synthetic and real data sets. The simulations were performed on a 700MHz Pentium-III IBM Thinkpad T20 computer with 128M of memory, running on octave 2.1.34[3] on Linux 2.4.10.

3.1   A Continuous Synthetic Data Set

In this experiment we attempted to cluster a continuous data set. We used the method described in [2] to generate a data set W_1. W_1 has $N = 100,000$ data points in a 20-dimensional space, with $K = 5$. All input classes were generated in some 7-dimensional subspace. Five percent of the data points was chosen to be outliers, which were distributed uniformly at random throughout the entire space. Using the second translation method described in Section 2.4, we mapped all the data point into a binary space with 41 features. Then, 1000 data points were randomly chosen as the bootstrap data set. By running CoFD algorithm on the bootstrap data set, we obtained clustering of the bootstrap data set. Using the bootstrap data set as the seed points, we ran the algorithm on the entire data set. Figure 4 shows the confusion matrix of this experiment. About 99.65% of the data points were recovered. The conditional entropy $H(I|O)$ is 0.0226 while the input entropy $H(I)$ is 1.72. The recovering rate is thus $1 - H(I|O)/H(I) = 0.987$. We made a rough comparison with the result reported in [2]. From the confusion matrix reported in the paper, their recovering rate is calculated as 0.927, which seems to indicate that our algorithm is better than theirs in terms of recovering rate.

Output \ Input	A	B	C	D	E	O.
1	1	0	1	17310	0	12
2	0	15496	0	2	22	139
3	0	0	0	0	24004	1
4	10	0	17425	0	5	43
5	20520	0	0	0	0	6
Outliers	16	17	15	10	48	4897

Output \ Input	1	2	3	4	5	6	7
A	0	0	0	0	0	0	1
B	0	20	0	0	0	0	0
C	39	0	0	0	0	0	0
D	0	0	2	0	0	0	0
E	2	0	1	13	0	0	4
F	0	0	0	0	0	8	5
G	0	0	2	0	0	3	0

Fig. 4. Confusion matrix for Continuous Synthetic Data Set

Fig. 5. Confusion matrix of Zoo

We made a rough comparison with the result reported in [2]. Computing from the confusion matrix reported in their paper, their recovering rate is 0.927.

---

[3] GNU Octave is a high-level language, primarily intended for numerical computations. The software can be obtained from http://www.octave.org/.

3.2   Zoo Database

We also evaluated the performance of the *CoFD* algorithm on the zoo database available at the UC Irvine Machine Learning Repository. The database contains 100 animals, each of which has 15 boolean attributes and 1 categorical attribute[4]. We translated each boolean attribute into two features, whether the feature is active and whether the feature is inactive. We translated the numeric attribute, "legs", into six features, which correspond to 0, 2, 4, 5, 6, and 8 legs, respectively. Figure 4 shows the confusion matrix of this experiment. The conditional entropy $H(I|O)$ is 0.317 while the input entropy $H(I)$ is 1.64. The recovering rate of this algorithm is $1 - H(I|O)/H(I) = 0.807$. In the confusion matrix, we found that the clusters with a large number of animals are likely to be correctly clustered.[5]

CoFD comes with an important by-product that the resulting classes can be easily described in terms of features, since the algorithm produces an explicit feature map. For example, the positive features of class B are "feather," "airborne," and "two legs." Hence, class B can be described as animals having feather and two legs, and being airborne, which are the representative features of the *birds*.[6]

3.3   Clustering of Technical Reports

We applied our *CoFD* algorithm to cluster the collection of technical reports published in the years 1989–2000 in our department based on the words in their abstracts. We obtained data points from the abstracts by removing stop words and then applying words stemming operations. Then we computed the frequency of each remaining word. We selected the top 500 frequent words and transformed the original dataset into a categorical data set according to the occurrence of these 500 words. The recovering rate is 0.5762 and the confusion matrix is shown in Table 6. We loosely divided the research areas into four groups: Symbolic-AI, Spatial-AI, Systems, and Theory. Thus there are four clusters in the result. The columns of the confusion matrix are the four groups in the order they are mentioned. The result shows that Systems and Theory are much different from each other, and are different both from Symbolic-AI and from Spatial-AI, that Symbolic-AI and Spatial-AI are similar to each other, and that Symbolic-AI is more similar to Spatial-AI. We also used *K-means* to this task, whose recovering rate was about 0.27.

---

[4] The original data set has 101 data points but one animal, "frog," appears twice. So we eliminated one of them. We also eliminated two attributes, "animal name" and "type."

[5] For example, cluster no. 1 is mapped into cluster C; cluster no. 2 is mapped into cluster B; etc.

[6] Animals "dolphin" and "porpoise" are in class 1, but were clustered into class E, because their attributes "aquatic" and "fins" make them more like animals in class E than their attribute "milk" does for class C.

3.4   Dermatology Database

We also evaluated our algorithms on the dermatology database from the UC Irvine Machine Learning Repository. The database is used for the differential diagnosis of erythemato-squamous diseases. These diseases all share the clinical features of erythema and scaling, with very little differences. The dataset contains 366 data points over 34 attributes and was previously used for classification. In our experiment, we use it to demonstrate our clustering algorithm. The first translation method described in Section 2.4 was used for preprocessing. The confusion matrix of *CoFD*, on this dataset is presented in Figure 7.

Output \ Input	1	2	3	4
A	8	9	5	109
B	9	3	83	5
C	7	44	0	3
D	74	8	6	3

Fig. 6. Confusion matrix of technical reports.

Output \ Input	1	2	3	4	5	6
A	0	5	0	1	0	20
B	112	13	0	2	4	0
C	0	0	72	1	0	0
D	0	14	0	15	5	0
E	0	7	0	4	43	0
F	0	22	0	26	0	0

Fig. 7. Confusion matrix of Dermatology Database.

Our algorithm scales linearly with the number of points and features. More detailed experiment results are presented in [21].

4   Relative Work

Traditional clustering techniques can be broadly classified into partitional clustering, hierarchical clustering, density-based clustering and grid-based clustering [14]. Most of the traditional clustering methods use the distance functions as objective criteria and are not effective in high dimensional spaces. Next we review some recent clustering algorithms which have been proposed for high dimensional spaces or without distance functions and are largely related to our work.

CLIQUE [3] is an automatic subspace clustering algorithm for high dimensional spaces. It uses equal-size cells and cell density to find dense regions in each subspace of a high dimensional space. CLIQUE does not produce disjoint clusters and the highest dimensionality of subspace clusters reported is about 10. *CoFD* produces disjoint clusters.

In [1,2], the authors introduced the concept of projected clustering and developed algorithms for discovering interesting patterns in subspaces of high dimensional spaces. The core idea of their algorithm is a generalization of feature selection which allows the selection of different sets of dimensions for different subsets of the data sets. However, their algorithms are based on the Euclidean distance or Manhattan distance and their feature selection method is a variant of singular value decomposition (SVD). Also their algorithms assume that the number of projected dimensions are given beforehand. *CoFD* does not need the distance measures and the number of dimensions for each cluster. Also it does not require all projected clusters to have the same number of dimensions.

Cheng[9] proposed an entropy-based subspace clustering for mining numerical data. There are also some recent work on clustering categorical datasets, such as ROCK and CACTUS, and on clustering based on decision tree. Our algorithm can be applied to both categorical and numerical data.

Strehl and Ghosh[19] proposed OPOSSUM, a similarity-based clustering approach based on constrained,weighted graph-partitioning. OPOSSUM is based on *Jaccard Similarity* and is particularly attuned to real-life market baskets, characterized by high-dimensional sparse customer-product matrices.

Fasulo[11] also gave a detailed survey on clustering approaches based on mixture models, dynamical systems and clique graphs. The relationship between maximum likelihood and clustering is also discussed in [16]. Similarity based on shared features has also been analyzed in cognitive science such as the *Family resemblances* study by Rosch and Mervis.

5   Conclusions

In this paper, we proposed a novel clustering method which does not require the distance function for high dimensional spaces. The algorithm performs clustering by iteratively optimize the data map and the feature map. We have adopted several approximation methods to maximize the likelihood between the given data set and the generated model. Extensive experiments have been conducted and the results show that *CoFD* is both efficient and effective.

Our future work includes developing more direct methods to optimize the data map and the feature map, designing the parallel and distributed versions of our algorithm and the incremental clustering algorithm based on our algorithm.

References

1. C. Aggarwal and P. S. Yu. Finiding generalized projected clusters in high dimensional spaces. In *SIGMOOD-00*, 2000.
2. C. C. Aggarwal, J. L. Wolf, P. S. Yu, C. Procopiuc, and J. Soo Park. Fast algorithms for projected clustering. In *ACM SIGMOD Conference*, 1999.
3. R. Agrawal, J. Gehrke, D. Gunopulos, and P. Raghavan. Automatic subspace clustering for high dimensional data for data mining applications. In *SIGMOD-98*, 1998.
4. J. S. Albus. A new approach to manipulator control: The cerebellar model articlatioon controller (CMAC). *Trans. of the ASME, J. Dynamic Systems, Meaasurement, and Control*, 97(3):220–227, sep 1975.
5. M. Berger and I. Rigoutsos. An algorithm for point clustering and grid generation. *IEEE Trans. on Systems, Man and Cybernetics*, 21(5):1278–1286, 1991.

6. K. Beyer, J. Goldstein, R. Ramakrishnan, and U. Shaft. When is nearest neighbor meaningful? In *ICDT Conference*, 1999.
7. M.R. Brito, E. Chavez, A. Quiroz, and J. Yukich. Connectivity of the mutual K-Nearest-Neighbor graph for clustering and outlier detection. *Statistics and Probability Letters*, 35:33–42, 1997.
8. P. Cheeseman, J. Kelly, and M. Self. AutoClass: A bayesian classification system. In *ICML'88*, 1988.
9. C-H Cheng, A. W-C Fu, and Y. Zhang. Entropy-based subspace clustering for mining numerical data. In *KDD-99*, 1999.
10. P. A. Chou, T. Lookabaugh, and R. M. Gray. Entropy-constrained vector quantization. *IEEE Trans.*, ASSP-37(1):31, 1989.
11. D. Fasulo. An analysis of recent work on clustering algorithms. Technical Report 01-03-02, U. of Washington, Dept. of Comp. Sci. & Eng., 1999.
12. Douglas H. Fisher. Iterative optimization and simplification of hierarchical clusterings. Technical Report CS-95-01, Vanderbilt U., Dept. of Comp. Sci., 1995.
13. S. Guha, R. Rastogi, and K. Shim. CURE: An efficient clustering algorithm for large database. In *Proceedings of the 1998 ACM SIGMOD Conference*, 1998.
14. Jiawei Han and Micheline Kamber. *Data Mining: Concepts and Techniques*. Morgan Kaufmann Publishers, 2000.
15. T. Hastie, R. Tibshirani, and J. Friedman. *The Elements of Statistical Learning: Data Mining,Inference, and Prediction*. Springer, 2001.
16. Michael I. Jordan. *Graphical Models: Foundations of Neural Computation*. MIT Press, 2001.
17. R. Kohavi and D. Sommerfield. Feature subset selection using the wrapper method: overfitting and dynamic search space technology. In *KDD-95*, 1995.
18. R. Srikant and R. Agrawal. Mining quantitative association rules in large relational tables. In *SIGMOD-96*, 1996.
19. A. Strehl and J. Ghosh. A scalable approach to balanced, high-dimensional clustering of market-baskets. In *HiPC-2000*, 2000.
20. T. Zhang, R. Ramakrishnan, and M. Livny. BIRCH: An efficient data clustering method for very large databases. In *ACM SIGMOD Conference*, 1996.
21. Shenghuo Zhu and Tao Li. An algorithm for non-distance based clustering in high dimensional spaces. Technical Report 763, University of Rochester, Computer Science Department, Rochester, NY, 2002.
22. Shenghuo Zhu and Tao Li. A non-distance based clustering algorithm. In *Proc. of IJCNN 2002*, 2002. To appear.

An Efficient K-Medoids-Based Algorithm Using Previous Medoid Index, Triangular Inequality Elimination Criteria, and Partial Distance Search

Shu-Chuan Chu[1], John F. Roddick[1], and J.S. Pan[2]

[1] School of Informatics and Engineering,
Flinders University of South Australia,
PO Box 2100, Adelaide 5001, South Australia.
{jan, roddick}@cs.flinders.edu.au
[2] Department of Electronic Engineering,
Kaohsiung University of Applied Sciences
415 Chien Kung Road,
Kaohsiung, Taiwan
jspan@cc.kuas.edu.tw

Abstract. Clustering in data mining is a discovery process that groups similar objects into the same cluster. Various clustering algorithms have been designed to fit various requirements and constraints of application. In this paper, we study several k-medoids-based algorithms including the PAM, $CLARA$ and $CLARANS$ algorithms. A novel and efficient approach is proposed to reduce the computational complexity of such k-medoids-based algorithms by using previous medoid index, triangular inequality elimination criteria and partial distance search. Experimental results based on elliptic, curve and Gauss-Markov databases demonstrate that the proposed algorithm applied to $CLARANS$ may reduce the number of distance calculations by 67% to 92% while retaining the same average distance per object. In terms of the running time, the proposed algorithm may reduce computation time by 38% to 65% compared with the $CLARANS$ algorithm.

1 Introduction

The goal of clustering is to group sets of objects into classes such that similar objects are placed in the same cluster while dissimilar objects in separate clusters. Clustering (or classification) techniques are common forms of data mining [1] and have been applied in a number of areas including image compression [2], computer vision [3], psychiatry [4], medicine and marketing. A number of clustering algorithms have been proposed including k-means [5], k-medoids [6], $BIRCH$ [7], $CURE$ [8], $CACTUS$ [9], $CHAMELEON$ [10] and $DBSCAN$ [11]. Clearly, no single algorithm is suitable for all forms of input data, nor are all algorithms appropriate for all problems, however, the k-medoids algorithms

Y. Kambayashi, W. Winiwarter, M. Arikawa (Eds.): DaWaK 2002, LNCS 2454, pp. 63–72, 2002.
© Springer-Verlag Berlin Heidelberg 2002

have been shown to be robust to outliers and are not generally influenced by the order of presentation of objects. Moreover, k-medoids algorithms are invariant to translations and orthogonal transformations of objects [6].

Partitioning Around Medoids (PAM) [6], *Clustering LARge Applications (CLARA)* [6] and *Clustering Large Applications based on RANdomized Search (CLARANS)* [12] are three popular k-medoids-based algorithms. In other work, our *Clustering Large Applications based on Simulated Annealing (CLASA)* algorithm applies simulated annealing to select better medoids [13]. Fuzzy theory can also be employed to develop fuzzy k-medoids algorithms [14] and while genetic algorithms can also be used [15]. The drawback of the k-medoids algorithms is the time complexity in calculating the medoids. However, there are many efficient algorithms developed for VQ-based clustering. These efficient codeword search algorithms used in VQ-based signal compression have not, to our knowledge, been applied to k-medoids-based algorithms.

In this paper, a novel and efficient k-medoids-based algorithm is proposed by using previous medoid index, triangular inequality elimination and partial distance search.

2   Existing Algorithms

2.1   *PAM* Algorithm

The k-medoids clustering algorithm evaluates a set of k objects considered to be representative objects (medoids) for k clusters within T objects such that the non-selected objects are clustered with the medoid to which it is the most similar. The total distance between non-selected objects and their medoid may be reduced by the swap of one of the medoids with one of the objects iteratively. The *PAM* (Partitioning Around Medoids) algorithm can be depicted as follows:

Step 1: Initialization - choose k medoids from T objects randomly.
Step 2: Evaluation - calculate the cost $D_t' - D_t$ for each swap of one medoid with another object, where D_t is the total distance before the swap and D_t' is the total distance after the swap.
Step 3: Selection - if the cost is negative, accept the swap with the best cost and go to step 2; otherwise record the medoids and terminate the program.

2.2   *CLARA* Algorithm

The computational complexity of the *PAM* algorithm is $O((1 + \beta)k(T - k)^2)$ which is based on the number of partition per object, where β is the number of successful swaps. It can also be expressed as $O'((1 + \beta)k^2(T - k)^2)$ based on the number of distance calculations. Obviously, *PAM* can be time consuming even for a moderate number of objects and small number of medoids. The *CLARA* algorithm [6] reduces the computational complexity by drawing multiple samples of the objects and applying the *PAM* algorithm on each sample. The final medoids are obtained from the best result of these multiple draws. The computational complexity of the $CLARA$ algorithm is $O(\alpha(ks^2 + (T - k)) + \lambda ks^2)$ or $O'(\alpha(k^2s^2 + k(T - k)) + \lambda k^2s^2)$, where α, s, k, λ and T are the number of samples, object size per sample, number of medoids, the number of successful swaps for all samples test and the total number of objects, respectively. The $CLARA$ algorithm can be depicted as follows:

Step 1: Repeat the following steps q times.
Step 2: Call PAM algorithm with a random sample, s objects from the original set of T objects.
Step 3: Partition the T objects based on the k medoids obtained from previous step. Update the better medoids based on the average distortion of the partition.

2.3 $CLARANS$ Algorithm

If the sample size s is not large enough, the effectiveness (average distortion) of the $CLARA$ algorithm is lower. However, the efficiency (computation time) is not good if the sample size is too large. It is thus a tradeoff between the effectiveness and efficiency. The best clustering cannot be obtained in $CLARA$ if one of the best medoids is not included in the sample objects. In order to retain the efficiency and but get acceptable performance in terms of the average distance per object, the $CLARANS$ (Clustering Large Applications based on RANdomized Search) algorithm [12] was proposed.

The clustering process in $CLARANS$ algorithm is formalized as searching through a certain graph where each node is represented by a set of k medoids, and two nodes are neighbours if they only differ by one medoid. Each node has $k(T - k)$ neighbors, where T is the total number of objects. $CLARANS$ starts with a selected node randomly. It moves to the neighbor node if a test for the *maxneighbor* number of neighbors is successful; otherwise it records the current node as a local minimum. Once a node representing a local minimum is found, it starts with a new randomly selected node and repeats the search for a new local minimum. The procedure continues until the *numlocal* numbers of local minima have been found, and returns the best node. The computational complexity is $O((p + numlocal)(T - k))$ based on the number of partition per object or $O'((p + numlocal)k(T - k))$ based on the number of distance calculation, where p is the number of successful move between nodes. The $CLARANS$ algorithm can be described as follows:

Step 1: Repeat the following steps for *numlocal* times.
Step 2: Select a current node randomly and calculate the average distance of this current code, where node is the collection of k medoids.
Step 3: Repeat *maxneighbor* times.
 − Select a neighbour node randomly and calculate the average distance for this node. If the average distance is lower, set current node to be the neighbour node.

3   Proposed Algorithm

3.1   Literature Review

Although k-medoids-based algorithms are designed for clustering large datasets, all existing k-medoids-based algorithms are time consuming. The computational complexity of k-medoids-based algorithms can be reduced by applying the concepts used in VQ-based codeword search. The efficient codeword searching algorithms used in VQ-based signal compression have not, to our knowledge, been applied to k-medoids-based algorithms. The partial distance search (PDS) algorithm [16] is a simple and efficient codeword search algorithm which allows early termination of the distortion calculation between a test vector and a codeword by introducing a premature exit condition in the search process.

Vidal proposed the approximating and elimination search algorithm ($AESA$) [17] whose computation time is approximately constant for a codeword search in a large codebook size. The high correlation characteristics between data vectors of adjacent speech frames and the triangular inequality elimination (TIE) criterion were utilized in the VQ-based recognition of isolated words [18]. The *equal-average nearest neighbor search* ($ENNS$) algorithm [19] uses the mean of an input vector to eliminate the impossible codewords. This algorithm reduces a great deal of computation time compared with the conventional full-search algorithm with only k additional memory, where k is the number of codewords (or the number of medoids for k-medoids-based algorithms). The improved algorithm [20] uses the variance as well as the mean of an input vector. It can be referred to as the *equal-average equal-variance nearest neighbor search* ($EENNS$) algorithm. This algorithm reduces more computation time with $2k$ additional memory. The improved algorithm [21] presented by Baek *et. al.* using the mean and the variance of an input vector such as $EENNS$ to develop a new inequality between these features and the distance. The bound for Minkowski metric and quadratic metric was derived and applied to codeword search [22]. The partial distance search (PDS) [16] and absolute error inequality criterion (AEI) [23] are all special cases in the bound for Minkowski metric. An inequality for fast codeword search based on the mean-variance pyramid was also derived [24].

3.2   Partial Distance Search

Given the squared Euclidean distance measure, one object $x = \{x_1, x_2, \ldots, x_d\}$ and two medoids (representative objects) $o_t = \{o_{t1}, o_{t2}, \ldots, o_{td}\}$ and $o_j = \{o_{j1}, o_{j2}, \ldots, o_{jd}\}$, assume the current minimum distance is

$$D(x, o_t) = \sum_{i=1}^{d} (x_i - o_{ti})^2 = D_{min}, \tag{1}$$

$$if \qquad \sum_{i=1}^{h} (x_i - o_{ji})^2 \geq D_{min}, \tag{2}$$

$$\text{then} \qquad D(x, o_j) \geq D(x, o_t), \tag{3}$$

where $1 \leq h \leq d$. The efficiency of PDS is derived from the elimination of an unfinished distance computation if its partial accumulated distortion is larger than the current minimum distance. This will reduce $(d - h)$ multiplications and $2(d - h)$ additions at the expense of h comparisons.

3.3   Triangular Inequality Elimination Criteria

Triangular inequality elimination (TIE) criteria are efficient methods for applying to codeword search. Let X be the set of objects and O be the set of medoids and x, y, z belong to the set X. Assume the distance measure existing for defining the mapping $d : X \times X \rightarrow R$, is used to fulfill the following metric properties:

$$d(x, y) \geq 0; \tag{4}$$

$$d(x, y) = 0 \;\; iff \;\; x = y \tag{5}$$

$$d(x, y) = d(y, x) \tag{6}$$

$$d(x, y) + d(y, z) \geq d(x, z) \tag{7}$$

Let o_1, o_2, o_3 be three different medoids and t be an object, then three criteria are obtained as follows:

– Criterion 1.

$$\textit{Given the triangular inequality}: \quad d(t, o_2) + d(t, o_1) \geq d(o_1, o_2); \tag{8}$$

$$if \qquad d(o_1, o_2) \geq 2d(t, o_1), \tag{9}$$

$$then \qquad d(t, o_2) \geq d(t, o_1). \tag{10}$$

– Criterion 2.

$$\textit{Given the triangular inequality}: \quad d(o_3, o_2) \leq d(t, o_2) + d(t, o_3); \tag{11}$$

$$if \qquad d(t, o_1) + d(t, o_2) \leq d(o_3, o_2), \tag{12}$$

$$then \qquad d(t, o_1) \leq d(t, o_3). \tag{13}$$

– Criterion 3.

$$Assume \qquad d(t, o_1) \leq d(t, o_2); \tag{14}$$

$$Given \qquad d(t, o_2) - d(t, o_3) \leq d(o_3, o_2), \tag{15}$$

$$if \qquad d(o_3, o_2) \leq d(t, o_2) - d(t, o_1) \tag{16}$$

$$then \qquad d(t, o_3) \geq d(t, o_1). \tag{17}$$

In Criterion 1, these distances between all pairs of medoids are computed in advance. If $Eq.$ 9 is satisfied, then we omit the computation of $d(t, o_2)$ if $d(t, o_1)$ has already been calculated. In this paper, Criterion 1 is modified for a squared error distance measure. A table is made to store the one-fourth of squared distance between medoids, if $d^2(o_1, o_2)/4 \geq d^2(t, o_1)$ then $d(t, o_2) \geq d(t, o_1)$. Only Criterion 1 is used for the preliminary experiments.

3.4   Previous Medoid Index and Proposed Method

Most k-medoids-based algorithms check whether the designation of medoid needs to be transferred to another object. Since only one medoid is changed, most of the objects will continue to belong to the cluster represented by the same medoid. By using this property, we may calculate the distance between the object and its previous medoid index firstly. Since the probability is high that the object belongs to the same medoid index, the distance will tend to be small. If we get a small distance between the object and one medoid, then it is easier to use Criterion 1 of TIE and partial distance search to reduce the distance computation.

The proposed efficient searching algorithm using previous medoid index, triangular inequality elimination (TIE) and partial distance search (PDS) algorithm applied to $CLARANS$ will be referred to as $CLARANS\text{-}ITP$, and can be described as follows:

Step 1: Repeat the following steps for *numlocal* times.
Step 2: Select a current node randomly and calculate the distances between medoids, where each node is the collection of k medoids. The average distance of this current node is computed using TIE and PDS. Record the index of the medoid for each object.
Step 3: Repeat the following step for *maxneighbor* times.
  - Select a neighbor node randomly and update the medoid distances between medoids.
  - Calculate the distance between the object and the previous medoid index of this object – this distance is referred to as D_{min}.
  - Calculate the average distance for this node by using D_{min}, medoid distances, TIE and PDS.
  - Update D_{min} and the previous medoid index if the distance between the object and one medoid is lower than D_{min}. If the average distance is lower, set current node to be the neighbor node; otherwise recover the previous medoid distances.

4   Experimental Results

4.1   Databases

Three artificial databases were used for the experiments as follows:

1. 3,000 objects with 8 dimensions are generated from the Gauss-Markov source which is of the form $y_n = \alpha y_{n-1} + w_n$ where w_n is a zero-mean, unit variance, Gaussian white noise process, with $\alpha = 0.5$.
2. 12,000 objects with 2 dimensions collected from twelve elliptic clusters.
3. 5,000 objects with 2 dimensions are generated from curve database. The object (x, y) is collected from the form $-2 \le x \le 2$ and $y = 8x^3 - x$.

4.2   Experiments

Two enhanced versions of $CLARANS$, one with triangular inequality elimination (TIE) and partial distance search (PDS) and one with previous medoid index, TIE and PDS are used and are referred to as $CLARANS$-TP and $CLARANS$-ITP, respectively. Experiments were carried out to test the number of distances calculation and the average distance per object for $CLARA$, $CLARANS$, $CLARANS$-TP and $CLARANS$-ITP algorithms. Squared Euclidean distance measure is used for the experiments. The Gauss-Markov source was used for the first experiment. 32 medoids are selected from 3000 objects. For the $CLARA$ algorithm, the parameter q was set to 5 and s was set to $320 + 2 * k$ for the sample size, where k is the number of medoids. For $CLARANS$ algorithm, the parameters numlocal and *maxneighbor* are set to 5 and 1200, respectively. Experimental results are shown in Table. 1. Comparing with $CLARANS$, $CLARANS$-ITP and $CLARANS$-TP will reduce the computational complexity by 67% and 53%, respectively.

Table 1. Results of Experiment for Gauss-Markov Source

seed	CLARA		CLARANS		CLARANS-TP		CLARANS-ITP	
	Average distance	Count of distances(10^5)	Average distance	Count of distances(10^5)	Average distance	Count of distances(10^5)	Average distance	Count of distances(10^5)
1	4.55877	154809	4.43227	37604	4.43227	17658	4.43227	12572
2	4.59175	163692	4.35912	53234	4.35912	24865	4.35912	17678
3	4.55139	178918	4.38063	37512	4.38063	17629	4.38063	12346
4	4.57830	172574	4.39766	40559	4.39766	19101	4.39766	13342
5	4.55919	182725	4.36724	39694	4.36724	18521	4.36724	13058
6	4.52568	167498	4.38396	41370	4.38396	19318	4.38396	13672
7	4.52725	185263	4.37978	32312	4.37978	14962	4.37978	10566
8	4.48292	162423	4.39364	39600	4.39364	18442	4.39364	12956
9	4.54490	190338	4.37717	36707	4.37717	17091	4.37717	11972
10	4.51372	180187	4.40632	35835	4.40632	16671	4.40632	11879
Ave.	4.54339	173843	4.38778	39443	4.38778	18426	4.38778	13004

Table 2. Results of Experiment for twelve elliptic clusters

seed	CLARA		CLARANS		CLARANS-TP		CLARANS-ITP	
	Average distance	Count of distances(10^5)	Average distance	Count of distances(10^5)	Average distance	Count of distances(10^5)	Average distance	Count of distances(10^5)
1	0.94030	115659	0.93121	91792	0.93121	35186	0.93121	14302
2	0.94220	92528	0.94334	63512	0.94334	24810	0.94334	10032
3	0.95640	122462	0.93531	76873	0.93531	29623	0.93531	11984
4	0.95144	103413	0.92793	79582	0.92793	30677	0.92793	12496
5	0.94601	111577	0.94903	90014	0.94903	34436	0.94903	14240
6	0.96015	108856	0.93616	72069	0.93616	28226	0.93616	11362
7	0.97183	77562	0.93580	84914	0.93580	33286	0.93580	13247
8	0.94376	93889	0.93388	93092	0.93388	35682	0.93388	14611
9	0.95432	84365	0.93005	59242	0.93005	23383	0.93005	9361
10	0.94236	84365	0.93072	75053	0.93072	29331	0.93072	11838
Ave.	0.95088	99467	0.93534	78615	0.93534	30464	0.93534	12347

The twelve elliptic clusters were used for the second experiment. 12 medoids are selected from 12000 objects. For $CLARA$ algorithm, the parameter q was set to 5 and s was set to $960 + 2 * k$. For $CLARANS$ algorithm, the parameters *numlocal* and *maxneighbor* are set to 5 and 1800, respectively. As shown in Table. 2 and Fig. 1, comparing with $CLARA$ and $CLARANS$, the $CLARANS\text{-}ITP$ may reduce the computation time by more than 87% and 83%.

The curve database was used for the third experiment. 20 medoids are selected from 5000 objects. For $CLARA$ algorithm, the parameter q was set to 5 and s was set to $400 + 2 * k$. For $CLARANS$ algorithm, the parameters *numlocal* and *maxneighbor* are set to 5 and 1250, respectively. As shown in Fig. 2, the $CLARANS\text{-}ITP$ and $CLARANS\text{-}TP$ may reduce the computation time by more than 92% and 74% by comparing with $CLARANS$.

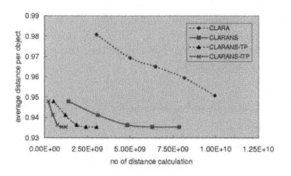

Fig. 1. Performance comparison of $CLARA$, $CLARANS$, $CLARANS\text{-}TP$ and $CLARANS\text{-}ITP$ for twelve elliptic clusters

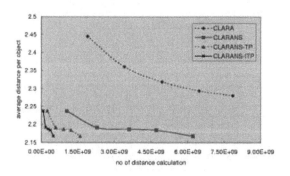

Fig. 2. Performance comparison of $CLARA$, $CLARANS$, $CLARANS\text{-}TP$ and $CLARANS\text{-}ITP$ for curve clusters

The running time of any algorithm depends on the computing facility and also on the skill of programmer. The Pentium III with CPU speed 850 MHZ is used to compute the running time of these four algorithms. As shown in Table 3, the proposed $CLARANS - ITP$ algorithm may reduce the running time from 38.7% to 65.4% compared with the $CLARANS$ algorithm.

Table 3. Performance comparison of running time

Database	CLARA		CLARANS		CLARANS-TP		CLARANS-ITP	
	Average distance	Time (sec.)	Average distance	Time (sec.)	Average distance	Time (sec.)	Average distance	Time (sec.)
Gauss-Markov	4.5433876	3128.2824	4.387779	693.6608	4.387779	540.8585	4.387779	425.8361
12 elliptic clusters	0.9598786	586.2521	0.935343	599.3182	0.935343	474.8397	0.935343	314.6202
Curve	2.280965	455.4464	2.168127	372.5514	2.168127	226.8398	2.168127	128.744

5   Conclusions and Future Work

In this paper, we have presented a novel and efficient method for improving k-medoids-based approach. Our experimental results demonstrate that applying the proposed hybrid method using previous medoid index, triangular inequality elimination and partial distance search to $CLARANS$ can reduce the number of distance calculation from 67% to 92% compared with $CLARANS$. In terms of the running time, the proposed algorithm may reduce 38.7% to 65.4% computation time compared with $CLARAN$ algorithm. Moreover, the proposed method may also apply to other k-medoids-based algorithms. For the preliminary experiments, only Criterion 1 of triangular inequality elimination is used. The other criteria of TIE, the improved absolute error inequality criterion and some other codeword search techniques may combine with the technique of previous medoid index to obtain a yet more efficient algorithm. This is the subject of future work.

References

1. J. Han, M. Kamber, and A. K. H. Tung, "Spatial clustering methods in data mining: A survey," in *Geographic Data Mining and Knowledge Discovery* (H. Miller and J. Han, eds.), Research Monographs in Geographic Information Systems, London: Taylor and Francis, 2001.
2. A. Gersho and R. M. Gray, *Vector Quantization and Signal Compression*. Boston, MA: Kluwer, 1992.
3. J. Jolion, P. Meer, and S. Bataouche, "Robust clustering with applications in computer vision," *IEEE Transactions on Pattern Analysis and Machine Intelligence*, vol. 13, no. 8, pp. 791–802, 1991.
4. D. Lecompte, L. Kaufman, and P. Rousseeuw, "Hierarchical cluster analysis of emotional concerns and personality characteristics in a freshman population," *Acta Psychiatrica Belgica*, vol. 86, pp. 324–333, 1986.
5. J. MacQueen, "Some methods for classification and analysis of multivariate observations," in *5th Berkeley symposium on mathematics, statistics and Probability*, vol. 1, pp. 281–296, 1967.
6. L. Kaufman and P. Rousseeuw, *Finding groups in data: an introduction to cluster analysis*. New York: John Wiley and Sons, 1990.
7. T. Zhang, R. Ramakrishnan, and M. Livny, "Birch: An efficient clustering method for very large databases," in *ACM SIGMOD Workshop on Research Issues on Data Mining and Knowledge Discovery*, (Montreal, Canada), pp. 103–114, 1996.
8. S. Guha, R. Rastogi, and K. Shim, "Cure: an efficient clustering algorithm for large databases," in *ACM SIGMOD International Conference on the Management of Data*, (Seattle, WA, USA), pp. 73–84, 1998.

9. V. Ganti, J. Gehrke, and R. Ramakrishnan, "Cactus-clustering categorical data using summaries," in *International Conference on Knowledge Discovery and Data Mining*, (San Diego, USA), pp. 73–83, 1999.
10. G. Karypis, E.-H. Han, and V. Kumar, "Chameleon: a hierarchical clustering algorithm using dynamic modeling," *Computer*, vol. 32, pp. 32–68, 1999.
11. M. Ester, H.-P. Kriegel, J. Sander, and X. Xu, "A density-based algorithm for discovering clusters in large spatial databases with noise," in *Second International Conference on Knowledge Discovery and Data Mining* (E. Simoudis, J. Han, and U. Fayyad, eds.), (Portland, Oregon), pp. 226–231, AAAI Press, 1996.
12. R. Ng and J. Han, "Efficient and effective clustering methods for spatial data mining," in *Twentieth International Conference on Very Large Data Bases* (J. B. Bocca, M. Jarke, and C. Zaniolo, eds.), (Santiago, Chile), pp. 144–155, Morgan Kaufmann, 1994.
13. S. C. Chu, J. F. Roddick, and J. S. Pan, "A comparative study and extensions to k-medoids algorithms," in *Fifth International Conference on Optimization : Techniques and Applications*, (Hong Kong, China), pp. 1708–1717, 2001.
14. R. Krishnapuram, A. Joshi, and L. Yi, "A fuzzy relative of the *k*-medoids algorithm with application to web document and snippet clustering," in *IEEE International Fuzzy Systems Conference*, (Seoul, Korea), pp. 1281–1286, 1999.
15. C. B. Lucasius, A. D. Dane, and G. Kateman, "On *k*-medoid clustering of large data sets with the aid of a genetic algorithm: background, feasibility and comparison," *Analytica Chimica Acta*, pp. 647–669, 1993.
16. C. D. Bei and R. M. Gray, "A improvement of the minimum distortion encoding algorithm for vector quantization," *IEEE Transactions on Communication*, vol. COM-33, no. 10, pp. 1132–1133, 1985.
17. E. Vidal, "An algorithm for finding nearest neighbours in (approximately) constant average time," *Pattern Recognition Letters*, vol. 4, pp. 145–157, 1986.
18. S. H. Chen and J. S. Pan, "Fast search algorithm for vq-based recognition of isolated word," *IEE Proc. I*, vol. 136, no. 6, pp. 391–396, 1989.
19. L. Guan and M. Kamel, "Equal-average hyperplane partitioning method for vector quantization of image data," *Pattern Recognition Letters*, pp. 693–699, 1992.
20. C. H. Lee and L. H. Chen, "Fast closest codeword search algorithm for vector quantization," *IEE Proc. Vision Image and Signal Processing*, vol. 141, no. 3, pp. 143–148, 1994.
21. S. J. Baek, B. K. Jeon, and K. M. Sung, "A fast encoding algorithm for vector quantization," *IEEE Signal Processing Letters*, vol. 4, no. 2, pp. 325–327, 1997.
22. J. S. Pan, F. R. McInnes, and M. A. Jack, "Bound for minkowski metric or quadratic metric applied to vq codeword search," *IEE Proc. Vision Image and Signal Processing*, vol. 143, no. 1, pp. 67–71, 1996.
23. M. R. Soleymani and S. D. Morgera, "A heigh-speed algorithm for vector quantization," *IEEE International Conference on Acoustics, Speech and Signal Processing*, pp. 1946–1948, 1987.
24. J. S. Pan, Z. M. Lu, and S. H. Sun, "A fast codeword search algorithm for image coding based on mean-variance pyramids of codewords," *IEE Electronics Letters*, vol. 36, no. 3, pp. 210–211, 2000.

A Hybrid Approach to Web Usage Mining

Søren E. Jespersen, Jesper Thorhauge, and Torben Bach Pedersen

Department of Computer Science, Aalborg University
{sej,jespert,tbp}@cs.auc.dk

Abstract. With the large number of companies using the Internet to distribute and collect information, knowledge discovery on the web has become an important research area. Web usage mining, which is the main topic of this paper, focuses on knowledge discovery from the clicks in the web log for a given site (the so-called click-stream), especially on analysis of *sequences* of clicks. Existing techniques for analyzing click sequences have different drawbacks, i.e., either huge storage requirements, excessive I/O cost, or scalability problems when additional information is introduced into the analysis.

In this paper we present a new *hybrid* approach for analyzing click sequences that aims to overcome these drawbacks. The approach is based on a novel combination of existing approaches, more specifically the Hypertext Probabilistic Grammar (HPG) and Click Fact Table approaches. The approach allows for additional information, e.g., user demographics, to be included in the analysis without introducing performance problems. The development is driven by experiences gained from industry collaboration. A prototype has been implemented and experiments are presented that show that the hybrid approach performs well compared to the existing approaches. This is especially true when mining sessions containing clicks with certain characteristics, i.e., when constraints are introduced. The approach is not limited to web log analysis, but can also be used for general sequence mining tasks.

1 Introduction

With the large number of companies using the Internet to distribute and collect information, knowledge discovery on the web, or *web mining* has become an important research area. Web mining can be divided into three areas, namely *web content mining*, *web structure mining* and *web usage mining* (also called web log mining) [8]. Web content mining focuses on discovery of information stored on the Internet, i.e., the various search engines. Web structure mining can be used when improving the structural design of a website. Web usage mining, the main topic of this paper, focuses on knowledge discovery from the usage of individual web sites. Web usage mining is mainly based on the activities recorded in the *web log*, the log file written by the web server recording individual requests made to the server. An important notion in a web log is the existence of *user sessions*. A user session is a sequence of requests from a single user within a certain time window. Of particular interest is the discovery of frequently performed *sequences* of actions by web user, i.e., frequent sequences of visited web pages.

The work presented in this paper has been motivated by collaboration with the Zenaria company [21]. For more on this collaboration, please consult the full paper[10].

Y. Kambayashi, W. Winiwarter, M. Arikawa (Eds.): DaWaK 2002, LNCS 2454, pp. 73–82, 2002.

Much work has been performed on extracting various pattern information from web logs and the application of the discovered knowledge range from improving the design and structure of a web site to enabling companies to provide more targeted marketing. One line of work features techniques for working directly on the log file [8,9]. Another line of work concentrates on creating aggregated structures of the information in the web log [13,16]. The Hypertext Probabilistic Grammar (HPG) model [3,4], utilizing the theory of grammars, is such an aggregated structure. Yet another line of work focuses on using database technology in the clickstream analysis [1,7], building so-called "data webhouses" [12]. Several database schemas have been suggested, e.g. the click fact star schema where the individual click is the primary fact[12]. Several commercial tools for analyzing web logs exist [15,19,20], but their focus is mostly on statistical measures, e.g., most frequently visited pages and they provide only limited facilities for click-stream analysis. Finally, a prominent line of work focuses on mining *sequential patterns* in general sequence databases [2,13,14,17]. However, all the mentioned approaches have inherent weaknesses in that they either have huge storage requirements, slow performance due to many scans over the data, or problems when additional information, e.g., user demographics, are introduced into the analysis.

In this paper we present a new *hybrid* approach for analyzing click sequences that aims to overcome these drawbacks. The approach is based on a novel combination of existing approaches, more specifically the HPG and Click Fact Table [12] approaches. The new approach attempts to utilize the quick access and the flexibility with respect to additional information of the click fact table, and the capability of the HPG model to quickly mine rules from large amounts of data. Specialized information is extracted from the click fact schema and presented using the HPG model. The approach allows for additional information, e.g., user demographics, to be included in the analysis without introducing performance problems. A prototype has been implemented and experiments are presented that show that the hybrid approach performs very well compared to the existing approaches. This is especially true when mining sessions containing clicks with certain characteristics, i.e., when constraints are introduced. The approach is not limited to web log analysis, but can also be used for general sequence mining tasks.

We believe this paper to be the first to present an approach for mining frequent sequences in web logs that at the same time provides small storage requirements, very fast rule mining performance, and the ability to introduce additional information into the analysis with only a small performance penalty. This is done by exploiting existing data warehouse technology.

The paper is organized as follows. Section 2 describes the techniques on which we base our new hybrid approach. Section 3 describes the hybrid approach in detail. Section 4 describes the prototype implementation. Section 5 examines the performance of the hybrid approach. Section 6 concludes and points to future work.

2   Background

This section briefly describes the approaches underlying our hybrid approach. For a more in-depth discussion of the various technologies, please consult the full paper[10].

Database-Based Approaches. These include storing the web log data in either a *click fact schema*[12], which holds the clickstream data at a very fine granularity but have problems presenting sequences of clicks effectively or in a *subsession fact schema*[1], which stores the clickstream data explicitly as sequences (subsessions) in the data warehouse and is therefore effective in extracting sequences of clicks but requires a significant storage overhead.

Hypertext Probabilistic Grammars. An HPG creates a compact, aggregated representation of a website, effectively mapping all web pages to states in a grammar and adding two additional artificial states, the start state S and the end state F, to form all states of a grammar. We will throughout the paper use the terms state and page interchangeably.

The probability of a production is assigned based on the information in the web log so that the probability of a production is proportional to the number of times the given link was traversed relative to the number of times the state on the left side of the production was visited. An HPG specifies a threshold η against which all strings are evaluated. If the probability of the string is below the threshold, the string will not be included in the language of the HPG (with the assigned threshold). This will generate a complete language for a given HPG with a given threshold, L^η. Mining an HPG is essentially the process of extracting high-probability strings from the grammar. These strings are called *rules*. These rules will describe the most preferred trails on the web site since they are traversed with a high probability. Mining can be done using both a breath-first and a depth-first search algorithm[3] and can be expanded using various heuristics [5,6] to allow for better control of the resulting ruleset. An example of an HPG is shown in Figure 2.1.

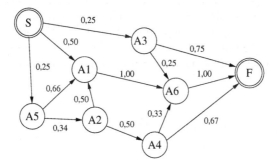

Fig. 2.1. Example of a Hypertext Probabilistic Grammar.

An HPG inherently uses the assumption of limited browsing history, due to the mapping of webpages directly to states, as can be seen in Figure 2.1. The HPG can also be generated with a *history-depth* N above 1. With a history-depth of e.g. 2 each state represents two web pages requested in sequence. The structure of the HPG remains the same but each state now has a "memory" of the N last states traversed. By using a larger history-depth cannot however gurantee against *false trails*, i.e. knowledge discovered without being correctly supported in session collection. The HPG has decisive problems containing information at a low granularity since it only holds aggregated clickstream data and is therefore not able to represent properties of individual clicks. Furthermore, the possibility of extracting false trails as knowledge is a decisive weakness.

Summary. As mentioned in the preceding paragraphs, each approach has some inherent strengths and weaknesses. The click and subsession fact approaches handle additional information easily, but result either in huge I/O or huge storage requirements. On the other hand, an HPG can efficiently mine long rules for a large collection of sessions, but is not able to represent additional information in a scalable way. To remedy this situation, we now present a new approach for extracting information about the use of a web site, utilizing the potential for mining very specific rules present in the HPG approach while still allowing for the representation of additional information using a click fact schema in a data warehouse, utilizing existing DW technology. The main idea is to create HPGs on demand, where each dynamically created HPG represents a specific part of the information in the web log.

3   The Hybrid Approach

Our proposal for a hybrid approach combines the click fact schema with the HPG model, creating a flexible technique able to answer both general *and* detailed queries regarding web usage. Using the detailed information from the click fact schema results in almost no data being lost in the conversion from web log to database. However, we also need some kind of abstraction or simplification applied to the query results. In short, we want to be able to specify exactly what subset of the information we want to discover knowledge for. An HPG provides us with a simple technique to create an overview from detailed information. The scalability issues and somewhat lack of flexibility in the HPG model must though also be kept in mind as we want to be flexible with regards to querying possibilities. The concept of the hybrid approach is shown in Figure 3.1.

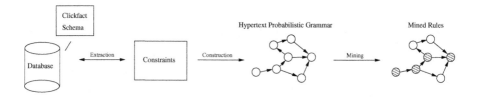

Fig. 3.1. Overview Of The Hybrid Approach.

Creating specialized HPGs would require storing the original web log information and creating each specialized HPG when required. Storing the original web log file is not very efficient since e.g. a lot of non-optimized string-processing would be required, so some other format needs to be devised. The click fact schema described above provides this detailed level, since it preserves the ordering of the web log and furthermore offers database functionality such as backup, optimized querying and the possibility of OLAP techniques such as pre-aggregation being applied. However, a more subtle feature of the click fact schema actually offers itself directly to the HPG model and proves useful in our solution. The database schema for the click fact table includes unique keys for both the *referrer* and the *destination* for each click. These two keys uniquely identify a specific production within a grammar since each key is a reference to a page and thus a state. Thereby we are able to extract all productions from the click fact table simply by returning all combinations of url_key and referer_key. Each occurrence of a specific combination of keys will represent a single traversal of the corresponding link on the website. Retrieving all states from an HPG is immediately possible from the click fact schema. The url_dimension table holds information about each individual page on the web site, therefore a single query could easily retrieve all states in the grammar and a count of how many times the state was visited, both in total and as first or last in a session. The queries can be used to initialize an HPG. This would normally be done using an algorithm iterating over all states in the sessions[3] but using the database representation, the required information can retrieved in a few simple database queries. Note that some post-processing of the query results are necessary for a nice in-memory representation. For further detail, please consult the full paper[10].

Constructing Specialized HPGs. Creating specialized HPGs is indeed possible with this approach. Inserting a *constraint* layer between the database software and the creation process for an HPG will allow for restrictions on the information represented in the HPG. Extending the queries described above to only extract information for clicks with certain characteristics will allow for creation of an HPG only representing this information. Thereby rules mined on this HPG will be solely for clicks with the specific characteristics. Using this concept, specialized HPGs can be created on-demand from the database. For instance, the user might be interested in learning about the usage characteristics of all male users with a college degree. The user will specify this constraint and the queries above are modified to only extract the productions and the states that apply to the constraint. The queries will therefore only extract the sessions generated by male users with a college degree and the HPG built from these sessions will produce rules telling about the characteristic behavior of exactly this user group.

This approach utilizes some of the techniques earlier described but combines them to utilize the strong sides and avoid some of the weak sides.

Pros: The limitations of the "simple" HPG model of not being able to efficiently represent additional information are avoided with this hybrid approach. The ability to easily generate a specialized HPG overcome the shortcomings of not being able to pre-generate all possible specialized HPGs. Saving the web log information in the click fact table (and thus in the database) gives us a tool for storing information which arguably is preferred to storing the original log file. A DBMS has many techniques for restoring, querying and analyzing the information with considerable performance gains over processing on raw textual data such as a log file. Combining the click fact schema, which offers a detailed level of information, and the HPG model, which offers a more generalized and compact view of the data will allow for different views on the same data within the same model, without storing information redundantly on non-volatile storage.

Cons: As the hybrid approach mine results using the HPG, false trails might be presented to the user, which is a characteristic inherited from the general HPG approach. This is obviously a critical issue since this might lead to misinterpretations of the data. Using a history depth greater than 1 might reduce the number of false trails.

The complexity considerations surrounding the HPG can be split into three separate parts, which are presented below. In the following, C is the number of clicks, P represents the number of productions and S represents the number of states.

Database access: the aggregate results obtained from the database can, using hash-based aggregation, be computed by two single scans of the clicks, i.e., in time $O(C)$. If the DBMS supports pre-aggregated data, this can be computed in time $O(P) + O(S) = O(P)$. *Constructing the HPG*: the HPG is a compact, aggregated representation and the size is dependent upon the number of productions it must represent, not the number of sessions since they are aggregated into each state. Therefore, the creation of the HPG has complexity $O(P)$. *Mining the HPG*: the mining of an HPG can be performed using both a general Breath First Search(BFS) and a Depth First Search(DFS) algorithm[3]. The complexity of mining an HPG using the BFS algorithm is $O(S + P)$[18].

Open Issues: The performance of generating specialized HPG's using queries on top of a database is an open issue that will be explored in Section 5.

4   Prototype Description

The architecture of the hybrid approach prototype can be seen in Figure 4.1. All modules within the system are implemented in the Java programming language. The weblog is cleaned, transformed and loaded into the data warehouse by the *Data Warehouse Loader*. The *Constraint Layer* presents a way of specifying what information should be represented in the HPG, which is extracted from the data warehouse and created in memory by the *HPG* module.

Constraint Layer Implementation. The main idea of combining a data warehouse with the HPG technique is to achieve the ability to constrain the data upon which the HPG is built. A detailed description of how this constraining is achieved is presented along with additional prototype details in the full paper[10]. We need SQL queries to extract our constrained set of data and then pass it on to a module initializing our HPG. However, the constraints must first be categorized into *session specific* and *click specific* information. This distinction is very important, as the constructed HPG could otherwise be incorrect.

Session specific: Dimensions holding information which are specific to an entire session will, when constrained on one or more of their attributes, *always* return entire sessions as the result. One such dimension is the session dimension. If the click fact schema is constrained to only return clicks referencing a subset of all sessions in the session dimension, it is assured that the clicks returned will form complete sessions. In an HPG context it means that the constructed HPG never has any *disconnected* states - states where no productions are going either to or from.

Click specific: Dimensions containing information relating to single clicks will, if the click fact table is constrained on a subset of these keys, produce a set of single clicks which are *probably not* forming complete sessions. The probability of this will increase

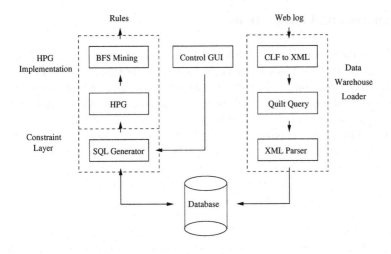

Fig. 4.1. Overview of the prototype architecture.

as the cardinality of the attribute grows or the number of selected attributes shrinks. The created HPG will contain a number of disconnected states which will invalidate the mining process (since they do not assure consistency in the HPG).

As we want the approach to provide the overview as well as the detail, these two types of dimensions must be dealt with *before* the HPG is built. The solution proposed here is to constrain the data in two stages. The two stages can briefly be described as follows. First, we retrieve a temporary result using dimensions which are thought to be *click* specific. The temporary result comes from joining the click specific dimensions with the click fact schema on *all* constrained attributes. The distinct session keys from the temporary result can be used to get the subset of all clicks having these session keys. These distinct keys are session specific and will assure an interconnected HPG. Second, we constrain the result using dimensions which are thought to be *session* specific and the distinct session keys. *All* constrains must be fulfilled on the dimension when joining with the click fact schema. The collection of clicks retrieved are interconnected.

HPG Implementation. The HPG implementation consists of two parts; The HPG creation method and a Breadth First Search (BFS) mining algorithm. The BFS algorithm is chosen instead of the Depth First Search (DFS) algorithm as the latter has a higher memory consumption [3]. We have chosen to implement both parts using algorithms and specifications as presented by Borges[3]. As our work is focused on creating a hybrid between the standard click fact schema and the standard HPG model we are not interested in altering any of these techniques. The only difference between the prototype implementation and the work by Borges[3] is, that rules and productions are stored in main memory instead of a database.

5   Experimental Evaluations

In evaluating the hybrid approach we decided to evaluate the performance of the creation of HPGs on-the-fly both by it self and against a straight-forward SQL-query on a subsession schema (see Section 2). The experiments were performed on both a non-optimized and an optimized implementation of the hybrid approach. We decided not to evaluate against a straight forward click fact schema since they perform porly on sequences of clicks[1] and techniques requiring a number of scans of the database for mining the patterns [2,13,14,17] would perform too poorly to be used for on-line mining. An extended description of the experimental results can be found in the full paper[10]. The *goals* of these experiments is to retrieve information concerning the performance of creating HPGs on-the-fly on top of a database.

Experimental Settings. We have used the web log from the Computer Science Department at Aalborg University for October 2001, containing 33000 sessions for a total of 115000 valid clicks divided amongst 27400 unique pages.

The DBMS used in the evaluation is a MySQL 4.0.1 running on an Intel^{TM} 933 Mhz machine. The prototype described in Section 4 is running on an AMD Athlon^{TM} 1800 Mhz machine.

We adopted the suggested convention[1] of limiting the subsession length to 10 clicks to avoid a massive blowup in number of subsessions generated. Insertion of subsessions yielded a total of 620000 entries in the subsession fact table divided amongst 490000 different subsessions. We now turn to the actual experimental results.

Analysis of The Hybrid Approach. In the process of extracting rules from the data warehouse, three main tasks are performed. First, the database is queried for data used to initialize the HPG. Second, the HPG is built in main memory based on the extracted data and third, the BFS mining algorithm extracts rules from the HPG. To test how the approach performs as the number of states increase, a range query test was performed.

By far the most time consuming part in the hybrid approach is the database query time. In most cases, more than 90% of the total time is spent in this part. The time used for the BFS mining very short. The time spent on initializing the HPG only adds little processing time to the overall processing time, usually 5–10%. Thus, it seems that a possible tuning effort should focus on the database query part.

One of the most obvious ways to optimize the database, is to create indexes on the key attributes in the click fact schema. Materialized views is another promising opportunity for tuning.

Comparative Analysis. We now compare the hybrid approach to the subsession schema on extraction of information for *all* sessions, *session* specific constraints and *click* specific constraints

All sessions: It is found that the non-optimized hybrid approach performs poorer than the subsession schema by a factor of approximately 25. However, the hybrid approach where both the database querying and the BFS mining is optimized, takes only 30% longer than the subsession approach. The small performance advantage of the subsession approach comes at a large price: the storage requirements are more than 5 times higher than for the hybrid approach, due to the need to store subsession of all lengths.

Click specific constraints: The test is performed by extracting information for all sessions containing requests including the string *tbp*, which is a specific personal home-page on the web site. The hybrid approach proves to be a factor of 10 faster than the subsession schema approach, even in the non-optimized case, the optimized version is 20 times faster.

Session specific constraints: The session specific constraint is evaluated using a constraint on the `total_session_seconds` field from the `session_dimension` table. The optimized hybrid approach outperforms all the other approaches by an average factor of 3–4. All the other approaches are rather similar in performance. Again, the superior performance of the optimized hybrid approach is accompanied by a storage requirement that is more than 5 times smaller than the subsession approach.

Experiment Summary. To conclude, our evaluation of the hybrid approach has shown that the optimized hybrid approach is very competitive when compared to the subsession fact approach. Even with a storage requirement that is more than 5 times smaller than for the subsession fact approach, the optimized hybrid approach performs 3–20 times faster. Only for mining all rules the performance is a little slower, making the hybrid approach the clear winner.

6   Conclusion and Future Work

Motivated by the need for an efficient way of mining sequence rules for large amounts of web log data, we presented a hybrid approach to web usage mining that aims to overcome some of the drawbacks of previous solutions. The approach was based on a novel combination of existing approaches, more specifically the HPG and Click Fact Table approaches. The new approach attempted to utilize the quick access and the flexibility with respect to additional information of the click fact table, and the capability of the HPG model to quickly mine rules from large amounts of data. Specialized information was extracted from the click fact schema and presented using the HPG model. The approach allows for additional information, e.g., user demographics, to be included in the analysis without introducing performance problems. A prototype has been implemented and experiments are presented that show that the hybrid approach performs very well compared to existing approaches, especially when mining sessions containing clicks with certain characteristics, i.e., when constraints are introduced.

In future work, the mining process should be modified to include the heuristics mentioned in Section 2, which will allow for a better control of rule extraction. Optimization of the prototype, especially the database querying is also an area of future improvement. The hybrid approach inherits the risk of presenting false trails from the HPG. Developing a method to work around this risk, potentially utilizing history depth or some other technique is an interesting way to go. Finally, an expansion of the HPG mining process where individual pages could be assigned a measure of importance in the mining process is desirable. Such an expansion would improve the capability of users to tune the mining process to specific pages in the interactive stories.

References

1. J.Andersen, A. Giversen, A. H. Jensen, R. S. Larsen, T. B. Pedersen, and J. Skyt. Analyzing clickstreams using subsessions. In *Proceedings of the Second International Workshop on Data Warehousing and OLAP*, 2000.
2. R. Agrawal and R. Srikant. Mining sequential patterns. In *Proceedings of the 11th International Conference on Data Engineering*, 1995.
3. J. Borges. *A Data Mining Model to Capture User Web Navigation Patterns*. PhD thesis, Department of Computer Science, University College London, 2000.
4. J. Borges and M. Levene. Data mining of user navigation patterns. In *Proceedings of WEBKDD*, 1999.
5. J. Borges and M. Levene. Heuristics for mining high quality user web navigation patterns. Research Note RN/99/68. Department of Computer Science, University College London, Gower Street, London, UK, 1999.
6. J. Borges and M. Levene. A fine grained heuristic to capture web navigation patterns. *SIGKDD Explorations*, 2000.
7. A.G. Büchner, S.S. Anand, M.D. Mulvenna, and J.G. Hughes. Discovering internet marketing intelligence through web log mining. In *Proceedings of UNICOM99*, 1999.
8. R. Cooley, J. Srivastava, and B. Mobasher. Web mining: Information and pattern discovery on the world wide web. In *Proceedings of the 9th IEEE International Conference on Tools with Artificial Intelligence (ICTAI'97)*, 1997.
9. R. Cooley, P. Tan, and J. Srivastava. Websift: the web site information filter system. In *Proceedings of the 1999 KDD Workshop on Web Mining*, 1999.
10. S. Jespersen, T. B. Pedersen, and J. Thorhauge. A Hybrid Approach to Web Usage Mining - Technical Report R02-5002 *Dept. of CS, Aalborg University, 2002*
11. J. Han and M. Kamber. *Data Mining - Concepts and Techniques*. Morgan Kaufmann, 2000.
12. R. Kimball and R. Merz. *The Data Webhouse Toolkit*. Wiley, 2000.
13. J. Pei, J. Han, B. Mortazavi-Asl, and H. Zhu. Mining access patterns efficiently from web logs. In *Proceedings of the Pacific-Asia Conference on Knowledge Discovery and Data Mining*, 2000.
14. J. Pei, J. Han, B. Mortazavi-Asl, H. Pinto, Q. Chen, U. Dayal, and M. Hsu. PrefixSpan: Mining Sequential Patterns by Prefix-Projected Growth. In *Proceedings of the 17th International Conference on Data Engineering*.
15. Sawmill, http://www.sawmill.net.
16. M. Spiliopoulou and L. C. Faulstich. WUM: a Web Utilization Miner. In *Proceedings of the Workshop on the Web and Data Bases*, 1998.
17. R. Srikant and R. Agrawal. Mining Sequential Patterns: Generalizations and Performance Improvements. In *Proceedings of the EDBT Conference*, 1996.
18. T. Cormen et. al. *Introduction to Algorithms* MIT Press, 2001.
19. WebTrends LogAnalyzer. http://www.webtrends.com/products/log/.
20. K.-L. Wu, P. S. Yu, and A. Ballman. Speedtracer: A web usage mining and analysis tool. *IBM System Journal, Internet Computing, Volume 37*, 1998.
21. Zenaria A/S. http://www.zenaria.com.

Building and Exploiting Ad Hoc Concept Hierarchies for Web Log Analysis

Carsten Pohle and Myra Spiliopoulou

Department of E-Business, Leipzig Graduate School of Management
{cpohle,myra}@ebusiness.hhl.de

Abstract. Web usage mining aims at the discovery of interesting usage patterns from Web server log files. "Interestingness" relates to the business goals of the site owner. However, business goals refer to business objects rather than the page hits and script invocations recorded by the site server. Hence, Web usage analysis requires a preparatory mechanism that incorporates the business goals, the concepts reflecting them and the expert's background knowledge on them into the mining process. To this purpose, we present a methodology and a mechanism for the establishment and exploitation of application-oriented concept hierarchies in Web usage analysis. We demonstrate our approach on a real data set and show how it can substantially improve both the search for interesting patterns by the mining algorithm and the interpretation of the mining results by the analyst.

Keywords: Concept hierarchies, taxonomy construction, pre-mining, data preparation, association rules' discovery, pattern matching, data mining

1 Introduction

The success of data mining projects depends heavily on the analyst's ability to translate a domain expert's problem statement into the semantics of the data to be mined. The complexity of this problem depends on the application domain and the data sources.

For example, when mining a retail store's transaction data for items frequently bought together, the store manager's notion of *item* or *product* can usually be directly transferred to the analyzed data, because products are represented by their respective product codes. Market basket analysis would then return rules like ProdA→ProdB, denoting that buyers of product A are likely to purchase product B, too. The data analyst's task becomes more complicated when the management is not interested in association patterns at the product level but in generic rules on product categories, like SkimmedMilk→OatmealCereals. If these product categories differ from those depicted in the company's warehouse, as is the case when new business opportunities are sought for, then the new categories must be established during data preparation.

The mapping of business concepts upon raw data is even more acute in web usage mining applications. Web servers record invocations of URLs, scripts, images and frames, while Web site owners are interested in patterns like "Users inspect three to five products before adding something to the shopping cart". As in the market basket analysis example, the analyst must formulate concept hierarchies in order to map object

Y. Kambayashi, W. Winiwarter, M. Arikawa (Eds.): DaWaK 2002, LNCS 2454, pp. 83–93, 2002.

invocations into business concepts. A *concept hierarchy* or *taxonomy* defines a sequence of mappings from detailed concepts into higher level abstractions.

Concept hierarchies are well-known from the research on data warehousing [3]: The corporate data warehouse is associated with multiple hierarchical views over the data, conceptualized as the dimensions of an OLAP cube. However, data mining often requires the exploitation of *ad hoc* taxonomies, which, in contrast to the rather static OLAP taxonomies, are tailored to the specific business problem specification for the data mining process. For example, a new marketing campaign of a large store may require that the products are observed in a different context than the general-purpose product classification available in the company warehouse.

The establishment of concept hierarchies is a human-centric task. Although text mining can be used to extract representative concepts from web pages, the specification of the concepts of interest for the analysis can only be done by the analyst. In this study, we do not attempt to delegate the analyst's work to the software, but rather propose a methodology for the establishment of application-oriented ad hoc concept hierarchies and provide tools that support the steps of this methodology.

We first provide a formal definition of concept hierarchies, introduce our Web usage environment WUM and briefly discuss related work. In section 3, we discuss the notion of *application-oriented* concept hierarchies, describe our methodology to establish them and explain how the data preparation module of WUM supports the exploitation of taxonomies by the miner. Section 4 contains a case study, in which we applied concept hierarchies for the behavioural analysis of the visitors of a Web site. The last section summarizes our results and provides an outlook of future work.

2   Concept Hierarchies

In OLAP applications, each dimension of a data warehouse's cube is statically pre-defined by a hierarchy of concepts. "Roll-up" operations fold the data into a more abstract level, while "drill-down" operations unfold them into more detailed concepts. Concept hierarchies are subject to formal constraints, intended to prevent the establishment of ill-formed taxonomies. Mutual exclusiveness of the concepts at the same level of the hierarchy is one such constraint; completeness is another.

2.1   Fundamentals of Concept Hierarchies

Our understanding of concepts and concept hierarchies goes back to the formal concept analysis developed by Wille et al. [7]. The authors define a formal context $(\mathcal{O}, \mathcal{A}, \mathcal{R})$ as two sets $\mathcal{O}$ and $\mathcal{A}$ and a relation $\mathcal{R} \subseteq \mathcal{O} \times \mathcal{A}$ between them. The elements of $\mathcal{O}$ are called *objects*, those of $\mathcal{A}$ are *attributes*. For each set of objects $O \subseteq \mathcal{O}, O' := \{a \in \mathcal{A} | (o, a) \in \mathcal{R} \forall o \in O\}$ denotes the set of attributes common to the objects in O. Accordingly, the set $A' := \{o \in O | (o, a) \in \mathcal{R} \forall a \in A\}$ is the set of objects sharing the attributes for each $A \subseteq \mathcal{A}$.

A *(formal) concept* of the context $(\mathcal{O}, \mathcal{A}, \mathcal{R})$ is a pair (O, A) with $O \subseteq \mathcal{O}, A \subseteq \mathcal{A}, O' = A$ and $A' = O$. The set O is called the concept's *extension*, the set A is its *intension*. The hierarchical *subconcept-superconcept relationship* is formalized as $(O_1, A_1) \leq (O_2, A_2) \iff O_1 \subseteq O_2 (\iff A_1 \supseteq A_2)$.

Let $c_1 = (O_1, A_1)$ and $c_2 = (O_2, A_2)$ be concepts of a context $(\mathcal{O}, \mathcal{A}, \mathcal{R})$. c_1 is a *subconcept* of c_2 and c_2 is a *superconcept* of c_1 iff $O_1 \subseteq O_2$. We denote this relationship as $c_1 \leq c_2$. Further, c_2 is called a *lower neighbor* of c_1, if $c_2 < c_1$ and there exists no concept c_3 with $c_2 < c_3 < c_1$. Then, c_1 is an *upper neighbor* of c_2, denoted as $c_2 \prec c_1$. The set of all lower neighbors $c_2 \ldots c_n$ of a concept c_1 is the set of *siblings under c_1*.

Using the ordering relation $\leq$ and the set $\mathcal{H}(\mathcal{O}, \mathcal{A}, \mathcal{R})$ of all concepts of a context $(\mathcal{O}, \mathcal{A}, \mathcal{R})$, one establishes a *complete lattice $H = (\mathcal{H}, \leq)$*, or *concept lattice (concept hierarchy)* of $(\mathcal{O}, \mathcal{A}, \mathcal{R})$. This means that for each set of concepts $V \subseteq \mathcal{H}(\mathcal{O}, \mathcal{A}, \mathcal{R})$, there exists a unique greatest subconcept (*infimum*) and a unique smallest superconcept (*supremum*). The supremum $\bigvee H$ of H is the *root* of the concept hierarchy, written as $\top$. The infimum of H, $\bigwedge H$, is called *null element* and is written as $\bot$.

These mathematical foundations have led to numerous applications in information retrieval [12], artificial intelligence [6], knowledge discovery [9] and knowledge management [14]. In many of them, concept lattices have a network structure, which means that concepts are allowed to have multiple superconcepts.

2.2 Constraints on Concept Hierarchies

In knowledge discovery applications, the mapping of data into abstract concepts must be non-ambiguous. Otherwise, the statistic operations on the data will produce erroneous results. For the general case of a lattice, one must specify which upper neighbour of a concept should be selected in any context. We rather enforce the following constraints:

C–1. Each concept c has at most one upper neighbour c'.
  This implies that we concentrate on concept hierarchies rather than generic lattices.
C–2. If $\{c_1, \ldots, c_n\}$ is the set of siblings under a concept c, then for each c_i, c_j belonging to this set and $c_i \neq c_j$ the condition $c_i \wedge c_2 = \bot$ holds.
  This means that the siblings under a concept are mutually exclusive.
C–3. For each item m in the dataset there is exactly one concept $c \in H$, such that m is mapped to c *and* c has no lower neighbour.
  This means that all items in the dataset can be mapped into concepts at the lowermost level of the concept hierarchy.

We refer to a mapping of items to concepts as *conceptual scaling*. A conceptual scaling that satisfies the second and third constraints is *non-ambiguous* and *complete*. The first constraint ensures that only trees of concepts are permitted. This implies that the application may need to establish multiple, partially overlapping concept hierarchies. For example, if a market store observes apple juice as "an apple product" and as "a product sold in a glass bottle", then two concept hierarchies are needed, one referring to the contents of the product and one to the packaging. We distinguish three kinds of concept hierarchies with respect to conceptual scaling:

Implicit concept hierarchies are already incorporated to the semantics of the schema. Time is an example of such a hierarchy: $\{minute \prec hour \prec day \prec month \prec year\}$

Generic concept hierarchies are those capturing the semantics of multiple applications in the business domain.

The static concept hierarchies established in the warehouse are expected to be of generic nature. Most data mining projects will exploit at least one concept hierarchy of this kind. However, the concepts captured in it may not be sufficient for the complete problem specification.

Ad hoc concept hierarchies are pertinent to a specific data mining project.

While an intuitively generic concept hierarchy is one that categorizes web pages by content, an ad hoc one may categorize them as heavily or rarely visited.

The type of a concept hierarchy influences the effort required for each implementation. While implicit concept hierarchies can be established almost trivially, and while generic concept hierarchies are often in place before a data mining project starts, ad hoc concept hierarchies call for sophisticated tools that must support the analyst in (i) the establishment of the taxonomy itself and (ii) the mapping of data items to concepts. In this study, we concentrate on the second aspect.

2.3   Concept Hierarchies in Data Mining

The KDD literature provides numerous reports about concept hierarchies for data mining. In [4], Han et al. present their method of attribute-oriented induction as a way of knowledge extraction from data. Concept hierarchies have also been used as a vehicle to incorporate domain knowledge into the mining process, as proposed by Anand, Büchner et al. [1]. Here, concept hierarchies enhance both the visibility of mined patterns and their usefulness to the user. In a similar way, Michalski and Kaufmann [11] show how attributes structured by concept hierarchies can support the interpretation of mining results. Srikant and Agrawal [17] proposed to utilize concept hierarchies for mining generalized association rules, where the mining algorithm autonomously chooses the maximal abstraction level, given statistical thresholds for interestingness.

Web usage mining deals with the extraction of patterns from Web server log data. Log files store timestamped information about the URL of the requested document, the objects (images, frames etc) comprising this document, the IP address of the accessing host, the volume of transferred data, the Web browser and operating system used etc. Although frequent patterns upon page objects can be identified, a frequent sequence

```
/shop/products/prodlist.cgi?pgroup=243 →
/shop/products/proddetail.cgi?prodId=243756 →
/shop/basket.cgi?custID=8893A87DC
```

is of limited use for understanding user behavior, while pattern like

```
Catalog → ProdDetails → ProdDetails → ShoppingBasket
```

can lead to valuable insights on site usage.

An early application of concept hierarchies in Web usage mining has been presented by Pirolli et al. [13]. The authors classified Web pages into several categories like index, reference or content pages along a single dimension representing their functional roles. In the following section, we extend this idea and provide support for arbitrary concept hierarchies to Web server logs.

3   Establishing Application-Oriented Concept Hierarchies

The core of our mechanism for the establishment of ad hoc concept hierarchies lays in the mapping of *named* data objects into the leaf concepts of a hierarchy. Currently, it is implemented in Perl and incorporated into the data preparation phase of the *Web Utilization Miner* WUM [15], [16]. This mechanism is part of our conceptual methodology on how an ad hoc conceptual hierarchy should be established. This methodology is part of the KDD process depicted in Fig. 1.

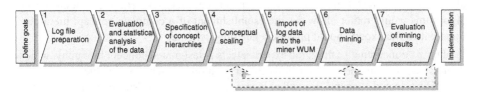

Fig. 1. The Web usage mining process with WUM

Fig. 1 shows the iterative mining process supported by WUM, following the process model proposed by Büchner et al. in [2]. The first five tasks constitute the data preparation phase, involving filtering of undesirable entries from the Web server log, resolution of IP addresses to DNS names, identification of accesses by robots and spiders, mapping of requests to visitors and partitioning sequences of visitor requests to sessions. The establishment of concept hierarchies corresponds to tasks 3 and 4 of Fig. 1. These tasks constitute a separate subprocess, which we model as follows:

Task 3.   Specification of concept hierarchies (cf. Fig. 1):
  3.1 Specification of the abstraction dimensions over the pages of the site according to the data mining problem at hand.
  3.2 Specification of a concept hierarchy that satisfies the constraints of subsection 2.2 for each dimension.
Task 4.   Conceptual scaling (cf. Fig. 1):
  4.1 Selection of a "designated" concept hierarchy as a basis for the analysis
  4.2 Identification of concepts in the other concept hierarchies, which should also be considered in the analysis
  4.3 Merging of the additional concepts in the designated concept hierarchy
  4.4 Selection of a level of generalization for each leaf concept:
      This results in a set of concepts, upon which the URLs should be mapped.
  4.5 Mapping of each URL into one of the selected concepts:
      Since the concepts of the designated concept hierarchy are mutually exclusive, each URL is mapped into a single concept.

Task 3 is an intellectual task and has to be performed manually. For the special case of an ad hoc concept hierarchy that reflects the contents of the pages, text clustering techniques could be applied. Then, the label of each cluster becomes a concept representing the pages in the cluster. Two issues should be considered in this context: First, in order to ensure that constraint C-2 in subsection 2.2 is satisfied, i.e. that sibling concepts are mutually exclusive, only clustering techniques that produce disjoint groups are appropriate. Second, while the literature provides a plethora of text clustering algorithms, the assignment of labels to clusters is a separate and difficult issue. For example, clustering the pages of a concert-hall site on content is easy; deriving automatically that "cluster 6 contains pages on midnight events for strings" while "cluster 7 contains pages on free-entrance jam sessions not involving strings" is less straightforward. We investigate the issue of semi-automated cluster labelling for text documents in [8], whereby our algorithm would result in an one-level deep concept hierarchy. Hierarchical clustering algorithms would rather allow for the establishment of a complete concept hierarchy, upon which the expert should provide a labelling scheme.

During conceptual scaling, the expert selects a designated concept hierarchy, which depicts the most important dimension in her opinion. In step 4.3, this hierarchy is extended by selected concepts from other hierarchies. Since the constraint on mutual exclusiveness among sibling concepts must be preserved, concepts from the other hierarchies cannot be simply added to the designated one. Assuming that a common concept has the same name in all hierarchies, and the tree of subconcepts T below a selected concept c can be added to the designated hierarchy if none of its concepts is there. If this does not hold, the designated concept hierarchy can be expanded in three steps: (i) The selected concept c is located in the designated concept hierarchy. (ii) The analyst specifies a level of generalization for concept c in T, so that not the whole tree needs to be integrated. This corresponds to a set of subconcepts $\{c_1, \ldots, c_n\}$. (iii) Each subconcepts d below c in the designated hierarchy is replaced by n subconcepts $dc_1, \ldots, dc_n$. This last step is supported by our data preparation tool WUMprep.

The last step of conceptual scaling is the most laborious one, since we deal with individual URLs. We exploit the fact that URLs are *named objects* and that their names follow conventions. To exploit these conventions, the expert just associates each concept with a regular expression. WUMprep replaces all URLs satisfying this regular expression with the associated concept.

Mutual exclusiveness among sibling concepts is imperative, but is difficult to enforce among the associated regular expressions. Therefore, our mapping tool accepts an *sequence* of regular expressions and checks each URL against it. This allows the analyst to map the most specific URLs to concepts first and map a large set of uninteresting URLs with the concept "OTHER" as last step, by associating "OTHER" with a very generic regular expression.

Summarizing, our generic methodology for concept hierarchy establishment involves the human-intensive specification task and the software-supported task of conceptual scaling. Our WUMprep prototype supports currently the mapping of URLs to concepts by means of user-specified regular expressions, as well as the expansion of a concept in the designated hierarchy by a set of mutually exclusive subconcepts from other hierarchies. The support of the whole process of hierarchy specification and selection of a generalization level by a graphical user interface is envisaged as future work.

4   A Case Study

To show the positive impact of concept hierarchies on the effectiveness of Web usage analysis, we report on the analysis of a Web site in a student project performed at the Leipzig Graduate School of Management. The major findings of this analysis can be found in [10]. The data preparation was performed with the WUMprep module of WUM, exploiting the concept hierarchy construction service. The analysis involved sequence mining and association rules' discovery.

4.1   The Web Site and Its Goals

Subject of the analysis was the Thomas Church in Leipzig, in which Bach has been active as cantor and composer of some of his most famous works. The site of the Thomas Church has several target groups: the religious community, fans of Bach all over the world, friends of classic music, and of course the tourists that visit the site before and after visiting the church building. The site's services include (a) invariant information on Bach, on the church building, its treasures and the Bach-organ, (b) a calendar of religious and secular events, among them many concerts, (c) contact points and (d) a shop of souvenirs, the ThomasShop. The site has two servers with interlinked contents.

One of the site's purposes is the contribution to the church's income through purchases and donations. Our analysis aimed at evaluating the site with respect to this goal. Of interest were not the volumina of purchases but the potential of the site in converting visitors to customers or donors, and the ways of maximizing this potential.

4.2   Mapping the Log Data onto Application Concepts

The site consists of two interlinked subsites operated by different servers. The dataset input to the analysis comes from the www.thomaskirche-bach2000.de server, here-after denoted as the "Thomaskirche server" for short. The log comprised 29231 entries including invocations of images and frameset components, which have been removed at the beginning of the data preparation phase. The sessions were reconstructed on the basis of IP-address and agent, using a page stay limit of 30 minutes. Applying the heuristic generated 1107 sessions.

The implicit concept hierarchy reflected in the site structure organized the pages in themes such as musical events. However, some of these events are for free, while for others tickets are sold online. Hence, ad-hoc hierarchies had to be established, capturing (a) the behavior and (b) the preferences of the users.

Concept Hierarchy for the Navigational Behavior. Each URL in each session was mapped onto a concept that expressed its *potential* in motivating a visitor to buy or to donate. For example, the conversion potential of the product order form is higher than that of a product inspection page, because a visitor filling a product order form has almost decided to perform the purchase. Fig. 2 shows the hierarchy of pages with respect to the conversion potential they exhibit during navigation through them. Ideally, visitors would move from low potential pages towards high potential ones. In the analysis of [10], the taxonomy in Fig. 2 was built together with the business expert in order to capture the

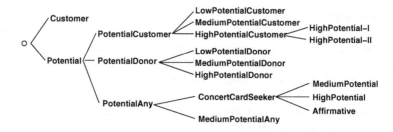

Fig. 2. Concept hierarchy for the conversion of customers and donors

underlying business goal. Then the page invocations were mapped onto the leaf concepts of this hierarchy using the scaling tool of WUMprep together with a manually encoded regular expression ruleset.

A page is mapped onto the concept "Customer", if its invocation means that the visitor is indeed converted to a customer. Only the confirmation of a submitted product order form in the ThomasShop corresponds to this concept. The two entry pages of the ThomasShop are mapped onto the concept "LowPotentialCustomer". The product inspection pages, organized in categories by item type, are all assigned to the concept "MediumPotentialCustomer". There are two "HighPotentialCustomer" concepts, namely the invocation of the shopping cart to place a product in it (type I) and the invocation of the product order form (type II).

The concept "HighPotentialDonor" is assigned to pages from which a donation-purpose mail can be submitted. These special pages are in the subsite of the "Association Thomas Church Bach 2000" (in the following simply referred to as "Association"). Financial support of the Thomas Church through donations and memberships is one of the primary tasks of this society. Its subsite is designed accordingly and was therefore characterized as "MediumPotentialDonor". The invocation of the entry page in the Association's subsite corresponds to the concept "LowPotentialDonor".

The Thomas Church is regularly organizing concerts. Forthcoming musical events are listed in the site, and concert cards can be ordered for concerts with card pre-sales. The links to such events appear in the entry page of the Association and are assigned to the concept "ConcertCardSeeker". Their mere invocation implies a "MediumPotential", the invocation of the card order page corresponds to "HighPotential", the confirmation of the order signals successful conversion ("Affirmative"). All remaining pages of the Association's subsite are assigned to the concept "MediumPotentialAny". This concept refers to donations, to concert card purchases and to purchases of products from the ThomasShop, which is linked to the Association's pages.

The concept hierarchy of Fig. 2 is intended to reflect how visitors move through the site. Ideally, visitors should move from low potential towards high potential pages. Moves in the opposite direction indicate that the underlying pages do not fullfill their purpose. These moves are actually frequent sequences of adjacently invoked concepts. Hence, our ad hoc concept hierarchy allows for a straightforward interpretation of the frequent sequences to be returned by the mining software.

Fig. 3. Thematic taxonomies for the conversion of customers and donors

Fig. 4. Ideal route for customer conversion

Concept Hierarchies for Visitor Preferences. In the taxonomy of Fig. 2, the concepts "MediumPotential[Customer|Donor|ConcertCardSeeker]" encompass a variety of subjects: A potential customer inspects a variety of products, a potential donor studies several information assets and finds a lot of event announcements, a potential concert card seeker has many concerts to choose upon before deciding to buy a concert card. A refinement of these concepts is necessary to identify items that have larger conversion potential than others. Fig. 3 depicts this refinement towards the concepts of Fig. 2.

The simple taxonomy below "MediumPotentialCustomer" (cf. 3 left side) categorizes the products sold in the ThomasShop. The other taxonomy is more sophisticated: It refers to the pages of the Association's subsite, joins the concepts of "MediumPotentialDonor", "MediumPotentialAny" and "ConcertCardSeeker.MediumPotential" and provides new refinements for them. This taxonomy covers information assets on several subjects, including membership to the Association, musical events and appropriate "targets" for donations. One such popular target is the restoration of the Bach organ.

4.3   Analysis upon the Ad Hoc Concept Hierarchies

For the data mining phase, we have used sequence mining. Our purpose, however, was not the discovery of frequent sequences but the acquisition of insights about the conversion efficiency of the site's components.

Evaluating Ideal Routes. Most well-designed sites contain routes which the owner considers as most appropriate for the visitors to follow. This comes close to the notion of *optimal path* introduced in [5] and will be referred to as *ideal route* hereafter, to reflect the facts that (a) it may contain an arbitrary number of cycles and (b) it is ideal according to the non-formal perceptions of a Web site owner.

We used the concept hierarchy of Fig. 2 as designated hierarchy and mapped the URLs into its leaf concepts.Then, we formulated the ideal route for customer conversion in Fig. 4. For example, the confidence of the sequence "MediumPotential-Customer→HighPotential I" indicates how efficient a page of the former concept is in converting a visitor to a very likely customer [16].

Hence, we used the sequence miner to return all frequent paths of length 2 containing adjacent nodes of the ideal path, along with their confidences. The mining result showed that the conversion from low to medium potential is circa 55%, while the conversion from medium to high potential (type I) is lower. The conversion from type I to type II high potential seems to be higher, but the support is inadequate for generalizations. Hence, the pages characterized as "medium potential" must be improved with highest priority. The page invocations characterized as "medium potential" for donors, concert card seekers etc., were also found to lead to high potential pages with low confidence only. The concept hierarchy granted a level of abstraction, at which the presentations of the individual products are generalized. Thus, the overall presentatin metaphor should be reconsidered rather than the product.

Evaluating the Preferences of the Visitors. The next iteration of our analysis was devoted in a more detailed investigation of the pages of medium potential. The taxonomies of Fig. 3 refine the pages of medium potential into groups of products (ThomasShop) and services (Association). We used this refinement to trace the preferences of the users that reach the ThomasShop entry page and of the users accessing the entry page of the Association. Visitors reaching these pages still have only low potential to become customers, resp. donors. Hence, it is of interest to identify the pages of the medium potential group that are most attractive to them. Sequence mining upon the groups of ThomasShop products showed that CDs are the most frequently inspected product group, followed by the group of souvenirs. When restricting the analysis to the patterns of customers only, it was found that CDs lead to a purchase with a confidence of more than 50%, while the confidence for souvenirs is slightly lower.

5 Conclusions

Web mining is launched to support a strategic decision, which is often of ad hoc nature. The concepts associated with a certain decision are rarely reflected in the data warehouse, since warehouses are built to serve OLAP applications of regular and static nature. In this paper, we have proposed a methodology for the establishment of concept hierarchies in web usage analysis and a mechanism that performs the mapping of URLs to concepts associated with regular expressions.

We have demonstrated the effectiveness of our approach through a case study. The existing implicit taxonomy of the site's contents was not appropriate for the goal of Web usage analysis, so that two complementary concept hierarchies were introduced. The subsequent analysis lead to the discovery of interesting patterns and to concrete indications for site improvement.

Our regular expression-based mechanism for the mapping of page invocations onto concepts is incorporated into our methodology for Web data preparation. One of its central task is the mapping of the business goal onto operations that can be performed by a mining tool. Ad hoc concept hierarchies are used to materialize one aspect of this mapping, namely the association of business terms with page invocations. The second aspect of this mapping, the association of business measures (e.g., ROI) with statistic measures (e.g., support and confidence) is subject of ongoing work. Further future work includes a coupling of our mapping tool with text mining tools that can categorize pages by content *and* provide labels for the categories.

References

1. Sarabjot S. Anand, David A. Bell, and John G. Hughes. The role of domain knowledge in data mining. In *CIKM'95*, pages 37–43, Baltimore MD, USA, 1995.
2. Alex G. Büchner, Maurice D. Mulvenna, Sarab S. Anand, and John G. Hughes. An internet-enabled knowledge discovery process. In *Proc. of the 9th Int'l Database Conference*, 1999.
3. Surajit Chaudhuri and Umeshwar Dayal. An overview of data warehousing and olap technology. *ACM SIGMOD Record*, 26(1), 1997.
4. Ming-Syan Chen, Jiawei Han, and Philip S. Yu. Data mining: An overview from database perspective. *IEEE Trans. on Knowledge and Data Engineering*, 9:866–883, 1996.
5. Mat Cutler and Jim Sterne. E-metrics – business metrics for the new economy. Whitepaper, NetGenesis Corp., Cambridge, MA, 2000.
6. T. Ellman. Explanation-based learning: A survey of programs and perspectives. *ACM Comput. Serveys*, 21:162–222, 1989.
7. Bernhard Ganter and Rudolf Wille. *Formale Begriffsanalyse: Mathematische Grundlagen.* Springer-Verlag, 1996.
8. Henner Graubitz, Myra Spiliopoulou, and Karsten Winkler. The DIAsDEM framework for converting domain-specific texts into XML documents with data mining techniques. In *Proc. of the 1st IEEE Intl. Conf. on Data Mining,*, pages 171–178, San Jose, CA, Nov. 2001. IEEE.
9. J. Hereth, G. Stumme, R. Wille, and U. Wille. Conceptual knowledge discovery and data analysis. In B. Ganter and G. Mineau, editors, *Proc. of Eight International Conference on Conceputel Structures: Logical, Linguistic, and Computational Issues*, volume 1867 of *Lecture Notes in Artificial Intelligence (LNAI)*, pages 421–437, Heidelberg, Aug 2000. Springer.
10. Patrik Jernmark, Nitin Mittal, Ramesh Narayan, Suresh Subudhi, and Kristian Wallin. Analysis of the Thomaskirche website. Kdd-course project report, Leipzig Graduate School of Management, Dec 2001.
11. Ryszard S. Michalski and Kenneth A. Kaufman. Data mining and knowledge discovery: A review of issues and a multistrategy approach. In R.S. Michalski, I. Bratko, and M. Kubat, editors, *Machine Learning and Data Mining: Methods and Applications.* John Wiley & Sons Ltd., 1997.
12. B. Mobasher, H. Dai, T. Luo, and M. Nakagawa. Effective personalization based on association rule discovery from web usage data. In *Proceedings of the 3rd ACM Workshop on Web Information and Data Management (WIDM01), held in conjunction with the International Conference on Information and Knowledge Management (CIKM 2001)*, Atlanta, Georgia, Nov 2001.
13. Peter Pirolli, James Pitkow, and Ramana Rao. Silk from a sow's ear: Extracting usable structures from the web. In *Conf. on Human Factors in Computing Systems (CIH'96)*, Vancouver, British Columbia, Canada, Apr 13–18 1996.
14. Giovanni M. Sacco. Dynamic taxonomies: A model for large information bases. *IEEE Transactions on Knowledge and Data Engineering*, 12(3):468–479, May/Jun 2000.
15. Myra Spiliopoulou and Lukas C. Faulstich. WUM: A web utilization miner. In *EDBT Workshop WebDB98*, Valencia, Spain, 1998. Springer Verlag.
16. Myra Spiliopoulou and Carsten Pohle. Data mining for measuring and improving the success of web sites. *Journal of Data Mining and Knowledge Discovery, Special Issue on E-Commerce*, 5:85–114, Jan–Apr 2001.
17. Ramakrishnan Srikant and Rakesh Agrawal. Mining generalized association rules. In *Proc. 21st Conf. on Very Large Databases (VLDB) Zurich, Switzerland*, 1995.

Authorization Based on Evidence and Trust*

Bharat Bhargava and Yuhui Zhong

Center for Education and Research in Information Assurance and Security (CERIAS),
and Department of Computer Sciences
Purdue University, West Lafayette, IN 47906-1398, USA {bb, zhong}@cs.purdue.edu

Abstract. Developing authorization mechanisms for secure information access by a large community of users in an open environment is challenging. Current research efforts grant privilege to a user based on her objective properties that are demonstrated by digital credentials (evidences). However, holding credentials is not sufficient to certify that a user is trustworthy. Therefore, we propose using the notion of trust to characterize the probability that a user will not harm an information system. We present a trust-enhanced role-mapping server, which cooperates with RBAC (Role-Based Access Control) mechanisms to together implement authorization based on evidence and trust. A prerequisite for this is our proposed formalization of trust and evidence.

1 Introduction

Research is needed to develop authorization mechanisms for a large and open community of users. In such an environment, prior knowledge about a new user normally does not exist [20]. For authorization, the permission set for each user must be determined. Current research efforts grant privilege to a user based on her objective properties that are demonstrated by digital credentials (evidences) issued by third parties [4],[9]. Credentials are not sufficient to certify that a user is trustworthy. Therefore, a formalized notion of trust is used by us to characterize the probability that a user or an issuer of credentials will not carry out harmful actions [6]. Next, the impact of users' behavior on system's trust towards them needs to be quantified. Furthermore, the reliability of evidence or credentials from different issuers might be different. Authorization based on evidence as well as trust makes access control adaptable to users' or issuers' behavior. The research requires: (1) an appropriate representations of the evidence and trust, so that their manipulation can be automated, (2) a suitable authorization architecture that can incorporate the evidence and trust, and (3) integration of this scheme with existing access control mechanisms. We investigate these issues and propose a trust-enhanced role-mapping (TERM) server architecture, which can cooperate with RBAC (Role-Based Access Control) mechanisms for authorization based on evidence and trust.

---

* This research is supported by CERIAS and NSF grants CCR-9901712 and CCR-0001788.

Y. Kambayashi, W. Winiwarter, M. Arikawa (Eds.): DaWaK 2002, LNCS 2454, pp. 94–103, 2002.

This paper is organized as follows. Section 2 introduces related research. Section 3 presents the fundamental concepts in our system, and their formal definitions. The architecture of a TERM server is described in section 4. The algorithms and implementation are in section 5. We focus on the role-assignment policy language and the algorithms that evaluate the reliability of evidence and role-assignment policies. Conclusions are in section 6.

2   Related Work

Authorization in an open environment: This is an active area of research. One direction is *trust management* [4],[5]. A trust management system provides a language allowing system administrators to define authorization policies based on credentials, and an engine to enforce the authorization polices. These systems design their own access control mechanisms instead of taking advantage of the existing ones such as RBAC [9].

Another direction of research divides the authorization problem into two sub-problems: (1) determine the permission set of a user (2) enforce access control by using existing mechanisms like RBAC. These approaches have the advantage of easy integration with existing systems. Our research effort is in this direction. Others determine users' permission set only according to evidence/credentials. Our work is distinguished by using evidence and trust.

Trust Models: Several researchers have proposed algorithms to summarize trust opinions from third parties. The summarization includes evaluating an opinion from an issuer, or combining opinions from different issuers [1],[11],[14]. Little research has been done to quantify trust based on direct experience. Because personal experience plays an important role when forming trust opinion in real life, we consider this first-hand information in our framework.

RBAC: RBAC has emerged as a promising technology for efficiently managing and enforcing security in large organizations [2],[17]. A role is an entity with some semantics regarding the authority and responsibility. The authorization process is divided into two parts: role-permission mapping and user-role mapping. Role-permission mapping associates roles with permission sets. User-role mapping assigns roles to users.

3   Concepts and Formal Definitions

The following concepts, definitions and representations are used in our research.

3.1   Concepts

Evidence: Evidences (also called credentials) are statements about certain properties of an entity (called subject). An evidence can come from internal or external sources. Evidence can be information stored in a local database (e.g, user name and password) or public key certificate (e.g, X.509 V3) [8],[10], digitally signed document (e.g, PICS rating) [18], etc.

Issuer's opinion about evidence: Current credentials do not provide a way for issuers to express their opinions towards the statements they make. When an issuer makes a statement, she is assumed to be 100% sure about it. This is not necessarily true in many cases. An issuer's opinion about an evidence characterizes the degree to which the issuer is sure about the statement he/she makes.

Reliability of evidence: The reliability of an evidence represents the subjective degree of belief in the evidence of the entity relying on the evidence. The reliability of an evidence depends on issuer's opinion and relying party's opinion about the issuer.

Trust towards a user or an issuer: Trust is a subjective degree of belief [15] in harmlessness of a user. The aspects forming the trust and the weights of the aspects might be different for different entities (users or issuers), or for a given entity in different environments.

Direct experience and recommendation: The interactions between the observer and the observed entity are called "direct experience", and are first-hand information. The opinions about an entity obtained from other entities are called "recommendations," and are second-hand information. Because trust is not transitive [1], recommendations cannot be directly used. Trust opinion is formed mainly based on direct experience and, to a lesser degree, on recommendations.

Trust associated with an issuer and with a regular user: Trust associated with an issuer should be distinguished from one associated with a regular user. The former impacts the trust towards the evidence provided by the issuer. The latter characterizes the trust towards the user's own behavior.

Trust environment: Trust is environment-specific [15]. Different aspects of trust might be emphasized in different environments. The measurement of the same aspect of trust may vary in different environments. Representing an environment and propagating trust in different environments are the issues we investigate.

3.2   Definitions and Representations

Definition: An *evidence type* is a 2-tuple (*et_id, attrs*) where *et_id* is the identifier of this evidence type and *attrs* is a set of attributes. Each attribute is represented as a triple (*attr_name, attr_domain, attr_type*). Attr_type ∈ {opt, mand} specifies whether the attribute type is optional or mandatory. Evidence type specifies information that is required by different kind of evidences.

Example: (student,{(name, string, mand), (university, string, mand), (department, string, opt)}) is an evidence type. It indicates that "name" and "university" are required for this kind of evidence while "department" is optional.

Evidence type hierarchy: The whole set of evidence types forms an evidence type hierarchy as shown in Figure 1. The first level of the hierarchy represents the two subsets of evidence types that we consider: *credentials_evidence* and *trust_evidence*. Credentials_evidence includes the set of all possible credential types recognized by the role server. Trust_evidence includes the set of all possible trust types used by the TERM server to describe trustworthiness. Level 2 consists of access_credentials, access_trust, testify_credentials, and testify_trust. Access_credentials and access_trust represent credential/trust related to regular user. Testify_credentials and testify_trust are used to represent credential/trust related to an issuer. The remaining evidence types inherit properties of one of the four Level 2 evidence types.

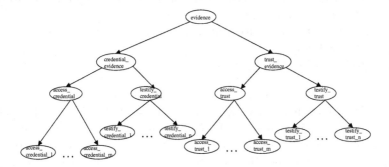

Fig. 1. Evidence Hierarchy

Definition: An *evidence* is a triple (*e_id, et_id, state*), where *e_id* is the identifier of this evidence, *et_id* is an evidence type identifier, $state = (a_1:v_1,\ldots, a_n:v_n)$, where $a_1, \ldots, a_n$ are the names of attributes, $v_1, \ldots, v_n$ are their values. Evidence is an instance of an evidence type. (Cf. the credentials model [3].)

Example: (proof_of_Michael_as_a_student, student, (name: "Michael", university: "Purdue")) is an evidence. The type of this evidence is *student*. It proves that the holder of the evidence has certain specified properties that are required for this type of evidence: his name is "Michael" and his university is "Purdue".

Definition: *Opinion* is a triple (*b, d, u*) where *b, d* and *u* designate belief, disbelief and uncertainty respectively. They satisfy the equation: b+d+u=1, b, d, u ∈ [0, 1]

Definition: Let *w*=(*b, d, u*) be an opinion. The *probability expectation* of w, denoted by *E(w)*, characterizes the degree of truth represented by an opinion. E(w) is defined as: E(w) = b + 0.5*u

We assume here that uncertainty about belief and disbelief can be split equally between them based on the principle of insufficient reason [19].

Definition: An *evidence statement* is a quadruple (*issuer, subject, evidence, opinion*). *Issuer* is the entity, which provides the evidence. *Subject* is the entity to which the evidence refers. *Evidence* contains properties of the subject, which can be either credential or trust information. *Opinion* characterizes the issuers belief related to the *evidence*.

An evidence statement provides a uniform view of different kinds of credential and trust information. It associates credentials or trust with different belief degree (expressed by an opinion), and makes it easy to adopt new type of credentials.

Role classification: Without a loss of generality, roles are classified into two non-overlapping categories.

Access role: A role is an *access role* if its permission set includes particular types of access to one or more objects of the system. A regular user must hold certain access roles.

Testifying role: A role is a *testifying role* if its permission set includes providing evidence for other entities. An issuer must hold certain testifying roles. The system accepts the evidence only from issuers holding appropriate testifying roles specified in the mapping policies.

Representation of trust information: Evidence statements are used to convey trust information.

Trust related to access roles: Trust for access roles is represented as $(I, u, access\_trust, opinion)$. I denotes the TERM server itself, u refers to the user, *opinion* denotes how much TERM server believes the above statement, and *access_trust* is an evidence type, which shows trust that the user will not harm the system. It contains three attributes (ua, mc, il), with the domains $[0, 1]$. Each attribute characterizes one aspect of user's potential harmful actions. The higher the value, the higher the probability that a user will not carry out such harmful actions.

1. Attribute ua denotes trust that the user will not attempt to get unauthorized access.

2. Attribute mc characterizes trust that the user will not try malicious consumption of enormous amounts of resources.

3. Attribute il shows a belief that the user will not try to cause an information leak.

Trust related to testifying roles: Trustworthiness for testifying role is represented as $(I, u, testify\_trust, opinion)$. I, u and *opinion* are the same as above. *Testify_trust* is an evidence type, which shows trust that the user will provide accurate information about other users. *Testify_trust* contains one attribute (t) with the domain $[0, 1]$. The higher the value, the higher belief that an evidence provided by the corresponding user is trustworthy.

4   Architecture of TERM Server

The proposed TERM server collaborates with an RBAC-enhanced web server for authorization in open environments. The task of the TERM server is to map users to roles based on evidence and trust. Clients obtain the roles from a TERM server and present them to RBAC-enhanced web server. Upon receiving a request from a client, the RBAC-enhanced Web server checks if the user holds the appropriate roles, and sends back the object if the answer is true. The focus of this paper is on the TERM server.

The TERM server first collects credentials and transforms them to evidence statements. Then, it evaluates the reliability of the evidence based on the *opinion* attribute of the evidence statement, and on testify_trust related to issuer. Finally it maps users to roles based on assignment policies, evidence reliability, and users' trustworthiness.

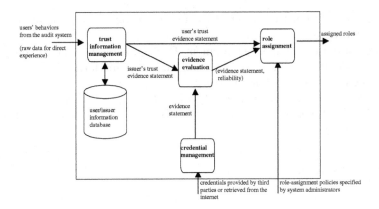

Fig. 2. Architecture of a TERM server

The top-level view of the architecture of a TERM server is shown in Figure 2. There are four components that exchange information using evidence statements presented. *Credentials Management* transforms different formats of credentials to evidence statements. *Evidence Evaluation* evaluates the reliability of evidence statements. *Role Assignment* maps roles to users based on the evidence statements and role assignment policies. *Trust Information Management* evaluates user/issuer's trust information based on system's direct experience and issuers' recommendations.

5   Algorithm and Implementation

A role-assignment policy declaration language has been designed to specify the requirements for assigning a role to a user. The algorithms to evaluate the reliability of evidence, and role-assignment policies have been developed. A prototype including *Evidence Evaluation* and *Role Assignment* and a part of *Trust Information Management* has been implemented (the *Credentials Management* component is still under development).

5.1   Evidence Evaluation

The *Evidence Evaluation* component determines the reliability of evidences for the TERM server. The reliability is computed on the basis of the opinions included in the evidence statements, and the issuers *testify_trust*. The ratio of belief to disbelief may affect the distribution of uncertainty. We plan to investigate this topic in our future research.

Algorithm to evaluate reliability of evidence
Input: an evidence statement $E_1=(issuer, subject, evidence, opinion_1)$
Output: The reliability of the evidence statement RE (E_1)
Step1: get $opinion_1 = (b_1, d_1, u_1)$ and *issuer* attribute from E_1

Step2: get testify_trust of *issuer*: $E_2 = (I, issuer, testify\_trust, opinion_2)$ from the local database

Step3: Create a new evidence statement $E_3 = (I, subject, evidence, opinion_3)$. Compute $opinion_3 = (b_3, d_3, u_3)$ by using the following formulas (the discounting operator is defined in [19]):

$$b_3 = b_1 * b_2, \ d_3 = b_1 * d_2, \ u_3 = d_1 + u_1 + b_2 * u_1$$

Step4: The *probability expectation* for (b_3, d_3, u_3) gives us the reliability for E_1, hence RE $(E_1) = b_3 + 0.5 * u_3$

5.2   Role Assignment

For this component, we devised a role-assignment policy declaration language, and developed algorithms to assign roles to users.

Policy declaration language: The policy declaration language is used to specify: (1) the content and the number of evidence statements needed for role assignment; (2) a threshold value that characterizes the minimal reliability expected for each evidence statement. If the reliability associated with an evidence does not exceed the minimum threshold, this evidence will be ignored.

Syntax
Policy::= (PolicyDeclaration)*
PolicyDeclaration::= Role_Name = UnitDeclarations
Role_Name::=*string*
UnitDeclarations::=Unit ("$\bigwedge$" Unit)*
Unit::= "[" *IssuerRole, EvidenceType,* "{" Exp "}", Threshold, Nr_Stmts "]"
Threshold::=*float*
Nr_Stmts::=*integer*
Exp::= AndExp "||" Exp
AndExp::= OpExp "&&" AndExp
OpExp::= *attr* Op Constant
Constant::= *integer* | *float* | *string*
Op::= = | $\neq$ | > | < | $\geq$ | $\leq$

A policy file can include several policy declarations. The name of a role is on the left hand side of a policy declaration. The right hand side of a policy declaration includes unit declarations. Each *UnitDeclarations* consists of one or more *Units*. A *Unit* is composed of *IssuerRole, EvidenceType, Exp, Threshold* and *Nr_Stmts*. *IssuerRole* is the role a qualified issuer should hold. *EvidenceType* specifies the required evidence type. Conditions on the attributes of evidence are specified by using *Exp*. *Threshold* specifies the minimum required value for the reliability of evidence. *Nr_Stmts* is used to determine how many evidences satisfying the above conditions are needed.

Example: VIP::=["Company", "Manager", {rank = "senior" && department = "sales" || salary > 100,000}, 0.75, 1] $\bigwedge$ ["I", "access_trust", {ua>0.75 && mc>0.5 && il>0.8}, 1, 1]. This policy specifies the conditions to get a VIP role. It consists of two units. The first unit requires that a user presents one evidence which says that she is a senior manager in sales department, or her salary is greater than 100,000. The reliability of this evidence should not be lower than 75%. The second unit is the constraint on the user's access_trust.

Evaluation policy: When a user presents a set of evidences, we need to determine a set of role-assignment policies that are satisfied by this set of evidences. Several policies may be associated with a role. The role is assigned if and only if any of the policies is satisfied. A policy may contain several units. The policy is satisfied if and only if its units evaluate to *True*.

Algorithm to assign a role to a user
Input: a set of evidences E with their reliabilities for a user, a role R
Output: *True/False*
P is the set of policies with role R on their left hand side
while P is not empty
 p = a policy in P
 satisfy = *True*
 for each unit u in p
   if Evaluate_unit(u, e, $RE(e)$) is *False* for all evidence statements e in E
     then satisfy = *False*
 if satisfy = *True* then return *True* else remove p from P
return *False*

The algorithm to evaluate a unit is based on two assumptions: (1) the domains of attributes are infinite; (2) the distribution of attribute values is uniform.

Algorithm to evaluate a unit of a role-assignment policy
Input: an evidence statement $E_1 = (issuer, subject, evidence, opinion_1)$ and its reliability RE (E_1), a unit U of a policy
Output: *True/False*
Step1: if *issuer* does not hold the *IssuerRole* specified in U, or the type of *evidence* does not match *EvidenceType* in U, return *False*.
Step2: Evaluate each *Exp* of U as follows:
if Exp = "$Exp_1 \parallel Exp_2$" then result(Exp) = max(result(Exp_1), result(Exp_2))
else if Exp = "Exp_1 && Exp_2" then result(Exp) = min (result(Exp_1), result(Exp_2))
else if Exp = "*attr* Op Constant" then
 if *attr* OP Constant = *True* then result(Exp) = RE(E_1)
 else if OP = $\neq$ then result(Exp) = 1 - RE(E_1)
 else result(Exp) = 0
Step3: if min (result(Exp), RE (E_1)) $\geq$ *Threshold* in unit U, output *True*. Otherwise, output *False*.

5.3   Trust Information Management

The trust information management component executes two important steps. First, it maps mistrust events to evidence statements, and then it appropriately updates trust values in the user/issuer trust information database.

Mapping mistrust events to evidence statements: A user's misbehavior is perceived by the system as a *mistrust event* [13]. Mistrust events are categorized. One category of mistrust events corresponds to one evidence type. Each category of mistrust events is represented by a set of characteristic features. The feature set of a category corresponds to the attribute set of an evidence type. Different mistrust event categories might have some common features. For example, *criticality* and *lethality*[16] can be used as such common features. Criticality measures the importance of the target of mistrust events. Lethality measures the degree of damage that could potentially be caused by mistrust events. Given a mistrust event, how to determine quantitative measures of its features is application-specific [7][12]. A mistrust event discovered by intrusion detection or data mining (both are external to our TERM server) is associated with a probability provided by them. This probability characterizes the confidence that a user caused a harm to the system. The probability impacts the opinion parameter in the evidence statement.

Updating trust values in the user/issuer trust information database: A user who visits the system for the first time is assigned a trust value based on the default/average trust value of her trust environment or a similar one. A trust environment consists of the role that the user requests, the domain/subnet from which the user comes, the trust opinion from third parties if available, and the trustworthiness of these third parties. With time the user becomes known to the system. Now her trust value is adjusted mainly based on her behavior. Trust values are modified periodically. The *access_trust* values of a user decrease if she was involved in any mistrust event. The *testify_trust* of a user u is modified periodically in the following way. Suppose u_1, u_2, ..., u_n are assigned to access roles based on the evidences provided by u. The modification of *testify_trust* of u is related to the changes of *access_trust* of all u_i's.

6   Conclusions

In this paper, we propose a detailed architecture for a TERM server. This server collaborates with an RBAC-enhanced web server to solve the authorization problem in open environments. The TERM server determines a user's permission set based on trust and evidence. Representations for evidence and trust, and evaluation of both of them are discussed. The algorithms for evaluation of evidence reliability and for role-assignment policies are presented.

In addition to showing our authorization solution, our result can contribute to solving the issues of trust and proof on the semantic web. An ultimate goal for the semantic web research is gaining the capability of machine understanding of information. Our research on quantification and formalization of evidence and trust could also help to enhance machine reasoning and proof. It could lead to an efficient way for determining trustworthiness of information on the semantic web. Another area, which could benefit from our research is decision-making in e-commerce, especially in effective trust management. Misuse of company information even through authorized access should be denied, therefore the question of trust and evidence is extremely important.

References

1. A. Abdul-Rahman and S. Hailes. Supporting trust in virtual communities. In *Hawaii International Conference on System Sciences*, Hawaii, January 2000.
2. G. Ahn and R. Sandhu. Role-based authorization constraints specification. *ACM Transactions on Information and System Security*, 3(4), November 2000.
3. E. Bertino, E. Ferrari, and E. Pitoura. An access control mechanism for large scale data dissemination Systems. In *RIDE-DM 2001*, 2001.
4. M. Blaze, J. Feigenbaum, and J. Ioannidis. The keynote trust-management System Version 2, http:// www.ietf.org/rfc/rfc2704.txt.
5. M. Blaze, J. Feigenbaum, and J. Lacy. Decentralized trust management. In *the 17th Symposium on Security and Privacy*, 1996.
6. Y. H. Chu, J. Feigenbaum, B. LaMacchia, P. Resnick, and M. Strauss. Referee: Trust management for web applications. *Word Wide Web Journal*, 1997.
7. D. Denning. *Information Warefare and Security*. Addison Wesley, 1999.
8. S. Farrell and R. Housley. An internet attribute certificate profile for authorization, http://www.ietf.org/internet-drafts/draft-ietf-pkix-ac509prof-OS.txt.
9. A. Herzberg, Y. Mass, J. Mihaeli, D. Naor, and Y. Ravid. Access control meets public key infrastructure, or: Assigning roles to strangers. In *IDEE Symposium on Security and Privacy*, CA, 2000.
10. R. Housley, W. Ford, W. Polk, and D. Solo. Internet x.509 public key infrastructure certificate and cr1 profile, http://www.ietf.org/rfc/rfc2459.txt.
11. A. Josang. A logic for uncertain probabilities. *International Journal of Uncertainty, Fuzziness and Knowledge-based Systems*, 9(3), June 2001.
12. W. Lee, W. Fan, M. Miller, S. Stolfo, and F. Zadok. Toward test-sensitive modeling for intrusion detection and response. *Journal of Computer Security*, 2001.
13. M. Mahoui, B. Bhargava, and Y. Zhong. Separating between trust and access control policies: A necessity for web applications. In *the IEEE Workshop on Security in Distributed Data Warehousing*, New Orleans, 2001.
14. S. Marsh. *Formalizing Trust as a Computational Concept*. PhD thesis, University of Stirling, UK, 1994.
15. D. McKnight and N. Chervany. Conceptualizing trust: A typology and ecommerce customer relation model. In *the 34th Hawaii ICSS-2001*, Hawaii, 2001.
16. S. Northcutt, J. Novak, and D. McLachlan. *Network Intrusion Dectection: Analyst's Handbook*. New Riders Publishing, 1999.
17. J. Park and R. Sandhu. Role-based access control on the web. *ACM Transactions on Information and System Security*, 4(1), February 2001.
18. P. Resnick and J. Miller. Pics: Internet access controls without censorship. *Communications of the ACM*, 39(10), 1996.
19. G. Shafer. *A Mathematical Theory of Evidence*. Princeton University Press, 1976.
20. M. Winslett, N. Ching, V. Jones, and I. Slepchin. Using digital credentials on the world-wide web. *Journal of Computer Security*, 1997.

An Algorithm for Building User-Role Profiles in a Trust Environment[1]

Evimaria Terzi[1], Yuhui Zhong[1], Bharat Bhargava[1], Pankaj[2], and Sanjay Madria[3]

[1] Center for Education and Research in Information Assurance and Security
(CERIAS)
and Department of Computer Sciences,
Purdue University, West Lafayette, IN-47907, USA
{edt,zhong,bb}@cs.purdue.edu
[2] Department of Management Information Systems,
Krannert Graduate School of Management,
Purdue University, West Lafayette, IN – 47907, USA
pankaj@mgmt.purdue.edu
[3] Department of Computer Science, University of Missouri-Rolla,
Rolla, MO- 65409, USA
madrias@umr.edu

Abstract. A good direction towards building secure systems that operate efficiently in large-scale environments (like the World Wide Web) is the deployment of Role Based Access Control Methods (RBAC). RBAC architectures do not deal with each user separately, but with discrete roles that users can acquire in the system. The goal of this paper is to present a classification algorithm that during its training phase, classifies roles of the users in clusters. The behavior of each user that enters the system holding a specific role is traced via audit trails and any misbehavior is detected and reported (classification phase). This algorithm will be incorporated in the Role Server architecture, currently under development, enhancing its ability to dynamically adjust the amount of trust of each user and update the corresponding role assignments.

1 Introduction

The goal of this paper is to provide a solution to the problem of classifying role profiles. The notion of the role is adopted for wide environments like the World Wide Web (WWW) that allow for wide range information exchange and access. In such a context, where accessibility to large amount of data is provided, certain security concerns about the data itself are also raised. In such an environment, there is no guarantee that all the users entering a system behave appropriately. Establishing security and access control mechanisms in particular is a rather difficult task mainly because of two

---

[1] This research is supported by the CERIAS and NSF grants CCR-9901712 and CCR-0001788

Y. Kambayashi, W. Winiwarter, M. Arikawa (Eds.): DaWaK 2002, LNCS 2454, pp. 104–113, 2002.

reasons: 1) the large number of users that want to access the applications and 2) the fact that these users are mainly unknown. RBAC has emerged as a promising technology for efficient security management and enforcement [1,6] in such large-scale environments. Adapting RBAC to enforce security in the Web is increasingly seen as a solution for scalability issues, because permissions are associated to roles instead of users and the number of roles is much smaller compared to the number of users [28,29]. Therefore, the notion of role that can be assigned to a group of users is vital for such applications. However the problem that remains unsolved is how to trace the users' behavior dynamically and guarantee that their behavior is within the limits imposed by the role they hold. This paper deals mainly with this problem and proposes an algorithm that will be a part of the Role Server architecture as described below.

1.1 The Role Server Architecture

The formalization of trustworthiness of users that enter large scale environments is a major research direction. The main goals of this research involve: (a) designing a trustworthiness model, (b) determining the permission set granted to a user, and (c) evaluating the reliability of credentials that a user obtains from third parties. The overall goal of our research is to build a prototype of a Role Server that securely assigns roles to users. The main components of this Role Server are shown in Figure 1.

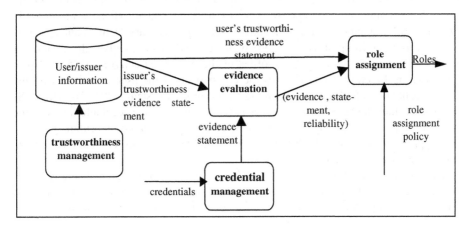

Fig. 1. Role Assignment

The main components of the Role Server architecture presented in Figure 1 are (a) the trustworthiness management, (b) the evidence evaluation, (c) the credential management, and (d) the role assignment component. The functionality of these components are described in [32].

2 Related Work

Our research on building role profiles is primarily inspired by the work done in three main research areas, namely, data mining, classification and clustering; intrusion detection and; user profile building.

Clustering can be loosely defined as the process of organizing objects into groups whose members are similar in some way. An introduction to clustering techniques is given in [11,13,15,17] while a brief overview of the existing clustering techniques is given in [14,12]. Generally, there are two major styles of clustering: *partitioning* (often called *k-clustering*), in which every object is assigned exactly to one group, and *hierarchical clustering,* in which each group of size greater than one is in turn composed of smaller groups. Clustering algorithms for user profiles extraction have been employed in [16]. In order to extract users access profiles, the user sessions are clustered based on the pair-wise dissimilarities and using a fuzzy clustering algorithm. An extension of the previous work is given in [18] where new algorithms for fuzzy clustering of relational data are presented. The basics of fuzzy clustering techniques are presented in [19].

Closely related to our work is the research being conducted in the area of Intrusion Detection (ID). The major objective of these research efforts is to determine whether the behavior of a user within the system is normal or intrusive. There are mainly two techniques towards Intrusion Detection namely *anomaly detection* and *misuse detection.* A taxonomy and an overview of the existing ID Systems (IDS) is presented in [7]. Generally, anomaly detection identifies activities that vary from established patterns for users or group of users. Anomaly detection typically involves the creation of knowledge bases that contain the profiles of the monitored activities ([25]). Misuse detection on the other hand, involves the comparison of the users activities with the known behaviors of attackers attempting to penetrate a system ([20,21]). The IDSs specify whether the behavior of the user is (is not) within the acceptable limits of the behavior that the system can (cannot) tolerate. The classification algorithm presented in this paper is based on [31]. In this paper the authors build clusters that characterize normal and intrusive behaviors.

Building user profiles is another important related area of research. There is a considerable amount of work that has been done on building users group profiles for web sites access, and which mainly lays in the area of web mining. The researchers involved in this area have noticed that as the complexity of the Web sites increases the statistics provided by existing Web log analysis tools [1,2,3] may prove to be inadequate, and more sophisticated types of analyses is necessary. *Web Usage Mining,* which is application of data mining techniques to large Web data repositories, adds powerful techniques to the tools available to Web site administrators for analyzing Web Site usage. Web Usage Mining Techniques developed in [8,9,10,27,30] have been used to discover frequent itemsets, association rules [5], clusters of similar pages and users, sequential patterns [26], and perform path analysis. In web usage mining the group profiles are constructed based on the user's navigation patterns within the web site and not based on the actions that have been conducted by the users on the system in terms of commands, memory and disk usage etc. In other words, the web profiles are based on the web log analysis, while the building role profiles in our case is based on the audit data analysis.

3 The Algorithm

The proposed algorithm can be described as follows:

The initial input to this algorithm is a data record of the audit log from which the system administrator can select n attributes which are the most appropriate ones. Therefore, each data-point is a value in the n-dimensional space. An additional field needs to be added in each record and this field will denote the role of the user the specific data record represents. Therefore a record – input to our algorithm will look as follows as $[X_1, X_2, \ldots X_n, R_1]$. This implies that the values of the attributes of the log file for the specific user are $X_1, X_2, \ldots X_n$ and that the role of this user is R_1. The goal of the algorithm is the following: Having a certain number of such data records, a certain number of clusters should be formed. The minimum number of these clusters will be equal to the number of different roles. But this is just the lower bound. The upper bound can obviously be the number of users, a case that will rarely occur given that the behaviors of users holding the same role will not be completely diverse. Each cluster can contain users that belong only to one role, and each one of them will actually, be a profile for the behavior of the users that have acquired that specific role. After the training phase, the system should be able to deal with new users coming to the system on its own. The algorithm should also be able to perform often updates, without deteriorating the performance of the system. This requires that the algorithm should be incremental.

Notice that the algorithm operates under the assumption that every user can only hold one role, and therefore there cannot be entries in the audit data that correspond to the same user, and are of the form $[X_1, X_2, \ldots X_n, R_1]$, $[X_1, X_2, \ldots X_n, R_2]$ with $R_1 ? R_2$.

3.1 The Phases

The algorithm consists of three phases. The first one is the training phase. During this phase the system is trained and the clusters that correspond to the role profiles are built based on the training data. The second phase is the classification phase. In this phase the algorithm actually detects whether the users behave according to the role that has been assigned to them. Since new users and new requirements arise, there is a need for periodical update. The frequency of functionality updates will depend on the system's requirements.

3.1.1 Training Phase – Building the Clusters

The algorithm starts by creating a number of dummy clusters, say d. This number d is equal to the number of discrete roles that can possibly exist in the system. The centroid of each one of these clusters is the mean vector, containing the average values of the selected audit data attributes) of all the users that belong to the specific role (note that in this stage the role of each user is known). It is also supposed that the training data consists of roles of the normal behaving entities. Although this may seem restrictive and enough to cause biased results, this is not the case since a legitimate user of a role R_1 is classified as a malicious user when he/she tries to acquire one of the other roles. This allows abnormal behaviors for each role also to be considered.

After the first step d discrete clusters exist. The next step is to deal with each one of the data records of the training data separately. For each training data record, the distance between this record and each one of the clusters is calculated. This distance calculation takes into consideration only the previously selected n attributes of the data records that come from the log data. The cluster C_{cur} that is closer to the current data record R_{cur} is therefore specified. The data record is not assigned immediately into its closest cluster. One more check, regarding the role of the current record and the role represented by the cluster, needs to be done. In other words if the role of the record R_{cur} is the same as the role of the cluster C_{cur} then the current data record is assigned to this cluster, the mean vector of the cluster is reevaluated and the procedure continues with the next record of the training set that becomes the current record R_{cur}. On the other hand, if the role of the current record R_{cur} is different from the role whose profile is represented by the cluster C_{cur} then a new cluster is created. This cluster will contain the current record and it will be another representative cluster of the role the record R_{cur} holds. This step is repeated until all the data that is available in the training set is processed.

Notice that form the above description of the above algorithm it can be concluded that each cluster contains behaviors of users that belong to a single role. However, there can be multiple different clusters that capture divergent behaviors of users holding a single role.

3.1.2 Classification Phase

The problem this phase deals with is that, given the behavior of a specific user U, represented by an *n-dimension* data point, the algorithm should verify whether the user U behaves according to the role he/she claims to have. If this is not the case, then the system should trigger an alarm, or take other measures as per the policy decided. Notice, that if the behavior of the user is not within the ranges of acceptable behavior of his role, the system is also able to determine which one of the other roles the user is attempting to acquire.

One of the ways of verifying (or not verifying) that a user behaves according to the role he/she has, is to calculate the distance between the n attributes that represent the user's U behavior in the audit data record with the centroids of the existing clusters.

Then take the closest cluster to the user U and check whether the role whose profile is represented by this cluster is the same as the role of the user U. If this is the case, then the user's behavior is within acceptable limits for the role he holds. Otherwise, a warning should be raised.

4 Experimental Results

The experimental data were collected from a standard NT server. We have experimented with 2000 records that have been selected for training the data and other 1800 records of user transactions have been used for testing. Three attributes of the audit log record have been selected as the most representative ones and they correspond to the command the user uses, the protocol he uses to access the server and the location he uses for his accesses.

4.1 Experiment I

Problem Statement: The goal of the first experiment is to test the classification accuracy of the proposed algorithm. Given a training data set what is the accuracy of classification that can be achieved when the testing set contains new records, other than those included in the training set?

Hypothesis: Intuitively it is expected that when the testing and the training data are identical the classification accuracy of the algorithm would be 100%, since the system has a clear idea of how to classify each one of the testing records. The higher the percentage of new (previously unknown) records in the testing set the less the classification accuracy of the algorithm.

Another parameter that is expected to have an impact to the classification accuracy of the algorithm is the number of distinct roles of the system. The more the number of roles, the less accuracy expected. And this is because the borders between the clusters become less distinct as the number of roles increase. Large number of roles inevitably means more clusters, whose centroids are closer to each other, making classification process less accurate.

Both hypotheses are experimentally tested below:

Input Parameters: For the first experiment we have used the training data set consisting of 2000 records describe above. For the testing phase we have substituted a certain percentage (ranging from 0 to 90%) of the training data set with new records from the other set of 1800 records.

Regarding the roles the input parameters were the following:

- For the experiment with 6 roles we discriminate six roles from the audit data ("system administrators", "faculty members", "staff", "graduate students", "undergraduate students", "visitors"). These roles are discriminated from the audit data and verified by the system administrator himself.
- For the 4 role experiments we have put some of the above roles under the same new (hyper)-role. In this case the roles that have been discriminated are: ("system ad-

ministrators", "academic staff", "students", "visitors"). Here the "academic staff" (hyper)-role refers to both the faculty and the staff members of the university. The same way the (hyper)-role "students" includes both the graduate and the undergraduate students referred previously.

- Finally the two-roles that have been discriminated for the two role experiments are the "recognized users" and the "visitors". The correspondence to the above categories is rather straightforward.

Output – Data Observations: The output data of the first experiment have been gathered and presented in Figure 2. The y-axis of the graph shows the classification accuracy of the algorithm for the various percentage of new records inserted in the testing phase (x-axis) and for different number of roles (2, 4, 6). For example, it is found that the classification accuracy is 80% when there are 4 distinct roles in the system and 50% of new records inserted in the testing data set with respect to the training data set. This implies that the testing set consists of 1000 records that are the same as in the records used in the training phase; and additional 1000 records that are new to the system and not used for training. Classification accuracy of 80% means that 1600 out of the total 2000 records of the testing data set were classified correctly.

Conclusions: The experimental results that we gather verify that our classification algorithm is capable of achieving satisfactory classification rates. The main parameters that have an impact on the performance of the algorithm are the percentage of new records in the test data with respect to the records of the training data set, and the number of distinct roles. The less the number of roles and the less new data records the better the classification rate obtained.

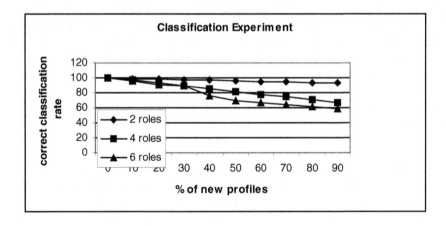

Fig. 2. Classification Experiment

4.2 Experiment II

Problem Statement: The second experiment's goal is to test the ability of the algorithm to point out misbehaviors of the users and to additionally specify the type of their misbehavior.

Hypothesis: Based on our intuition and on the results obtained from the previous experiment, we hypothesize that the two main parameters that have an impact on the performance of the algorithm in this experiment are the percentage of misbehaviors that appear in the testing data set, and the number of discrete roles that are discriminated in the system.

Input Parameters: For the second experiment we have used the same training data set constituting 2000 data records. For the testing phase we do not use any of the additional 1800 new data records. Instead we have modified the role attribute of a certain percentage of the records of the initial data set varying from 0 to 90%. Therefore, if an initial record of the training data set is like $[X_1,X_2,X_3,R_1]$ and this records is going to be changed for the testing phase, then its changed format is $[X_1,X_2,X_3,R_2]$. The algorithm is expected to point out that this is a misbehavior in the system of the form $R_1 \rightarrow R_2$. The rest of the input parameters remain the same as in experiment I.

Output – Data Observations: We compare the algorithm's output regarding the misbehavior of the users with the initial unmodified records and check the output of the algorithm in terms of how successfully the misbehaved users were classified. Figure 3 presents the output of the experiment II. The y-axis of the graph shows the misclassification accuracy, while the x-axis shows the percentage of the original data records that have been changed to be misbehaviors for their roles.

Conclusions: The experimental results have pointed out the ability of the algorithm to find misbehaviors in the system and to point out the type of this misbehavior in terms of the role that a user is illegally trying to acquire. The number of distinct roles and the percentage of misbehaviors play an important role in this context.

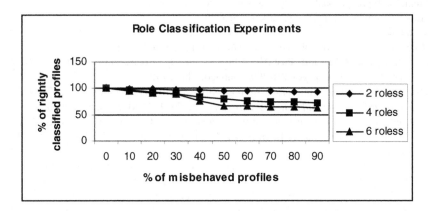

Fig. 3. Misclassification Experiment

5 Conclusions and Future Work

This paper presents an algorithm for building user role profiles. This algorithm will be used in the Role Server architecture [32] and can also be adopted within any RBAC system to examine whether a user behaves according to the role he/she holds. The algorithm has been presented in detail and evaluated by a small-scale experimental process.

Among our future research plans are extensive experimental evaluation of the algorithm and its incorporation as a component of the trustworthiness manager of the Role Server presented in Figure 1. We also plan to compare the performance of the algorithm with similar classification algorithms and cross validate experiments. Attempts will be made to check the impact of larger data sets, number of roles and attributes, on the accuracy of the algorithm. Experiments with larger data sets would give a better insight into other aspects of the algorithm, e.g., efficiency, accuracy and scalability etc.

Acknowledgements. We would like to acknowledge Dr. Mukesh Mohania, IBM India Research Laboratory, IIT Delhi Campus, Hauz Khas, New Delhi, India for his useful contribution to this research through numerous discussions and written exchanges.

References

1. Funnel web professional. http://www.activeconcepts.com
2. Hit list commerce. http://www.marketwave.com
3. Webtrends log analyzer. http://www.webtrends.com
4. Role Based Access Control website, http://csrc.nist.gov/rbac/, 2001.
5. R. Agrawal and R. Srikant: "Fast Algorithms for mining association rules". In *Proc. Of the 20th VLDB Conference,* pages 487-499, Santiago, Chile, 1994
6. G-J. Ahn, R. Sandhu: "Role-based Authorization Constraints Specification". *ACM Transactions on Information and System Security,* Vol. 3, No. 4, ACM, November 2000.
7. S. Axelsson: " Intrusion Detection Systems: A Survey and Taxonomy", Technical Report No 99-15, Dept. of Computer Engineering, Chalmers University of Technology, Sweden, March 2000
8. A. Buchner and M. Mulvenna: "Discovering internet marketing intelligence throughout online analytical web usage mining". SIGMOD Record, 27(4):54-61, 1998.
9. M.S. Chen, J.S. Park and P.S. Yu: "Data Mining for path traversal patterns in web environment". In 16th International Conference on Distributed Computing Systems, pages 385-392, 1996.
10. R. Cooley, B. Mobasher and J. Srivastave: "Data preparation for mining world wide web browsing patterns". Knowledge and Information Systems, 1(1), 1999.
11. B.S. Everitt: "Cluster Analysis", Halsted Press, Third Edition, 1993
12. D. Fasulo: "An Analysis of Recent Work on Clustering Algorithms", TR. Computer Sciences Dpt., Washington University, 1999.

13. A.D. Gordon: "Classification: Methods for Exploratory Analysis of Multivariate Data". Chapman and Hall, 1981.

14. J. Han and M. Kambler: "Data Mining, Concepts and Techniques ", Morgan Kaufmann Publishers

15. A.K. Jain and R.C. Dubes: "Algorithms for Clustering Data". Prentice Hall, 1988.

16. A. Joshi and R. Krishnapuram: "On Mining Web Access Logs". ACM SIGMOD Workshop on Research Issues in Data Mining and Knowledge Discovery, 2000

17. L. Kaufman and P.J. Rousseeuw: "Finding Groups in Data: An Introduction to Cluster Analysis", John Wiley & Sons, Inc, 1990.

18. R. Krishnapuram, A. Joshi, L. Yi : "A Fuzzy Relative of the k-Medoids Algorithm with Application to Web Document and Snippet Clustering".

19. R. Krishnapuram and J. M. Keller: "A possibilistic approach to clustering". IEEE Transactions on Fuzzy Systems, 1(2):98-110, May 1993

20. S. Kumar and E. Spafford: "A pattern Matching Model for Misuse Intrusion Detection". In Proc. Of the 17th National Computer Security Conference, pp. 11-21, 1994.

21. S. Kumar and E. Spafford: "A software Architecture to Support Misuse Intrusion Detection". Dpt. Of Computer Sciences, Purdue University, CDS_TR_95-009, 1995.

22. Terran Lane and Carla E. Brodley: "Temporal sequence learning and data reduction for anomaly detection", ACM Transactions on Information Systems Security 2(3) (Aug. 1999), Pages 295 - 331.

23. W. Lee and S.J. Stolfo: "A Framework for Constructing Features and Models for Intrusion Detection Systems", ACM Transactions on Information and Security, Vol.3, No. 4, pp. 227- 261, November 2000,

24. T. Lunt: "Detecting Intruders in Computer Systems". Conference on Auditing and Computer Technology, 1993

25. T. Lunt, A. Tamaru, F. Gilham, R. Jagannathan, P. Neumann, H. Javitz, A. Valdes and T. Garvey: "A real-time intrusion detection expert system (IDES) – final technical report. Technical Report, Computer Science Laboratory, SRI International, Menlo Park, California, 1992.

26. H. Mannila, H. Toivonen and A.I. Verkamo: "Discovering Frequent Episodes in Sequences". In Proc. Of the 1st International Conference on Knowledge Discovery and Data Mining, 1997.

27. O. Nasraoui, R. Krishnapuram and A. Joshi: " Mining web access logs using fuzzy relational clustering algorithm based on robust estimator". In 18th International World Wide Web Conference, Toronto , Canada, 1999.

28. J. S. Park, R. S. Sandhu, S. Ghanta: "RBAC on the Web by Secure Cookies". Proc. of the IFIP Workshop on Database Security, pp. 49-62, 1999.

29. J. S. Park, R. S. Sandhu: "Smart certificates: Extending x.509 for secure attribute services on the web". Proc. of the 22nd NIST-NCSC National Information Systems Security Conference, Arlington, VA, October 1999.

30. C. Shahabi, A. Zarkesh, J. Adibi and V. Shah: "Knowledge Discovery from users web page navigation". In Workshop on Research Issues in Data Engineering, Birmingham, England , 1997.

31. N. Ye and X. Li: " A Scalable Clustering Technique for Intrusion Signature Recognition", Proc. Of Workshop on Information Assurance and Security, NY – USA, June 2001

32. Y. Zhong, B. Bhargava, M. Mahoui: "Trustworthiness Based Authorization on WWW". Proc. of the Workshop on Security in Distributed Data Warehousing. New Orleans, 2001

Neural-Based Approaches for Improving the Accuracy of Decision Trees

Yue-Shi Lee[1] and Show-Jane Yen[2]

[1] Department of Information Management, Ming Chuan University,
5 The-Ming Rd., Gwei Shan District, Taoyuan County 333, Taiwan, R.O.C.
leeys@mcu.edu.tw
[2] Department of Computer Science & Information Management, Fu Jen Catholic University,
510 Chung Cheng Rd., Hsinchuan, Taipei 242, Taiwan, R.O.C.
sjyen@csie.fju.edu.tw

Abstract. The decision-tree learning algorithms, e.g., C5, are good at dataset classification. But those algorithms usually work with only one attribute at a time. The dependencies among attributes are not considered in those algorithms. Unfortunately, in the real world, most datasets contain attributes, which are dependent. Generally, these dependencies are classified into two types: categorical-type and numerical-type dependencies. Thus, it is very important to construct a model to discover the dependencies among attributes, and to improve the accuracy of the decision-tree learning algorithms. Neural network model is a good choice to concern with these two types of dependencies. In this paper, we propose a Neural Decision Tree (NDT) model to deal with the problems described above. NDT model combines the neural network technologies and the traditional decision-tree learning capabilities to handle the complicated and real cases. The experimental results show that the NDT model can significantly improve the accuracy of C5.

1 Introduction

The decision-tree algorithms, e.g., C5, are good at dataset classification. They build decision trees by recursively partitioning the dataset according to the selected attributes [1, 2]. However, those algorithms usually work with only one attribute at a time. The dependencies among attributes are not considered in those algorithms. Unfortunately, in the real world, most datasets contain attributes, which are dependent. Thus, it is very important to construct a model to discover the dependencies among attributes, and to improve the accuracy of the decision tree algorithms.

Generally, these dependencies are classified into two types: categorical-type and numerical-type dependencies. Chen [3] proposed the concepts for categorical-type dependencies. However, they did not describe how these dependencies could be obtained. Kim and Lee [4] proposed a method for numerical-type dependencies using

Y. Kambayashi, W. Winiwarter, M. Arikawa (Eds.): DaWaK 2002, LNCS 2454, pp. 114–123, 2002.
© Springer-Verlag Berlin Heidelberg 2002

multilayer perceptron. Nevertheless, the categorical-type dependencies are not considered in their works.

This paper proposes a Neural Decision Tree (NDT) model to deal with both categorical-type and numerical-type dependencies. It combines the neural network technologies and the traditional decision-tree learning capabilities to handle the complicated and real cases. This paper is organized as follows. Section 2 introduces two types of dependencies. Section 3 then describes our NDT model. Before concluding, the experimental results are demonstrated in Section 4.

2 Types of Dependencies

The following subsections will illustrate two types of attribute dependencies: categorical-type and numerical-type dependencies.

2.1 Categorical-Type Dependency

Table 1 shows a transportation dataset with 8 records. It illustrates the relationships among gender (male or female), income (roughly classify into low or high), distance (away from home) and the target – vehicle (bike or car).

Table 1. Transportation Dataset with 8 Records

ID	Gender	Income	Distance	Target: Vehicle
01	Male	Low	Far	Car
02	Male	Low	Far	Car
03	Female	High	Far	Car
04	Female	High	Near	Car
05	Male	High	Near	Bike
06	Male	High	Near	Bike
07	Female	Low	Near	Bike
08	Female	Low	Far	Bike

Based on the entropy-based decision-tree learning algorithm, i.e., C5, the decision tree returned by the algorithm is shown in Fig. 1. If we consider more than one attribute, e.g., gender and income, at a time, a more compact decision tree can be obtained shown in Fig. 2. This example illustrates the drawbacks of the traditional decision tree algorithms because they usually work with only one attribute at a time.

2.2 Numerical-Type Dependency

Table 2 shows a stock price dataset with 18 records. It is generated by the following two simple rules [5].

IF the stock price on date T is greater than the forecast price on date T+1, sell it.
IF the stock price on date T is less than the forecast price on date T+1, buy it.

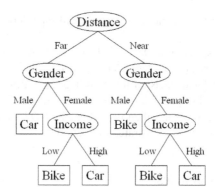

Fig. 1. A decision tree for the concept vehicle

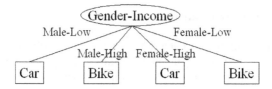

Fig. 2. A compact decision tree for the concept vehicle

Table 2. Stock Price Dataset with 18 Records

ID	Price on Day T	Forecast Price on Day T+1	Target: Decision
01	17.60	17.72	Buy
02	17.70	17.60	Sell
03	17.70	17.71	Buy
04	17.71	17.94	Buy
05	17.72	17.70	Sell
06	17.75	17.84	Buy
07	17.84	17.97	Buy
08	17.90	17.75	Sell
09	17.92	18.09	Buy
10	17.94	18.08	Buy
11	17.97	18.08	Buy
12	18.02	17.92	Sell
13	18.08	17.90	Sell
14	18.08	18.10	Buy
15	18.08	18.16	Buy
16	18.09	18.08	Sell
17	18.10	18.11	Buy
18	18.16	18.02	Sell

Based on the C5, no rules can be generated. After we remove the 17th record, C5 obtains four rules, which are listed below. The relationships between dataset and rules are shown in Fig. 3.

If Forecast Price on Day T+1 > 18.02, Buy the Stock.
If Forecast Price on Day T+1 <= 18.02 and Price on Day T > 17.84, Sell the Stock.
If Forecast Price on Day T+1 <= 18.02, Price on Day T <= 17.84 and
    Forecast Price on Day T+1 > 17.7, Buy the Stock.
If Forecast Price on Day T+1 <= 18.02, Price on Day T <= 17.84 and
    Forecast Price on Day T+1 <= 17.7, Sell the Stock.

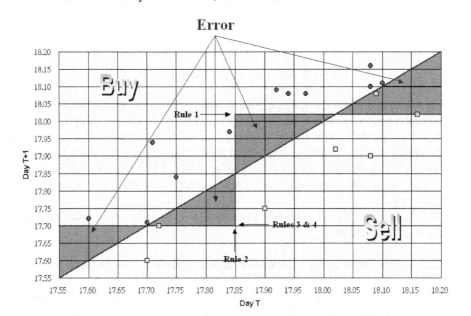

Fig. 3. The relationship between dataset and rules

According to the four induction rules listed above, we will make wrong prediction if the data fell into the four darker areas. The above example shows that even a simple rule "If Forecast Price on Day T+1 is greater than Price on Day T, Buy the Stock" cannot be correctly generated by C5.

3   Neural Decision Tree (NTD) Model

To deal with the dependency problems described in Section 2, a Neural Decision Tree (NDT) model is proposed. NDT model combines the neural network technologies and traditional decision-tree learning capabilities to discovery a more compact and correct rules. The architecture of NDT model is depicted in Fig. 4.

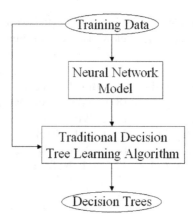

Fig. 4. The architecture of NDT model

In this architecture, the training data is firstly sent to the neural network model. Artificial neural networks were inspired from biology. It has been applied to many applications for different purposes. In this paper, the neural network is used to find the dependencies among attributes. The model used in this paper is the Back-Propagation (BP) model. The training data and the results obtained by the neural network model are then sent to the traditional decision-tree learning algorithm, C5, to improve the accuracy of C5.

The following illustrates the rule extraction steps in NDT model over numerical-categorical-mixed dataset.

1.   We separate the numerical-categorical-mixed dataset into two parts, e.g., numerical subset and nominal subset.
2.   For numerical subset, we train a feed-forward back-propagation neural network and collect weights between the input layer and the first hidden layer. Then, we change each attribute value according to the weights generated by the neural network model.
3.   For categorical subset, we also train a back-propagation neural network and classify categorical attributes according to the weights generated by the neural network model.
4.   We combine the new numerical subset and new categorical subset into a new numerical-categorical-mixed dataset.
5.   The new dataset is sent to the C5 system to generate the decision tree and rules.

To clearly describe the NDT model, the following two subsections will describe the details about how to infer the decision tree and rules for Tables 1 (categorical dataset) and 2 (numerical dataset).

3.1 NDT Model for Nominal Dataset

Because the neural network model only accepts numerical data as input, we prepare the transportation dataset in Table 1 by encoding each categorical attribute value into a numerical one. The encoded results are shown in Table 3.

Table 3. Encoded Transportation Dataset

ID	Gender	Income	Distance	Target: Vehicle	
				Car	Bike
01	1.0	0.0	1.0	1.0	0.0
02	1.0	0.0	1.0	1.0	0.0
03	0.0	1.0	1.0	1.0	0.0
04	0.0	1.0	0.0	1.0	0.0
05	1.0	1.0	0.0	0.0	1.0
06	1.0	1.0	0.0	0.0	1.0
07	0.0	0.0	0.0	0.0	1.0
08	0.0	0.0	1.0	0.0	1.0

Based on Table 3, we then train a feed-forward back-propagation neural network with the following parameters: input nodes: 3, hidden nodes: 2, output nodes: 2, training cycles: 30,000, learning rate: 2.0, decreased by: 0.95, lower bound for learning rate: 0.5, and momentum: 0.5. The training results are shown below.

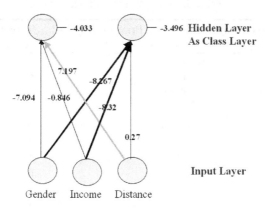

Fig. 5. Training results for encoded transportation dataset

Using the absolute value of link weight between the input layer and the first hidden layer, we classify the attributes into two groups: Group 1: "Distance" and Group 2: "Gender and Income". Because the "Distance" has a larger contribution (7.197) for Group 1 rather than Group 2 (0.27), "Distance" is classified into Group1. Based on the absolute value of link weights, "Gender" and "Income" are classified into Group 2. According to this classification, the attributes can be combined and transformed into

Table 4. After putting the combined dataset into C5, we got the compact decision tree as Fig. 2.

Table 4. Combined Transportation Dataset

ID	Gender-Income	Distance	Target: Vehicle
01	Male-Low	Far	Car
02	Male-Low	Far	Car
03	Female-High	Far	Car
04	Female-High	Near	Car
05	Male-High	Near	Bike
06	Male-High	Near	Bike
07	Female-Low	Near	Bike
08	Female-Low	Far	Bike

3.2 NDT Model for Numerical Dataset

In order to generate the correct decision rules for the stock price dataset shown in Table 2, we prepare the training data by normalizing each attribute value. The normalized results are shown in Table 5. The attribute values of "Price on Day T" and "Forecast Price on Day T+1" are normalized by the following formula: New Value = (Old Value - 1.76) / 0.56.

Table 5. Normalized Stock Price Dataset

ID	Price on Day T	Forecast Price on Day T+1	Target: Decision	
			Buy	Sell
01	0	0.214	1	0
02	0.179	0	0	1
03	0.179	0.196	1	0
04	0.196	0.607	1	0
05	0.214	0.179	0	1
06	0.268	0.429	1	0
07	0.429	0.661	1	0
08	0.536	0.268	0	1
09	0.571	0.875	1	0
10	0.607	0.857	1	0
11	0.661	0.857	1	0
12	0.750	0.571	0	1
13	0.857	0.536	0	1
14	0.857	0.893	1	0
15	0.857	1	1	0
16	0.875	0.857	0	1
17	0.893	0.911	1	0
18	1	0.750	0	1

Based on Table 5, we then train a feed-forward back-propagation neural network with the following parameters: input nodes: 2, hidden nodes: 2, output nodes: 2, training cycles: 30,000, learning rate: 2.0, decreased by: 0.95, lower bound for learning rate: 0.5 and momentum: 0.5. The training results are shown below.

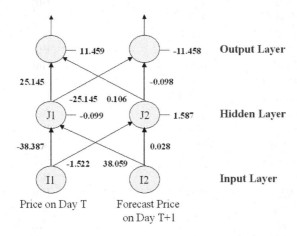

Fig. 6. Training results for normalized stock price dataset

We examine the link weights between the input layer and the first hidden layer. Then, we change the attribute values according to these weights. That is, we transform the normalized stock price dataset into a new one by the following formula.

J1 = (-38.387) * I1 + (38.059) * I2 - (-0.099)
J2 = (-1.522) * I1 + (0.028) * I2 - (-1.587)

I1 means "Normalized Price on Day T", I2 means "Normalized Forecast Price on Day T+1", J1 means "New Price on Day T" and J2 means "New Forecast Price on Day T+1". The transformed results generated by this way are shown in Table 6. The transformed dataset is then sent to the C5 and the C5 generate the following rule.

If Price on Day T (in Table 6) <= -1.066, Sell the Stock, Otherwise Buy the Stock.

"Price on Day T (in Table 6) <= -1.066" can be rewritten as follows.

Price on Day T (in Table 6) <= -1.066 ≡
-38.387 * (Price On Day T (in Table 2) - 17.6) / 0.56 + 38.059 *
(Price On Day T+1 (in Table 2) - 17.6) / 0.56 - 0.099 > -1.066 ≡
Price On Day T+1 + 0.15 > 1.009 * Price On Day T ≒
Price On Day T+1 (in Table 2) > Price On Day T (in Table 2)

Table 6. Transformed Stock Price Dataset

ID	Price on Day T	Forecast Price on Day T+1	Target: Decision
01	8.057	1.593	Buy
02	-6.954	1.315	Sell
03	0.522	1.321	Buy
04	15.468	1.305	Buy
05	-1.529	1.266	Sell
06	5.930	1.191	Buy
07	8.596	0.953	Buy
08	-10.469	0.779	Sell
09	11.267	0.742	Buy
10	9.217	0.687	Buy
11	7.160	0.605	Buy
12	-7.141	0.462	Sell
13	-12.613	0.297	Sell
14	0.979	0.307	Buy
15	5.057	0.310	Buy
16	-1.066	0.279	Sell
17	0.288	0.254	Buy
18	-9.942	0.086	Sell

Therefore, the correct rule "If Price on Day T+1 (in Table 2) > Price On Day T (in Table 2), Sell the Stock, Otherwise Buy the Stock" can be obtained.

4   Experimental Results

The dataset used for the following experiments is the 1985 Auto Imports Database, which has 205 records (records which has missing values have been removed) with 25 attributes (16 continuous and 9 nominal). This dataset can be obtained from the following web site: "http://www1.ics.uci.edu/~mlearn/MLRepository.html".

For the sake of the validity, we took the ten-fold cross-validation method for all the following experiments. It could make the results more objectively. Following the steps in Section 3, we separated the dataset into numerical subset and categorical subset. The experimental results are listed in Table 7.

In numerical subset, the NDT model reduces 29.6% errors and generates less decision rules than C5. In categorical subset, the NDT model reduces 7.14% errors. In entire database, the NDT model reduces 25% errors and generates less decision rules than C5. The experimental results show that the NDT model can significantly improve the accuracy of C5.

Table 7. Experimental Results for the 1985 Auto Imports Database

Model	Average Number of Rules	Average Errors
C5 for Numerical Subset	08.90	12.5%
NDT Model for Numerical Subset	06.10	08.8%
C5 for Categorical Subset	11.95	35.0%
NDT Model for Categorical Subset	12.40	32.5%
C5 for Entire Database	09.30	10.0%
NDT Model for Entire Database	06.15	07.5%

5   Conclusions

In this paper, we propose a model, Neural Decision Tree (NDT) Model, to deal with the problems of attribute dependencies. It combines the neural network technologies and traditional decision tree learning capabilities to handle the complicated and real cases. The experimental results show that the NDT model can significantly improve the accuracy of C5.

Although the preliminary tests give very encouraging results, some important issues especially for the number of nodes in the hidden layer must be concerned. They must be investigated further.

Acknowledgement. Research on this paper was partially supported by National Science Council grant NSC90-2213-E130-003 and NSC90-2213-E030-003.

References

1. Quinlan J.R: Improved Use of Continuous Attributes in C4.5. Journal of Artificial Intelligence Approach, Vol. 4, (1996) 77-90
2. Han J., Kamber M. (ed.): Data Mining: Concepts and Techniques. Morgan Kaufmann Publishers, (2000)
3. Chen, M.S.: Using Multiple Attribute for Mining Classification Rules. Proceedings of the 22nd Annual International Computer Software and Application Conference, (1998)
4. Kim D., Lee J.: Rule Reduction over Numerical Attributes in Decision Trees Using Multilayer Perceptron. Proceedings of the 5th Pacific Area Conference on Knowledge Discovery and Data Mining, (2001) 538-549
5. Kovalerchuk B., Vityaev E. (ed.): Data Mining In Finance: Advances in Relational and Hybrid Methods. Kluwer Academic Publishers, (2000)

Approximate k-Closest-Pairs with Space Filling Curves

Fabrizio Angiulli and Clara Pizzuti

ISI-CNR
c/o DEIS, Università della Calabria
87036 Rende (CS), Italy
{angiulli,pizzuti}@isi.cs.cnr.it

Abstract. An approximate algorithm to efficiently solve the k-*Closest-Pairs* problem in high-dimensional spaces is presented. The method is based on dimensionality reduction of the space $\mathbb{R}^d$ through the Hilbert space filling curve and performs at most $d+1$ scans of the data set. After each scan, those points whose contribution to the solution has already been analyzed, are eliminated from the data set. The pruning is lossless, in fact the remaining points along with the approximate solution found can be used for the computation of the exact solution. Although we are able to guarantee an $\mathcal{O}(d^{1+\frac{1}{t}})$ approximation to the solution, where $t = 1, \dots, \infty$ denotes the used L_t metric, experimental results give the exact k-Closest-Pairs for all the data sets considered and show that the pruning of the search space is effective.

1 Introduction

The k-*Closest-Pairs problem* is a classical problem in computational geometry that received a lot of attention in other fields such as statistics [1], pattern recognition [7] and, more recently, spatial databases [4] and data mining [14]. In this problem we are given a set $\mathcal{D}$ of n points in $\mathbb{R}^d$ and an integer k, $1 \leq k \leq \frac{n(n-1)}{2}$. The k-*Closest-Pairs* (CP_k) problem consists in finding the k *closest pairs of* $\mathcal{D}$ *under the* L_t *metric.* The L_t distance $d_t(p,q)$ between two points $p = (p_1, \dots, p_d)$ and $q = (q_1, \dots, q_d)$ is defined as $d_t(p,q) = (\sum_{i=1}^{d} |p_i - q_i|^t)^{1/t}$ for $1 \leq t < \infty$ and $\max_{1 \leq i \leq d} |p_i - q_i|$, for $t = \infty$. We denote by $CP_k(\mathcal{D})$ the output of the CP_k problem on an input data set $\mathcal{D}$. Several algorithms have been given for this problem [2,9,10,12]. A comprehensive overview on algorithms regarding closest-pair and related problems can be found in [18]. When the dimension d is constant, such algorithms are very efficient. However a thorough analysis reveals that their time requirements grow exponentially with d. As a consequence, when the dimensionality d is a parameter, the *brute force* approach, i.e. the simple enumeration of all the pairs of points, can outperform such methods, even for very small values of d. Thus, when d grows, the solution of the problem can be very time expensive. Then, it makes sense to search for an approximate solution in a reasonably amount of time. The paper intends to give a contribution in this setting.

Y. Kambayashi, W. Winiwarter, M. Arikawa (Eds.): DaWaK 2002, LNCS 2454, pp. 124–134, 2002.

In [12], Lopez and Liao present an approach to solve the k-Closest-Pairs problem based on multiple shifted copies of the input data set ordered with respect to the Z-order (Peano space filling curve). Their method consists of two phases, an approximate phase, where the approximate solution is guaranteed within a small factor of the exact one, and an exact phase, in which the k closest pairs are obtained.

In this paper we present an approximate algorithm to solve the k-*Closest-Pairs* problem. The method, named ASP, Approximate k-Closest-Pairs with SPace-filling Curves, analogously to [12], is based on dimensionality reduction of the space $\mathbb{R}^d$ through a space filling curve, in our case the Hilbert curve, and performs at most $d + 1$ scans of the data set by using shifted copies of the input data set. Our approach however, differs substantially from that of [12] since it is based on a property that allows us to eliminate those points whose contribution to the solution has already been analyzed. At each iteration, after the transformation of the d-dimensional points into one dimensional points, the input points are examined with respect to the order induced by the Hilbert curve. By exploring the $2m$ (m predecessors and m successors) nearest approximate neighbors of each point p on the line, we define a property that allows us to determine, among such $2m$ points, the true $l \leq 2m$ nearest neighbors of p and to establish a lower bound to the distance from p to the $(l+1)$-th nearest neighbor. Such a property is very useful since it permits to detect the points that do not need to be considered any more and thus that can be discarded. The main contributions of our work can be summarized as follows:

- We define a general property related to space-filling curves, that we employ to solve the k-Closest-Pairs problem, but that can be exploited to solve other proximity problems.
- We give an approximate algorithm that performs no more than $d + 1$ scans of the input data set in at most $\mathcal{O}(dn(d(\log n + m) + m \log k))$ time, which is able to eliminate points from the data set after each scan. The pruning of the search space is *lossless* thus our algorithm could constitute a *preprocessing step* for an exact algorithm. Furthermore we define the worst case condition allowing a point to be pruned from the input data set.
- Although the algorithm is approximate, and guarantees an $\mathcal{O}(d^{1+\frac{1}{t}})$ approximation to the solution, when a particular condition is satisfied, we are able to state that the returned solution is the exact one.
- The experimental results (a) give the *exact closest pairs* for all the considered high dimensional data sets and for different values of k, (b) confirm that the pruning of the search space is effective, that is that the size of the data set at the end of the algorithm is significantly reduced, and (c) show that the algorithm outperforms brute force enumeration by some order of magnitude.

The paper is organized as follows. Next section gives an overview of space filling curves. Section 3 gives definitions and properties necessary to introduce the algorithm. Section 4 presents the method. In Section 5 experimental results on several data sets are reported.

2   Space Filling Curves

The concept of *space-filling curve* came out in the 19-th century and is accredited to Peano [16] who, in 1890, proved the existence of a continuous mapping from the interval $I = [0, 1]$ onto the square $Q = [0, 1]^2$, thus settling a question posed almost ten years before, about the existence of a curve that passes through every point of a closed unit square. Curves of this type are called *Peano curves* or *space-filling curves*. Peano discovered the first space-filling curve, but it was Hilbert in 1891 who defined a general procedure to generate an entire class of space-filling curves. Hilbert observed that if the interval I can be mapped continuously onto the square Q then, after partitioning I into four congruent subintervals and Q into four congruent sub-squares, each subinterval can be mapped onto one of the sub-squares. Sub-squares are ordered such that each pair of consecutive sub-squares shares a common edge. If this process is continued ad infinitum, I and Q are partitioned into 2^{2h} replicas for $h = 1, 2, 3 \ldots$ Figure 1 (on the left) shows the second step of this process. Sub-squares are arranged so that the inclusion relationships and adjacency property are always preserved. In practical applications the partitioning process is terminated after h steps to give an approximation of a space-filling curve of order h. For $h \geq 1$ and $d \geq 2$, let $\mathcal{H}_h^d$ denote the h-th order approximation of a d-dimensional Hilbert space-filling curve that maps 2^{hd} subintervals of length $1/2^{hd}$ into 2^{hd} sub-hypercubes whose centre-points are considered as points in a space of finite granularity. The Hilbert curve, thus, passes through every point in a d-dimensional space once and once only in a particular order. This establishes a mapping between values in the interval I and the coordinates of d-dimensional points. Let D be the set $\{p \in \mathbb{R}^d : 0 \leq p_i \leq 1, 1 \leq i \leq d\}$ and p a d-dimensional point in D. The inverse image of p under this mapping is called its *Hilbert value* and is denoted by $\mathcal{H}(p)$. Let $\mathcal{D}$ be a set of points in D. These points can be sorted according to the order in which the curve passes through them. We denote by $\mathcal{H}(\mathcal{D})$ the set $\{\mathcal{H}(p) \mid p \in \mathcal{D}\}$ sorted with respect to the order relation induced by the Hilbert curve. Given a point p the predecessor and the successor of p, denoted $\mathcal{H}_{pred}(p)$ and $\mathcal{H}_{succ}(p)$, in $\mathcal{H}(\mathcal{D})$ are thus the two closest points with respect to the ordering induced by the Hilbert curve. The m-th predecessor and successor of p are denoted by $\mathcal{H}_{pred}(p, m)$ and $\mathcal{H}_{succ}(p, m)$.

Space filling curves have been studied and used in several fields [5,6,8,13,19]. A useful property of such a mapping is that if two points from the unit interval I are close then the corresponding images are close too in the hypercube D. The reverse statement, however, is not true because two close points in D can have non-close inverse images in I. This implies that the reduction of dimensionality from d to one can provoke the loss of the property of nearness. In order to preserve the closeness property, approaches based on the translation and/or rotation of the hypercube D have been proposed [17,12,19]. Such approaches assure the maintenance of the closeness of two d-dimensional points, within some factor, when they are transformed into one dimensional points. In particular, in [12], the number of shifts depends on the dimension d. Given a data set $\mathcal{D}$ and the vector $v^{(j)} = (j/(d+1), \ldots, j/(d+1)) \in \mathbb{R}^d$, each point $p \in \mathcal{D}$ can be translated

$d + 1$ times along the main diagonal in the following way: $p^j = p + v^{(j)}$, for $j = 0, \ldots, d$. The shifted copies of points thus belong to $[0, 2)^d$ and, for each p, $d + 1$ Hilbert values in the interval $[0, 2)$ can be computed. In this paper we make use of this family of shifts to overcome the loss of the nearness property.

3   Preliminaries

In this section we give preliminary definitions and notations used in the paper, and we state the property, coming from space-filling curves, necessary to show the correctness of our algorithm. Without loss of generality, we assume that the given data set $\mathcal{D}$ has been normalized so that it is constituted by points in D. The original and the shifted data points thus belong to $[0, 2)^d$, hence in the following we consider data sets on $[0, 2)^d$. Furthermore we fix the value h of the h-th order approximation of the Hilbert curve $\mathcal{H}_h^d$.

Definition 1. An r-*region* is an open ended hypercube in $[0, 2)^d$ with side length of $r = 2^{1-s}$ having the form $\prod_{i=0}^{d-1}[a_i r, (a_i + 1)r)$, where each a_i, $0 \le i < d$, and s are in $\mathbb{N}$.

Notice that every r-region contains one and only one contiguous segment of a space filling curve.

Definition 2. Given three points p, q_1, and q_2, we denote by $MaxReg(p, q_1, q_2)$ the side r of the greatest r-region containing p but neither q_1 nor q_2.

The function $MaxReg$ can be calculated in time $\mathcal{O}(d)$ working on the bit-string representation of $\mathcal{H}(p)$, $\mathcal{H}(q_1)$, and $\mathcal{H}(q_2)$.

Definition 3. Let p be a point, and let r be the side of a r-region. We denote by $MinDist(p, r)$ the value $\min_{i=1}^{d}\{\min\{\mathrm{mod}(p_i, r), r - \mathrm{mod}(p_i, r)\}\}$ where $\mathrm{mod}(x, r) = x - \lfloor x/r \rfloor r$, and p_i denotes the value of p along the i-th coordinate.

Hence $MinDist(p, r)$ is the perpendicular distance from the point p to the nearest face of the r-region of side r containing p, i.e. a lower bound to the distance between p and a point lying out of this region.

Definition 4. Let p be a point in $\mathbb{R}^d$, and let r be a non-negative real number. $\mathcal{B}(p, r)$ is defined as the set of points whose distance from p is less than or equal to r, i.e. $\mathcal{B}(p, r) = \{q \in \mathbb{R}^d \mid \mathrm{d_t}(p, q) \le r\}$.

Definition 5. Let $\mathcal{D}$ be a data set, p a point in $\mathcal{D}$ and m be a positive integer. The m-*nearest-neighbor* of p in $\mathcal{D}$, written $\mathrm{NN}_m^{\mathcal{D}}(p)$, is a point q of $\mathcal{D}$ such that there exist $m - 1$ points $q_1, \ldots, q_{m-1}$ in $\mathcal{D}$ with $\mathrm{d_t}(p, q_1) \le \mathrm{d_t}(p, q_2) \le \ldots \le \mathrm{d_t}(p, q_{m-1}) \le \mathrm{d_t}(p, q)$, and for each $x \in \mathcal{D}, x \neq p, q_i, i = 1, \ldots, m - 1$, $\mathrm{d_t}(p, x) \ge \mathrm{d_t}(p, q)$.

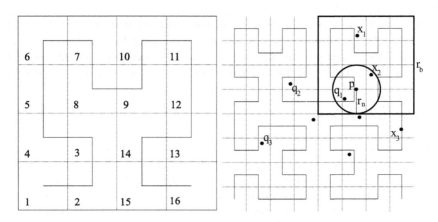

Fig. 1. Hilbert curve (left) and an example of application of Lemma 1 with $m = 3$ (right).

Definition 6. Given a data set $\mathcal{D}$, a point p of $\mathcal{D}$, and a positive integer m, the interval $\mathcal{I}_{\mathcal{H}}(p, m) \subseteq \mathcal{D}$ of the $2m$ points that precede and follow p in the Hilbert order is denoted by

$$\mathcal{I}_{\mathcal{H}}(p, m) = \{q_m, \dots, q_1, x_1, \dots, x_m \mid q_m = \mathcal{H}_{pred}(p, m), \dots, q_1 = \mathcal{H}_{pred}(p, 1),$$

$$x_1 = \mathcal{H}_{succ}(p, 1), \dots, x_m = \mathcal{H}_{succ}(p, m)\}$$

Notice that $\mathcal{I}_{\mathcal{H}}(p, m)$ are the $2m$ nearest neighbors of p with respect to the Hilbert order and thus they constitute an approximation of the true closest neighbors. The following lemma allows us to determine, among such $2m$ points, the exact $l \leq 2m - 2$ nearest neighbors of p, i.e. $\mathrm{NN}_1^{\mathcal{D}}(p), \dots, \mathrm{NN}_l^{\mathcal{D}}(p)$, and to establish a lower bound to the distance from p to the $(l+1)$-th nearest neighbor $\mathrm{NN}_{l+1}^{\mathcal{D}}(p)$.

Lemma 1. *Given a data set $\mathcal{D}$, a point p of $\mathcal{D}$, a positive integer m and the interval $\mathcal{I}_{\mathcal{H}}(p, m)$, let $r_b = MaxReg(p, q_m, x_m)$, $r_n = MinDist(p, r_b)$, and $S_n = \mathcal{I}_{\mathcal{H}}(p, m) \cap \mathcal{B}(p, r_n)$. Then*

1. *The points in S_n are the true first $|S_n|$ nearest-neighbors of p in $\mathcal{D}$;*
2. $\mathrm{d_t}(p, \mathrm{NN}_{|S_n|+1}^{\mathcal{D}}(p)) > r_n$.

Figure 1 shows an example of application of Lemma 1, and shows the r_b-region, the distance r_n, and $\mathcal{B}(p, r_n)$, for $m = 3$ and $t = 2$.

4   Algorithm

In this section we give the description of the ASP algorithm. The method does $d + 1$ scans of the input data set. During each scan it works on a shifted version of the data set. Exploiting the property defined in Lemma 1, at each iteration, it eliminates those points that do not need to be considered any more. This pruning of the search space allows to obtain a fast approximate algorithm for the k-Closest-Pairs problem in high dimensional spaces, as experimental results show in Section 5. Before starting with the description, we introduce the concept of *point feature* that contains, for each point of the input data set, its Hilbert value and a value that represents the radius of its maximum d-dimensional neighborhood explored.

Definition 7. A *point feature* f is a triple $\langle point, h\_key, lb \rangle$, where *point* is a point in $[0, 2)^d$, h_key is the Hilbert value associated to *point* in the h-th order approximation of the d-dimensional Hilbert space-filling curve mapping the hypercube $[0, 2)^d$ into the integer set $[0, 2^{hd})$, and lb is a distance representing the radius of the maximum d-dimensional neighborhood of *point* explored during the execution of the algorithm.

In the following with the notation $f.point$, $f.h\_key$, and $f.lb$ we refer to the *point*, h_key, and lb value of the point feature f respectively.

```
algorithm ASP ;
input:    D = {p₁,...,pₙ} : dataset;
k : integer; (* closest-pairs requested *)
m : integer; (* lookups allowed *)
begin
    INIT(Q_CP, k);
    for i := 1 to n do begin
        F_i.point := p_i; F_i.lb := 0;
    end;
    j := 0;
    while F ≠ ∅ and j ≤ d do begin
        HILBERT(F, v^(j));
        SCAN(F, v^(j), m, Q_CP);
        PRUNE(F, MAX(Q_CP));
        j := j + 1;
    end;
    return P(Q_CP);
end.
```

```
procedure SCAN(var F : features;
    v : point;
    m : integer;
    var Q_CP : queue);
begin
    for i := 1 to |F| do begin
        for j := i + 1 to min{i + m, |F|}
        do begin
            δ := d_t(F_i.point, F_j.point);
            UPDATE(Q_CP, F_i.point, F_j.point, δ);
        end;
        r_b := MaxReg(F_i.point + v,
            F_{i-m}.point + v, F_{i+m}.point + v);
        r_n := MinDist(F_i.point + v, r_b);
        if r_n > F_i.lb then
            F_i.lb := r_n;
    end;
end; { SCAN }
```

Fig. 2. The algorithm ASP and the procedure SCAN

The algorithm is reported in Figure 2. Two data structures are employed, a priority queue Q_{CP} and a list of point features F. Q_{CP} is a priority queue whose elements are triples of the form $\langle p, q, \delta \rangle$, where p and q are distinct points of the input data set, and δ is the associated distance $d_t(p, q)$. Every triple contained in Q_{CP} is one of the nearest pairs met during the execution of the algorithm. F is a list of point features, while F_i denotes the i-th element of the list F. In the following we denote by $\mathcal{P}(Q_{CP})$ the set $\{\langle p, q \rangle \mid \langle p, q, \delta \rangle \in Q_{CP}\}$, and by $\mathcal{P}(F)$ the set $\{\langle p, q \rangle \mid \exists f, g \in F : f \neq g \wedge p = f.point \wedge q = g.point\}$. The algorithm receives as input the data set $\mathcal{D}$, the number k of closest pairs to find and the number m of neighbors that the algorithm is allowed to consider on the line

(m predecessors and m successors). The procedure INIT initializes the priority queue Q_{CP} as an empty queue of size at most k, the number of closest pairs to find. The initialization phase builds also the list F associated to the input data set. The value of lb for each point feature of F is set to the value 0. The main cycle, consists of at most $d+1$ steps. We explain the single operations performed during each step of this cycle.

The HILBERT procedure calculates the value $\mathcal{H}(F_i.point + v^{(j)})$ of each point feature F_i of F, places this value in $F_i.h\_key$, and sorts the point features in the list F using as order key the values $F_i.h\_key$. Thus it performs the Hilbert mapping of a shifted version of the input data set. As $v^{(0)}$ is the zero vector, at the first step ($j = 0$) no shift is performed. Thus during this step we work on the original data set.

The procedure SCAN is reported in Figure 2. To update the priority queue Q_{CP} the procedure UPDATE is employed. UPDATE(Q, p, q, δ) modifies Q as follows: unless the triple $\langle p, q, \delta \rangle$ is already present in Q, if the size of Q is less than the maximum size allowed (we recall that, in the case of the queue Q_{CP}, this size is k, the number of closest-pairs we are searching for), then the triple $\langle p, q, \delta \rangle$ is inserted in the queue Q. Otherwise, if δ is less than the maximum distance associated to a triple in Q, then this triple is erased from Q and the triple $\langle p, q, \delta \rangle$ is inserted in Q. The procedure SCAN performs a sequential scan of the list F. For each point feature F_i, the distances between the point $F_i.point$ and the points $F_{i+1}.point, \ldots, F_{i+m}.point$ are calculated. At the same time the priority queue Q_{CP} is updated through the procedure UPDATE. After having examined the m point features consecutive to F_i, the size r_n of the greatest r-region containing $F_i.point$ but neither $F_{i-m}.point$ nor $F_{i+m}.point$ is calculated. Finally, if the value of r_n is greater than the value of $F_i.lb$ already determined, this value is set to r_n.

The procedure PRUNE deletes from F all the point features F_i such that $F_i.lb > \text{MAX}(Q_{CP})$ where $\text{MAX}(Q_{CP}) = \max\{\delta \mid \langle p, q, \delta \rangle \in Q_{CP}\}$. Hence, the list of features processed at the next step of the cycle is a subset (not necessarily proper) of the current list. The main cycle stops when F is an empty list or after at most $d + 1$ steps. This terminates the description of the algorithm. Now we state the main property of the algorithm.

Theorem 1. *Let $\overline{F}$ and $\overline{Q}_{CP}$ be the current list of point features F and the current priority queue Q_{CP}. Then, during the execution of the ASP algorithm, the following holds:*

$$CP_k(\mathcal{D}) \subseteq \mathcal{P}(\overline{Q}_{CP}) \cup \mathcal{P}(\overline{F})$$

Theorem 1 proves the correctness of the algorithm. Furthermore, it establishes that the pruning operated by ASP is *lossless*, that is the remaining points along with the approximate solution found can be used for the computation of the exact solution. In the following with the notation F^* and Q^*_{CP} we refer to the value of the list of point features F and of the priority queue Q_{CP} at the end of the ASP algorithm, respectively. Moreover, we denote by ϵ_d the value $2d^{\frac{1}{t}}(2d+1)$, and by δ_k the distance between the two points composing the k-closest-pair of points in $\mathcal{D}$. The following Corollary gives the first important result regarding the algorithm, i.e. when the list F^* is empty then we can assert that the solution returned is the exact one.

Corollary 1. $F^* = \emptyset$ implies that $CP_k(\mathcal{D}) = \mathcal{P}(Q_{CP}^*)$.

Now we give some definitions and results useful to state the approximation error order for the value of δ_k guaranteed by the algorithm.

Definition 8. A point p is α-central in an r-region iff for each $i = 1, \ldots, d$, we have $\alpha r \leq \mathrm{mod}(p_i, r) < (1 - \alpha)r$, where $0 \leq \alpha < 0.5$.

The following result is from [3].

Lemma 2. Suppose d is even. Then, for any point $p \in \mathbb{R}^d$ and $r = 2^{-s}$ ($s \in \mathbb{N}$), there exists $j \in \{0, \ldots, d\}$ such that $p + v^{(j)}$ is $1/(2d + 2)$-central in its r-region.

The previous lemma states that if we shift a point p of $\mathbb{R}^d$ at most $d + 1$ times in a particular manner, i.e. if we consider the set of points $\{p + v^{(0)}, \ldots, p + v^{(d)}\}$, then, in at least one of these shifts, this point must become *sufficiently* central in an r-region, for each admissible value of r. As we use this family of shifts, we are able to state an upper bound for the approximation error of the algorithm similar to that defined in [12], that employed the same family of shifts.

Theorem 2. $\mathrm{MAX}(Q_{CP}^*) \leq \epsilon_d \delta_k$.

Thus, the algorithm guarantees an $\mathcal{O}(d^{1 + \frac{1}{i}})$ approximation to the solution. Now we define the worst case condition allowing a point to be pruned from the input data set by the ASP algorithm.

Theorem 3. The list F^* does not contain at least those points p of $\mathcal{D}$ such that $\delta > \epsilon_d^2 \delta_k$, where δ is the distance between p and its nearest neighbor in $\mathcal{D}$.

Thus, let Δ be the distribution of the nearest-neighbor distances of the points of $\mathcal{D}$, i.e. the distribution of the distances in the set $\{d_t(p, \mathrm{NN}_1^{\mathcal{D}}(p)) \mid p \in \mathcal{D}\}$. Theorem 3 asserts that the ability of the ASP algorithm to prune points increases when the distribution Δ accumulates around and above the value $\epsilon_d^2 \delta_k$.

Now we give time and space cost analysis of the algorithm. In the worst case the HILBERT procedure requires $\mathcal{O}(dn \log n)$ time, while the procedure PRUNE requires $\mathcal{O}(n)$ time. The procedure SCAN requires in the worst case $\mathcal{O}(m(d + \log k))$ time to execute the inner cycle and $\mathcal{O}(d)$ time to calculate r_n, thus in total $\mathcal{O}(n(d + m(d + \log k)))$ time. Thus, in the worst case the algorithm runs in $\mathcal{O}(dn(d(\log n + m) + m \log k))$ time. Since the algorithm enumerating all the possible pairs in the data set requires $\mathcal{O}(n^2(d + \log k))$ time, it must be the case that k and m are such that the following inequality holds

$$n \geq (d(d(\log n + m) + m \log k))/(d + \log k)$$

otherwise the algorithm could be outperformed by the brute force approach. As the point features considered in the current iteration could be a proper subset of those considered in the preceding iteration, the effective execution time of the algorithm could be sensibly less than the expected. Finally, regarding the space cost analysis, the algorithm requires $\mathcal{O}(n + k)$ space to store the list F and the queue Q_{CP}.

5   Experimental Results

We implemented the algorithm using the C programming language on a Pentium III 800MHz based machine having 256Mb of main memory. We used a 64 bit floating-point type to represent point coordinates and distances, and the 32th order approximation of the d-dimensional Hilbert curve to map the hypercube $[0, 2)^d$ onto the set of integers $[0, 2^{32d})$. We set $m = k$ for all the experiments.

The data sets we used to test the algorithm are: *Cure* ($d = 2$, $n = 100000$), *ColorMoments* ($d = 9$, $n = 68040$), *CoocTexture* ($d = 16$, $n = 68040$), *ColorHistogram* ($d = 31$, $n = 68040$). Cure is the two dimensional very large synthetic data set described in [15] (referred as Data set 1) and widely used to test clustering algorithms. The other three data sets corresponds to a collection of real images. Each point of these data sets represents an image of the collection (see http://kdd.ics.uci.edu/databases/CorelFeatures/CorelFeatures.html for more information). We consider only the first 31 dimensions of the 32 dimensional data set *ColorHistogram* as our actual implementation does not go beyond 31 dimensions.

We search the k closest pairs under the L_2 metric. Although we are able to guarantee an $\mathcal{O}(d^{\frac{3}{2}})$ approximation to the solution, the algorithm calculates the *exact solution* for all the experiments, even when F^* was not empty. Hence, we report only the evaluation of the *pruning effectiveness* and of the *running time* of the algorithm.

Table 1. The size of F^*

Dataset \ k	1	10	100	1000
Cure	0	0	0	0
ColorMoments	0	0	0	35732
CoocTexture	0	0	0	25558
ColorHistogram	0	0	0	0

Table 1 reports the size of the list F^* for different values of k. The results show the effectiveness of the algorithm in reducing the size of the input data set. In practice the algorithm is able to prune points having distance δ to their nearest-neighbor significantly more less than $\epsilon_d^2 \delta_k$, the worst case stated by Theorem 3. For the experiments done we verified that the pruning effectiveness deteriorates when δ_k and the mode of the distribution Δ have the same order of magnitude (this is the case of *ColorMoments* and *CoocTexture* for $k = 1000$).

Figure 3 shows the *speed up* obtained in the experiments, i.e. the ratio $\frac{T}{T'}$ where T' is the execution time of our algorithm and T is the execution time of the brute force enumeration algorithm on the same input. We plot also the curves of the theoretical speed up associated to the data sets considered (represented as dotted curves), i.e. the speed up obtained in the worst case execution time of the algorithm. The experimental results show that in practice our algorithm

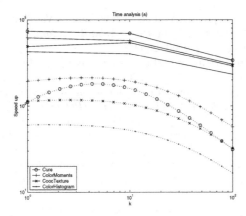

Fig. 3. Execution time

outperforms brute force enumeration by some order of magnitude, and that it guarantees, in all the cases considered, a speed up greater than those predicted by the theory.

Acknowledgments. Special thanks to Jonathan Lawder who provided us his source code implementing the multidimensional Hilbert mapping.

6 Conclusions

In this paper an approximated algorithm, based on dimensionality reduction through space-filling curves, to solve the k-Closest- Pairs problem on high dimensional spaces has been presented. The method exploits a property of such curves to prune the search space. Experimental results give the exact closest pairs for all the considered data sets, confirm that the pruning is effective and show that the algorithm outperforms brute force enumeration by some order of magnitude. We intend to build a disk-based version of ASP to explore how the algorithm scales for data sets that do not fit into main memory. The introduced property can be fruitfully used for other classical proximity problems. Currently, we are investigating its application to different data mining tasks, such as the discovery of outliers.

References

1. H. C. Andrews. *Introduction to Mathematical Techniques in Pattern Recognition.* Wiley-Interscience, New York, 1972.
2. J. L. Bentley and M. I. Shamos. Divide-and-conquer in multidimensional space. In *Proc. of the 8th ACM Symp. on Theory of Computing*, pages 220–230, 1996.
3. T. Chan. Approximate nearest neighbor queries revisited. In *Proc. of the 13th ACM Symp. on Computational Geometry*, pages 352–358, 1997.

4. A. Corral, Y. Manolopoulos, Y. Theodoridis, and M.Vassilakopoulos. Closest pair queries in spatial databases. In *Proc. ACM Int. Conf. on Managment of Data (SIGMOD'00)*, pages 189–2000, 2000.

5. C. Faloutsos. Multiattribute hashing using gray codes. In *Proceedings ACM Int. Conf. on Managment of Data (SIGMOD'86)*, pages 227–238, 1986.

6. C. Faloutsos and S. Roseman. Fractals for secondary key retrieval. In *Proc. ACM Int. Conf. on Principles of Database Systems (PODS'89)*, pages 247–252, 1989.

7. J. A. Hartigan. *Clustering Algorithms*. Wiley, New York, 1975.

8. H.V. Jagadish. Linear clustering of objects with multiple atributes. In *Proc. ACM Int. Conf. on Managment of Data (SIGMOD'90)*, pages 332–342, 1990.

9. N. Katoh and K. Iwano. Finding k furthest pairs and k closest/farthest bichromatic pairs for points in the plane. In *Proc. of the 8th ACM Symp. on Computational Geometry*, pages 320–329, 1992.

10. H.P. Lenhof and M. Smid. Enumerating the k closest pairs optimally. In *Proc. of the 33rd IEEE Symp. on Foundation of Computer Science (FOCS92)*, pages 380–386, 1992.

11. S. Liao, M. Lopez, and S. Leutenegger. High dimensional similarity search with space filling curves. In *Proc. of the 17th Int. Conf. on Data Engineering (ICDE)*, pages 615–622, 2001.

12. M. Lopez and S. Liao. Finding k-closest-pairs efficiently for high dimensional data. In *Proc. of the 12th Canadian Conf. on Computational Geometry (CCCG)*, pages 197–204, 2000.

13. B. Moon, H.V. Jagadish, C. Faloutsos, and J.H.Saltz. Analysis of the clustering properties of the Hilbert space-filling curve. *Technical Report 10, Department of Computer Science, University of Arizona, Tucson*, August 1999.

14. A. Nanopoulos, Y. Theodoridis, and Y. Manolopoulos. C^2P : Clustering based on closest pairs. In *Proc. of the 27th Conf. on Very Large Database (VLDB'01)*, pages 331–340, 2001.

15. K. Shim S. Guha, R. Rastogi. Cure: An efficient clustering algorithm for large databases. In *Proc. ACM Int. Conf. on Managment of Data (SIGMOD'86)*, pages 73–84, 1998.

16. Hans Sagan. *Space Filling Curves*. Springer-Verlag, 1994.

17. J. Shepherd, X. Zhu, and N. Megiddo. A fast indexing method for multidimensional nearest neighbor search. In *Proc. of SPIE Vol. 3656, Storage and retrieval for image and video databases*, pages 350–355, 1998.

18. M. Smid. Closest-point problems in computational geometry. In *Tech. Report, Univ. Magdeburg, Germany*, pages 1–63, 1997.

19. Roman G. Strongin and Yaroslav D. Sergeyev. *Global Optimization with Non-Convex Costraints*. Kluwer Academic, 2000.

Optimal Dimension Order: A Generic Technique for the Similarity Join

Christian Böhm[1], Florian Krebs[2], and Hans-Peter Kriegel[2]

[1] University for Health Informatics and Technology, Innsbruck
Christian.Boehm@umit.at
[2] University of Munich
{krebs,kriegel}@dbs.informatik.uni-muenchen.de

Abstract. The similarity join is an important database primitive which has been successfully applied to speed up applications such as similarity search, data analysis and data mining. The similarity join combines two point sets of a multidimensional vector space such that the result contains all point pairs where the distance does not exceed a given Parameter ε. Although the similarity join is clearly CPU bound, most previous publications propose strategies that primarily improve the I/O performance. Only little effort has been taken to address CPU aspects. In this Paper, we show that most of the computational overhead is dedicated to the final distance computations between the feature vectors. Consequently, we propose a generic technique to reduce the response time of a large number of basic algorithms for the similarity join. It is applicable for index based join algorithms as well as for most join algorithms based on hashing or sorting. Our technique, called Optimal Dimension Order, is able to avoid and accelerate distance calculations between feature vectors by a careful order of the dimensions. The order is determined according to a probability model. In the experimental evaluation, we show that our technique yields high performance improvements for various underlying similarity join algorithms such as the R-tree similarity join, the breadth-first-R-tree join, the Multipage Index Join, and the ε-Grid-Order.

1 Introduction

The similarity join is a database primitive which gains increasing importance for similarity search [2] and data mining [4]. Like the relational join, the similarity join combines tuples (vectors) of two sets into one such that a join condition is fulfilled. The join condition of the similarity join is the similarity between the two objects (vectors) according to some suitable metric $\| \cdot \|$. In most cases, the Euclidean distance metric is used. Formally, the similarity join $P \underset{sim}{\bowtie} Q$ between two finite sets $P = \{p_i, \dots, p_n\}$ and $Q = \{q_i, \dots, q_m\}$ is defined as the set

$$P \underset{sim}{\bowtie} Q := \{(p_i, q_j) | \|p_i - q_j\| \leq \varepsilon\}$$

and can also be expressed in a SQL like fashion as

SELECT * FROM P, Q **WHERE** $\|P.\text{vector} - Q.\text{vector}\| \leq \varepsilon$.

Y. Kambayashi, W. Winiwarter, M. Arikawa (Eds.): DaWaK 2002, LNCS 2454, pp. 135–146, 2002.
© Springer-Verlag Berlin Heidelberg 2002

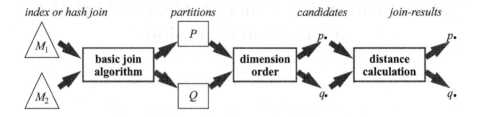

Fig. 1. Integration of the dimension-order-algorithm

Due to its high importance, many different algorithms for the similarity join have been proposed, operating on multidimensional index structures [9,14,11], multidimensional hashing [15,16], or various sort orders [19,12,7]. In contrast to algorithms for simple similarity queries upon a single data set (such as *range queries* or *nearest neighbor queries*), all of these algorithms are clearly CPU bound. In spite of the filtering capabilities of the above algorithms the evaluations cost are dominated by the final distance calculations between the points. This is even true for index structures which are optimized for minimum CPU cost [8].

Therefore, in the current paper, we propose a technique for the effective *reduction* of the high number of the distance calculations between feature vectors. Our method shows some resemblance to the paradigm of plane-sweep algorithms [17] which is extended by the determination of an optimal order of dimensions. A design objective of our technique was generality, i.e. our method can be implemented on top of a high number of basic algorithms for the similarity join such as R-tree based joins [9,14,11], hashing based methods [15,16], and sort orders [19,12,7]. A precondition for our optimal dimension order is to have some notion of *partitions* to be joined having a position and extension in the data space. This is given for all techniques mentioned above. Our technique is not meaningful on top of the simple nested loop join [20].

Organization Section 2 is dedicated to our technique, the *Optimal Dimension Order*. The experimental evaluation of our approach is presented in section 3 and section 4 concludes the paper.

2   Optimal Dimension Order

In this section we will develop a criterion for ordering the dimensions to optimize the distance computations. We assume that our join algorithm with optimal dimension order is preceded by a filter step based on some spatial index structure or spatial hash method which divides the point sets that are to be joined into rectangular partitions and only considers such partitions that have a distance to each other of at most ε. Suitable techniques are depth-first-and breadth-first-R-tree-Join [9,11], Spatial Hash Join [15,16], Seeded Trees [14], the ε-dB-tree [19], the Multidimensional Join (MDJ) [13], or the ε-grid-order [7].

2.1 Algorithm

The integration of the dimension order is shown in figure 1. Our dimension order algorithm receives partition pairs (P, Q) from the basic technique for the similarity join and generates point-pairs as candidates for the final distance calculations. The general idea of the dimension order is as follows:

If the points of one partition, say Q are sorted by one of the dimensions, then the points of Q which can be join mates of a point p of P form a contiguous sequence in Q (cf. figure 2). A large number of points which are excluded by the sort dimension can be ignored. In most cases, the points which can be ignored, are located at the lower or upper end of the sorted sequence, but it is also possible, that the se-

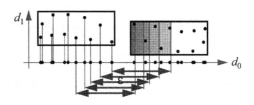

Fig. 2. Idea of the Dimension Order

quence of points that must be processed are in the middle of the sequence. In the latter case, the start and end of the sequence of relevant points must be searched e.g. by binary search, as depicted in the algorithm in figure 3. In the other cases, it is actually not necessary to determine the first (last) point before entering the innermost loop. Here, we can replace the search by a suitable break operation in the innermost loop.

2.2 Determining the Optimal Sort Dimension

We will show in section 3 that the proposed algorithm gains much performance only if the optimal sort dimension is selected for each partition pair individually. If two partitions are joined by the basic technique, we can use the following information in order to choose the optimal dimension:

- The distance of the two partitions with respect to each other or the overlap (which we will interpret as *negative* distance from now on) in each case projected on the one single dimension of the data space. We observe that the overall distance of the two partitions as well as the distance projected on each of the dimensions cannot exceed ε otherwise the whole partition pair would have been eliminated by the *preprocessing step* in the basic technique.
- The extent of the two partitions with respect to each of the single dimensions

In order to demonstrate in a 2-dimensional example that both distance as well as extent, really do matter, see figure 4: In both cases the distance of the two partitions is the same. For simplification we show one exemplary point with its

```
algorithm optimal_dimension_order_join (index M₁, M₂)
    the similarity-join basic method
    generates partition pairs from M₁ and M₂;
        for all parition pairs (P,Q) with dist(P,Q) ≤ ε
        determine best sort dimension s according to Eq. (9);
        sort (indirectly) points in Q according to dimension s;
        for all points p ∈ P
            determine the first point a ∈ Q: |aₛ − pₛ| ≤ ε;
            determine the last point b ∈ Q: |bₛ − pₛ| ≤ ε;
            for all points q ∈ Q with aₛ ≤ qₛ ≤ bₛ
                if dist(p,q) ≤ ε
                    output (p,q);
    end;
```

Fig. 3. Algorithmic Scheme

ε-neighborhood in partitions Q and Q' although in our further discussion we assume uniform distribution of points within the two partitions i.e. we will not consider one specific point.

On the left side of figure 4 both of the partitions are roughly square. Let us first look at the projection on the d_0-axis: We observe that about 70% of the projected area of P lies within the projected ε-neighborhood of our sample point in Q. If we were to choose d_0, as sort-dimension only about 30% of the points can be excluded as join-

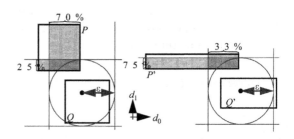

Fig. 4. Distance and extension of partitions

mates for our sample point in the first step. For the remaining 70% we still have to test dimension d_1 i.e. we have to compute the overall point distance. If we now look at the projection on dimension d_1: here only 25% of the area of P lies within the ε-neighborhood of our sample point in Q. If we choose d_1 as start-dimension as much as 75% of the points are already eliminated in the first step of our dimension ordering algorithm. In the case of quadratic partitions it is thus advisable to choose the dimension within which the partitions have the largest distance with respect to each other as this minimizes the area of the projected ε-neighborhood.

The right side of figure 4 shows the two partitions P' and Q' which have a much larger extent in dimension d_0, than in dimension d_1. For this reason the projection on the d_0-axis, with a portion of 33% of the area, is much better than the projection on the d_1-axis (75%). In this case the dimension d_0, should be chosen as sort-dimension.

We can note the following as a first rule of thumb for the selection of the dimension: for approximately square partitions choose the dimension with the greatest distance, otherwise the dimension with the greatest extent.

2.3   Probability Model

In the following we will propose a model which grasps this rule of thumb much more precisely. Our model is based on the assumption that the points within each partition follow a uniform distribution. Data from real life applications such as those used in our experimental evaluation are far from being uniformly distributed. In our previous work, however, it has been shown that the conclusions which are drawn from such models with respect to optimization in multidimensional index structures are good enough to clearly improve the performance of multidimensional query processing [5].

Our model determines for each dimension the probability $W_i[\varepsilon]$ (termed *mating probability* of dimension d_i) that two points in partitions P and Q with given rectangular boundaries $P.\mathrm{lb}_i$, $P.\mathrm{ub}_i$, $Q.\mathrm{lb}_i$, $Q.\mathrm{ub}_i$ ($0 \leq d$; lb and ub for lower bound and upper bound, respectively) have at most the distance ε with respect to dimension d_i.

Definition 1
Given two partitions P and Q, let $W_i[\varepsilon]$ denote the probability for each dimension d_i that an arbitraty pair of points (p, q) with $p \in P$ and $q \in Q$ has a maximal distance of ε with respect to d_i:

$$W_i[\varepsilon] := W(|p_i - q_i| \leq \varepsilon), (p, q) \in (P, Q) \tag{1}$$

If $P.\#$ denotes the number of points within partition P, then the expectation of the number of point pairs which are excluded by the optimal dimension order equals to

$$E_i[\varepsilon] := P.\# \cdot Q.\# \cdot (1 - W_i[\varepsilon]) \tag{2}$$

This means that exactly the dimension d_i should be chosen as sort dimension that minimizes the mating probability $W_i[\varepsilon]$.

We will now develop a universal formula to determine the mating probability. We assume uniform distribution within each of the partitions P and Q. Thus the i-th component p_i of the point $p \in P$ is an arbitrary point from the uniform interval given by $[P.\mathrm{lbi}_i \ldots P.\mathrm{ub}_i]$. The pair (p_i, q_i) is chosen from an independent and uniform distribution within the two-dimensional interval $[P.\mathrm{lb}_i \ldots P.\mathrm{ub}_i] \times [Q.\mathrm{lb}_i \ldots Q.\mathrm{ub}_i]$ because of the independence of the distributions within P and Q, which we can assume for $P \neq Q$. Hence the event space of dimension d_i is given by

$$F_i = (P.\mathrm{ub}_i - P.\mathrm{lb}_i) \cdot (Q.\mathrm{ub}_i - Q.\mathrm{lb}_i) \tag{3}$$

$W_i[\varepsilon]$ is therefore given by the ratio of the portion of the area of F_i where p_i and q_i have a distance of at most ε to the whole area F_i. This can be expressed by the following integral:

$$W_i[\varepsilon] = \frac{1}{F_i} \cdot \int_{P.lb_i}^{P.ub_i} \int_{Q.lb_i}^{Q.ub_i} \begin{cases} 1 \; for \, |x - y| \leq \varepsilon \\ 0 \; otherwise \end{cases} dy \, dx \qquad (4)$$

We can now simplify the integral of formula (4) by case analysis looking at the geometric properties of our configuration, i.e. we can transform our problem into d distinct two-dimensional geometric problems. To illustrate this, we look at the join of the two partitions P and Q in two-dimensional space as shown on the left hand side of figure 5. In this case, it is not directly obvious which dimension yields better results. The projection on d_0, which is the transformation that is used to determine $W_0[\varepsilon]$ is shown on the right hand side of figure 5. The range with respect to d_0, of points which can be stored in P is shown on the x-axis while the range with respect to d_0, of points which can be stored in Q is shown on the y-axis. The projection (p_0, q_0) of an arbitrary pair of points $(p, q) \in (P, Q)$ can only be drawn inside the area denoted as event space (cf. equation 3), as all points of P with respect to dimension d_0, are by definition within $P.lb_0$ and $P.ub_0$. The same holds for Q.

The area within which our join condition is true for dimension d_0, i.e. the area within which the corresponding points have a distance of less than ε with respect to d_0, is marked in gray in figure 5. All these projections of pairs of points which fall into the gray area are located within a stripe of width 2ε (the ε-stripe) which is centered around the 45° main diagonal. All projections outside this stripe can be excluded from our search as the corresponding points already have a distance with respect to d_0 that exceeds our join condition. The intersection of this stripe with the event space represents those point pairs that cannot be excluded from our search using d_0 alone. The mating probability is given by the ratio of the intersection to the whole event space which equals 18% in our example.

2.4   Efficient Computation

In the previous section, we have seen that the exclusion probability of a dimension d_i corresponds to the proportion of the event space which is covered by the ε-stripe. In this section, we show how this proportion can be efficiently determined. Efficiency is an important aspect here because the exclusion probability must be determined for each pair of mating pages and for each dimension d_i.

Throughout this section we will use the shortcut PL for $P.lb_i$ and similarly PU, QL, and QU. Considering figure 6 we can observe that there exists a high number of different shapes that the intersection of the event space and the ε-stripe can have. For each shape, an individual formula for the intersection area applies. We will show

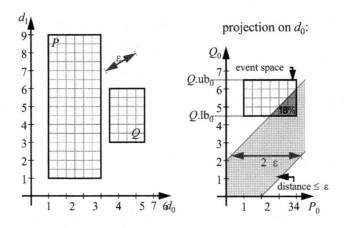

Fig. 5. Determining the mating probability $W_0[\varepsilon]$

- that exactly 20 different shapes are possible,
- how these 20 cases can be efficiently distinguished, and
- that for each case a simple, efficient formula exists.

Obviously, the shape of the intersection is determined by the relative position of the 4 corners of the event space with respect to the ε-stripe. E.g. if 3 corners of the event space are *above* (or *left* from) the ε-stripe, and 1 corner is *inside* the ε-stripe, the intersection shape is always a triangle. For the relative position of a corner and the ε-stripe, we define the following cornercode cc of a point:

Definition 2 Cornercode (cc) of a point in the event space
A point (p, q) in the event space has the corner code $cc(p, q)$ with

$$cc(p, q) = \begin{cases} 1 \text{ if } q > p + \varepsilon \\ 2 \text{ otherwise} \\ 3 \text{ if } q < p - \varepsilon \end{cases} \tag{5}$$

Intuitively, the cornercode is 1 if the point is left (or above) from the ε-stripe, 3 if it is right (or underneath) from the ε-stripe, and 2 if it is inside the ε-stripe (cf. figure 8). For an event space given by its upper and lower bounds (PL,PU,QL,QU), the corners are denoted as C_1, C_{2a}, C_{2b}, and C_3, as depicted in figure 7. We induce the cornercode for the event space given by lower and upper bounds.

Definition 3 Cornercode $cc(ES)$ of the event space
The cornercode of the event space ES given by the lower and upper limits $ES = $ (PL,PU,QL,QU) is the 4-tuple:

$$cc(ES = (cc(C_1), cc(C_{2a}), cc(C_{2b}), cc(C_3)) \tag{6}$$

Formally, there exist $3^4 = 81$ different 4-tuples over the alphabet $\{1,2,3\}$. However, not all these 4-tuples are geometrically meaningful. For instance it is not

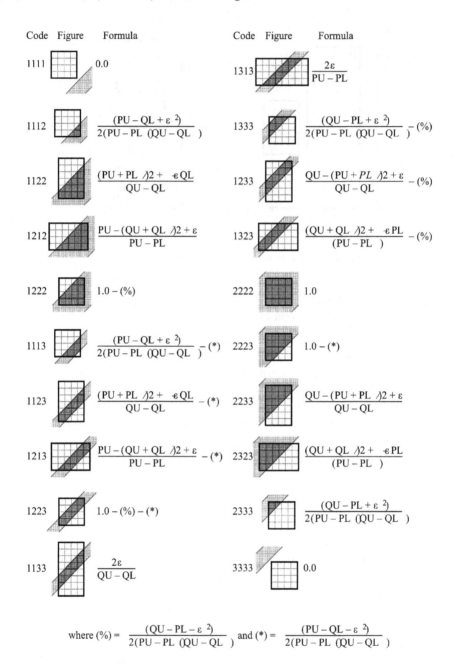

Fig. 6. Relative Positions of Event Space and ε-Stripe and Corresp. Probability Formulas

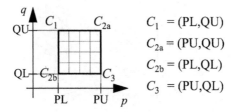

$C_1 = (PL, QU)$

$C_{2a} = (PU, QU)$

$C_{2b} = (PL, QL)$

$C_3 = (PU, QL)$

Fig. 7. Identifiers for the Corners of the Event Space

possible that simultaneously C_1 is below and C_3 above the ε-stripe. As C_1 is left from C_{2a} and C_{2a} is above C_3 we have the constraint:

$$cc(C_1) \leq cc(C_{2a}) \leq cc(C_3) \tag{7}$$

And as C_1 is above C_{2a} and C_{2b} is left from C_3 we have the constraint:

$$cc(C_1) \leq cc(C_{2b}) \leq cc(C_3) \tag{8}$$

The corner code of C_{2a} may be greater than, less than, or equal to the corner code of C_{2b}. The following lemma states that there are 20 different 4-tuples that fulfill the two constraints above.

Lemma 1. Completeness of Case Distinction
There are 20 different intersection shapes for the event space and the ε-tripe.

Proof. By complete enumeration of all four-tuples: There are 3 tuples where $cc(C_1) = cc(C_3)$: 1111, 2222, and 3333. If the difference between $cc(C_1)$ and $cc(C_3)$ is equal to 1 (i.e. tuples like 1??2 or 2??3), we obtain 2 possibilities for each of the corner Codes $cc(C_{2a})$ and $cc(C_{2b})$, i.e. $2 \cdot 2^2 = 8$ different tuples. For a difference of two between $cc(C_1)$ and $cc(C_3)$ which corresponds to tuples like 1??3, we have a choice out of three for each of the corners C_{2a} and C_{2b}, i.e. $3^2 = 9$ tuples. Summarized, we obtain 20 different tuples □

Note that the cornercodes 1111 and 3333 which are associated with a probability of 0.0 actually are never generated because the corresponding partitions have a distance of more than ε and, thus, are excluded by the preceding filter step.

Each corner code of the event space is associated with a geometric shape of the intersection between event space and ε-stripe. The shape varies from a triangle (e.g. $cc = 1112$) to a six-angle ($cc = 1223$). The fact that only 45° and 90° angles occur facilitates a simple and fast computation. Figure 6 shows the complete listing of all 20 shapes along with the corresponding corner codes and the formulas to compute the intersection area.

The concept of the cornercodes is not only a formal means to prove the completeness of our case distinction but also provides an efficient means to implement the area determination. Our algorithm computes the corner code for each of the 4 corners of the event space, concatenates them using arithmetic operations and performs a case analysis between the 20 cases.

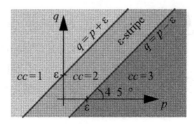

Fig. 8. The ε-stripe

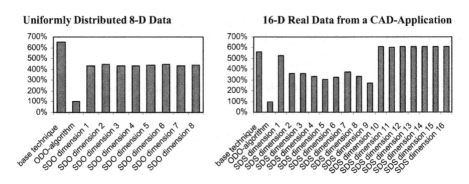

Fig. 9. Experimental Results for MuX: Plain Basic Technique, ODO and Simple DS

2.5   Determining the Optimal Sort Dimension

Our algorithm determines the sort dimension such that the mating probability $W_i[\varepsilon]$ is minimized. Ties are broken by random selection, i.e.

$$d_{\text{sort}} = \text{some}\{d_i | 0 \leq i < d, \quad W_j[\varepsilon] \forall j, 0 \leq j < d\}. \tag{9}$$

Thus, we have an easy way to evaluate the formula for the sort dimension. As $W_i[\varepsilon]$ merely is evaluated for each dimension d_i, thus keeping the current minimum and the corresponding dimension in local variables, the algorithm is linear in the dimensionality d of the data space and independent of all remaining parameters such as the number of points stored in the partitions, the selectivity of the query, etc. Moreover, the formula must be evaluated only once per pair of partitions. This constant (with respect to the capacity of the partition) effort is contrasted by potential savings which are quadratic in the capacity (number of points stored in a partition). The actual savings will be shown in the subsequent section.

3   Experimental Evaluation

In order to show the benefits of our technique we implemented our optimal dimension order on top of several basic similarity join methods and performed an extensive experimental evaluation using artificial and real data sets of varying size and dimensionality. For comparison we tested our algorithm not only against plain basic techniques, but also against a simple version of the dimension-order algorithm which does not calculate the best dimensions for each partition pair, but chooses one dimension which then is used globally for all partition pairs. In the following we will not only observe that our algorithm can improve CPU-efficiency by an important factor, but we will also see that it performs much better than the simple dimension-ordering algorithm – even if this algorithm chooses the best global dimension.

We integrated the ODO-algorithm into two index-based techniques, namely the *Multipage Index Join (MuX)* [8] and the *Z-order-RSJ* which is based on the *R-tree Spatial Join (RSJ)*[9] and employs a page scheduling strategy using Z-ordering. The latter is very similar to the *Breadth-First-R-tree-Join (BFRJ)* proposed in [11]. We also implemented the ODO-algorithm into the recently proposed *Epsilon Grid Order (EGO)* [7] which is a technique operating without preconstructed index.

The Multipage Index (MuX) is an index structure in which each page accommodates a secondary main-memory search structure which effectively improves the CPU performance of the similarity join. We implemented ODO on top of this secondary search structure, i.e. we measured the improvement that ODO brings on top of this secondary search structure. For comparison, we used the original MuX code which also exploited the secondary search structure.

All our experiments were carried out under Windows NT4.0 on Fujitsu-Siemens Celsius 400 machines equipped with a Pentium III 700 MHz processor and 256 MB main memory (128 MB available). The installed disk device was a Seagate ST3 10212A with a sustained transfer rate of about 9 MB/s and an average read access time of 8.9ms with an average latency time of 5.6ms.

Our 8-dimensional synthetic data sets consisted of up to 800,000 uniformly distributed points in the unit hypercube. Our real-world data set is a CAD database with 16-dimensional feature vectors extracted from geometrical parts.

The Euclidean distance was used for the similarity join. We determined the distance parameter ε for each data set such that it is suitable for clustering following the selection criteria proposed in [18] obtaining a reasonable selectivity.

Figure 9 shows our experiments comparing the overall runtime i.e. I/O- and CPU-time for the plain basic technique MuX either to MuX with integrated ODO or integrated simple dimension-order (SDO) for all possible start dimensions. The left diagram shows the results for uniformly distributed 8-dimensional artificial data while the right diagram shows results for 16-dimensional real data from a CAD-application. The database contained 100,000 points in each case. The SDO-algorithm depends heavily on the shape of the page regions i.e on the split algorithm used by the index employed by the basic technique. For uniformly distributed artificial data the loading procedure used by MuX treats all dimensions equally and therefore the results for the simple dimension-ordering algorithm are roughly the same for all start dimensions. ODO performs 6 times faster than plain MuX and 4 times faster than the best SDO while SDO itself is about 1.5 times faster than plain MuX. Note again that our algorithm chooses the most suitable dimension *for each pair of partitions.* Therefore, it is possible that ODO clearly outperforms the simple dimension ordering technique (SDO) even for its best dimension. For our real data set SDO shows varying performance with varying start dimension. We can even observe that for some start dimensions the overhead of SDO outweighs the savings and overall performance degrades slightly compared to the plain basic technique. This shows that it can be disadvantageous to apply dimension-ordering for one fixed start dimension. MuX with integrated ODO is about 5.5 times faster for the real data set than plain MuX while it is still 3 times faster than the SDO with the best performance, however it is more than 6 times faster than SDO with the worst performance.

Figure 10 shows all results for the uniformly distributed artificial data set for varying database size, including the diagram with distance calculations. We can see that the plain MuX performs up to 50 times more distance calculations than with ODO. The diagrams for the real data set are left out due to space restrictions.

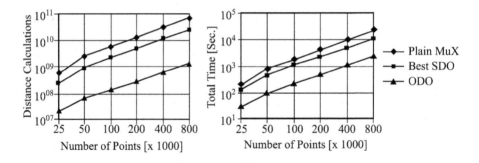

Fig. 10. Experimental Results for MuX: Uniformly Distributed 8-D Data

In order to show that the optimal dimension-ordering algorithm can be implemented on top of other basic techniques as well, we show the results for the *Z-order-RSJ* with uniformly distributed data in figure 11. Z-order-RSJ without ODO is up to 7 times slower than with integrated ODO and performs up to 58 times more distance calculations. The results for *Z-order-RSJ* with real data are shown in figure 12. We can see a speedup factor of 1.5 for SDO vs. plain *Z-order-RSJ* with respect to total time and of 1.8 with respect to distance calculations. ODO performs 3.5 times faster and performs 17 times fewer distance calculations than SDO while it performs 5.5 times faster and up to 25 times less distance calculations than SDO.

EGO was used to demonstrate integration of ODO with a basic technique that does not use a preconstructed index. The results are given in figure 13 where

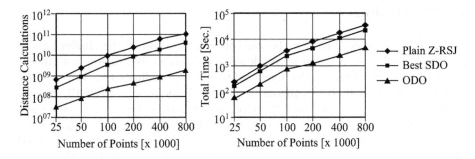

Fig. 11. Experimental Results for Z-RSJ: Uniformly Distributed 8-D Data

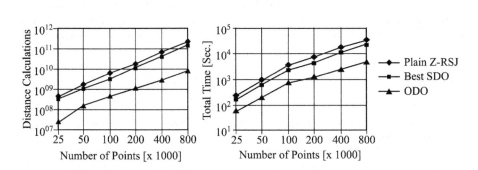

Fig. 12. Experimental Results for Z-RSJ: 16-D Real Data from a CAD-Application

EGO with SDO, as well as plain EGO clearly perform worse than ODO i.e. SDO is about 1.5 times faster than plain EGO, but ODO is twice as fast as SDO and outperforms plain EGO by a factor of 3.5.

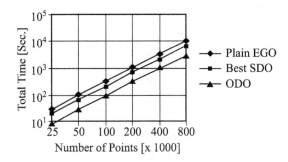

Fig. 13. Experimental Results for EGO (16d CAD data)

4   Conclusions

Many different algorithms for the efficient computation of the similarity join have been proposed in the past. While most well-known techniques concentrate on disk I/O operations, relatively few approaches are dedicated to the reduction of the computational cost, although the similarity join is clearly CPU bound. In this paper, we have proposed the Optimal Dimension Order, a generic technique which can be applied on top of many different basic algorithms for the similarity join to reduce the computational cost. The general idea is to avoid and accelerate the distance calculations between points by sorting the points according to a specific dimension. The most suitable dimension for each pair of pages is carefully chosen by a probability model. Our experimental evaluation shows substantial performance improvements for several basic join algorithms such as the multipage index, the ε-grid-order and the breadth-first-R-tree join.

References

1. Ankerst M., Breunig M.M., Kriegel H.-P., Sander J.: *OPTICS: Ordering Points To Identify the Clustering Structure*, ACM SIGMOD Int. Conf. on Management of Data, 1999.
2. Agrawal R., Lin K., Sawhney H., Shim K.: *Fast Similarity Search in the Presence of Noise, Scaling, and Translation in Time-Series Databases*, Int. Conf. on Very Large Data Bases (VLDB), 1995.
3. Arge L., Procopiuc O., Ramaswamy S., Suel T., Vitter J.S.: *Scalable Sweeping-Based Spatial Join*, Int. Conf. on Very Large Databases (VLDB), 1998.
4. Böhm C., Braunmüller B., Breunig M.M., Kriegel H.-P.: *Fast Clustering Based on High-Dimensional Similarity Joins*, Int. Conf. on Information Knowledge Management (CIKM), 2000.
5. Berchtold S., Böhm C., Jagadish H.V., Kriegel H.-P., Sander J.: *Independent Quantization: An Index Compression Technique for High Dimensional Spaces*, IEEE Int. Conf. on Data Engineering (ICDE), 2000.
6. Berchtold S., Böhm C., Keim D., Kriegel H.-P.: *A Cost Model For Nearest Neighbor Search in High-Dimensional Data Space*, ACM Symposium on Principles of Database Systems (PODS), 1997.
7. Böhm C., Braunmüller B., Krebs F., Kriegel H.-P.: *Epsilon Grid Order: An Algorithm for the Similarity Join on Massive High-Dimensional Data*, ACM SIGMOD Int. Conf. on Management of Data, 2001.
8. Böhm C., Kriegel H.-P.: *A Cost Model und Index Architecture for the Similarity Join*, IEEE Int. Conf. on Data Engineering (ICDE), 2001.
9. Brinkhoff T., Kriegel H.-P., Seeger B.: *Efficient Processing of Spatial Joins Using R-trees*, ACM SIGMOD Int. Conf. on Management of Data, 1993.
10. Brinkhoff T., Kriegel H.-P., Seeger B.: *Parallel Processing of Spatial Joins Sing R-trees*, IEEE Int. Conf. on Data Engineering (ICDE), 1996.
11. Huang Y.-W., Jing N., Rundensteiner E. A.: *Spatial Joins Using R-trees: Breadth-First Traversal with Global Optimizations*, Int. Conf. on Very Large Databases (VLDB), 1997.
12. Koudas N., Sevcik C.: *Size Separation Spatial Join*, ACM SIGMOD Int. Conf. on Managern. of Data, 1997.

13. Koudas N., Sevcik C.: *High Dimensional Similarity Joins: Algorithms and Performance Evaluation*, IEEE Int. Conf. on Data Engineering (ICDE), Best Paper Award, 1998.
14. Lo M.-L., Ravishankar C.V.: *Spatial Joins Using Seeded Trees*, ACM SIGMOD Int. Conf., 1994.
15. Lo M.-L., Ravishankar C.V.: *Spatial Hash Joins*, ACM SIGMOD Int. Conf, 1996.
16. Patel J.M., DeWitt D.J., *Partition Based Spatial-Merge Join*, ACM SIGMOD Int. Conf., 1996.
17. Preparata F.P., Shamos M.I.: 'Computational Geometry', Chapter 5 ('Proximity: Fundamental Algorithms'), Springer Verlag New York, 1985.
18. Sander J., Ester M., Kriegel H.-P., Xu X.: *Density-Based Clustering in Spatial Databases: The Algorithm GDBSCAN and its Applications*, Data Mining and Knowledge Discovery, Vol. 2, No. 2, 1998.
19. Shim K., Srikant R., Agrawal R.: *High-Dimensional Similarity Joins*, Int. Conf. on Data Engineering, 1997.
20. Ullman J.D.: *Database and Knowledge-Base Systems*, Vol. II, Computer Science Press, Rockville MD, 1989

Fast Discovery of Sequential Patterns by Memory Indexing

Ming-Yen Lin and Suh-Yin Lee

Department of Computer Science and Information Engineering
National Chiao Tung University, Taiwan 30050, R.O.C.
{mylin, sylee}@csie.nctu.edu.tw

Abstract. Mining sequential patterns is an important issue for the complexity of temporal pattern discovering from sequences. Current mining approaches either require many times of database scanning or generate several intermediate databases. As databases may fit into the ever-increasing main memory, efficient memory-based discovery of sequential patterns will become possible. In this paper, we propose a memory indexing approach for fast sequential pattern mining, named *MEMISP*. During the whole process, *MEMISP* scans the sequence database only once for reading data sequences into memory. The find-then-index technique recursively finds the items which constitute a frequent sequence and constructs a compact index set which indicates the set of data sequences for further exploration. Through effective index advancing, fewer and shorter data sequences need to be processed in *MEMISP* as the discovered patterns getting longer. Moreover, the maximum size of total memory required, which is independent of minimum support threshold in *MEMISP*, can be estimated. The experiments indicates that *MEMISP* outperforms both *GSP* and *PrefixSpan* algorithms. *MEMISP* also has good linear scalability even with very low minimum support. When the database is too large to fit in memory in a batch, we partition the database, mine patterns in each partition, and validate the true patterns in the second pass of database scanning. Therefore, *MEMISP* may efficiently mine databases of any size, for any minimum support values.

1   Introduction

Sequential pattern mining is a very complicated issue in data mining which aims at discovering frequent sub-sequences in a sequence database. The problem is more difficult than association rule mining because the patterns are formed not only by combinations of items but also by permutations of item-sets. Enormous patterns can be formed as the length of a sequence is not limited and the items in a sequence are not necessarily distinct. For example, given 50 possible items in a sequence database, the number of potential patterns is 50*50+(50*49)/2 regarding two items, and 50*50*50 + 50*[(50*49)/2]*2 + (50*49*48)/(2*3) regarding three items, ..., etc. Owing to the challenge of exponential possible combinations, improving the efficiency of sequential pattern mining has been the focus of recent research in data mining [2, 3, 8, 11, 12].

In general, we may categorize the mining approaches into the generate-and-test framework and the pattern-growth one, for sequence databases of horizontal layout. Typifying the former approaches [2, 6, 10], the *GSP* (**G**eneralized **S**equential **P**attern) algorithm [10] generates potential patterns (called *candidates*), scans each data sequence in the database to compute the frequencies of candidates (called *supports*), and then identifies candidates having sufficient supports as sequential patterns. The

Y. Kambayashi, W. Winiwarter, M. Arikawa (Eds.): DaWaK 2002, LNCS 2454, pp. 150-160, 2002.

sequential patterns in current database pass become seeds for generating candidates in the next pass. This generate-and-test process is repeated until no more new candidates are generated. When candidates cannot fit in memory in a batch, *GSP* re-scans the database to test the remaining candidates that have not been loaded into memory. Consequently, *GSP* scans at least *k* times of the in-disk database if the maximum size of the discovered patterns is *k*, which incurs high cost of disk reading. Despite that *GSP* was good at candidate pruning, the number of candidates is still very huge that might impair the mining efficiency.

The *PrefixSpan* (**Prefix**-projected **S**equential **pattern** mining) algorithm [8], representing the pattern-growth methodology [4, 8], finds the frequent items after scanning the sequence database once. The database is then projected into several smaller databases according to the frequent items. Finally, all sequential patterns are found by recursively growing subsequence fragments in each projected database. Two optimizations for minimizing disk projections were described in [8]. The *bi-level projection* technique, dealing with huge databases, scans each sequence twice in the (projected) database so that fewer and smaller projections are generated. The *pseudo-projection* technique, avoiding physical projections, keeps the sequence-postfix by a pointer-offset for each sequence in the projection. However, according to [8], maximum mining performance can be achieved only when the database size is reduced to the size accommodable by the main memory by employing *pseudo-projection* after using *bi-level* optimization. Although *PrefixSpan* successfully discovered patterns employing the divide-and-conquer strategy, the cost of disk I/O might be high due to the creation and processing of the sub-databases.

Besides the horizontal layout, the sequence database can be transformed into a vertical format consisting of items' id-lists [7, 12]. The id-list of an item is a list of (*sequence-id*, *timestamp*) pairs indicating the occurring timestamps of the item in that *sequence*. Searching in the lattice formed by id-list intersections, the *SPADE* (**S**equential **PA**ttern **D**iscovery using **E**quivalence classes) algorithm [12] completed the mining in three passes of database scanning. Nevertheless, additional computation time is required to transform a database of horizontal layout to vertical format, which also requires additional storage space several times larger than that of the original sequence database.

With rapid cost down and the evidence of the increase in installed memory size, many small or medium sized databases will fit into the main memory. For example, a platform with 256MB memory may hold a database with one million sequences of total size 189MB. Pattern mining performed directly in memory now becomes possible. However, current approaches discover the patterns either through multiple scans of the database or by iterative database projections, thereby requiring abundant disk operations. The mining efficiency could be improved if the excessive disk I/O is reduced by enhancing memory utilization in the discovering process.

Therefore, we propose a memory-indexing approach for fast discovery of sequential patterns, called *MEMISP* (**MEM**ory **I**ndexing for **S**equential **P**attern mining). The features of the *MEMISP* approach lie in no candidate generation, no database projection, and high CPU and memory utilization for sequential pattern mining. *MEMISP* reads data sequences into memory in the first pass, which is the only pass, of database scanning. Through index advancement within an index set comprising pointers and position indices to data sequences, *MEMISP* discovers patterns by a recursive finding-then-indexing technique. The conducted experiments show that *MEMISP* runs faster than both *GSP* and *PrefixSpan* algorithms, even for the database with one million sequences. When the database is too large to fit into the memory, we still can mine patterns efficiently in two database scans by running *MEMISP* with a partition-and-validation technique with discussion in Section 3.3.

The remaining paper is organized as follows. We formulate the problem in Section 2. Section 3 presents the *MEMISP* algorithm. The experimental evaluation is described in Section 4. We discuss the performance factors of *MEMISP* in Section 5. Section 6 concludes the study.

2   Problem Statement

A *sequence s*, denoted by $<e_1e_2...e_n>$, is an ordered set of n elements where each *element* e_i is an itemset. An *itemset*, denoted by $(x_1, x_2,..., x_q)$, is a nonempty set of q items, where each *item* x_j is represented by a literal. Without loss of generality, we assume the items in an element are in lexicographic order. The *size* of sequence s, written as $|s|$, is the total number of items in all the elements in s. Sequence s is a k-*sequence* if $|s| = k$. For example, $<(a)(c)(a)>$, $<(a,c)(a)>$, and $<(c)(a,e)>$ are all 3-sequences. A sequence $s = <e_1e_2...e_n>$ is a *subsequence* of another sequence $s' = <e_1'e_2'...e_m'>$ if there exist $1 \le i_1 < i_2 < ... < i_n \le m$ such that $e_1 \subseteq e_{i_1}'$, $e_2 \subseteq e_{i_2}'$, ..., and $e_n \subseteq e_{i_n}'$. Sequence s' *contains* sequence s if s is a subsequence of s'. For example, $<(b)(a,e)>$ is a subsequence of $<(b,c)(c)(a,c,e)>$.

Each sequence in the sequence database *DB* is referred to as a *data sequence*. The *support* of sequence s, denoted by $s.sup$, is the number of data sequences containing s divided by the total number of data sequences in *DB*. The *minsup* is the user specified minimum support threshold. A sequence s is a *frequent sequence*, or called *sequential pattern*, if $s.sup \ge minsup$. Given the *minsup* and the sequence database *DB*, the problem of sequential pattern mining is to discover *the set of all sequential patterns*.

An example database *DB* having 6 data sequences is listed in the first column in Table 1. Take the data sequence *C6* for instance. It has three elements (i.e. three itemsets), the first having items b and c, the second having item c, and the third having items a, c and e. The support of $<(b)(a)>$ is 4/6 since all the data sequences, except *C2* and *C3*, contain $<(b)(a)>$. The $<(a,d)(a)>$ is a subsequence of both *C1* and *C4*, thus $<(a,d)(a)>.sup = 2/6$. Given $minsup = 50\%$, $<(b)(a)>$ is a sequential pattern while $<(a,d)(a)>$ is not. The set of all sequential patterns is shown in the second column in Table 1.

Table 1. Example sequence database *DB* and the sequential patterns

Sequence	Sequential patterns (*minsup=50%*)
C1=$<(a,d)(b,c)(a,e)>$	$<(a)>$, $<(a)(a)>$, $<(a)(b)>$, $<(a,c)>$, $<(a,c)(a)>$, $<(a,e)>$,
C2=$<(d,g)(c,f)(b,d)>$	$<(b)>$, $<(b)(a)>$, $<(b)(a,e)>$, $<(b)(e)>$, $<(b,c)>$,
C3=$<(a,c)(d)(f)(b)>$	$<(b,c)(a)>$, $<(b,c)(a,e)>$, $<(b,c)(e)>$, $<(b,d)>$,
C4=$<(a,b,c,d)(a)(b)>$	$<(c)>$, $<(c)(a)>$, $<(c)(a,e)>$, $<(c)(b)>$, $<(c)(e)>$,
C5=$<(b,c,d)(a,c,e)(a)>$	$<(d)>$, $<(d)(a)>$, $<(d)(b)>$, $<(d)(c)>$,
C6=$<(b,c)(c)(a,c,e)>$	$<(e)>$

3   MEMISP: Memory Indexing for Sequential Pattern Mining

In this section, the proposed method for sequential pattern mining, named *MEMISP*, is described. *MEMISP* uses a recursive find-then-index strategy to discover all the sequential patterns from in-memory data sequences. The algorithm is illustrated by mining an example database in Section 3.1. Section 3.2 presents the algorithm. The procedure for dealing with extra-large databases beyond memory space is described in Section 3.3.

3.1   Mining Sequential Patterns by *MEMISP*: An Example

Definition (Type-1 pattern, type-2 pattern, stem, P-pat) Given a pattern ρ and a frequent item x in the sequence database *DB*, ρ' is a *type-1 pattern* if it can be formed by appending the itemset (x) as a new element to ρ, and is a *type-2 pattern* by extending the last element of ρ with x. The frequent item x is called the *stem-item* (abbreviated as *stem*) of the sequential pattern ρ' and ρ is the **prefix pattern** (abbreviated as *P-pat*) of ρ'.

For example, given a pattern <(a)> and the frequent item b, we have the *type-1* pattern <(a)(b)> by appending (b) to <(a)> and the *type-2* pattern <(a,b)> by extending <(a)> with b. The <(a)> is the *P-pat* and the b is the *stem* of both <(a)(b)> and <(a,b)>. As to a *type-2* pattern <(c)(a,e)>, its *P-pat* is <(c)(a)> and its *stem* is e. Note that the null sequence, denoted by <>, is the *P-pat* of any frequent 1-sequence.

Example 1: Given *minsup*=50% and the *DB* in Table 1. *MEMISP* mines the patterns by the following steps.

Step 1. Read *DB* into memory and find frequent 1-sequences. The count of every item is accumulated while reading data sequences from *DB* into memory. The in-memory *DB* is referred to as *MDB* hereafter. Hence, we have frequent items a (count=5 for appearing in 5 data sequences *C1, C3, C4, C5, C6*), b (count=6), c (count=6), d (count=5), and e (count=3). All these frequent items are stems of the *type-1* patterns with respect to the *P-pat* = <>. **Loop steps 2 and 3 on each stem to find all the sequential patterns.**

Step 2. Output the sequential pattern ρ formed by current *P-pat* and stem x, and construct the index set ρ-idx. A sequential pattern ρ generated by current *P-pat* and stem x is outputted. Next, a (*ptr_ds*, *pos*) pair for each data sequence *ds* in *MDB* is allocated if and only if *ds* contains x, where *ptr_ds* is a pointer to *ds* and *pos* is the first occurring position of x in *ds*. Index set ρ-idx is the collection of these (*ptr_ds*, *pos*) pairs.

Take stem $x = a$ for instance. Now, the *P-pat* is <>. The *type-1* sequential pattern ρ = **<(a)>** is outputted and the index set **<(a)>-idx** in Fig. 1-(1) is constructed. For instances, the *pos* is 1 for *C1*=<(**a**,d)(b,c)(a,e)> and 4 for *C6*=<(b,c)(c)(**a**,c,e)>.

Step 3. Use index set ρ-idx and *MDB* to find stems with respect to *P-pat* = ρ. We are going to find any sequential pattern having current pattern ρ as its *P-pat*. Now, the *ptr_ds* of each (*ptr_ds*, *pos*) pair in ρ-idx points to a data sequence *ds* which contains ρ. Any item appearing after the *pos* position in *ds* could be a potential stem (with respect to ρ). Thus, for every *ds* existing in ρ-idx, the count of such item (item appearing after the *pos* in *ds*) is increased by one, and then the stems having enough support counts are found.

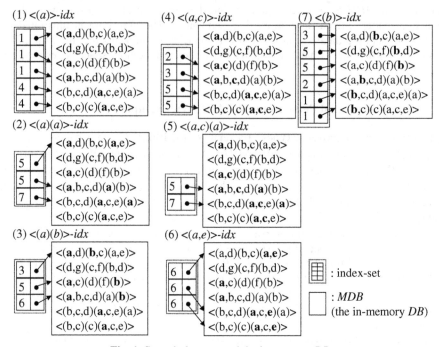

Fig. 1. Some index sets and the in-memory *DB*

We continue with <(a)>-*idx*. The **pos** of the (**ptr_ds, pos**) pointing to *C1* is 1. Only those items occurring after position 1 in *C1* need counting. The count of potential stem *d* (for potential *type-2* pattern <(a,d)>) is increased by one (also potential stem *e* for <(a,e)>). The count of potential stem *b* (also *c*, *a*, and *e*) for potential *type-1* pattern <(a)(b)> (<(a)(c)>, <(a)(a)>, and <(a)(e)>) is increased by one. Analogously, we count items occurring after position 1, 1, 4, 4 for data sequences *C3*, *C4*, *C5*, and *C6*, respectively. After validating the support counts, we obtain stems *a*, *b* of *type-1* patterns and stems *c*, *e* of *type-2* patterns with respect to *P-pat* = <(a)>. Steps 2 and 3 will be recursively applied on stems *a*, *b*, *c*, and *e* with *P-pat* = <(a)>. The mining with *P-pat* = <(a)> and stem *a* is proceeded in the following.

Sequential pattern ρ = <(a)(a)> is generated and outputted by applying step 2. Again, a new (*ptr_ds, pos*) pair for a data sequence *ds* will be inserted into ρ-*idx* (<(a)(a)>-*idx*) if and only if *ds* contains ρ. While constructing <(a)(a)>-*idx*, we simply check the data sequences indicated by current index set, i.e. <(a)>-*idx*, rather than in *MDB*. Assume that a pair (*ptr_ds, pos*) in <(a)>-*idx* points to *ds*. The search for the occurring position of stem **a** (with respect to *P-pat* = <(a)>) starts from position **pos+1** in *ds*. Item *a* occurs at 5 in *C1* and in *C4*, and at 7 in *C5*. No entry is created for *C3* and *C6* since item *a* cannot be found after position 1 and 4, respectively. Hence, we have the new index set <(a)(a)>-*idx* as shown in Fig. 1–(2).

Note that current index set is 'pushed' for later mining before the new index set becomes active.

Applying step 3 with *<(a)(a)>-idx* and *MDB*, no stems can form sequential patterns further. Therefore, we stop this mining and 'pop' the previous index set, i.e. *<(a)>-idx*. The mining goes on with stem *b*. The creation and mining of *<(a)(b)>-idx* outputs pattern **<(a)(b)>** but finds no more patterns. Next, the *<(a,c)>-idx* is constructed. The result of applying step 2 with this index set generates **<(a,c)>** and discovers next stem *a*. Thus, *<(a,c)>-idx* is 'pushed' and we create the *<(a,c)(a)>-idx*.

After the mining with *<(a,c)(a)>-idx*, which stops with nothing found but generates the pattern **<(a,c)(a)>**, the pattern **<(a,e)>** is generated while mining with *<(a,e)>-idx*. All the subsequent find-then-index processes regarding stem *a* with *P-pat* = <> now finish.

By collecting the patterns found in the above process, *MEMISP* efficiently discovers all the sequential patterns.

3.2 The *MEMISP* Algorithm

The central idea of *MEMISP* is to utilize the memory for both data sequences and indices in the mining process. A memory size of 256MB is very common in nowadays computer installation, which can accommodate a sequence database having one million sequences of size 189MB as indicated in our experiments. Processing sequences in-memory is more efficient than disk-based processing, either multiple scans or iterative projections. *MEMISP* scans only one pass over the database, which reads data sequences into memory, in the whole mining process. Starting from sequential patterns of size one, *MEMISP* then discovers all the frequent sequences of larger size recursively by searching the set of data sequences having common sub-sequences. Fig. 2 outlines the proposed *MEMISP* algorithm.

In order to speed up mining by „focused search", we construct a set grouping the data sequences to check. A data sequence *ds* participates in the finding of pattern ρ' only when *ds* contains the *P-pat* (prefix-pattern) ρ of pattern ρ'. Therefore, for each *ds* containing ρ, we create a pointer *ptr_ds* pointing to *ds* in the set for exploring patterns ρ' having *P-pat* ρ. The set is denoted by ρ–*idx*. For each data sequence *ds* pointed in the ρ–*idx*, we associate *ptr_ds* with a position index *pos* indicating where (in *ds*) to find the potential stems.

Take the data sequence *C6*=<(**b,c**)(c)(**a**,c,e)> in memory for instance. We may find <(b)> occurring at position **1**, <(b,c)> occurring at composite position (1, **2**), and <(b,c)(a)> occurring at composite position (1, 2, **4**). Assume that items b, c, and a are frequent. While mining patterns having *P-pat* <(b)>, we include *C6* in the index set with ***pos*=1**, suggesting that only items appearing after position 1 in *C6* should engage in the mining. Similarly, *C6* will be included in the index set for patterns having *P-pat* <(b,c)> with ***pos*=2**, *P-pat* <(b,c)(a)> with ***pos*=4**. As the discovered *P-pat* becomes longer, the index set will contain fewer data sequences to process. Moreover, the number of items in each data sequence remaining to be processed becomes fewer. Through recursive finding-then-indexing, the proposed *MEMISP* algorithm efficiently discovers sequential patterns.

Algorithm *MEMISP*
Input: *DB* = a sequence database; *minsup* = minimum support.
   Output: the set of all sequential patterns.
   Method:
   1. Scan *DB* into *MDB* (the in-memory *DB*), find the set of all frequent items.
   2. For each frequent item *x*,
      (i) form the sequential pattern ρ = <(*x*)> and output ρ.
      (ii) call *IndexSet*(*x*, <>, *MDB*) to construct the index set ρ-*idx*.
      (iii) call *Mine*(ρ, ρ-*idx*) to mine patterns with index set ρ-*idx*.

Subroutine *IndexSet*(*x*, ρ, *range-set*)
Parameters: *x* = a stem-item; ρ = a (*P-pat*) pattern; *range-set* = the set of data sequences for indexing. /* If *range-set* is
      an index set, each data sequence for indexing is pointed by the **ptr_ds** of the (**ptr_ds**, **pos**) entry in the index set */
Output: index set ρ'-*idx*, where ρ' denotes the pattern formed by stem-item *x* and *P-pat* ρ.
   Method:
   1.   For each data sequence *ds* in *range-set*,
      (i) if *range-set* = *MDB* then *start-pos* = 0; otherwise *start-pos* = *pos*.
      (ii) starting from position (*start-pos*+1) in *ds*,
            if the stem-item *x* is first found at position **pos** in *ds*, we insert a (**ptr_ds**, **pos**) pair to the index set ρ'-*idx*,
               where **ptr_ds** points to *ds*.
   2. Return index set ρ'-*idx*.

Subroutine *Mine*(ρ, ρ-*idx*)
Parameter: ρ = a pattern; ρ-*idx* = an index set.
   Method:
   1.   For each data sequence *ds* pointed by the *ptr_ds* of an entry (*ptr_ds*, *pos*) in ρ-*idx*,
      (i) starting from position (*pos*+1) to |*ds*| in *ds*, we increase the support count of each potential stem *x* by one.
   2. Find the set of stems *x* having enough support count to form a sequential pattern.
   3. For each stem *x*,
      (i) form the sequential pattern ρ' with *P-pat* ρ and stem *x*, output ρ'.
      (ii) call *IndexSet*(*x*, ρ, ρ-*idx*) to construct the index set ρ'-*idx*.
   (iii) call *Mine*(ρ', ρ'-*idx*) to mine patterns with index set ρ'-*idx*.

Fig. 2. Algorithm *MEMISP*

3.3 Dealing with Extra-Large Databases

With more and more memory installed, many databases will fit into the main memory
without difficulty. Still, some databases might be too large for the main memory to
accommodate in a batch. In this case, we discover the sequential patterns by a
partition-and-validation technique, as shown in Fig. 3. The extra-large database is
partitioned so that each partition can be handled in memory by *MEMISP*. The set of
potential patterns is obtained by collecting the discovered patterns after running
MEMISP on these partitions. The true patterns can be identified through support
counting against the data sequences with only one extra database pass. Therefore, we
may employ *MEMISP* to mine databases of any size, in two passes of database
scanning.

4   Experimental Results

Several experiments were conducted to assess the performance of the *MEMISP* algorithm. The experiments used an 866 MHz Pentium-III PC with 256MB memory

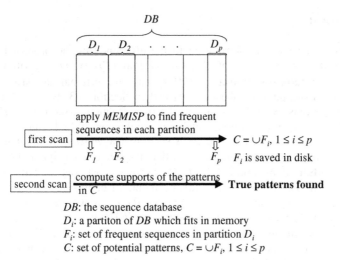

Fig. 3. Partition the database and discover patterns for extra-large databases

running the Windows NT. Like most studies on sequential pattern mining [2, 4, 8, 9, 10, 12], the synthetic datasets for these experiments were generated using the conventional procedure described in [2]. Here, we report the results on dataset C10–T2.5–S4–I1.25 having 100,000 sequences. Readers can refer to [2] for the details of the parameters. Results on other datasets are of similar performance.

The total execution times of sequence mining with various *minsup* values by algorithms *GSP*, *PrefixSpan*, and *MEMISP* using horizontal layout are compared. The *PrefixSpan* was implemented without further optimizations like pseudo-projection or bi-level projection. The *SPADE* algorithm was not implemented in the comparison because additional storage space and computation time are required to transform the database to vertical format. In these experiments, *MEMISP* and *PrefixSpan* are faster than *GSP* for all *minsup* values. *MEMISP* outperforms *PrefixSpan* about 13%~38% for low *minsup*. As shown in Fig. 4, the total execution times of the three algorithms are nearly the same for *minsup* = 2% and 1.5% because only few (less than 200) patterns have enough supports and most patterns are short. However, the performance gaps become clear as *minsup* decreases.

Fig. 5 depicts that *MEMISP* scales up linearly as the number of data sequences increases, from 100K to 1000K. The performance of *MEMISP* is very stable even when *minsup* is very low for large databases, if the database can fit into memory. Given *minsup*=0.25%, *MEMISP* can perform well in processing one million data sequences of total size 189MB with a 256MB main memory in our experiments. Nevertheless, just for the mining of 100K sequences with *minsup* = 0.5%, *GSP* scanned the database 4 times to test the 4.4 million candidates in pass two (more passes to go), and *PrefixSpan* generated sub-databases which amounts to 9.6 times the size of the original database.

5 Discussion

We summarize the factors contributing to the efficiency of the proposed *MEMISP* algorithm by comparing with the well-known *GSP* and *PrefixSpan* algorithms.

- **One pass database scanning.** *MEMISP* reads the original database only once, except for extra-large databases described in Section 3.3. However, *GSP* must read the database at least k times to discover frequent k-sequences. *PrefixSpan* reads one pass over the original database, and then writes and reads once for each projected sub-database. In some cases such as low *minsup*, the total size of sub-databases might be several times larger than the size of the original database.

- **No candidate generation.** *MEMISP* discovers patterns directly from data sequences in-memory by index advancement. In contrast to *GSP*, the time in candidate generation and testing. Moreover, the unknown sized (and often huge) space for candidate storage is unnecessary in *MEMISP*.

- **No database projection.** The pure and simple index advancing in *MEMISP* creates no new databases so that the intermediate storage, which *PrefixSpan* needs, is not needed here.

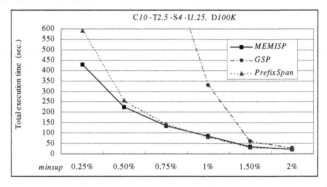

Fig. 4. Total execution times with respect to various *minsup* values

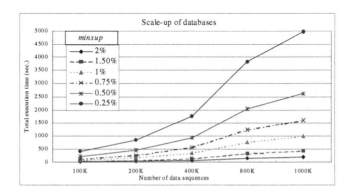

Fig. 5. Linear scalability of *MEMISP*

- **Focused search and effective indexing.** *MEMISP* considers those data sequences indicated by current index set only instead of searching every data sequence in the database. Furthermore, each position index keeps moving forward along a data sequence as the discovered pattern gets longer. Consequently, fewer and fewer items in a data sequence need to be considered as a prefix pattern getting longer.
- **Compact index storage.** In an index set, the maximum number of indices required equals to the number of data sequences, no matter how small the *minsup* value is. Assume that the database has *m* million sequences. In a *4*-byte addressing mode, *MEMISP* demands maximum $(4+4)*m$ MB for an index set. The required total memory would be less than $k*(8*m)$ MB for discovering the frequent *k*-sequences with respect to any *minsup* value. Nevertheless, we can hardly estimate the memory requirement in *GSP* without giving the *minsup*.
- **High CPU and memory utilization.** *PrefixSpan* needs only little memory space during the mining process. It solved the mining problem successfully by sub-database searching, though, with possible CPU idle while projecting sub-databases. *MEMISP*, by contrast, uses all the available memory and maximizes CPU utilization without extra disk operations.

6 Conclusions

Speeding up the discovery of sequential patterns has been the focus of data mining research. In this paper, we present a memory indexing approach for fast discovery of sequential patterns, called *MEMISP*. *MEMISP* mines the set of all sequential patterns without generating candidates or sub-databases. The performance study exhibits that *MEMISP* is more efficient than both *GSP* and *PrefixSpan* algorithms, and has good linear scalability even for very low minimum support. The compact indexing and the effective find-then-index technique together makes *MEMISP* a promising approach for fast discovery of sequential patterns in sequence databases of any size.

In addition to sequential pattern mining, the technique could be extended to the discovery of maximum patterns [1] and constrained/generalized sequential patterns [10], and incremental sequence discovery after database updating [5, 7]. It is also interesting toward integrating the proposed index sets with database systems for efficient queries.

Acknowledgements. The authors thank the reviewers' comments for improving the quality of the paper. This research is supported partially by National Science Council of R.O.C. and the LEE and MTI Center for Networking Research at National Chiao Tung Univ., R.O.C.

References

1. Agarwal, R. C., Aggarwal, C. C., Prasad, V. V. V.: Depth First Generation of Long Patterns. Proce. 6th SIGKDD (2000) 108-118
2. Agrawal, R., Srikant, R.: Mining Sequential Patterns. Proc. 11th ICDE (1995) 3–14

3. Garofalakis, M. N., Rastogi, R., Shim, K.: SPIRIT: Sequential Pattern Mining with Regular Expression Constraints. Proc. 25th VLDB (1999) 223–234
4. Han, J., Pei, J., Mortazavi-Asl, B., Chen, Q., Dayal U., Hsu, M.-C.: FreeSpan: Frequent Pattern-projected Sequential Pattern Mining. Proc. 6th SIGKDD (2000) 355–359
5. Lin, M. Y., Lee, S. Y.: Incremental Update on Sequential Patterns in Large Databases. Proc. 10th ICTAI (1998) 24–31
6. Masseglia, F., Cathala, F., Poncelet, P.: The PSP Approach for Mining Sequential Patterns., Proc. 2nd Euro. Symp. PKDD (1998) 176–184
7. Parthasarathy, S., Zaki, M. J., Ogihara, .M., Dwarkadas, S.: Incremental and Interactive Sequence Mining. Proc. 8th CIKM (1999) 251–258
8. Pei, J., Han, J., Pinto, H., Chen, Q., Dayal, U., Hsu, M.-C.: PrefixSpan: Mining Sequential Patterns Efficiently by Prefix-projected Pattern Growth., Proc. 2001 ICDE (2001) 215–224
9. Shintani, T., Kitsuregawa, M.: Mining Algorithms for Sequential Patterns in Parallel: Hash Based Approach. Proc. 2nd PAKDD (1998) 283–294
10 Srikant, R., Agrawal, R.: Mining Sequential Patterns: Generalizations and Performance Improvements. Proc. 5th EDBT (1996) 3–17
11. Thomas, S., Sarawagi, S.: Mining Generalized Association Rules and Sequential Patterns Using SQL Queries. Proc. 4th SIGKDD (1998) 344–348
12. Zaki, M. J.: SPADE: An Efficient Algorithm for Mining Frequent Sequences. Machine Learning Journal, Vol. 42, No. 1/2, (2001) 31–60

Dynamic Similarity for Fields with NULL Values

Li Zhao[1], Sung Sam Yuan[1], Qi Xiao Yang[2], and Sun Peng[1]

[1] Department of Computer Science, National University of Singapore
3 Science Drive 2, Singapore 117543
{lizhao,ssung,sunpeng1}@comp.nus.edu.sg
[2] Institute of High Performance of Computing
89B Science Park Drive, Singapore 118261
qixy@ihpc.nus.edu.sg

Abstract. One of the most important tasks in data cleansing is to de-duplicate records, which needs to compare records to determine their equivalence. However, existing comparison methods, such as Record Similarity, Equational Theory, implicitly assume that the values in all fields are known, and NULL values are treated as empty strings, which will result in a loss of correct duplicate records. In this paper, we solve this problem by proposing a simple yet efficient method, Dynamic Similarity, which dynamically adjusts the similarity for field with NULL value. Performance results on real and synthetic datasets show that Dynamic Similarity method can achieve more correct duplicate records and without introducing more false positives as compared with Record Similarity. Furthermore, the percentage of correct duplicate records obtained by Dynamic Similarity but not obtained by Record Similarity will increase if the number of fields with NULL values increases.

1 Introduction

Organizations today are confronted with the challenge of handling an ever-increasing amount of data. The data is very likely to be dirty because of misuse of abbreviations, data entry mistake, control information hiding, missing fields, spelling errors, outdated codes etc [9]. Since dirty data will distort information obtained from it because of the 'garbage in, garbage out' principle, data cleansing is very important and necessary.

Data cleansing is critical for many industries over a wide variety of applications [6], including marketing communications, commercial householding, customer matching, merging information systems, medical records etc. It is often studied in association with data warehousing, data mining and database integration, which have received much attention from the database research community in recent years. Especially, data warehousing [2,5] requires and provides extensive support for data cleansing. In [11], data cleansing was identified as one of the database research opportunities for data warehousing into the 21st century.

Y. Kambayashi, W. Winiwarter, M. Arikawa (Eds.): DaWaK 2002, LNCS 2454, pp. 161–169, 2002.

1.1　Related Works

Data cleansing deals with detecting and removing errors and inconsistencies from data in order to improve its quality. One of the most important tasks in data cleansing is to de-duplicate records (detect and remove duplicate records).

Given a dirty database, the standard method to detect exact duplicates is to sort the database and then check if the neighboring records are identical [1]. To detect inexact duplicate records, which are records that refer to the same real world entity while not being syntactically equivalent, the Sorted Neighborhood Method(SNM) was proposed in [4]. SNM first sorts the database on a key and then makes pair-wise comparisons of nearby records by sliding a window over the sorted database. Clustering SNM [4] first partitions the database into independent clusters using a key extracted from the data, then applies SNM to each individual cluster independently. Multi-pass SNM [4] is to execute several independent runs of SNM, each time using a different key and a relatively small window. Duplicate Elimination SNM (DE-SNM) [3] sorts the records on a chosen key and then divides the sorted records into two lists: a duplicate list and a no-duplicate list. The duplicate list contains all records with exact duplicate keys. All the other records are put into the no-duplicate list. A small window scan is first performed on the duplicate list to find the lists of matched and unmatched records. The list of unmatched records is merged with the original no-duplicate list and a second window scan is performed. Priority queue [10] uses a priority queue of sets of records belonging to the last few clusters detected. The algorithm scans the database sequentially and determines whether each record scanned is or is not a member of a cluster represented in a priority queue. Representative records are chosen for each cluster and heuristics need to be developed for choosing the representative records, which will affect the results greatly.

As the above cleansing method determine which records need to be compared, comparison methods perform the actual comparison on records to determine their equivalence. Hence the comparison methods are essential in detecting duplicate records.

Equational Theory was proposed in [4] to compare records. The approach uses a declarative rule language to specify an equational theory. The following is a simplified rule that exemplifies one axiom of equational theory:

> Given two records, r1 and r2.
> IF the last name of r1 equals the last name of r2,
> 　　AND the first names differ slightly,
> 　　AND the address of r1 equals the address of r2
> THEN
> 　　r1 is equivalent to r2.

The implementation of "differ slightly" specified here is based upon the computation of a distance function applied to the first name fields of two records, and the comparison of its results to a threshold to capture obvious typographical errors that may occur in the data. The selection of a distance function and proper threshold is a knowledge intensive activity that demands experimental evaluation. An improperly chosen threshold will lead to either an increase in the number of false positives (non-duplicate records that are falsely detected as duplicate) or to a decrease in the number of correct duplicate records.

Record Similarity (RS) was introduced in [8]. It compares two records to determine their degree of similarity. Two records are treated as a duplicate pair if their Record Similarity exceeds a certain threshold. Section 2 gives its description in details and our discussion will largely base on it.

Smith-Waterman algorithm [12] was employed in [10] to compare records. The Smith-Waterman was originally developed for finding evolutionary relationships between biological protein and DNA sequences.

1.2   Our Approach

The comparison methods prove to have good performances in capturing duplicate records. However, they all have a common drawback, that is, they implicitly assume that the values in all fields are known, and NULL values on fields are simply treated as empty strings. However, in practice, databases to be cleansed very likely have records with NULL values. Treating the NULL values as empty strings is definitely not a good method and will result in a loss of correct duplicate records. Table 1 gives an example showing that while treating NULL values as empty strings in Record Similarity, a correct duplicate pair is lost. More analysis on the table is in Section 3. Thus, the fields with NULL values need to be specially treated. In this paper, we propose a simple yet efficient method, called *Dynamic Similarity*, which solves the "NULL field problem" by dynamically adjusting the similarity for field with NULL value. For each field, there are a set of dependent fields associated with it. For any field with NULL value, the dependent fields will be used to determine its similarity.

To test our method, we compare it with Record Similarity. The performance result shows that Dynamic Similarity can get more correct duplicate records and does not introduce new false positives as compared with Record Similarity.

The rest of the paper is organized as follows. In next section, we introduce the Record Similarity method. In Section 3, we then propose the Dynamic Similarity. We give the performance results in Section 4 and conclude in Section 5.

2   Record Similarity

In this section, we introduce Record Similarity, on which Dynamic Similarity is based, in details.

Record Similarity is proposed in [8] and it is an efficient method to compare two records to determine their degree of similarity. In order to calculate the degree of similarity between two records, it is crucial to know that the importance of each field. Therefore, *field weightage* is introduced. The field weightage of each field has to be provided by users and the sum of all field weightages should equal to 1.

Each Field is identified as tokens by using a set of delimiters such as space and punctuations. The process of computing the similarity between two records begins with comparing the sorted tokens of the corresponding fields. The tokens are compared using exact string matching, single-error matching and abbreviation matching. Based on the field token comparison results, the similarity between the entire fields is computed. Finally, the Record Similarity can be computed from the field similarity and the field weightage.

Tokens comparison: When comparing tokens to calculate the degree of similarity, if two tokens are an exact match, they will have a degree of similarity of 1. Otherwise, if there is a total of x characters in the token, then $\frac{1}{x}$ is deducted from the maximum degree of similarity of 1 for each character that is not found in the other token. For any two tokens x_1 and x_2, $DoS_{(x_1,x_2)}$ is used to denote the degree of similarity of comparing x_1 with x_2. For example, if comparing tokens "cat" and "late", then $DoS_{(cat,late)} = 1 - 1/3 = 0.67$ since the character c in "cat" is not found in "late" and $DoS_{(late,cat)} = 1 - 2/4 = 0.5$ since the characters l and e are not found in "cat".

Field Similarity: Suppose a field F in record X has tokens $t_{x_1}, t_{x_2}, \cdots, t_{x_n}$ and the corresponding field in record Y has tokens $t_{y_1}, t_{y_2}, \cdots, t_{y_m}$. For token t_{x_1}, it is compared with tokens $t_{y_j}, 1 \leq j \leq m$. Let $DoS_{x_1} = max\{DoS_{(t_{x_1},t_{y_1})}, \cdots, DoS_{(t_{x_1},t_{y_m})}\}$. Similarly, we get $DoS_{x_2}, \cdots, DoS_{x_n}, DoS_{y_1}, DoS_{y_2}, \cdots, DoS_{y_m}$. Then the field similarity for record X and record Y is given as

$$Sim_F^{RS}(X,Y) = \frac{\sum_{i=1}^n DoS_{x_i} + \sum_{i=1}^m DoS_{y_i}}{n+m}.$$

Record Similarity: Suppose a database has fields $F_1, F_2, \cdots, F_n$ with field weightages $W_1, W_2, \cdots, W_n$ respectively, where $\sum_{i=1}^n W_i = 1$. Given two records X and Y, let $Sim_{F_1}^{RS}(X,Y), Sim_{F_2}^{RS}(X,Y), \cdots, Sim_{F_n}^{RS}(X,Y)$ be the field similarities computed. Then the Record Similarity for record X and record Y is given as

$$Sim^{RS}(X,Y) = \sum_{i=1}^n (Sim_{F_i}^{RS}(X,Y) \times W_i).$$

Obviously, for any record X and record Y, we have $0 \leq Sim^{RS}(X,Y) \leq 1$. Two records are treated as a duplicate pair if their similarity exceeds a certain threshold such as 0.8. The threshold is a knowledge intensive activity and demands experimental evaluation.

3   Dynamic Similarity

In this section, we propose the *Dynamic Similarity*, which is based on the Record Similarity.

Suppose that a database has fields $F_1, F_2, \cdots, F_n$ with field weightages $W_1, W_2, \cdots, W_n$ respectively. Let $\mathcal{F} = \{F_1, F_2, \cdots, F_n\}$. Given two records X and Y, let X_{F_1} and Y_{F_1} be the values of field F_1 of X and Y respectively. The fields $F_2, \cdots, F_n$ are similarly defined.

Intuitively, for field with NULL value, there could be some fields that affect its similarity. These fields are called *dependent fields*. Furthermore, for each field, its dependent fields may have different importance. Thus weightages are assigned to dependent fields. To distinguish from the field weightages defined previously, these weightages are called *dependent weightages*. A formal definition is given as follows.

Definition 1. *Formally, a weighted dependent function on $\mathcal{F}$ is a function Φ: $\mathcal{F} \mapsto 2^{\mathcal{F} \times [0,1]}$ such that, $\forall F_i \in \mathcal{F}$,*

$$- \ \forall (F_j, v_j) \in \Phi(F_i) \Rightarrow F_j \neq F_i;$$
$$- \ \sum_{(F_j, v_j) \in \Phi(F_i)} v_j = 1.$$

The weighted dependent function defines a dependent relation on fields. It may not be symmetric, i.e., $(F_j, -) \in \Phi(F_i)$ does not imply $(F_i, -) \in \Phi(F_j)$. For example, the same value in "name" field in two records imply the "age" field in the two records having the same value with large chance. However, the reverse could not be true. The dependent relation is highly domain dependent and need experimental tests to decide. Experts on the database to be cleansed will lead to a better dependent relation.

One special case of weighted dependent function is that all dependent fields have the same weightage. For simplicity, we call the special case as *dependent function*, which can be formally defined as follows with equal weightage.

Definition 2. *Formally, a dependent function on $\mathcal{F}$ is a function Φ: $\mathcal{F} \mapsto 2^{\mathcal{F}}$ such that $\forall F_i \in \mathcal{F}, F_i \notin \Phi(F_i)$.*

One simple and commonly used dependent function is: $\Phi(F_i) = \mathcal{F} - \{F_i\}$, that is, each field depends on all the other fields. Generally, this function works well. For some databases, a careful defined weighted dependent function may improve the performance in getting correct duplicate records.

With the weighted dependent function or dependent function, we can then compute the similarity for records with NULL values. Similar to Record Similarity, each field is identified as tokens by using a set of delimiters and tokens comparison is also the same. The difference is on how to compute the similarity for field with NULL value. In Record Similarity, similarity for NULL values is 0, while in Dynamic Similarity, similarity for NULL values is dynamically adjusted with its dependent fields and dependent weightages.

Field Similarity: Given a field F and two records X and Y, If $X_F \neq NULL \wedge Y_F \neq NULL$, then $Sim_F^{DS}(X,Y) = Sim_F^{RS}(X,Y)$. Otherwise, if Φ is a weighted dependent function, let

$$F' = \{(F_i, v_i) | (F_i, v_i) \in \Phi(F) \wedge X_{F_i} \neq NULL \wedge Y_{F_i} \neq NULL\}.$$

We have

$$Sim_F^{DS}(X,Y) = \sum_{(F_i, v_i) \in F'} (Sim_{F_i}^{DS}(X,Y) \times v_i) \tag{1}$$

If Φ is dependent function, i.e., $v_i = \frac{1}{|\Phi(F)|}$, then Formula (1) can be written as

$$Sim_F^{DS}(X,Y) = \frac{\sum_{(F_i, v_i) \in F'} Sim_{F_i}^{DS}(X,Y)}{|\Phi(F)|} \tag{2}$$

The field similarity is computed as follows. If the fields in two records are NOT NULL, we use the same method in Record Similarity to compute the field similarity. Otherwise, we compute it dynamically. In this case, the field

Table 1. Correct duplicate records obtained in Dynamic Similarity but missed in Record Similarity

	Code	Name	1st Addr.	2nd Addr.	Currency	Tel	Fax
X		JVC Elec.	79 AYE road	Ayer rajah ind., SG 139890	USD	7764711	
Y	JVC	JVC Elec.		Ayer rajah ind., SG 139890	USD	7764711	

similarity is computed from all the dependent fields with NOT NULL values, and the dependent weightages in these fields also affect the similarity.

We have defined the (weighted) dependent function and shown how to use it to compute the similarity for NULL field. The idea behind it is from Functional Dependency (FD). Given a clean database and an FD $\mathcal{F}_1 \to \mathcal{F}_2$, where $\mathcal{F}_1 \subseteq \mathcal{F}$ and $\mathcal{F}_2 \subseteq \mathcal{F}$. For any records X and Y, if $X.\mathcal{F}_1 = Y.\mathcal{F}_1$, we have $X.\mathcal{F}_2 = Y.\mathcal{F}_2$, where $X.\mathcal{F}_1$ denotes the projection of record X onto the fields in $\mathcal{F}_1$. That is, the FD $\mathcal{F}_1 \to \mathcal{F}_2$ says that if two records agree on the values in fields $\mathcal{F}_1$, they must also agree on the values in fields $\mathcal{F}_2$. Thus, for a clean database, from FDs, we can determine the values of some fields from the values of some other fields. However, in this paper, our discussion is on dirty databases and the values in some fields are likely having errors or missing. Therefore, we propose the (weighted) dependent function and field similarity, which says that if all fields in $\Phi(F_i)$ have large similarities, the similarity of F_i is to be large. From Formula (1), we can see that if $\forall F_j \in \Phi(F_i)$, $Sim_{F_j}(X,Y) = 1$, then $Sim_{F_i}(X,Y) = 1$. That is, if $X.\Phi(F_i) = Y.\Phi(F_i)$, then $X.\{F_i\} = Y.\{F_i\}$. Thus (weighted) dependent function and field similarity are an extension of FDs with similarity.

When the similarities of all fields are computed, the Dynamic Similarity of records is obtained by:

$$Sim^{DS}(X,Y) = \sum_{i=1}^{n}(Sim_{F_i}^{DS}(X,Y) \times W_i) \tag{3}$$

Obviously, we have $0 \leq Sim^{DS}(X,Y) \leq 1$.

We adopt Record Similarity as the base of Dynamic Similarity because Record Similarity is an efficient comparison method. However, Dynamic Similarity can be extended to any other similarity-based comparison methods easily.

We have shown the method to compute the Dynamic Similarity, which can well deal with the fields with NULL values. Table 1 gives an example, which shows that correct duplicate records are obtained in Dynamic Similarity but missed in Record Similarity. The records are from a real database which is used in the performance study. Some fields' values are shortened to fit in one line. The field weightages are 0.05, 0.3, 0.15, 0.25, 0.05, 0.1, 0.1 respectively and the threshold is 0.73. These values are obtained by experimental tests on the database. In Dynamic Similarity, we use $\Phi(F) = \mathcal{F} - \{F\}$ as the dependent function.

In Table 1, the record X and record Y are duplicate and each has fields with NULL values. The similarity computed by Record Similarity is 0.7, which is less than the threshold 0.73. Thus they are missed by Record

Table 2. False positives obtained if treating two NULL values as equal

Code	Name	1st addr.	2nd addr.	Currency	Tel	Fax
OMNI	Omni Elec.		#07-01/03, woodlands ave 5, SG	SGD		
OMNI-LD	Omni Elec.		lower delta road, #01-12/16, SG	SGD		

Similarity. However, with Dynamic Similarity, we have $Sim^{DS}_{Name}(X,Y) = Sim^{DS}_{2nd}(X,Y) = Sim^{DS}_{Cur}(X,Y) = Sim^{DS}_{Tel}(X,Y) = 1.0$. Form Formula (2), we have $Sim^{DS}_{Code}(X,Y) = 4/6 = 0.67$. Similarly, we have $Sim^{DS}_{1st}(X,Y) = Sim^{DS}_{Fax}(X,Y) = 0.67$. Thus from Formula (3), we have $Sim^{DS}(X,Y) = 0.9 > 0.73$. Then they are correctly obtained as duplicate records. An alternative solution is to decrease the threshold. For example, if the threshold is decreased to 0.7 for the above example, the two records can also be detected as duplicate by Record Similarity. However, this is far from a good solution since decreasing threshold obtained by experimental tests will largely increase the number of false positives. Another alternative solution is to treat two NULL values as equal, that is, $Sim_F(NULL, NULL) = 1$. Then the two records in Table 1 have similarity of 0.8 > 0.73. They are obtained as duplicate records. However, treating two fields with NULL values as equal will also increase the number of false positives. Table 2 gives such an example. In Table 2, the two records are non-duplicate and each has fields with NULL values. If two fields with NULL values are treated as equal, then the similarity computed by Record Similarity is 0.84, which is larger than the threshold 0.73. Thus they will be falsely obtained as duplicate with Record Similarity. With Dynamic Similarity, the similarity is 0.67 < 0.73. They can be correctly detected as non-duplicate with Dynamic Similarity.

4   Experimental Results

4.1   Databases

We test the performance on a real database, named company; and four synthetic databases, customers.

We get the company database from the authors of [7]. The company database has 856 records and each record has 7 fields: company code, company name, first address, second address, currency used, telephone number and fax number.

We generate the customers as follows. We first generate a clean database with 100000 records. Each record consists of 8 fields: name, gender, marital status, race, nation, education, phone and occupation. Then we add additional 50000 duplicate records into the clean database. The changes in duplicate records range from small typographical difference in some fields to loss of values in some fields (NULL values). Basing on how many fields with NULL values, we generate four databases, customer-0, customer-1, customer-2 and customer-3, with average 0, 1, 2 and 3 fields with NULL values respectively.

4.2   Platform

The databases are stored as relational table in Microsoft SQL server 7.0, which runs on windows 2000. The experiments on the databases are performed on a 500 MHz Pentium II machine with 256 MB of memory. The SQL server was connected with ODBC.

4.3   Performance

We compare the performance of Record Similarity and Dynamic Similarity on the company database and the customer databases. The performance result is shown in Table 3. The cleansing method we used is SNM and all results are obtained at the window size of 10. In Table 3, The "C" column under each method is the correct duplicate records obtained by that method. The "F. P." column under each method is the false positives obtained by that method. C_{DS} and C_{RS} denote the correct duplicate records obtained by Dynamic Similarity and Record Similarity respectively.

Table 3. Duplicate pairs obtained by Record Similarity and Dynamic Similarity

Database	Record Similarity			Dynamic Similarity			$C_{DS} - C_{RS}$
	Total	C	F. P.	Total	C	F. P.	
company	52	51	1	57	56	1	5
customer-0	62192	62155	37	62192	62155	37	0
customer-1	61918	61881	37	62145	62118	37	237
customer-2	60630	60593	37	61940	61903	37	1310
customer-3	56732	56685	37	61389	61352	37	4667

The results from all databases clearly show that Dynamic Similarity can obtain more correct duplicate records and does not introduce more false positives as compared with Record Similarity. For instance, in the company database, Record Similarity gets 51 correct duplicate records and introduces 1 false positive, while Dynamic Similarity gets 56 correct duplicate records and also introduces 1 false positive. There is 5 correct duplicate records increased. Furthermore, the results on customers show that when the average number of NULL fields increases, the Dynamic Similarity can get more correct duplicate records than Record Similarity dose. As we can see, in customer-1, Dynamic Similarity get 237 more correct duplicate records, while in customer-3, Dynamic Similarity get 4667 more correct duplicate records.

5   Conclusion

Existing comparison methods, such as Record Similarity, do not address the field with NULL value well, which lead to a decrease in the number of correct duplicate records. In this paper, we propose a simple yet efficient comparison method,

Dynamic Similarity, which deals with fields with NULL values. Performance results on real and synthetic datasets show that Dynamic Similarity can get more correct duplicate records and does not introduce more false positives as compared with Record Similarity. Furthermore, the percentage of correct duplicate records obtained by Dynamic Similarity but not obtained by Record Similarity will increase if the number of fields with NULL values increases.

References

1. D. Bitton and D. J. DeWitt. Duplicate record elimination in large data files. *ACM Transactions on Database Systems*, pages 8(2):255–265, 1983.
2. S. Chaudhuri and U. Dayal. An overview of data warehousing and olap technology. In *ACM SIGMOD Record*, page 26 (1), 1997.
3. M. Hernandez. A generalization of band joins and the merge/purge problem. Technical Report CUCS-005-1995, Columbia University, February 1996.
4. M. Hernandez and S. Stolfo. The merge/purge problem for large databases. In *Proceedings of the ACM SIGMOD International Conference on Managemnet of Data*, pages 127–138, May 1995.
5. M. L. Jarke, M. Vassiliou, and P. Vassiliadis. *Fundamentals of data warehouses*. Springer, 2000.
6. R. Kimball. Dealing with dirty data. *DBMS online*, September 1996. Available from `http://www.dbmsmag.com/9609d14.html`.
7. M. L. Lee, T. W. Ling, and W. L. Low. Intelliclean: A knowledge-based intelligent data cleaner. In *Proceedings of the sixth ACM SIGKDD international conference on Knowledge discovery and data mining*, pages 290–294, 2000.
8. M. L. Lee, H. J. Lu, T. W. Ling, and Y. T. Ko. Cleansing data for mining and warehousing. In *Proceedings of the 10th International Conference on Database and Expert Systems Applications (DEXA)*, pages 751–760, 1999.
9. Infoshare Limited. Best value guide to data standardizing. *InfoDB*, July 1998. Available from `http://www.infoshare.ltd.uk`.
10. A. E. Monge and C. P. Elkan. An efficient domain-independent algorithm for detecting approximately duplicate database records. In *Proceeding of the ACM-SIGMOD Workshop on Research Issues on Knowledge Discovery and Data Mining*, Tucson, AZ, 1997.
11. A. Silberschatz, M. StoneBraker, and J. Ullman. Database research: Achievements and opportunities into the 21st century. In *SIGMOD Record (ACM Special Interest Group on Management of Data)*, page 25(1):52, 1996.
12. T. F. Smith and M. S. Waterman. Identification of common molecular subsequences. *Journal of Molecular Biology*, pages 147:195–197, 1981.

Outlier Detection Using Replicator Neural Networks

Simon Hawkins, Hongxing He, Graham Williams, and Rohan Baxter

CSIRO Mathematical and Information Sciences
GPO Box 664, Canberra ACT 2601, Australia
`Firstname.Lastname@csiro.au`

Abstract. We consider the problem of finding outliers in large multi-variate databases. Outlier detection can be applied during the data cleansing process of data mining to identify problems with the data itself, and to fraud detection where groups of outliers are often of particular interest. We use replicator neural networks (RNNs) to provide a measure of the outlyingness of data records. The performance of the RNNs is assessed using a ranked score measure. The effectiveness of the RNNs for outlier detection is demonstrated on two publicly available databases.

1 Introduction

Outlier detection algorithms have application in several tasks within data mining. Data cleansing requires that aberrant data items be identified and dealt with appropriately. For example, outliers are removed or considered separately in regression modelling to improve accuracy. Detected outliers are candidates for aberrant data. In many applications outliers are more interesting than inliers. Fraud detection is a classic example where attention focuses on the outliers because these are more likely to represent cases of fraud. Fraud detection in insurance, banking and telecommunications are major application areas for data mining. Detected outliers can indicate individuals or groups of customers that have behaviour outside the range of what is considered 'normal' [8,6,21].

Studies from the field of statistics have typically considered outliers to be residuals or deviations from a regression or density model of the data:

An outlier is an observation that deviates so much from other observations as to arouse suspicion that it was generated by a different mechanism [9].

In this paper we employ multi-layer perceptron neural networks with three hidden layers, and the same number of output neurons and input neurons, to model the data. These neural networks are known as replicator neural networks (RNNs). In the RNN model the input variables are *also* the output variables so that the RNN forms an implicit, compressed model of the data during training. A measure of outlyingness of individuals is then developed as the reconstruction error of individual data points. The RNN approach has linear analogues in Principal Components Analysis [10].

Y. Kambayashi, W. Winiwarter, M. Arikawa (Eds.): DaWaK 2002, LNCS 2454, pp. 170–180, 2002.

The insight exploited in this paper is that the trained neural network will reconstruct some small number of individuals poorly and these can be considered as outliers. We measure outlyingness by ranking data according to the magnitude of the reconstruction error. This compares to SmartSifter [22] which similarly builds models to identify outliers but scores the individuals depending on the degree to which they perturb the model.

Following [22], [4] and [17] when dealing with large databases, we consider it more meaningful to assign each datum an *outlyingness score*. The continuous score reflects the fuzzy nature of outlyingness and also allows the investigation of outliers to be automatically prioritised for analysis.

2   Related Work

We classify outlier detection methods as either *distribution-based* or *distance-based*. However, a probabilistic interpretation can often be placed on the distance-based approaches and so the two categories can overlap. Other classifications of outlier detection methods are based on whether the method provides an outlyingness score or a binary predicate (which may also be based on a score), or whether the method measures outlyingness from the *bulk* (i.e., a convex hull) of the data, or from a regression surface. Distribution-based methods include mixture models such as SmartSifter [22]. Individuals are scored according to the degree to which they perturb the currently learnt model. Distance-based methods use distance metrics such as Mahalanobis distance [2,15] or Euclidean distance [11,13,12]. A prominent and useful technique for detecting outliers is to use a clustering algorithm, such as CURE or BIRCH, and then designate data occurring in very small clusters, or data distant from existing clusters as outliers [16,21,7,23,14]. Visualisation methods [3], based on grand tour projections, can also be considered distance-based since the distance between points is projected onto a 2-dimensional plane. Visualisations using immersive virtual environments [20] similarly explore the space for outliers allowing users to identify and view outliers in multiple dimensions. Despite the obvious issues of subjectiveness and scaling, visualisation techniques are very useful in outlier detection. Readily available visualisation tools such as *xgobi* [18] provide an effective, efficient, and interactive initial exploration of outliers in data (or necessarily a sample of the data). We are aware of only one other previous neural network method approach to detecting outliers [19]. Sykacek's neural network approach is to use a multi-layer perceptron (MLP) as a regression model and to then treat outliers as data with residuals outside the error bars.

3   Replicator Neural Network Outlier Detection

Although several applications in image and speech processing have used the Replicator Neural Network for its data compression capabilities [1,10], we believe the current study is the first to propose its use as a outlier detection tool.

As mentioned in Section 1, the RNN is a variation on the usual regression model. Normally, input vectors are mapped to desired output vectors in multi-layer perceptron neural networks. For the RNN, however, the input vectors are also used as the output vectors; the RNN attempts to reproduce the input patterns in the output. During training, the weights of the RNN are adjusted to minimise the mean square error (or mean reconstruction error) for all training patterns. As a consequence, common patterns are more likely to be well reproduced by the trained RNN so that those patterns representing outliers will be less well reproduced by a trained RNN and will have a higher reconstruction error. The reconstruction error is used as the measure of outlyingness of a datum.

3.1 RNN

The RNN we use is a feed-forward multi-layer perceptron with three hidden layers sandwiched between an input layer and an output layer. The function of the RNN is to reproduce the input data pattern at the output layer with error minimised through training. Both input and output layers have n units, corresponding to the n features of the training data. The number of units in the three hidden layers are chosen experimentally to minimise the average reconstruction error across all training patterns. Heuristics for making this choice are discussed later in this section. Figure 1 shows a schematic view of the fully connected Replicator Neural Network. The output of unit i of layer k is calculated by the

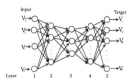

Fig. 1. A schematic view of a fully connected Replicator Neural Network.

activation function $S_k(I_{ki})$, where I_{ki}, denoted generically as θ, is the weighted sum of the inputs to the unit and defined as:

$$\theta = I_{ki} = \sum_{j=0}^{L_{k-1}} w_{kij} Z_{(k-1)j} \tag{1}$$

Z_{kj} is the output from the jth unit of the kth layer. L_k is the number of units in the kth layer.

The activation function for the two outer hidden layers ($k = 2, 4$) is then:

$$S_k(\theta) = \tanh(a_k\theta) \qquad k = 2, 4 \tag{2}$$

where a_k is a tuning parameter which is set to 1 for our experiments. For the middle hidden layer ($k = 3$), the activation function is staircase like with parameter N as the number of steps or activation levels and a_3 controlling the transition rate from one level to the next:

$$S_3(\theta) = \frac{1}{2} + \frac{1}{2(k-1)} \sum_{j=1}^{N-1} tanh[a_3(\theta - \frac{j}{N})] \qquad (3)$$

With a_3 set to a large value (we use $a_3 = 100$ throughout this work) and $N = 4$ the resulting activation function is shown in Figure 2. The activation levels of the hidden units are thus quantised into N discrete values: $0, \frac{1}{N-1}, \frac{2}{N-1}, \ldots 1$. The step-wise activation function used for the middle hidden layer divides the

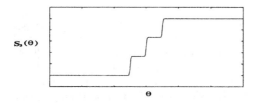

$S_r(\theta)$

θ

Fig. 2. Activation function of the units in the middle hidden layer.

continuously distributed data points into a number of discrete valued vectors. Through this mechanism data compression is achieved. The same architecture is adopted in this work for outlier detection. The mapping to the discrete categories in the middle hidden layer naturally places the data points into a number of clusters. The outliers identified by the RNN can be analysed further to identify individual outliers and small clusters. We discuss this further in later sections.

Training the RNN. We choose one of two candidate functions as the activation function for the output layer. The first is linear and is the weighted sum of the inputs using the formula in Equation 1, so that $S_5(\theta) = \theta$. The second is the Sigmoid function:

$$S_5(\theta) = \frac{1}{1 + e^{-a_5\theta}} \qquad (4)$$

We use an adaptive learning rate for training the neural network at each iteration level, l . The weights in the neural network are updated using:

$$w_{ij}^{l+1} = w_{ij}^l + \alpha_{l+1} \Delta w_{ij}^{l+1} \qquad (5)$$

The new learning rate at iteration $l + 1$, α_{l+1} is given by:

$$\alpha_{l+1} = \begin{cases} \beta_r * \alpha_l \text{ if } e_{l+1} > 1.01 * e_l \quad \text{(undo weight update)} \\ \beta_e * \alpha_l \text{ if } e_{l+1} < e_l \text{ and } \alpha_l < \alpha_{max} \\ \alpha_l \qquad \text{otherwise} \end{cases} \qquad (6)$$

Where e_l in equation 6 refers to the mean square error.

$$e_l = \frac{1}{mn} \sum_{i=1}^{M} \sum_{j=1}^{n} (x_{ij} - o_{ij}^l)^2 \tag{7}$$

In Equation 7, m is the number of records in the training set, n is the number of features, and x_{ij} is the input value and is also the targeted output value $(i = 1, 2, \ldots, m, j = 1, 2, \ldots, n)$ and o_{ij}^l is the value of the output from the RNN for the lth iteration. The Initial Learning Rate, α_0, the Maximum Learning Rate, α_{max}, the Learning Rate Enlargement Factor, β_e, and the Learning Rate Reduction Factor, β_r, are adjustable parameters.

In our experiment of Section 4, we use the fixed settings shown in Table 1. . For convergence some data sets require adjustment to the training parameters

Table 1. Parameter values used for updating the learning rate.

α_0	Initial Learning Rate	0.0001
α_{max}	Maximum Learning Rate	0.02
β_e	Learning Rate Enlargement Factor	1.005
β_r	Learning Rate Reduction Factor	0.98

and the number of units in the RNN architecture. Furthermore, in the experiments to be discussed in Section 4 we use different numbers of hidden units for different data sets, ranging over 15, 35, 40, and 45. Increasing the number of hidden units increases training time but convergence is more likely. The success of training is evaluated by the average reconstruction error. It is not very sensitive to most parameters, a few experiment may be needed in choosing the values of a couple of parameters to guarantee the convergence of the error.

3.2   Methodology for Applying RNN to Outlier Detection

We now describe the measure of outlyingness, the treatment of categorical variables, and the sampling scheme for large data sets.

Outlier Factor (OF). We define the *Outlier Factor* of the ith data record OF_i as our measure of outlyingness. OF_i is defined by the average reconstruction error over all features (variables)

$$OF_i = \frac{1}{n} \sum_{j=1}^{n} (x_{ij} - o_{ij})^2 \tag{8}$$

where n is the number of features. The OF is evaluated for all data records using the trained RNN.

Categorical Variables. For datasets with categorical variables, we split the dataset into a number of subsets, each corresponding to a set of particular values of the categorical variables. For example, if we have two categorical variables each with two categories, we split the data set into four disjoint subsets each corresponding to the unique combination of values of the two categorical variables. We then train an RNN for each subset individually. This is not an optimal way of treating categorical variables and a better method is being developed.

Sampling and Training. For each subset C_i, we sample a portion of data either randomly or by selecting every nth record to train the RNN.

Applying the Trained RNN. The trained RNN is used to calculate OF_i for all data points.

4   Experimental Results

We demonstrate the effectiveness of the RNN as an outlier detector on three data sets.

4.1   Network Intrusion Detection

We apply the RNN approach to the 1999 KDD Cup network intrusion detection data set [5]. Each event in the original data set of nearly 5 million events is labelled as an intrusion or not an intrusion. This class label is not included when training the RNN but is used to assess the RNN's performance in identifying intrusions. In summary we show that RNN outlier detection over the network intrusion data effectively identifies those events that are intrusions.

We follow the experimental technique employed in [22]. There are 41 attributes in the 1999 KDD Cup data set. There are 34 numerical variables and 7 categorical variables. The categorical variable *attack* originally had 22 distinct values (*normal, back, buffer_overflow* etc.). We map these 22 distinct values to a binary categorical variable by mapping all values, except *normal*, to *attack*. We use four of the 41 original attributes (*service, duration, src_bytes, dst_bytes*) because these attributes are thought to be the most important features [22]. *Service* is a categorical feature while the other three are continuous features. There are 41 original categories of *service* which are mapped into five categorical values: *http, smtp, ftp, ftp_data,* and *others*. Since the continuous features were concentrated around 0, we transformed each continuous feature by the log-transform $y = log(x + 1.0)$ for some subset. The original data set contained 4,898,431 data records, including 3,925,651 attacks (80.1%). This high rate is too large for attacks to be considered outliers. Therefore, following [22] we produced a subset consisting of 703,066 data records including 3,377 attacks (0.48%). The subset consists of those records with *logged_in* being positive. Attacks that successfully *logged_in* are called intrusions.

Sampling. The data set is then divided into five subsets according to the five values of *service*. The aim is to identify intrusions within each of the categories by identifying outliers using the RNN approach. For the smaller of the resulting subsets (*other* contained 5858 events and *ftp* contained 4091 events) all of the events were used to train the corresponding RNN. The subsets for *http*, *smtp* and *ftp-data* are considerably larger and were sampled in order to train the corresponding RNN within a feasible time. Note that scoring events for outlyingness is considerably more efficient than training and thus the trained RNN can be rapidly applied to very large datasets to score each event. The subsets were obtained by sampling every nth record from the data so that the subsets would be no larger than about 6K records. Details of the resultant training sets are listed in Table 2.

Table 2. Summary counts of the five KDD Cup data subsets used to train each of the RNNs.

Service	Events	Intrusions	Proportion Intrusions	Sample	Sample Intrusions	Proportion
http	567497	2211	3.9%	5674	22	0.4%
smtp	95156	30	0.3%	5597	4	0.1%
ftp-data	30464	722	2.4%	5077	122	2.4%
other	5858	98	1.7%	5858	98	1.7%
ftp	4091	316	7.7%	4091	316	7.7%
Total	703066	3377	0.5%	26297	562	2.1%

Training of the RNN. The training parameters used to train the five RNNs are listed in Table 3. The choices in the training parameters were made empirically to guarantee the convergence of the mean reconstruction error to a lowest possible value for the training set.

Table 3. Parameter values for training the RNNs on *kddcup* network intrusion data.

Parameter	http	smtp	ftp-data	other	ftp
Number of activation function steps	4	4	4	4	4
Log Transform of Continuous Features	Yes	Yes	No	Yes	No
Output Layer Activation Function	Sigmoid	Sigmoid	Sigmoid	Sigmoid	Sigmoid
Number of Units: Hidden Layer 1	35	40	40	40	45
Number of Units: Hidden Layer 2	3	3	3	3	3
Number of Units: Hidden Layer 3	35	40	40	40	45
Number of Iterations	1000	40000	10000	10000	40000

Results. The trained RNN is used to score each event with the value of OF. The data can then be reordered in descending order of OF. The records ranked higher are expected to be more likely intrusions. Figure 3 shows the overall ratio of the coverage of the intrusions plotted against the percentage of the data selected when ordered by OF. The combined result gives the overall performance of the outlier detector.

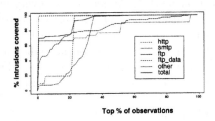

Top % of observations

Fig. 3. Ratio of detected intrusions found by the RNN method

Best results are obtained for service type *http*, which has the highest number of intrusions. Indeed, the top one percent of the ranked records contains all intrusions. In other words, all 2211 intrusions are included in the top 5670 patterns, identifying a small data subset which has a significant proportion of outliers.

Table 4 lists the distribution of all the patterns in the codebook (identifying clusters through combination of values) of the middle hidden layer. There are $N^{L_3} = 4^3 = 64$ possible codes (i.e., clusters) in the middle hidden layer. Only ten of these are non-empty clusters. It is clearly visible that cluster 48 has 2202 (99.6%) intrusion cases and only 31 normal cases. All other clusters have only normal cases (except cluster 51, which has only one intrusion cases).

Table 4. Results for *http*, according to middle hidden layer output

Cluster Index	Middle hidden layer output			Total Records	*normal* Records	*attack* Records
	Neuron 1	Neuron 2	Neuron 3			
0	0	0	0	21137	21131	6
1	0	0	1	103	102	1
2	0	0	2	409	408	1
16	1	0	0	539448	539448	0
17	1	0	1	50	50	0
18	1	0	2	2	2	0
32	2	0	0	4105	4105	0
48	3	0	0	2233	31	2202
49	3	0	1	9	9	0
51	3	0	3	1	0	1

4.2   Wisconsin Breast Cancer Dataset

The Wisconsin breast cancer data set is found in the UCI machine learning repository[5]. The dataset contains nine continuous attributes. Each record is labelled as *benign* (458 or 65.5%) or *malignant* (241 or 34.5%). We removed some of the *malignant* records to form a very unbalanced distribution for testing the RNN outlier detection method. When one in every six *malignant* records was chosen, the resultant data set had 39 (8%) *malignant* records and 444 (92%) *benign* records. The results are shown in Table 5. Within the top 40 ranked cases (ranked according to the Outlier Factor), 30 of the malignant cases (the outliers), comprising 77% of all malignant cases, were identified. There are 25 non-empty clusters out of 64 possible codes. Among the non-empty clusters eleven of them (0-15) form a super cluster. The common characteristic of this super cluster is that the output from the first neuron is 0. There are 53 records in this cluster and 36 of them are malignant cases (outliers). We can categorise this super cluster as an outlier cluster with 68% (36/53) confidence. On the other hand, the other three super clusters (where output from the first neuron of the middle hidden layer is 1, 2, and 3 respectively) contains mostly inliers.

Table 5. Results for Wisconsin breast cancer data according to outlier factor

Top % of record	Number of malignant	Number of record	% of malignant	Top % of record	Number of malignant	Number of record	% of malignant
0	0	0	0.00	12	35	48	89.74
1	3	4	7.69	14	36	56	92.31
2	6	8	15.38	16	36	64	92.31
4	11	16	28.21	18	38	72	97.44
6	18	24	46.15	20	38	80	97.44
8	25	32	64.10	25	38	100	97.44
10	30	40	76.92	28	39	112	100.00

5   Discussion and Conclusions

We have presented an outlier detection approach based on Replicator Neural Networks (RNN). An RNN is trained from a sampled data set to build a model that predicts the given data. We use this model to develop a score for outlyingness (called the Outlier Factor) where the trained RNN is applied to the whole data set to give a quantitative measure of the outlyingness based on the reconstruction error. Our approach takes the view of letting the data speak for itself without relying on too many assumptions. SmartSifter, for example, assumes a mixed Gaussian distribution for inliers. Distance-based outlier methods use a chosen distance metric to measure the distances between the data points with the number of clusters and the distance metric preset. The RNN approach also identifies cluster labels for each data record. The cluster label can often help to interpret the resulting outliers. For example, outliers are sometimes found to be concentrated in a single cluster (as in service type *http* of the KDD99 intrusion data) or in a group of clusters with common characteristics (as in the Wisconsin breast cancer data). The cluster label not only enables the individuals to be identified as outliers but also groups to identified as being outliers, as in [21]. We have demonstrated the method on two publicly available data sets. To test the accuracy of the method datasets with unbalanced distributions two or more classes were selected. The RNN was able to identify outliers (small classes) without using the class labels with high accuracy in both datasets. A paper comparing the RNN with other outlier detection methods is in preparation.

References

[1] D. H. Ackley, G. E. Hinton, and T. J. Sejinowski. A learning algorithm for boltzmann machines. *Cognit. Sci.*, 9:147–169, 1985.

[2] A. C. Atkinson. Fast very robust methods for the detection of multiple outliers. *Journal of the American Statistical Association*, 89:1329–1339, 1994.

[3] A. Bartkowiak and A. Szustalewicz. Detecting multivariate outliers by a grand tour. *Machine Graphics and Vision*, 6(4):487–505, 1997.

[4] M. Breunig, H. Kriegel, R. Ng, and J. Sander. Lof: Identifying density-based local outliers. In *Proc. ACM SIGMOD, Int. Conf. on Management of Data*, 2000.

[5] 1999 KDD Cup competition.
http://kdd.ics.uci.edu/databases/kddcup99/kddcup99.html.

[6] W. DuMouchel and M. Schonlau. A fast computer intrusion detection algorithm based on hypothesis testing of command transition probabilities. In *Proc. 4th Int. Conf. on Knowledge Discovery and Data Mining*, pages 189–193, 1998.

[7] M. Ester, H. P. Kriegel, J. Sander, and X. Xu. A density-based algorithm for discovering clusters in large spatial databases with noise. In *Proc. KDD*, pages 226–231, 1999.

[8] T. Fawcett and F. Provost. Adaptive fraud detection. *Data Mining and Knowledge Discovery Journal*, 1(3):291–316, 1997.

[9] D. M. Hawkins. *Identification of outliers*. Chapman and Hall, London, 1980.

[10] R. Hecht-Nielsen. Replicator neural networks for universal optimal source coding. *Science*, 269(1860-1863), 1995.

[11] E. Knorr and R. Ng. A unified approach for mining outliers. In *Proc. KDD*, pages 219–222, 1997.

[12] E. Knorr and R. Ng. Algorithms for mining distance-based outliers in large datasets. In *Proc. 24th Int. Conf. Very Large Data Bases, VLDB*, pages 392–403, 24–27 1998.

[13] E. Knorr., R. Ng, and V. Tucakov. Distance-based outliers: Algorithms and applications. *VLDB Journal: Very Large Data Bases*, 8(3–4):237–253, 2000.

[14] George Kollios, Dimitrios Gunopoulos, Nick Koudas, and Stefan Berchtold. An efficient approximation scheme for data mining tasks. In *ICDE*, 2001.

[15] A. S. Kosinksi. A procedure for the detection of multivariate outliers. *Computational Statistics and Data Analysis*, 29, 1999.

[16] R. Ng and J. Han. Efficient and effective clustering methods for spatial data mining. In *Proc. 20th VLDB*, pages 144–155, 1994.

[17] S. Ramaswamy, R. Rastogi, and K. Shim. Efficient algorithms for mining outliers from large data sets. In *Proceedings of International Conference on Management of Data, ACM-SIGMOD*, Dallas, 2000.

[18] D. F. Swayne, D. Cook, and A. Buja. XGobi: interactive dynamic graphics in the X window system with a link to S. In *Proceedings of the ASA Section on Statistical Graphics*, pages 1–8, Alexandria, VA, 1991. American Statistical Association.

[19] P. Sykacek. Equivalent error bars for neural network classifiers trained by bayesian inference. In *Proc. ESANN*, 1997.

[20] G. Williams, I. Altas, S. Bakin, Peter Christen, Markus Hegland, Alonso Marquez, Peter Milne, Rajehndra Nagappan, and Stephen Roberts. The integrated delivery of large-scale data mining: The ACSys data mining project. In Mohammed J. Zaki and Ching-Tien Ho, editors, *Large-Scale Parallel Data Mining*, LNAI State-of-the-Art Survey, pages 24–54. Springer-Verlag, 2000.

[21] G. Williams and Z. Huang. Mining the knowledge mine: The hot spots methodology for mining large real world databases. In Abdul Sattar, editor, *Advanced Topics in Artificial Intelligence*, volume 1342 of *Lecture Notes in Artificial Intelligenvce*, pages 340–348. Springer, 1997.

[22] K. Yamanishi, J. Takeuchi, G. Williams, and P. Milne. On-line unsupervised outlier detection using finite mixtures with discounting learning algorithm. In *Proceedings of KDD2000*, pages 320–324, 2000.

[23] T. Zhang, R. Ramakrishnan, and M. Livny. An efficient data clustering method for very large databases. In *Proc. ACM SIGMOD*, pages 103–114, 1996.

The Closed Keys Base of Frequent Itemsets

Viet Phan Luong

Laboratoire d'Informatique Fondamentale de Marseille, LIF-UMR CNRS 6166
C.M.I. de l'Université de Provence
39, rue F. Joliot Curie, 13453 Cedex 13, France
phan@gyptis.univ-mrs.fr

Abstract. In data mining, concise representations are useful and necessary to apprehending voluminous results of data processing. Recently many different concise representations of frequent itemsets have been investigated. In this paper, we present yet another concise representation of frequent itemsets, called the closed keys representation, with the following characteristics: (i) it allows to determine if an itemset is frequent, and if so, the support of the itemset is immediate, and (ii) basing on the closed keys representation, it is straightforward to determine all frequent key itemsets and all frequent closed itemsets. An efficient algorithm for computing the closed key representation is offered. We show that our approach has many advantages over the existing approaches, in terms of efficiency, conciseness and information inferences.

1 Introduction

Searching for frequent itemsets is a primary step in mining association rules, episode rules, sequential patterns, clusters, etc. The number of frequent itemsets in a real application can be exponential with respect to the number of items considered in the application. This is a problem not only to online data mining, but also to end-users to apprehending the mining results. A solution of this problem is the concise representations of frequent itemsets and association rules [3,7,10, 12,13,15]. Existing approaches to the concise representations of frequent itemsets are the representations based on closed itemsets [9,15], key (generator) itemsets [4], disjunction-free itemsets [5], and disjunction-free generator itemsets[8]. Each of these representations is lossless: it allows to determine if an itemset is frequent, and if so, the support of the itemset can be computed from the supports of the itemsets in the representation. However, as we shall see such a computation of the support is not straightforward. Moreover, in the applications of the concise representations of frequent itemsets, as the representations of association rules, we need to know both closed itemsets and key itemsets [7,12,13]. Searching for the key itemsets from the closed itemsets representation or the disjunction-free itemsets representation is not straightforward. It is the same to searching for the closed itemsets from the generators representation or the disjunction-free generarators representation.

In this paper, we present yet another concise representation of frequent itemsets, that we call the *closed keys representation*, with the following properties:

Y. Kambayashi, W. Winiwarter, M. Arikawa (Eds.): DaWaK 2002, LNCS 2454, pp. 181–190, 2002.
© Springer-Verlag Berlin Heidelberg 2002

(i) it is lossless, and (ii) basing on the representation, it is straightforward to determine the supports of all frequent itemsets, and to find all frequent key itemsets and all closed itemsets. An efficient algorithm for finding the representation is offered. Comparisons with related work, in terms of efficiency, conciseness and information inferences, are discussed. We show that our approach has many advantages over the existing approaches.

The paper is organized as follows. In Section 2, we remind the main concepts on frequent itemsets, closed itemsets and key itemsets. Properties concerning the inference of supports of itemsets are presented in Section 3. The concept of the closed keys representation is given at the end of Section 3. Section 4 is devoted to the algorithm for searching the closed keys representation. The correctness and completeness of the algorithm are proved. Related work is discussed in Section 5, which ends with remarks and conclusions.

2   Preliminaries

We consider a *dataset* which is a triple $\mathcal{D} = (\mathcal{O}, \mathcal{I}, \mathcal{R})$, where $\mathcal{O}, \mathcal{I}, \mathcal{R}$ are finite non-empty sets. An element in $\mathcal{I}$ is called an item, an element in O is called an object or a transaction. $\mathcal{R}$ is a binary relation on $\mathcal{O}$ and $\mathcal{I}$. A couple $(o, i) \in \mathcal{R}$ represents the fact that the object (transaction) o has the item i. A subset $I \subseteq \mathcal{I}$ is called an *itemset* of $\mathcal{D}$. An itemset consisting of k items is called a k-itemset. The *Galois connection* [6] between $2^{\mathcal{O}}$ and $2^{\mathcal{I}}$ is a couple of functions (f, g) where $g(I) = \{o \in \mathcal{O} \mid \forall i \in I, (o, i) \in \mathcal{R}\}$, and $f(O) = \{i \in \mathcal{I} \mid \forall o \in O, (o, i) \in \mathcal{R}\}$. Intuitively, $g(I)$ is the set of all objects in $\mathcal{O}$ that share in common all the items in I, and dually, $f(O)$ is the set of all items that the objects in O share in common. The functions g and f can be extended with $g(\emptyset) = \mathcal{O}$ and $f(\emptyset) = \mathcal{I}$. The function g is antimonotonic: for all $I_1, I_2 \subseteq \mathcal{I}$, if $I_1 \subseteq I_2$ then $g(I_2) \subseteq g(I_1)$. The function f is also antimonotonic. The *Galois closure operators* are the following functions: $h = f \circ g$ and $h' = g \circ f$, where $\circ$ denotes the composition of functions. h and h' are montonic. Given an itemset $I, h(I) = f(g(I))$ is called the *closure* of I. Indeed, for all $I \in \mathcal{I}, I \subseteq h(I)$ (Extension) and $h(h(I)) = h(I)$ (Idempotency). An itemset I is said to be *closed* if $I = h(I)$. An itemset I is called a *key* itemset or a *generator* if for every itemset $I' \subseteq I, h(I') = h(I)$ implies $I = I'$. That is I is a key itemset if there is no itemset I' strictly included in I and having the same closure as I.

The support of I, denoted by $sup(I)$, is $sup(I) = card(g(I))/card(\mathcal{O})$, where $card(X)$ denotes the cardinality of $X, \forall X \subseteq \mathcal{O}$. Given a support threshold, denoted by $minsup$, $0 \leq minsup \leq 1$, an itemset I is said to be *frequent* if $sup(I) \geq minsup$. An itemset I is called a frequent key (or closed) itemset if I is frequent and I is a key (respectively closed) itemset.

An *association rule* [1] is an expression of the form $I_1 \rightarrow I_2$, where $I_1, I_2 \subseteq \mathcal{I}$. Let r be an association rule, denoted by $r : I_1 \rightarrow I_2$. Its support and confidence, denoted by $sup(r)$ and $conf(r)$ respectively, are $sup(r) = sup(I_1 \cup I_2)$, and $conf(r) = sup(r)/sup(I_1)$. A general form of association rules, called *disjunctive association rules* [5], is $r : I \rightarrow I_1 \vee I_2$, where $I, I_1, I_2 \subseteq \mathcal{I}$, with support and confidence defined by $sup(r) = sup(I \cup I_1) + sup(I \cup I_2) - sup(I \cup I_1 \cup I_2)$, and $conf(r) = sup(r)/sup(I)$. Let r be an association rule (normal or disjunctive). r is said to be exact (certain) if $conf(r) = 1$; otherwise, r is said to be approximate.

Example 1. Consider a dataset represented in Table a. The itemsets of the dataset are classified with respect to their supports in Table b.

Table a

OID	Items
1	A - - D -
2	- B - - E
3	A B C - E
4	A - C - E
5	A B C - E

Table b

Supports	Itemsets
1/5	D, AD
2/5	AB, BC, ABC, ABE, BCE, ABCE
3/5	B, C, AC, AE, BE, CE, ACE
4/5	A, E,
1	∅

In short an itemset is denoted by juxtaposition of its items, so is the union of itemsets, when no confusion is possible. For example, ACE denotes the itemset $\{A, C, E\}$, and $I_1 I_2$ denotes $I_1 \cup I_1$, where I_1, I_2 are itemsets.

Let $minsup = 2/5$. The frequent closed itemsets of $\mathcal{D}$ are $ABCE$, ACE, BE, A, E, $\emptyset$. The frequent key itemsets of $\mathcal{D}$ are AB, AE, BC, A, B, C, E, $\emptyset$. The association rule $B \to ACE$ is approximate. The association rule $B \to C \vee E$ is disjunctive and exact.

3   Closed Keys Representation

We start this section by providing the basis for support inferences. Then we define the concept of the closed keys representation, and show how frequent itemsets can be determined on the representation. Some results are similar to the results in [4]. However, we shall show how our results are distinct from those in [4].

Lemma 1. *Let I, J be itemsets. Then $g(I \cup J) = g(I) \cap g(J)$.*

Proposition 1. *Let I_1, I_2 be itemsets such that $I_1 \subset I_2$. If $g(I_1) = g(I_2)$ then for every $I \supset I_2$, $g(I) = g(I_1 \cup (I - I_2))$.*

Proof. Suppose that $I_1 \subset I_2$ and $g(I_1) = g(I_2)$. Let I be an itemset such that $I \supset I_2$. I can be represented as $I = I_2 \cup (I_1 \cup (I - I_2))$. Therefore, by Lemma 1, $g(I) = g(I_2) \cap g(I_1 \cup (I - I_2))$. As $g(I_2) = g(I_1)$, we have $g(I) = g(I_1) \cap g(I_1 \cup (I - I_2))$. Now, as $g(I_1 \cup (I - I_2)) \subseteq g(I_1)$, we have: $g(I) = g(I_1 \cup (I - I_2))$. ◇

In [4], it was shown that $g(I) = g(I - (I_2 - I_1))$. In fact, $I_1 \cup (I - I_2) = I - (I_2 - I_1)$. However, $I_1 \cup (I - I_2)$ is computationally more efficient than $I - (I_2 - I_1)$, because under the condition $I_1 \subset I_2 \subset I$, we have $I_1 \cap (I - I_2) = \emptyset$, so the union of I_1 and $I - I_2$ can be implemented by just insertion.

The following corollaries are direct consequences of Proposition 1.

Corollary 1. *Let I_1, I_2 be itemsets such that $I_1 \subset I_2$. If $sup(I_1) = sup(I_2)$ then for every $I \supset I_2$, $sup(I) = sup(I_1 \cup (I - I_2))$.*

Corollary 2. *Let I be an itemset. If I is not a key itemset then for every $J \supset I$, J is not a key itemset.*

After Corollary 2, if we are only interested in key itemsets, then in an incremental method for generating key itemsets, we can discard non-key itemsets.

Definition 1. *An itemset K is called a maximal key itemset included in an itemset X if K is a key itemset and there is no key itemset K' such that $K \subset K'$ and $K' \subset X$.*

In the above definition, K is required to be a key itemset, but $sup(K)$ is not necessarily equal to $sup(X)$. However, the following property holds.

Lemma 2. *If X is a non-key itemset, then any key itemset K included in X, such that $sup(X) = sup(K)$, is a maximal key itemset included in X.*

Proposition 2. *Let X be an itemset. Let $K_1, K_2, .., K_m$ be maximal key itemsets included in X. Then $sup(X) = min\{sup(K_i) \mid K_i, i = 1..m\}$*

Proof. We have $sup(X) \leq min\{sup(K_i) \mid K_i, i = 1, .., m\}$. If X is a key itemset, then clearly $sup(X) = min\{sup(K_i) \mid K_i, i = 1..m\}$, where $m = 1$. Otherwise, X is not a key. Then there exists a key itemset K such that $K \subset X$ and $sup(K) = sup(X)$. Such a key itemset K is a maximal key itemset included in X (Lemma 2). Hence, $sup(X) = sup(K) \geq min\{sup(K_i) \mid K_i, i = 1..m\}$. Thus, $sup(X) = min\{sup(K_i) \mid K_i, i = 1..m\}$. ⋄

In [4], it was shown that if X is a non-key k-itemsets, $k \geq 2$, then the support of X is $sup(X) = min\{sup(I_{k-1}) \mid I_{k-1} \subset X\}$. Proposition 2 is distinct from this result on two points (i) Proposition 2 is valid not only for non-key itemsets, but also for key itemsets, and (ii) in order to compute the support of X, we do not need to consider all $(k-1)$-itemsets included in X, but only the maximal key itemsets included in X.

Proposition 2 means that if we know the supports of all key itemsets, then we can infer the support of any other itemset. However, if we are only interested in determining the frequent key itemsets with their supports, then we can base on only frequent key itemsets.

Theorem 1. *If there exists a frequent key itemset K such that $K \subseteq X$ and $X \subseteq h(K)$, then $sup(X) = sup(K)$. Otherwise, X is not frequent.*

Proof. If there exists a frequent key itemset K such that $K \subseteq X$ and $X \subseteq h(K)$, then $sup(X) \leq sup(K)$ and $sup(h(K)) \leq sup(X)$. As $sup(K) = sup(h(K))$, we have $sup(X) = sup(K) = sup(h(K))$. Otherwise, by contradiction suppose that X is frequent. We have either X is a key or X is not a key. In the former case, the contradition is immediate, because X is a frequent key itemset included in itself. In the latter case, there exists a key itemset $K \subset X$ such that $sup(K) = sup(X)$. Therefore $g(K) = g(X)$, and then $h(K) = f(g(K)) = f(g(X)) = h(X)$. Hence, $X \subseteq h(X) = h(K)$. As X is frequent, K is frequent. Thus, contradiction. ⋄.

Definition 2. *Let $\mathcal{D}$ be a dataset. The closed keys representation of $\mathcal{D}$, with respect to a support threshold minsup, denoted by $\mathcal{H}(\mathcal{D}, minsup)$, is the set*
$$\{(K, h(K) - K, sup(K)) \mid K \text{ is a key itemset of } \mathcal{D} \text{ and } sup(K) \geq minsup\}.$$

By Theorem 1, basing on the closed keys representation, it is straightforward to determine if an itemset I is frequent, and if so, its support already available, without any computation.

Example 1 (continued). The closed keys representation of the dataset in Table a, with respect to $minsup = 2/5$, consists of $(\emptyset, \emptyset, 1), (A, \emptyset, 4/5), (B, E, 3/5), (C, AE, 3/5), (E, \emptyset, 4/5), (AB, CE, 2/5), (AE, C, 3/5), (BC, AE, 2/5)$.

4 Generating the Closed Keys Representation

We propose an incremental algorithm as Apriori [2] to generate the closed keys representation. We start with the empty itemset, which is of course a key, with support 1. Then we compute the supports of all 1-itemsets. For each 1-itemset I, if $sup(I) = 1$, then I is a non-key itemset. The remaining 1-itemsets are key itemsets. Let Y_0 be the union of all non-key 1-itemsets. Clearly, Y_0 is the closure of the empty itemset. A triple $(\emptyset, Y_0, 1)$ is added to the closed keys representation. In step $i \geq 2$, we consider the i-itemsets built on the frequent $(i-1)$-itemsets, until the set of key $(i-1)$-itemsets is empty.

4.1 Generating Key Itemset Candidates

Let X and Y be frequent $(i-1)$-itemsets such that $X - Y$ and $Y - X$ are singletons and $X - Y > Y - X$ in lexicographic order. Then XY is an i-itemset candidate. We have the following cases:

(a) X is not key. Then XY is not key (Corollary 2). As X is frequent, there exists a frequent $(i-2)$-itemset Z such that $Z \subset X$ and $sup(Z) = sup(X)$. By Corollary 1, $sup(XY) = sup(Z \cup (XY - X)) = sup(Z \cup (Y - X))$. As Z is an $(i-2)$-itemset and $(Y - X)$ is disjoint from Z, we have $Z \cup (Y - X)$ is an $(i-1)$-itemset. Therefore, we search $(Z \cup (XY - X))$ among the frequent $(i-1)$-itemsets. If it is there, then XY is frequent, and the itemset $Z \cup (Y - X)$ is linked to XY, for use in the next step. Otherwise, XY is not frequent. The case where Y is not key is similar.

(b) Both X and Y are keys. There are two subcases:

(b.1) There exists a frequent non-key $(i-1)$-itemset Z such that $Z \subset XY$. In this case, XY is not a key. As Z is a frequent non-key itemset, there exists a frequent $(i-2)$-itemset T such that $T \subset Z$ and $sup(T) = sup(Z)$, and $sup(XY) = sup(T \cup (XY - Z))$. Similarly to case (a), by searching among the frequent $(i-1)$-itemsets previously discovered, we can see if XY is frequent, and if so, the itemset $T \cup (XY - Z)$ is linked to XY, for use in the next step. Otherwise, XY is infrequent.

(b.2) Else, if all $(i-1)$-itemsets which are subsets of XY are frequent then XY is a candidate. Otherwise, XY is deleted from the list of candidates.

The frequent i-itemsets generated in points (a) and (b.1) are not key itemsets. They are stored in a list denoted by F_i. The frequent i-itemsets generated in point (b.2) are stored in a list denoted by C_i.

Notations: For each i-itemset I, there are associated the following fields:
- $I.key$: to indicate if I is a key itemset, and
- $I.prev$: to represent an $(i-1)$-itemset I_{i-1} such that $I_{i-1} \subset I$ and $sup(I) = sup(I_{i-1})$, if such an itemset exists.

Algorithm GenCandidate

Input: F_{i-1}, C_{i-1}: lists of frequent $(i-1)$-itemsets.
Output: F_i: list of frequent i-itemsets, and C_i list of i-itemset candidates.
Method:
$F_i = \emptyset; C_i = \emptyset$;
For each pair of itemsets (X, Y), where $(X, sup(X)), (Y, sup(Y)) \in$
   $F_{i-1} \cup C_{i-1}$, such that $X - Y$ and $Y - X$ are singletons and $X - Y > Y - X$
   in lexicographic order, do
If *not X.key* then Begin
   $Z = X.prev$; // Z is an $(i-2)$-itemset: $Z \subset X$ and $sup(Z) = sup(X)$;
   If $Z \cup (Y - X)$ is a frequent $(i-1)$-itemset then begin
     $XY.key = false; sup(XY) = sup(Z \cup (Y - X))$;
     $XY.prev = Z \cup (Y - X)$; insert $(XY, sup(XY))$ in F_i
   end End
Else If *not Y.key* then Begin
   $Z = Y.prev$; // Z is an $(i-2)$-itemset: $Z \subset Y$ and $sup(Z) = sup(Y)$;
   If $Z \cup (X - Y)$ is a frequent $(i-1)$-itemset then begin
     $XY.key = false; sup(XY) = sup(Z \cup (X - Y))$;
     $XY.prev = Z \cup (X - Y)$; insert $(XY, sup(XY))$ in F_i
   end End
Else If there exists a frequent non-key $(i-1)$-itemset Z such that $Z \subset XY$
   then Begin
     $T = Z.prev$; // T is an $(i-2)$-itemset: $T \subset Z$ and $sup(T) = sup(Z)$;
     If $(T \cup (XY - Z))$ is a frequent $(i-1)$-itemset then begin
       $XY.key = false; sup(XY) = sup(T \cup (XY - Z))$;
       $XY.prev = T \cup (XY - Z)$; insert $(XY, sup(XY))$ in F_i
     end End
   Else If all $(i-1)$-itemsets which are subsets of XY are frequent
     then begin $sup(XY) = 0$; insert $(XY, sup(XY))$ into C_i end;

4.2   Generating the Closed Keys Representation

In step $i \geq 2$, GenCandidate is called with inputs F_{i-1} and C_{i-1}. It results in F_i and C_i. If C_i is not empty, then we access the dataset to compute the supports of the itemsets in C_i, and keep only those which are frequent. Next, we consider each frequent key itemset I_{i-1}. For each $I_i \in C_i \cup F_i$, if $sup(I_i) = sup(I_{i-1})$, then we add $I_i - I_{i-1}$ to Y_{i-1}, which is initially set to empty for each frequent key itemset I_{i-1}, and we set $I_i.prev = I_{i-1}$, if $I_i \in C_i$. In such a case clearly I_i is not a key itemset. We shall show that the union of I_{i-1} and the final value of Y_{i-1}, when all $I_i \in C_i \cup F_i$ are already considered, is the closure of I_{i-1}.

Algorithm FClosedKeys

Input: A dataset $\mathcal{D} = (\mathcal{O}, \mathcal{I}, \mathcal{R})$, and a support threshold *minsup*.

Output: The closed keys representation of $\mathcal{D}$, with respect to *minsup*.

Method:

$\emptyset.key = true$; $F_0 = \{(\emptyset, 1)\}$; $Y_0 = \emptyset$; $K_1 = \emptyset$;

Read the dataset to compute the support of each 1-itemset;

$F_1 = \{(I_1, sup(I_1)) \mid sup(I_1) \geq minsup\}$;

For each $(I_1, sup(I_1)) \in F_1$ do

    If $sup(I_1) = 1$ then begin $Y_0 = Y_0 \cup I_1$; $I_1.prev = \emptyset$; $I_1.key = false$ end

    else begin $I_1.key = true$; $K_1 = K_1 \cup \{(I_1, sup(I_1))\}$ end;

$\mathcal{H}_0 = \{(\emptyset, Y_0, 1)\}$; $i = 2$; $\mathcal{H} = \mathcal{H}_0$; $\mathcal{H}_{i-1} = \emptyset$; $C_1 = \emptyset$;

While $K_{i-1} \neq \emptyset$ do begin

    GenCandidate(F_{i-1}, C_{i-1}); // Results in F_i and C_i.

    If $C_i \neq \emptyset$ then begin

        Read the dataset to compute the support of each i-itemset in C_i;

        Delete from C_i all itemsets I_i such that $sup(I_i) < minsup$;

          For each $(I_i, sup(I_i)) \in C_i$ do $I_i.key = true$; // by default

    end;

    For each $(I_{i-1}, sup(I_{i-1})) \in K_{i-1}$ do begin

        $Y_{i-1} = \emptyset$;

        For each $(I_i, sup(I_i)) \in C_i$ do

          If $I_{i-1} \subset I_i$ and $sup(I_{i-1}) = sup(I_i)$ then begin

            $Y_{i-1} = Y_{i-1} \cup (I_i - I_{i-1})$; $I_i.prev = I_{i-1}$; $I_i.key = false$

          end;

        For each $(I_i, sup(I_i)) \in F_i$ do

          If $I_{i-1} \subset I_i$ and $sup(I_{i-1}) = sup(I_i)$ then $Y_{i-1} = Y_{i-1} \cup (I_i - I_{i-1})$;

        $\mathcal{H}_{i-1} = \mathcal{H}_{i-1} \cup \{(I_{i-1}, Y_{i-1}, sup(I_{i-1}))\}$;

    end;

    $\mathcal{H} = \mathcal{H} \cup \mathcal{H}_{i-1}$; $K_i = \{(I_i, sup(I_i)) \in C_i \mid I_i.key = true\}$;

    $i = i + 1$; $\mathcal{H}_{i-1} = \emptyset$;

end;

Return($\mathcal{H}$).

Example 1 (continued). Computing the closed keys representation of the dataset in Table a, with respect to $minsup = 2/5$.

    $K_1 = F_1 = \{(A, 4/5), (B, 3/5), (C, 3/5), (D, 1/5), (E, 4/5)\}$;

    $\mathcal{H}_0 = \{(\emptyset, \emptyset, 1)\}$; $C_1 = \emptyset$.

Call *GenCandidate*(F_1, C_1), and compute the supports of the itemsets in C_2:

$F_2 = \emptyset$; $C_2 = \{(AB, 2/5), (AC, 3/5), (AE, 3/5), (BC, 2/5), (BE, 3/5), (CE, 3/5)\}$.

For each key itemset in K_1: For A, $Y_1 = \emptyset$. For B, $Y_1 = E$, $BE.prev = B$, and BE is not a key itemset. For C, $Y_1 = AE$, $AC.prev = C$, $AE.prev = C$, and AC and CE are not key itemsets. For E, $Y_1 = \emptyset$. Hence,

    $\mathcal{H}_1 = \{(A, \emptyset, 4/5), (B, E, 3/5), (C, AE, 3/5), (E, \emptyset, 4/5)\}$,

and $K_2 = \{(AB, 2/5), (AE, 3/5), (BC, 2/5)\}$.

Call *GenCandidate*(F_2, C_2):

    $F_3 = \{(ABC, 2/5), (ABE, 2/5), (ACE, 3/5), (BCE, 2/5)\}$; $C_3 = \emptyset$;

For each key itemset in K_2: For AB, $Y_2 = CE$, and ABC and ABE are not key itemsets. For AE, $Y_2 = C$, and ACE is not a key itemset. For BC, $Y_2 = AE$, and ABC and BCE are not key itemsets. Hence,
$$\mathcal{H}_2 = \{(AB, CE, 2/5), (AE, C, 3/5), (BC, AE, 2/5)\}.$$
As $C_3 = \emptyset$, K_3 is also empty, the algorithm stops. The closed keys representation of the dataset $\mathcal{D}$, with respect to $minsup = 2/5$, is
$$\mathcal{H} = \{(\emptyset, \emptyset, 1), (A, \emptyset, 4/5), (B, E, 3/5), (C, AE, 3/5), (E, \emptyset, 4/5),$$
$$(AB, CE, 2/5), (AE, C, 3/5), (BC, AE, 2/5)\}.$$

Proposition 3. *In Algorithm* FClosedKeys, *for an itemset $I_i \in C_i$, if $I_i.key$ is not set to be false, then I_i is a frequent key itemset.*

Proposition 4. FClosedKeys *finds all frequent key itemsets.*

Proposition 5. *For each triple $(I_{i-1}, Y_{i-1}, sup(I_{i-1})) \in \mathcal{H}_{i-1}$, I_{i-1} is a frequent key itemset and $h(I_{i-1}) = I_{i-1} \cup Y_{i-1}$.*

Proof. By Proposition 3, I_{i-1} is a frequent key itemset. For each $A \in h(I_{i-1}) - I_{i-1}$, $I_{i-1} \cup \{A\}$ is a frequent i-itemset, which is either in F_i or in C_i. For each frequent key $(i-1)$-itemset I_{i-1}, FClosedKeys considers all i-itemsets I_i in C_i and F_i. If $I_{i-1} \subset I_i$ and $sup(I_{i-1}) = sup(I_i)$, then it set $Y_{i-1} = Y_{i-1} \cup (I_i - I_{i-1})$, where Y_{i-1} is initially set to empty. Thus, $h(I_{i-1}) = I_{i-1} \cup Y_{i-1}$. $\diamond$

Theorem 2. *The set $\mathcal{H}$ consists of all triples $(I_i, (h(I_i) - I_i), sup(I_i))$, where I_i is a frequent key itemset of the given dataset. That is $\mathcal{H}$ is the closed keys representation of the dataset, with respect to support threshold minsup.*

The proof of Theorem 2 is immediate by Propositions 4 and 5.

Let us conclude this section with some remarks about the complexities of the closed keys representation and the algorithms. For each triple $(I_i, (h(I_i) - I_i), sup(I_i))$ in the closed keys representation, the memory space required to store I_i and $(h(I_i) - I_i)$ can be estimated by the memory space required to store $h(I)$, the closure of I. In each step $i \geq 2$ of Algorithm FClosedKeys, the generation of an i-itemset candidate I_i, basing on two frequent $(i-1)$-itemsets X and Y, needs to know the $(i-2)$-itemsets $X.prev$ or $Y.prev$ or $Z.prev$, where Z is a frequent $(i-1)$-itemset included in XY. These $(i-2)$-itemsets are associated with the $(i-1)$-itemsets in step $(i-1)$. Thus in step i, the algorithm needs only the stored information in step $(i-1)$, and not the stored information in step $(i-2)$. The computation of the support of a frequent non-key i-itemset I_i is immediate, as well as the field $I_i.prev$. Only in the case of frequent key itemset candidates (case b.2 in Algorithm GenCandidate), the computation costs more: checking that all $(i-1)$-itemsets $I_{i-1} \subset I_i$ are frequent, accessing the dataset to compute the support of I_i, and checking that I_i is a key itemset. Finally, we observe that in Algorithm *FClosedKeys*, the number of dataset accesses is at most equal to the maximal size of the frequent key itemsets.

5 Related Work, Remarks, and Conclusions

AClose [9] is an Apriori-like algorithm that computes frequent closed itemsets in two phases. In the first phase, AClose uses a bottom-up search to identify all frequent key itemsets. In the second phase AClose computes the closure of each frequent key itemsets I as the intersection of all transactions in which I occurs. Apriori-Close[10] is another Apriori-like algorithm that computes simultaneously frequent and frequent closed itemsets. CHARM [14] is also a bottom-up algorithm that computes frequent closed itemsets. In contrast to AClose, it explores both itemset and transaction identifier set spaces. Moreover, when generating candidates, CHARM avoids enumerating all possible subsets of a closed itemset. CLOSET [11] is a recursive method for computing closed itemsets, that uses a compact representation of transactions, called the FP-tree, where each branch represents the transactions having a same prefix. Dually to Apriori-Close, Pascal [4] computes frequent and frequent key itemsets, with optimization by inferencing supports: Let I_k be a generated k-itemset, and p_{I_k} the minimum of the supports of $(k-1)$-itemsets I_{k-1} contained in I_k. If such an I_{k-1} is not a key itemset, then mark I_k as non-key, and set $sup(I_k) = p_{I_k}$.

Our algorithm is distinct from the above algorithms on the following points: (i) It computes both frequent key and closed itemsets, and in only one phase. (ii) It stops as soon as all frequent key itemsets are discovered. (iii) With respect to inferencing supports, it is distinct from Pascal: When generating candidates in step $k \geq 2$, for every candidate I_k, Pascal verifies if all $(k-1)$-itemsets which are subsets of I_k are frequent, in our algorithm, this verification only exists for candidates in case (b.2) (see GenCandidate). Moreover, if all $I_{k-1} \subset I_k$ are frequent, and such an I_{k-1} is not key, then our algorithm does not compute the minimum. It knows which itemset $I_{k-1} \subset I_k$ such that $sup(I_k) = sup(I_{k-1})$.

The *disjunction-free sets representation* [5] is an approach to concise representations of frequent itemsets, based on the concept of frequent disjunction-free itemset. An itemset X is called frequent disjunction-free if X is frequent and there are no items $A, B \in X$ such that $X - \{A, B\} \rightarrow A \vee B$ is an exact rule. Otherwise, X is called disjunctive. Work in [8] applied the notion of disjunction free to generators (key itemsets) to propose a more concise representation, called *disjunction-free generators representation*. However, computing the disjunction-free generators representation costs more than computing the closed keys representation, in time and in space. Inferencing frequent itemsets basing on the disjunction-free generators representation is a very complex operation and costs more than basing on the closed keys representation. Moreover, the conciseness of the two representations is not comparable.

The above discussion on related work has shown that our approach has many advantages over existing approaches, in terms of algorithms and frequent itemset inferences. In [3] an approach to online mining association rules was proposed, using an adjacency lattice structure to store all frequent itemsets in main memory. This structure allows not only to efficiently mining association rules, but also allows to avoid generating redundant rules. Instead of storing the adjacency lattice structure, we think it will be more efficient if we store the closed keys representation in an adequate structure. This is because the closed keys representation is clearly more compact than the adjacency lattice structure, yet the support of any frequent itemset is immediate in the representation, without any computation. The work is currently investigated.

References

1. R. Agrawal, T. Imielinski, and A. Swami, "Mining Association Rules between Sets of Items in Large Databases", in Proc. of the 1993 ACM SIGMOD Int'l Conf. on Management of Data, May 1993, pp. 207-216.
2. R. Agrawal, R. Srikant, "Fast Algorithms for Mining Association Rules in Large Databases", Proc. of the $20^t h$ Int'l Conference on Very Large Data Bases (VLDB), juin 1994, pp. 478-499.
3. C. C. Aggarwal, P.S. Yu, "Online Generation of Association Rules", in Proc. of the Int'l Conference on Data Engineering, Orlando, Florida, Feb. 1998.
4. Y. Bastide, R. Taouil, N. Pasquier, G. Stumme and L. Lakhal, "Mining frequent patterns with counting inference" ACM SIGKDD Explorations, vol. 2(2), December 2000, pp. 66-75.
5. A. Bykowski and C. Rigotti, "A condensed representation to find frequent patterns", in Proc. of the 12th ACM SIGACT-SIGMOD-SIGART PODS'01, May, 2001.
6. B. Ganter, R. Wille, "Formal concept Analysis: Mathematical Foundations", Springer, 1999.
7. M. Kryszkiewics, "Closed set based discovery of representative association rules", in Proc. of IDA'01, Springer, September 2001.
8. M. Kryszkiewics, "Concise Representation of Frequent Patterns based on Disjunction-free Generators", in Proc. of the 2001 IEEE International Conference on Data Mining (ICDM'01), 29-Nov. - 2-Dec. 2001, San Jose, California, USA, pp. 305-312.
9. N. Pasquier, Y. Bastide, R. Taouil, and L. Lakhal, "Discovering frequent closed itemsets for association rules", Proc. of the 7th Int'l Conf. on Database Theory (ICDT), jan. 1999, pp. 398-416.
10. N. Pasquier, Y. Bastide, R. Taouil, and L. Lakhal, "Efficient mining of association rules using closed itemset lattices", Information Systems, 24(1), 1999, pp. 25-46.
11. J. Pei, J. Han, R. Mao, "CLOSET: An Efficient Algorithm for Mining Frequent Closed Itemsets", in Proc. Workshop on Reasearch Issues on Data Mining and Knowledge Discovery (DMKD), May 2000, p. 21-30.
12. V. Phan-Luong, "The Representative Basis for Association Rules", in Proc. of the 2001 IEEE International Conference on Data Mining (ICDM'01), 29-Nov. - 2-Dec. 2001, San Jose, California, USA, poster paper pp. 639-640.
13. V. Phan-Luong, "Reasoning on Association Rules", 17e Journées Bases de Données Avancées (BDA'2001), Cépaduès Edition, pp. 299-310.
14. M.J Zaki, C.J. Hsiao, "CHARM: An efficient algorithm for closed association rules mining", Technical report 99-10, Computer Science Dept., Rensselaer Polytechnic Institute, Oct. 1999.
15. M.J Zaki, "Generating non-redundant association rules", proc. of the 6th ACM SIGMOD Int'l Conf. on Knowledge Discovery and Data Mining KDD 2000 Boston, MA, August 2000, pp. 34-43.

New Representation and Algorithm for Drawing RNA Structure with Pseudoknots*

Yujin Lee[1], Wootaek Kim[2], and Kyungsook Han[1]

[1] Department of Computer Science and Engineering, Inha University,
Inchon 402-751, South Korea
[2] Department of Automation Engineering, Inha University, Inchon 402-751, South Korea
http://wilab.inha.ac.kr/PseudoViewer/

Abstract. Visualization of a complex molecular structure is a valuable tool in understanding the structure. A drawing of RNA pseudoknot structures is a graph (and a possibly nonplanar graph) with inner cycles within a pseudoknot as well as possible outer cycles formed between a pseudoknot and other structural elements. Thus, drawing RNA pseudoknot structures is computationally more difficult than depicting RNA secondary structures. Although several algorithms have been developed for drawing RNA secondary structures, none of these can be used to draw RNA pseudoknots and thus visualizing RNA pseudoknots relies on significant amount of manual work. Visualizing RNA pseudoknots by manual work becomes more difficult and yields worse results as the size and complexity of the RNA structures increase. We have developed a new representation method and an algorithm for visualizing RNA pseudoknots as a two-dimensional drawing and implemented the algorithm in a program. The new representation produces uniform and clear drawings with no edge crossing for all kinds of pseudoknots, including H-type and other complex types. Given RNA structure data, we represent the whole structure as a tree rather than as a graph by hiding the inner cycles as well as the outer cycles in the nodes of the abstract tree. Once the top-level RNA structure is represented as a tree, nodes of the tree are placed and drawn in increasing order of their depth values. Experimental results demonstrate that the algorithm generates a clear and aesthetically pleasing drawing of large-scale RNA structures, containing any number of pseudoknots. This is the first algorithm for automatically drawing RNA structure with pseudoknots.

1 Introduction

For most people, graphical representation of data is much easier to understand than raw data. This is especially true for large-scale data of complex molecular structures. This paper describes a new representation and an algorithm for generating a clear and aesthetically appealing drawing of RNA pseudoknot structures.

---

* Research supported by the Korea Science and Engineering Foundation (KOSEF) under grant R05-2001-000-01037-0.

Y. Kambayashi, W. Winiwarter, M. Arikawa (Eds.): DaWaK 2002, LNCS 2454, pp. 191-201, 2002.

An RNA pseudoknot is a tertiary structural element formed when bases of a single-stranded loop pair with complementary bases outside the loop. Pseudoknots are not only widely occurring structural motifs in all kinds of viral RNA molecules, but also responsible for several important functions of RNA. Currently no automatic method for drawing RNA pseudoknot structures exists. Several programs are available for drawing RNA secondary structures (for example, [1, 4]), but none of these can be used to draw RNA pseudoknots. In the sense of graph theory, a drawing of RNA secondary structures is a tree, whereas a drawing of RNA pseudoknots is a graph with inner cycles within a pseudoknot as well as possible outer cycles formed between a pseudoknot and other structural elements. Thus, RNA pseudoknot structures are computationally more difficult to visualize than RNA secondary structures.

RNA pseudoknots are often represented by adding line segments to the secondary structure drawings to indicate base pairs formed by the pseudoknots. Alternatively, pseudoknots are drawn either manually by modifying the RNA secondary structure drawings or from scratch. In either case, drawing RNA pseudoknots manually becomes more difficult and yields unsatisfactory results as the size of the drawings increases. One of the difficulties in drawing RNA structures is an overlapping of structural elements, which reduces the readability of the drawing. In most drawing programs of RNA secondary structures, the computational load is increased because of the work associated with removing the overlap of structural elements, performed either by an iterative process of the programs or with user intervention.

We have developed a new representation method and an algorithm for automatically drawing RNA secondary structures with pseudoknots, and implemented the algorithm in a working program called PSEUDOVIEWER. To the best of our knowledge, this is the first algorithm for drawing RNA pseudoknot structures. We adopted two basic criteria when designing the algorithm: (1) overlapping of structural elements should be minimized to increase the readability of the drawing, and (2) not only the pseudoknots themselves but also the entire RNA structure containing them should be recognized quickly and easily. Experimental results demonstrate that the algorithm is capable of producing a clear and aesthetically appealing drawing of RNA structures. The rest of this paper describes the algorithm and its experimental results.

2   Representation of Pseudoknots

2.1   Pseudoknots of H-Type

In the classic type or H-type pseudoknots, bases in a hairpin loop pair with complementary bases outside the hairpin loop (see Figure 1). According to the broad definition of pseudoknots [6], 14 types of topologically distinct pseudoknots are possible in principle. However, the most commonly occurring pseudoknots are of the H-type, where H stands for hairpin loop.

Figure 1 displays typical representations of H-type pseudoknots [5]. All H-type pseudoknots are drawn with edge crossings. The edge crossings reduce the readability of the drawings and make it difficult to follow the RNA sequence from the 5'-end to

3'-end. The edge crossings, however, are inevitable in these drawings in order to stack the two stems coaxially. The coaxial stacking of the two stems has a biological meaning for the two stems of a pseudoknot to mimic a single stem, and has been confirmed by an NMR study [5]. However, the drawing of pseudoknots with RNA secondary structure describes a *topological* structure rather than a *geometric* structure. That is, the drawing of this type is intended to represent the connectivity relation between bases, so the drawing should focus on making the connectivity relation clear.

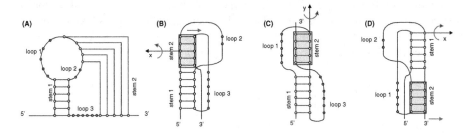

Fig. 1. Schematic representation of H-type pseudoknots, adapted from [5]. (A) General configuration. (B) Loop 1 is eliminated. (C) Loop 2 is eliminated. (D) Loop 3 is eliminated. The pseudoknot shown in (C) is the one most abundant in natural RNA.

We propose a new method for representing all H-type pseudoknots uniformly and without edge-crossings. The drawings shown in Figure 2A-2D represent exactly the same pseudoknots of Figure 1A-1D. The resulting drawings contain no edge-crossings and have similar shapes with exactly two inner cycles regardless of their types. Furthermore, it is much easier to follow the RNA sequence direction from the 5'-end to 3'-end. In the new representation, the two stems of a pseudoknot are not stacked coaxially, but they are parallel and adjacent to each other.

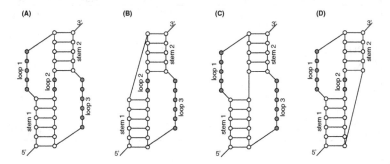

Fig. 2. New representation of H-type pseudoknots. (A) General configuration. (B) Drawing obtained from Figure 1B by flipping stem 2 (enclosed in a yellow box) with respect to a horizontal axis and by translating it horizontally by the stem width. (C) Drawing obtained from Figure 1C by flipping stem 2 with respect to a vertical axis. (D) Drawing obtained from Figure 1D by flipping stem 2 with respect to a horizontal axis and by translating it horizontally.

2.2 Pseudoknots of Other Types

Although the most commonly occurring pseudoknots are of the H-type, there are other types of pseudoknots. Basepairing of a hairpin loop with a single stranded part outside the hairpin loop forms the H-type pseudoknot, which has been discussed in the previous subsection. Basepairing of a hairpin loop with another hairpin loop forms a HH type pseudoknot, while basepairing of a hairpin loop with a single stranded part of a bulge, internal, or multiple loop forms a HL type (Figure 3). After analyzing all the pseudoknots of PseudoBase [7] for the purpose of drawing them in combination of basic pseudoknot types, we have concluded that there are 6 basic pseudoknot types — H-type and 5 other types displayed in Figure 3 (see also Table 1). All these pseudoknots can be drawn as planar graphs in our representation.

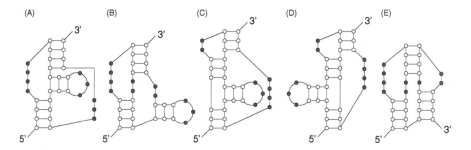

Fig. 3. Pseudoknots of other types. (A) LL type. (B) HL_{OUT} type. (C) HL_{IN} type. (D) HH type. (E) HHH type. H: hairpin loop, L: bulge loop, internal loop, or multiple loop.

Table 1. Classification of 236 pseudoknots in PseudoBase

Pseudoknot type	Number of occurrences	Ratio of occurrences
H	180	76.3%
LL	12	5.1%
HL_{OUT}	24	10.2%
HL_{IN}	11	4.7%
HH	1	0.4%
HHH	6	2.5%
Unclassified	2	0.8%
total	236	100.0%

3 Algorithm for Visualization

3.1 Preliminaries

In RNA secondary structures, there are two types of structural elements:

- Stem: double-stranded part, which is a contiguous region of base pairs.
- Regular loop: single-stranded part such as a hairpin loop, internal loop, bulge loop, multiple loop, or dangling end.

Since our algorithm draws pseudoknots as well as secondary structural elements, we considered additional structural elements as well:

- Pseudoknot: structural element formed by a pairing of bases in a regular loop with complementary bases outside the loop.
- Pseudoknot loop (PK loop): high-level loop that contains a pseudoknot as well as single-stranded part (see Figure 6B for an example).

A drawing of RNA pseudoknots is a graph with *inner* cycles within a pseudoknot as well as possible *outer* cycles formed between a pseudoknot and other structural elements. What we call a "PK loop" represents the outer cycle. Given RNA pseudoknots and secondary structures, we represent the whole structure as a tree rather than as a graph. This is possible by representing both regular loops and PK loops as nodes of the tree. Edges of the tree represent stems of the secondary structure. The root node of the tree is the loop with the smallest starting base number. A pseudoknot itself is not represented in the abstract tree; it is part of a node. By hiding the inner cycles as well as the outer cycles in the nodes of the abstract tree, we can represent the whole, top-level RNA structure as a tree, making the drawing process simple. Loops of the tree are placed and drawn in increasing order of their depth values (the root node has the smallest depth value). The outline of both a regular loop and a PK loop is drawn in a circle shape.

The algorithm of PSEUDOVIEWER is outlined as follows: (1) stems, regular loops, pseudoknots and PK loops are identified from the input structure data; (2) an abstract tree is constructed for representing the entire structure; (3) for each node and edge of the tree, its size and shape is determined; and (4) starting with the root node, each node and edge of the tree is positioned level by level by both translation and rotation. This section describes each step of the algorithm in detail.

3.2 Pseudoknots

PSEUDOVIEWER takes as input an ASCII file in pairing format, which is widely used for representing pseudoknots [7]. The paring format describes pseudoknots as well as secondary structures in the style of Figure 4A, which shows a H-type pseudoknot. Given this input, PSEUDOVIEWER identifies stems constituting a pseudoknot and computes the size of the pseudoknot. The size of a pseudoknot is the diagonal length of its bounding box. Figure 5 shows another example of a pseudoknot of more complex type, which is a combination of LL and HL$_{OUT}$ types.

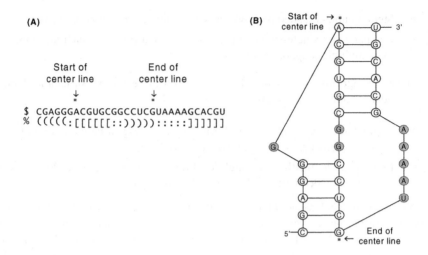

Fig. 4. (A) Input data for a H-type pseudoknot. (B) Drawing of the H-type pseudoknot.

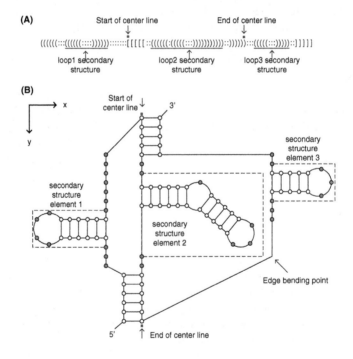

Fig. 5. (A) Input data for a nonclassic pseudoknot, which has 3 additional secondary structure elements in loop regions of the H-type pseudoknot. (B) Drawing of the nonclassic pseudoknot.

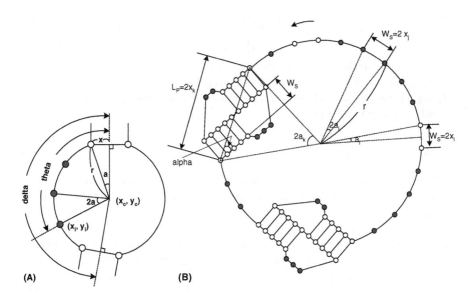

Fig. 6. (A) a regular loop. $2x$: distance between adjacent bases, $2a$: angle between adjacent bases. (B) a PK loop. Ws: width of a stem as well as the distance between adjacent bases, L_p: diagonal length of a pseudoknot, r: radius of a PK loop, α: angle between the diagonal direction and the stem direction of a pseudoknot

3.3 Regular Loops

The outline of a regular loop is drawn in a circle shape. In Figure 6A, the distance between adjacent bases of a regular loop is $2x$. Since a regular loop is considered to consist of several isosceles triangles, the vertical angle a of the isosceles triangle and the radius r of the regular loop can be computed using equations 1 and 2, respectively.

$$a = \frac{1}{2} \cdot \frac{2\pi}{n_{lb}} = \frac{\pi}{n_{lb}} \tag{1}$$

where n_{lb} is the number of bases on the regular loop.

$$r = \frac{x}{\sin a} \tag{2}$$

Once we determine the vertical angle a of the isosceles triangle, we can calculate the angle δ between adjacent stems and the angle θ_i between the i-th base of a regular loop and the positive y-axis. Let n_s be the number of stems connected to a regular loop, and n_b be the number of intervening bases between adjacent stems. Then,

$$\delta = 2a(n_b + 2) \tag{3}$$

$$\theta_i = (2i + 1)a, \quad i = 0, 1, 2, \ldots, n_{lb} - 1 \tag{4}$$

Using the angles computed by equations 1-4, the bases of a regular loop can be positioned as follows.

$$x_i = -r\sin\theta_i + x_c \tag{5}$$

$$y_i = r\cos\theta_i + y_c \tag{6}$$

x_i, y_i: x and y coordinates of the i-th base of a regular loop
x_c, y_c: x and y coordinates of the center of a regular loop
θ_i: angle between the i-th base of a regular loop and the positive y-axis
r: radius of a regular loop

3.4 Pseudoknot Loops

In order to handle a PK loop in a similar way to a regular loop, we should first determine the size of the PK loop. Since the outline of a PK loop is a circle shape, its radius can be computed from pseudoknots and bases contained in it. When a PK loop contains p pseudoknots and b bases, an inscribed polygon of the PK loop can be considered to consist of n (=$p+b$) isosceles triangles (see Figure 6B). Let x_i be the half of the base length of the i-th isosceles triangle. Then, equations 7 and 8 hold.

$$\sin a_i = \frac{x_i}{r} \quad\Rightarrow\quad a_i = \arcsin\left(\frac{x_i}{r}\right) \tag{7}$$

$$f = \sum_{i=1}^{n} \arcsin\left(\frac{x_i}{r}\right) - \pi = 0 \tag{8}$$

Equation 8 is solved for the radius r by incrementing r iteratively. For adjacent bases on a PK loop, the distance $2x_i$ between them is the same for every pair of adjacent bases. Thus, the value of $\arcsin(x_i/r)$ is calculated once and used for every pair of adjacent bases to efficiently determine r. Once we determine r, we can compute several angles shown in Figure 6B.

4 Implementation and Experimental Results

PSEUDOVIEWER is written in Java, so it is executable on any platform that supports Java. Figures 7 and 8 show the structures of odontoglossum ringspot virus (ORSV) and satellite tobacco necrosis virus 1 (STNV-1) RNAs [3], respectively. Bases are numbered in the frequency of 10. If a base number falls on a loop, it is shown in the drawing; otherwise, it is not shown to avoid overlaps. In addition to this, the starting base of each pseudoknot is shown in green background color with its base number. Pseudoknots are shown in yellow background color to make them easily distinguished from other parts. There is no overlapping of structural elements, and the PK loop with several pseudoknots takes on a circle shape similar to a regular loop.

In addition to the standard drawings, as shown in Figures 7 and 8, PSEUDOVIEWER produces outline drawings as well. The outline drawings display the structure in the form of a backbone in which loops are replaced by circles and helices by line segments. PSEUDOVIEWER also provides an interactive editing facility for manually fixing drawings when overlaps occur. In the editing mode, the user can drag a regular loop to any position. However, structural elements on a PK loop are not allowed to move because their relative positions are fixed.

Fig. 7. Structure of ORSV RNA with 11 pseudoknots

We have tested PSEUDOVIEWER on many RNA structures with pseudoknots in PseudoBase [7], and have not yet found the size limitation of the RNA imposed by the PSEUDOVIEWER algorithm. We suppose that the maximum size that can be visualized by PSEUDOVIEWER is limited by the computing power of the computer system and the bitmap size supported by the graphic device driver. Table 2 shows the execution time of PSEUDOVIEWER for 6 test cases. It follows from this result that the execution time is not proportional to the number of bases of RNA, but rather to the number of inscribed triangles of PK loops and the number of pseudoknots. An inscribed triangle of a PK loop corresponds to either a pseudoknot or a base of the PK loop. This is because the most time-consuming part of the PSEUDOVIEWER algorithm is the computation of the radius of a PK loop since it involves adding the arcsin values of n inscribed triangles of the PK loop in each step of the iteration.

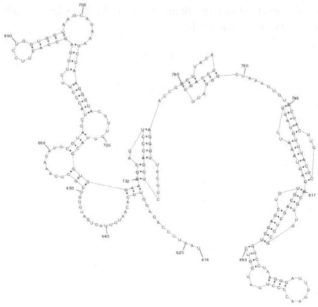

Fig. 8. Structure of STNV-1 with 4 pseudoknots

Table 2. Execution time of PSEUDOVIEWER

RNA	# bases	# pseudoknots	# inscribed triangles in PK loops	time (ms)
tobacco mosaic virus	214	5	34	62
satellite tobacco necrosis virus 1	252	4	45	125
E.coli tmRNA	363	4	49	172
satellite tobacco mosaic virus	421	8	75	218
odontoglossum ringspot virus	419	11	48	297
cyanophora paradoxa cyanelle tmRNA	291	1	153	390

5 Conclusions

A drawing of RNA pseudoknots is a graph (possibly nonplanar) with inner cycles within a pseudoknot as well as possible outer cycles formed between a pseudoknot and other structural elements. Thus, generating a clear representation of RNA pseudoknot structures is computationally harder than RNA secondary structures. We have developed a new representation method and an algorithm for visualizing RNA pseudoknots as a two-dimensional drawing and have implemented the algorithm in a working program called PSEUDOVIEWER. The new representation produces uniform and clear drawings with no edge crossing for all H-type pseudoknots as well as other types of pseudoknots.

Given the data of RNA pseudoknots and secondary structures, we represent the whole structure as a tree rather than as a graph by hiding the inner cycles as well as the outer cycles in the nodes of the abstract tree. Once the entire, top-level RNA structure is represented as a tree, nodes of the tree are placed and drawn in increasing order of their depth values. Experimental results have shown that PSEUDOVIEWER is capable of generating a clear and aesthetically pleasing drawing of RNA pseudoknots. The algorithm of PSEUDOVIEWER is the first one for automatically drawing RNA structures containing pseudoknots.

References

1. De Rijk, P., De Wachter, R.: RnaVIz, a program for the visualization of RNA secondary structure. Nucleic Acids Res. 25 (1997) 4679-4684
2. Du, Z., Hoffman, D.W.: An NMR and mutational study of the pseudoknot within the gene 32 mRNA of bacteriophage T2: insights into a family of structurally related RNA pseudoknots. Nucleic Acids Res. 25 (1997) 1130-1135
3. Gultyaev, A.P., van Batenburg, E., Pleij, C.W.A.: Similarities between the secondary structure of satellite tobacco mosaic virus and tobamovirus RNAs. J. Gen. Virology 75 (1994), 2851-2856
4. Han, K., Kim, D., Kim, H.-J.: A vector-based method for drawing RNA secondary structure. Bioinformatics 15 (1999) 286-197
5. Hilbers, C.W., Michiels, P.J.A., Heus, H.A.: New Developments in Structure Determination of Pseudoknots. Biopolymers 48 (1998) 137-153
6. Pleij, C.W.A.: Pseudoknots: a new motif in the RNA game. Trends in Biochemical Sciences 15 (1990) 143-147
7. van Batenburg, F.H.D., Gultyaev, A.P., Pleij, C.W.A.: PseudoBase: structural information on RNA pseudoknots. Nucleic Acids Res. 29 (2001) 194-195

Boosting Naive Bayes for Claim Fraud Diagnosis

Stijn Viaene[1], Richard Derrig[2], and Guido Dedene[1]

[1] KBC Insurance Research Chair,
Dept. of Applied Economic Sciences, K.U.Leuven,
Naamsestraat 69, B-3000 Leuven, Belgium
{stijn.viaene;guido.dedene}@econ.kuleuven.ac.be
[2] Automobile Insurers Bureau of Massachusetts &
Insurance Fraud Bureau of Massachusetts,
101 Arch Street, Boston, Massachusetts
richard@aib.org

Abstract. In this paper we apply the weight of evidence reformulation of AdaBoosted naive Bayes scoring due to Ridgeway et al. (1998) for the diagnosis of insurance claim fraud. The method effectively combines the advantages of boosting and the modelling power and representational attractiveness of the probabilistic weight of evidence scoring framework. We present the results of an experimental comparison with an emphasis on both discriminatory power and calibration of probability estimates. The data on which we evaluate the method consists of a representative set of closed personal injury protection automobile insurance claims from accidents that occurred in Massachusetts during 1993. The findings of the study reveal the method to be a valuable contribution to the design of effective, intelligible, accountable and efficient fraud detection support.

1 Introduction

Insurance fraud perpetrators range from opportunistic individuals to well-organized, criminal fraud rings. Insurance fraud is committed at underwriting time as well as at claim time. The latter is commonly termed claim fraud. It is generally believed that insurance fraud has evolved into one of the most prevalent and costly white collar crimes of which a sizeable amount remains undetected. The (US) Coalition Against Insurance Fraud estimates that insurance fraud costs Americans at least $80 billion a year. The Comité Européen des Assurances estimates that claim fraud cannot be less than €8 billion, which represents approximately 2% of the total annual premium income all classes combined for the European insurance industry (anno 1996). The Canadian Coalition Against Insurance Fraud estimates that $1.3 billion worth of general insurance claims paid in Canada every year are fraudulent. Most published material tends to confirm these orders of magnitude, at least using a wide definition of what constitutes a fraudulent claim. Producing exact figures, however, remains very hard as fraud, by its very nature, is a covert operation.

The most effective way to fight fraud is to prevent abuse of the system. Insurers have thereto been improving their applicant screening facilities, providing

Y. Kambayashi, W. Winiwarter, M. Arikawa (Eds.): DaWaK 2002, LNCS 2454, pp. 202–211, 2002.
© Springer-Verlag Berlin Heidelberg 2002

special training for front-office and claims handling personnel, establishing special investigative units, intensifying communication and cooperation within the industry and between the industry and prosecution and police authorities to fight insurance fraud, sponsoring state/country-level fraud bureaus, and committing to a policy to bring fraudsters before the courts. But fraudsters are renowned for their agility and creativity when it comes to finding new ways of exploiting the inertia of complex systems, especially when there is a lot of money involved. It then is imperative that fraud be detected at the earliest possible moment and that cheaters be swiftly tracked down. More systematic electronic collection and organization of, and company-wide access to coherent insurance data have stimulated data-driven initiatives aimed at analyzing and modelling the formal relations between fraud indicator combinations and claim suspiciousness to upgrade fraud detection with (semi-)automatic, intelligible, accountable tools.

In this paper we focus on the detection of suspicious personal injury protection automobile insurance claims. Previous work has been synthesized elsewhere [1]. We present the results of the successful application of the probabilistically interpretable weight of evidence reformulation of AdaBoosted naive Bayes scoring due to Ridgeway et al. [2] for the diagnosis of claim fraud. The paper is organized as follows. Sect. 2 briefly highlights the characteristics of the claims data used for this study. Sect. 3 covers the algorithmic details and the performance evaluation criteria, emphasizing both discriminatory power and calibration of probability estimates. Sect. 4 presents the results of an experimental assessment of the performance of the method. Sect. 5 wraps up the discussion.

2   Data Description

The study is based on a representative data set of 1,400 personal injury protection automobile insurance claims from accidents that occurred during 1993 and for which information was collected by the Automobile Insurers Bureau (AIB) of Massachusetts [3]. The data set is made up of closed claim files that were fully investigated and judged by experts. For all the claims the AIB carefully tracked 48 binary indicator variables (a.k.a. red flags), that were supposed to make sense to claims adjusters and fraud investigators. These indicators pertained to characteristics of the accident (12 variables), the claimant (5 variables), the insured driver (6 variables), the injury (11 variables), the treatment (7 variables) and lost wages (7 variables). For each of the 1,400 claim files senior claims adjusters recorded the presence or absence of each of the 48 indicator variables. Each claim file was reviewed by a senior claims manager on the basis of all available information. This closed claim reviewing was summarized into a 10-point scale expert assessment of suspicion of fraud, with 0 being the lowest and 10 the highest fraud suspicion score. Each definition threshold imposed on the 10-point scale then defines a specific (company) view/policy towards the investigation of claim fraud. Typically, a 4+ target encoding, i.e. IF suspicion rate < 4 THEN pass, ELSE no pass, is the operational domain expert choice [1]. For this scenario about 28% of the 1,400 claims were assigned to the latter category.

3   Method

3.1   Naive Bayes

The naive or simple Bayes classifier is well-known and widely-used. It builds on the conditional independence of predictors given the class label. Since probability estimates based on training data frequencies may be unreliable in sparsely populated regions, an additional smoothing operation can be applied. In this paper, smoothing is based on imposing a uniform Dirichlet prior on the tabular conditional probabilities (for individual predictors given the class) estimated from the training data [1,4]. Naive Bayes has a long history of empirical studies reporting often surprisingly good performance, even in cases where the independence assumption underlying naive Bayes was clearly unrealistic [1,5,6].

3.2   Boosting Naive Bayes

The AdaBoost or Adaptive Boosting algorithm was proposed by Freund and Shapire [7]. The mechanics of boosting rest on the construction of a sequence of classifiers, where each classifier is trained on a resampled (or reweighted) training set where those training instances that got poorly predicted in the previous runs receive a higher weight in the next run. At termination, i.e. after a fixed number of iterations, the constructed classifiers are then combined by weighted or simple voting schemes. The idea underlying the sequential perturbation of the training data is that the base learner, i.c. naive Bayes, gets to focus incrementally on those regions of the data that are harder to learn. The ground-breaking work of Freund and Shapire has since stimulated research on boosting (and other forms of model combination), and with success: for a variety of weak base learners, i.e. learners having a simple model bias (e.g. naive Bayes), boosting has been reported to reduce misclassification error, bias and/or variance (see e.g. [8,9]). We note that Elkan's application of boosted naive Bayes [10] won first prize in the KDD'97 data mining competition out of 45 entries. Ridgeway et al. [2] and O'Kane et al. [11] also report encouraging results from boosting naive Bayes.

AdaBoost [7], using the probabilistic predictions of the base learner, works as follows. For a training set $\{x_i, t_i\}_{i=1}^N$ with $x_i \in \mathbb{R}^n$ and $t_i \in \{0, 1\}$ let the initial instance weights be $w_i^{(1)} = \frac{1}{N}$. For run r from 1 to R proceed as follows:

1. Using weights $w_i^{(r)}$, learn model $H^{(r)}(x) : \mathbb{R}^n \to [0, 1]$.
2. Compute error of $H^{(r)}(x)$ as $\epsilon^{(r)} = \sum_{i=1}^N w_i^{(r)} \mid t_i - H^{(r)}(x_i) \mid$.
3. Let $\beta^{(r)} = \frac{\epsilon^{(r)}}{1-\epsilon^{(r)}}$ and $w_i^{(r+1)} = w_i^{(r)} (\beta^{(r)})^{1-|t_i - H^{(r)}(x_i)|}$.
4. Normalize $w_i^{(r+1)}$ by demanding that $\sum_{i=1}^N w_i^{(r+1)} = 1$.

The following final model combination hypothesis is then proposed for scoring a new case [7]:[1]

$$H(x) = \frac{1}{1 + \prod_{r=1}^R (\beta^{(r)})^{2Q(x)-1}} \quad \text{where} \quad Q(x) = \frac{\sum_{r=1}^R \log(\frac{1}{\beta^{(r)}}) H^{(r)}(x)}{\sum_{r=1}^R \log(\frac{1}{\beta^{(r)}})} . \qquad (1)$$

---

[1] Under the assumption that all models are useful, i.e. $\forall\, r \in \{1, ..., R\} : \epsilon^{(r)} < 0.5$.

Boosting naive Bayes then involves replacing $H^{(r)}(x)$ by the run r (smoothed) naive Bayes estimate of $p(t = 1 \mid x)$.

3.3 Weights of Evidence

Formulating the log-odds in favor of class $t = 1$ under the naive Bayes independence assumption, given discrete-valued predictors $x^{(m)}$ $(m = 1, ..., n)$ with values $a_k^{(m)}$ $(k = 1, ..., v^{(m)})$, yields:

$$\log(\tfrac{p(t=1|x)}{p(t=0|x)}) = \log(\tfrac{p(t=1)}{p(t=0)}) + \sum_{m=1}^{n} \log(\tfrac{p(x^{(m)}|t=1)}{p(x^{(m)}|t=0)})$$
$$= w_0 + \sum_{m=1}^{n} \sum_{k=1}^{v^{(m)}} I(x^{(m)} = a_k^{(m)}) w_{mk} \tag{2}$$

where $w_0 = \log(\tfrac{p(t=1)}{p(t=0)})$ and $I(\cdot)$ is 1 if its argument is true, 0 otherwise. The w_{mk} (or estimates $\hat{w}_{mk}$) are called weights of evidence [12,13]. They allow for a straightforward and intuitive interpretation of naive Bayes: a state of $x^{(m)}$ corresponding to a positive weight w_{mk} adds evidence to the hypothesis of suspicion of fraud, whereas a state of $x^{(m)}$ corresponding to a negative weight w_{mk} decreases the evidence. Accumulating all the evidence pro and contra automatically leads to an assessment of the case which can readily be transformed into posterior probabilistic instance scores. A variable that is missing scores 0 weight of evidence [13].

In order to restore the elegance and intuition characteristic of the weight of evidence formulation of simple Bayes – destroyed by the need to combine a sequence of boosted models – Ridgeway et al. [2] propose an equivalent for the case of AdaBoosted naive Bayes using a Taylor series approximation to the sigmoid transform up to the linear term. The estimate of the log-odds of the boosted model in Eq.(1) in favor of class $t = 1$ can then be formulated as:

$$\log(\tfrac{H(x)}{1-H(x)}) \approx \sum_{r=1}^{R} \alpha^{(r)} \log(\tfrac{\hat{p}^{(r)}(t=1)}{\hat{p}^{(r)}(t=0)}) + \sum_{m=1}^{n} \sum_{r=1}^{R} \alpha^{(r)} \log(\tfrac{\hat{p}^{(r)}(x^{(m)}|t=1)}{\hat{p}^{(r)}(x^{(m)}|t=0)})$$
$$\approx boosted \ prior \ weight \ of \ evidence \ estimate$$
$$+ \sum_{m=1}^{n} boosted \ weight \ of \ evidence \ estimate \ for \ x^{(m)}$$
$$\approx RHS \tag{3}$$

where $\alpha^{(r)} = \tfrac{\log(\frac{1}{\beta^{(r)}})}{\sum_{r=1}^{R} \log(\frac{1}{\beta^{(r)}})}$. A boosted estimate of $p(t = 1 \mid x)$ is then given by the sigmoid transform of RHS, i.e. $\tfrac{1}{1+\exp(-RHS)}$ [2].

3.4 Evaluation Criteria

Percentage correctly classified (PCC). PCC is the proportion of (test) instances that are correctly classified. PCC is the most widely-used measure of classifier discriminatory power (range $[0, 1]$; 1 being optimal) [14].

Receiver operating characteristic (ROC) curve. A ROC curve is a two-dimensional visualization of the false alarm rate (X-axis) versus the true alarm rate (Y-axis) for various values of the classification threshold imposed on the value range of a scoring rule or continuous-output classifier (e.g. for $\hat{p}(t = 1|x)$ i.e. $[0,1]$). It illustrates the classification properties of the scoring rule in terms of $\left(\frac{\text{False Positives}}{\text{False Positives} + \text{True Negatives}}, \frac{\text{True Positives}}{\text{True Positives} + \text{False Negatives}} \right)$ pairs for alternative operating conditions, i.c. summarized in the classification threshold. Informally, the closer the ROC curve is to the point $(0,1)$ (upper left) the better the scoring rule in general terms, i.e. taking into account the whole range of operating conditions. A specific operating condition coincides with a point on the ROC curve. For known operating conditions, scoring rules can be compared by contrasting the appropriate points on their ROC curves (or convex hull) [1,15,16,17].

Area under the ROC curve (AUROC). AUROC is a single-figure summary measure associated with ROC curve performance assessment (range $[0, 1]$; 1 being optimal). It is only appropriate as a performance measure for cases where specific operating conditions are unknown or vague, and more general evaluation/comparison of scoring rules over a range of operating conditions is in order. AUROC then provides a simple figure-of-merit for the expected performance of a scoring rule across a wide range of operating conditions. It is equivalent to the non-parametric Wilcoxon-Mann-Whitney statistic, which estimates the probability that a randomly chosen positive instance is correctly ranked higher than a randomly selected negative instance [15,16]. AUROC is based solely on the relative ranking of instances according to the continuous output of the scoring rule that underlies classification. This implies that AUROC analysis does not allow to assess whether probability estimates $\hat{p}(t \mid x)$ are well-calibrated [1,15, 16,17].

Logarithmic score $(\overline{L})$. Cross-entropy $\overline{CE}$ [18] is defined as follows for (test) data $\{x_i, t_i\}_{i=1}^N$ with $x_i \in \mathrm{IR}^n$ and $t_i \in \{0, 1\}$:

$$\overline{CE} = -\frac{1}{N} \sum_{i=1}^N \sum_{t^*=0}^1 p(t = t^* \mid x_i) \log(\hat{p}(t = t^* \mid x_i)). \tag{4}$$

However, since we do not have access to the true probabilities $p(t \mid x)$ and only the class labels are known, $p(t = t^* \mid x_i)$ is replaced in Eq.(4) by $\delta(t^*, t_i)$ where $\delta(\cdot, \cdot)$ is 1 if both arguments agree, 0 otherwise. This operation yields the logarithmic score $\overline{L}$. It is a widely-used minimization criterion for 2-class, single-output neural network classifiers (range $[0, +\infty]$; 0 being optimal) [18]. It takes account of the estimated probabilities $\hat{p}(t \mid x)$ and can thus be used as a measure for assessing the quality of the assigned probabilities. $\overline{L}$ is sensitive to small values of the assigned probabilities, an effect that can be dampened by setting a lower limit to $\hat{p}(t \mid x)$ [19].

Brier inaccuracy $(\overline{B})$. The Brier score $\overline{BS}$ (*Brier imprecision*) [15] is defined as follows for (test) data $\{x_i, t_i\}_{i=1}^N$ with $x_i \in \mathrm{IR}^n$ and $t_i \in \{0, 1\}$:

$$\overline{BS} = \frac{1}{N} \sum_{i=1}^N \sum_{t^*=0}^1 (\hat{p}(t = t^* \mid x_i) - p(t = t^* \mid x_i))^2. \tag{5}$$

This score coincides with the mean squared error (MSE) of the probability estimates. Again, since we do not have access to the true probabilities $p(t \mid x)$ and only the class labels are known, $p(t = t^* \mid x_i)$ is replaced in Eq.(5) by $\delta(t^*, t_i)$, as defined above. This operation yields the *Brier inaccuracy* $\overline{B}$ (range $[0, 2]$; 0 being optimal) [15]. $\overline{B}$ takes into account both the discriminatory power and the calibration of probability estimates [15,20].

Calibration plot. This plot depicts the agreement between the predicted probabilities $\hat{p}(t = 1 \mid x)$ (X-axis) and the observed proportions in the data (Y-axis) [21]. The golden standard is the diagonal from the point $(0,0)$ (bottom left) to the point $(1,1)$ (upper right). The closer the calibration plot is to the diagonal, the more reliable, i.e. well-calibrated, are the probability estimates. The plot is obtained by partitioning the measurement space spanned by x by means of grouping the values $\hat{p}(t = 1 \mid x)$ into G bins [15]. We then plot the average of $\hat{p}(t = 1 \mid x)$ over the instances within each bin versus the actual proportion of instances in the bin having $t = 1$. The latter serves as an estimate of the average true probability $\overline{p}(t = 1 \mid x)$ for the bin. Calibration can then be measured by the *grouped Brier imprecision* ($\overline{BS_c}$) [15] as follows for (test) data $\{x_i, t_i\}_{i=1}^N$ with $x_i \in \mathbb{R}^n$ and $t_i \in \{0, 1\}$:

$$\overline{BS_c} = \frac{1}{N} \sum_{g=1}^{G} \sum_{t^*=0}^{1} \nu_g (\overline{\hat{p}_g}(t = t^* \mid x) - \overline{\hat{p}_g}(t = t^* \mid x))^2 \tag{6}$$

where ν_g is the number of instances in bin g, $\overline{\hat{p}_g}(t \mid x)$ is the estimated average true probability $\overline{p}(t \mid x)$ for bin g and $\overline{\hat{p}_g}(t \mid x)$ the average of $\hat{p}(t \mid x)$ for bin g.

4   Discussion

Here we present the results of an experimental comparison of the methods discussed in Sect. 3 using the data described in Sect. 2. We used a split-sample experimental setup for evaluating the methods: $2/3$ of the data are used for training, the remaining $1/3$ is left for testing. The experiment was repeated 100 times, each time using a different randomization of the data. The same randomizations were used for the evaluation of all the methods. Each boosted classifier consisted of a sequence of 25 classifiers.

Table 1 presents the average test set results (standard deviation) for (smoothed) naive Bayes (NB), AdaBoosted naive Bayes (AB) and AdaBoosted weights of evidence (ABWOE). For comparison, we also give results for the MA-JORITY scoring rule, where each instance gets assigned a constant score equal to the base rate of positive instances in the training set. Results are reported in terms of percentage correctly classified (PCC), area under the receiver operating characteristic curve (AUROC), logarithmic score ($\overline{L}$), Brier inaccuracy ($\overline{B}$) and grouped Brier imprecision[2] $\overline{BS_c}$. The best mean per column has been underlined. For all performance measures ABWOE outperforms the rest. Most significant are the improvements for $\overline{L}$, $\overline{B}$ and $\overline{BS_c}$. The average test set ROC and calibration plots are given in Fig. 1. Each plot is provided with a subplot

---

[2] Not applicable for MAJORITY, where each instance gets the same base rate score.

Table 1. Average test set results (standard deviation)

	PCC	AUROC	$\overline{L}$	$\overline{B}$	$\overline{BS_c}$
NB	0.8303 (0.0141)	0.8856 (0.0128)	0.5670 (0.0655)	0.2768 (0.0247)	0.0433 (0.0108)
AB	0.8441 (0.0162)	0.8908 (0.0141)	0.8789 (0.1332)	0.2813 (0.0298)	0.0518 (0.0118)
ABWOE	<u>0.8443</u> (0.0155)	<u>0.8919</u> (0.0139)	<u>0.3697</u> (0.0237)	<u>0.2264</u> (0.0167)	<u>0.0109</u> (0.0039)
MAJORITY	0.7163 (0.0082)	0.5000 (0)	0.5941 (0.0151)	0.4042 (0.0141)	—

(bottom right) showing the standard deviation around the average. The calibration plot also depicts the distribution of data instances, totalling 100×466 (= number of randomizations × size test set), for the bins (bin width=0.1) imposed on the predicted probability range for NB, AB and ABWOE. The calibration plot clearly shows the improved calibration of probability estimates for ABWOE vis-à-vis NB and AB. From the ROC plot it can be observed that all methods tend to rank the test instances well. However, as can be observed from the calibration plot (and subplot), NB and AB (even more so) clearly tend to produce probability estimates $\hat{p}(t \mid x)$ that are too extreme, i.e. either close to 0 or to 1.[3] As noted by Ridgeway et al. [24], ABWOE, which relies on the Taylor series approximation to the sigmoid transform up to the linear term [2], seems to have a shrinking effect on the weights of evidence, similar to the logistic regression shrinkage proposed by Spiegelhalter and Knill-Jones [13], countering the classifier's over-confidence and yielding better-calibrated probabilities.

The claims manager now has an insightful balance of evidence [13] of the claim at his disposal. An example is given in Table 2. This evidence sheet is governed by a simple additivity principle: the total weight of evidence for a claim is determined by collecting the information on the available fraud indicators and summing their respective learned weights. Missing indicators score 0 weight of evidence. The sigmoid transform then maps this balance of evidence into a posterior fraud class membership probability estimate for the claim. Notice how boosting has set the initial score to (-43), which corresponds to a prior of 39%, whereas the actual data prior of positive instances amounted to 28% (see Sect. 2). This clearly illustrates that the boosting algorithm emphasized on learning the fraudulent cases in consecutive steps of the algorithm. As new information comes in, the balance of evidence can readily be updated. For example, information on the treatment, which is often very valuable for fraud detection purposes, is usually available later on in the life of a claim, e.g. the independent medical examiner may have questioned the extent of the injury, i.c. estimated weight of (+95). Also note that the actual classification threshold may be (iteratively) tuned to optimize for company-specific operating conditions and policy [13].

---

[3] This has been observed before for naive Bayes (see e.g. [6,22,23]).

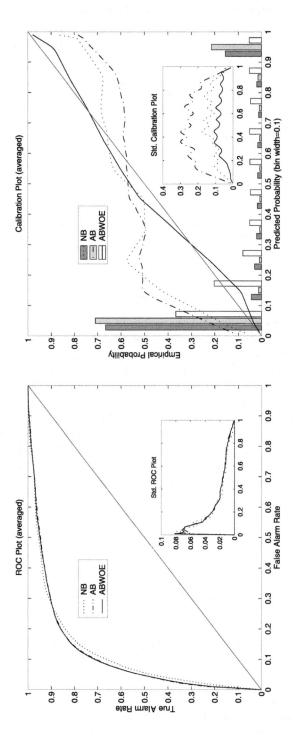

Fig. 1. Average test set ROC & calibration plots. Each plot is provided with a subplot (bottom right) showing the standard deviation around the average. The calibration plot also depicts the distribution of data instances, totalling 100×466 (= number of randomizations $\times$ size test set), for the bins (bin width=0.1) imposed on the predicted probability range for NB, AB and ABWOE

Table 2. Example balance of evidence

EVIDENCE PRO FRAUD		EVIDENCE CONTRA FRAUD	
Claimant in old, low-value vehicle	(+17)	Objective evidence of injury	(-36)
Two drivers related	(+49)	Insured driver was cooperative	(-5)
Claimant retained high-volume attorney	(+62)	Report police officer at scene	(-15)
Claimant appeared "claims-wise"	(+43)		
Insured driver appeared "claims-wise"	(+25)		
Injury consisted of strain/sprain only	(+27)		
	= (+223)		= (-56)
Balance of Evidence:	= (+167)		
Initial Score:	(-43)		
Final Score:	= (+124)	≈ 78% chance of fraud	

5 Conclusion

In this paper the weight of evidence reformulation of AdaBoosted naive Bayes scoring due to Ridgeway et al. (1998) was applied for the diagnosis of insurance claim fraud. The method was evaluated on closed personal injury protection automobile insurance claims from accidents in Massachusetts during 1993. On this real-life and representative data the algorithm showed good discriminatory ability and produced well-calibrated probability estimates. Moreover, the boosted weight of evidence framework offers a readily accessible and interpretable probabilistic model. It also naturally allows for human expert interaction and tuning. The framework effectively combines the advantages of AdaBoosted model ensemble learning with the modelling power and representational attractiveness of the probabilistic weight of evidence scoring framework.

References

1. Viaene, S., Derrig, R., Baesens, B., Dedene, G.: A comparison of state-of-the-art classification techniques for expert automobile insurance fraud detection. Journal of Risk and Insurance (2002) to appear
2. Ridgeway, G., Madigan, D., Richardson, T., O'Kane, J.: Interpretable boosted naive Bayes classification. In: Fourth International Conference on Knowledge Discovery and Data Mining, New York City (1998)
3. Weisberg, H., Derrig, R.: Identification and investigation of suspicious claims. AIB Cost Containment/Fraud Filing DOI Docket R95-12, AIB Massachusetts (1995) http://www.ifb.org/ifrr/ifrr170.pdf
4. Friedman, N., Geiger, D., Goldszmidt, M.: Bayesian network classifiers. Machine Learning **29** (1997) 131–163
5. Kohavi, R., Becker, B., Sommerfield, D.: Improving simple Bayes. In: Ninth European Conference on Machine Learning, Prague (1997)

6. Domingos, P., Pazzani, M.: On the optimality of the simple Bayesian classifier under zero-one loss. Machine Learning **29** (1997) 103–130
7. Freund, Y., Shapire, R.: A decision-theoretic generalization of on-line learning and an application to boosting. In: Second European Conference on Computational Learning Theory, Barcelona (1995)
8. Bauer, E., Kohavi, R.: An empirical comparison of voting classification algorithms: Bagging, boosting and variants. Machine Learning **36** (1999) 105–139
9. Shapire, R., Freund, Y., Bartlett, P., Lee, W.: Boosting the margin: A new explanation for the effectiveness of voting methods. The Annals of Statistics **26** (1998) 1651–1686
10. Elkan, C.: Boosting and naive Bayesian learning. Technical Report CS97-557, Department of Computer Science and Engineering, University of California, San Diego (1997)
11. O'Kane, J., Ridgeway, G., Madigan, D.: Statistical analysis of clinical variables to predict the outcome of surgical intervention in patients with knee complaints. Statistics in Medicine (1998) submitted
12. Good, I.: The estimation of probabilities: An essay on modern Bayesian methods. MIT Press, Cambridge (1965)
13. Spiegelhalter, D., Knill-Jones, R.: Statistical and knowledge-based approaches to clinical decision-support systems, with an application in gastroenterology. Journal of the Royal Statistical Society. Series A (Statistics in Society) **147** (1884) 35–77
14. Provost, F., Fawcett, T., Kohavi, R.: The case against accuracy estimation for comparing classifiers. In: Fifteenth International Conference on Machine Learning, Madison (1998)
15. Hand, D.: Construction and assessment of classification rules. John Wiley & Sons (1997)
16. Hanley, J., McNeil, B.: The meaning and use of the area under a receiver operating characteristic (ROC) curve. Radiology **143** (1982) 29–36
17. Provost, F., Fawcett, T.: Robust classification for imprecise environments. Machine Learning **42** (2001) 203–231
18. Bishop, C.: Neural networks for pattern recognition. Oxford University Press (1995)
19. Titterington, D., Murray, G., Murray, L., Spiegelhalter, D., Skene, A., Habbema, J., Gelpke, G.: Comparison of discrimination techniques applied to a complex data set of head injured patients. Journal of the Royal Statistical Society. Series A (Statistics in Society) **144** (1981) 145–175
20. Spiegelhalter, D.: Probabilistic prediction in patient management and clinical trials. Statistics in Medicine **5** (1986) 421–433
21. Copas, J.: Plotting p against x. Journal of the Royal Statistical Society. Series C (Applied Statistics) **32** (1983) 25–31
22. Bennett, P.: Assessing the calibration of naive Bayes' posterior estimates. Technical Report CMU-CS-00-155, Computer Science Department, School of Computer Science, Carnegie Mellon University (2000)
23. Zadrozny, B., Elkan, C.: Learning and making decisions when costs and probabilities are both unkown. In: Seventh ACM SIGKDD Conference on Knowledge Discovery in Data Mining, San Francisco (2001)
24. Ridgeway, G., Madigan, D., Richardson, T.: Boosting methodology for regression problems. In: Seventh International Workshop on Artificial Intelligence and Statistics, Fort Lauderdale (1999)

Optimization of Association Word Knowledge Base through Genetic Algorithm

Su-Jeong Ko and Jung-Hyun Lee

Department of Computer Science & Engineering
Inha University
Yong_hyen dong , Namgu, Inchon, Korea
{sujung@nlsun.inha.ac.kr},{jhlee@inha.ac.kr}

Abstract Query expansion in knowledge based on information retrieval system requires knowledge base being considered semantic relations between words. Since Apriori algorithm extracts association word without taking user preference into account, recall is improved but accuracy is reduced. This paper shows how to establish optimized association word knowledge base with improved accuracy only including association word that users prefer among association words being considered semantic relations between words. Toward this end, web documents related to computer are classified into eight classes, and nouns are extracted from web document of each class. Association word is extracted from nouns through Apriori algorithm, and association word that users do not favor is excluded from knowledge base through genetic algorithm.

1 Introduction

In Knowledge Based Query Processor system, if there is no index word that corresponds to query word, the word is retrieved through query expansion through word classification knowledge base[10,17]. Established word classification knowledge base is two fold: manual work by experts[11] and word clustering through co-occurrence between words as for corpus [4,7]. It takes a lot of time and efforts to establish word classification knowledge base through these methods, and it does not accurately reflect semantic relation between words.

In order to resolve this problem, we construct association word knowledge base by Apriori algorithm. But since Apriori algorithm extracts association word without taking user preference into account, recall is improved but accuracy is reduced. This

Y. Kambayashi, W. Winiwarter, M. Arikawa (Eds.): DaWaK 2002, LNCS 2454, pp. 212–221, 2002.
© Springer-Verlag Berlin Heidelberg 2002

paper shows how to establish optimized association word knowledge base with improved accuracy only including association word that users prefer among association words being considered semantic relations between words. In order to optimize the knowledge base, case base or user association feedback method can be used but these methods require existing cases or manual work by users[12,14].

This paper classified documents related to computer into eight classes, and association word is extracted through Apriori algorithm and then genetic algorithm[13] is applied for the purpose of optimization. Genetic algorithm optimizes knowledge base by excluding association word that users do not prefer among those extracted through Apriori algorithm.

2 Designing Optimized Association Word Knowledge Base

Fig. 1 is the whole system for extracting association word through Apriori-Genetic algorithm. System of Fig. 1 consists of HTTP down loader, text Engine, association word mining, association word refining and word rule set.

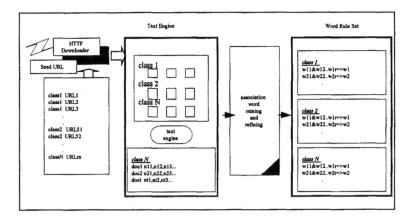

Fig. 1 System for implementing association word knowledge base

Association word group means association word mined in each class of class1,class2,...,classN. Association word is expressed in the form of {w11&w12,..,&w1r=>w1,   w21&w22,...,&w2r=>w2,..}. Each component of {w11,w12,...} included in association word means words that constitute association word and "&" symbolizes that words are associated. These words are based on nouns extracted from each web document. However, they are expressed differently as shown in {n11,..} and {w11,...} to demonstrate that {w11,...} is included in the association word. The association word group is optimized by genetic algorithm. HTTP down loader collects web document by class. Text engine conducts morphological analysis for web documents collected to each class and then extracts only nouns. Documents included into each class in text engine are expressed in the form of {doc1,doc2,...,doct} and nouns extracted from each document is expressed in the form of {n11,n12,n13,...}. In order to implement Fig. 1, flowchart of Fig. 2 has been suggested. Fig. 2 is divided into two; composition of knowledge base through extraction of association word from web document and refining of association word so that knowledge base is optimized. Block 1 and Block 2 of Fig. 2 are the stages where knowledge base is established and Block 3 and Block 4 are the stages where knowledge base is optimized.

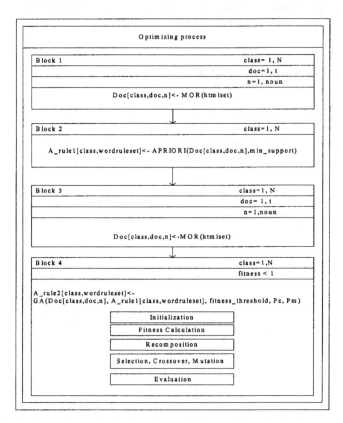

Fig. 2 Flowchart for implementing optimization of association word knowledge base

In Block 1, noun is extracted from web document through morphological analysis. The whole process is expressed as MOR( ) function. Doc[class,doc,n] is an array of result of extracting only nouns after morphological analysis of document collected in each class. "class" of Doc[class,doc,n] shows each class of {class1,...,classN}. "doc" of Doc[class,doc,n] indicates each document of {doc1,..,doct}, which is collected to each class of {class1,..,classN}. "n" of Doc[class,doc,n] indicates {n11,n12,...,ndocnoun} and means nouns extracted from each document of {doc1,...,doct}. In Block 2, mining association word from extracted nouns is conducted. A_rule1[class,wordruleset] of this stage indicates association word ground mined by each class. Here, class represents each class of {class1,...,classN} and wordruleset can be expressed in the form of {w11&w12,..,&w1r=>w1, w21&w22,...,&w2r=>w2,...}. APRIORI( ) indicates Apriori algorithm for mining association word, and min_support indicates minimal support used in Apriori algorithm. In Block 3, nouns are extracted from web document through morphological analysis as in Block 1. But it is different from Block 1 in that nouns are extracted from web document without consideration of user preference in Block 1 whereas nouns are extracted from web document that users prefer in Block 3. In Block 4, association word that users do not favor is excluded from knowledge base among association words of A_rule1[class,wordruleset] mined in Block 2 through nouns extracted from Block 3. GA( ) indicates genetic algorithm to remove association word that users do not favor from knowledge base, and fitness_threshold and Pc and Pm indicates fitness threshold, crossover probability and mutation probability. A_rule2[class,wordruleset] indicates array of saving optimal association word after removal of association word that users do not favor.

3 Process of Extracting and Refining of Association Word

Apriori algorithm[1,2] extracts association rule between words through data mining [16]. In order to extract association word from document, we use the method of [9]. Web documents related to computer are classified into eight in experiment for this paper. Its criteria are classification statistics used in existing information retrieval engine such as Yahoo, Altavista. APRIORI( ) shown in Block2 of Fig. 2 creates association word through application of Apriori algorithm as for result of Table 1.

Table 1. Association words in game class

(1)game&organization&athlete&participation=>selection	(10)game&utilization&problem=>rule
(2)domestic&newest&technology&installation=>development	(11)figure&popularity&service=>music
(3)game&participation&popularity&user&access=>event	(12)figure&data&service=>engine
(4)operation&selection&match&rank&rule=>assessment	(13)data&program=>music
(5)game&rank&name=>sports	(14)figure&data&program=>picture
(6)operation&sports&committee&athlete=>selection	(15)game&explanation&provision=>occupation
(7)game&organization&selection&rank=>match	(16)game&utilization&technology=>development
(8)game&schedule&athlete&participation&operation=>sports	(17)removal&game&individual match=>warning
(9)data&password&communicationnetwork=>affiliation	(18)game&provision&illustration=>explanation

Genetic algorithm optimizes knowledge base by excluding association word extracted through mining technique and that users do not favor. Association word that users favor is based on web document that users favor. Genetic algorithm optimizes association word knowledge base through initialization, fitness calculation, recomposition, selection, crossover, mutation, fitness evaluation.

GA( ) function shown in Fig. 2 refines association words from association word candidate that is result of APRIORI( ) function in Fig. 2. In initialization stage, document is expressed as collection of genes. In game class in Table 1, since eighteen association words exist, all chromosomes are expressed in eighteen bits. In order to remove improper association word from association words shown in Table 1, nouns shown in Table 2 have been extracted from ten web documents that users have selected through such process as morphological analysis. In addition, the second call of MOR( ) of Block 3 in Fig. 2 is conducted to extract nouns from ten web documents that users selected themselves, and Table 2 illustrates this case.

Table 2. Extracted nouns from web documents in population

Document	Nouns
Doc1	organization, page, genesis, rule, image, background, attack, gallery, link, explanation, ..
Doc2	participation, wedding, athlete, couple, gallery, attack, background, explanation, recording,..
Doc3	individual match, reorganization, game, warning, match, rule, group, standard, answer, ...
Doc4	technique, rule, athlete, attack, popularity, access, user, file, development, participation...
Doc5	list, game, button, tournament, event, computer, hardware, information, provision, purchase,..
Doc6	game, use, rule, explanation, provision, popularity, user, athlete, participation, operation,..
Doc7	sports, baseball, mercenary, location, match, organization, record, application, actual battle,..
Doc8	game, domestic, participation, popularity, access, work, technique, installation, operation,..
Doc9	multi-media, sound, domestic, provision, manufacturing, software, music, data, program, ..
Doc10	individual match, sports, group match, professional, amateur, application, tournament,..

For example of initialization, the first bit represents association word of (1) of Table 1 and the second bit expresses association word of (2), and so it consists of the total of 18 bits. If association word of Table 1 is included in nouns of Table 2, each bit of chromosome becomes 1(on) and otherwise, it is 0(off). Through this initialization, each document is expressed as a gene as shown in Table 3.

Table 3. Expressing web document as chromosome

Document	Chromosome(the first generation)
Doc1	101100000000100000
Doc2	001000000000001001
..	..
Doc10	101011010000000010

After expressing document as genes as shown in Table 3, fitness of document can be calculated as shown in second column of Table 4 through document fitness calculation by Equation (1). In Equation (1), #(doc$n$ U doc$m$) indicates the sum of the number of genes having the value of 1 in chromosome that represents doc n and the number of genes having the value of 1 in chromosome that represents doc m.

$$\text{Fitness}(docn,docm)=\#(docn \cap docm)/\#(docn \cup docm) \qquad (1)$$

Recomposed fitness of each document shown in third column of Table 4 is used through Equation (2) for adjustment. Equation (2) calculates ratio of fitness of each document against total fitness of all documents that belong to class.

Equation (2) calculates ratio of (Fitness[class,doc]) of each document against the total fitness of all documents that belong to class. According to this, fitness is readjusted and saved in Fitness-s[class,doc].

$$Fitness\_s[class,doc]=\frac{Fitness[class,doc]}{\sum_{doc=1}^{t}Fitness[class,doc]} \qquad (2)$$

Table 4. The calculation of fitness for web document

Document	Fitness	Recomposed fitness
Doc1	0.277170	5.354191
Doc2	0.275670	5.325215
..	..	..
Doc10	0.464354	8.97009
Average fitness	0.517669	10

In selection stage, select document subject to crossover based on recomposed fitness. In that case, doc3, doc4, doc5, doc6 in Table 4 are highly likely to be selected as parent chromosome because they have higher recomposed fitness than the others. In crossover stage, as for selected document, crossover is conducted according to crossover rate. This paper has used 1-point crossover method and crossover probability is 0.9. Selected chromosomes in Table 4 are subject to crossover as crossover stage. In mutation stage, according to mutation probability 0.01, one bit in chromosome after crossover is changed into another value as mutation stage. Table 5 is chromosome for the second generation, a child of the first generation, born after parent chromosome shown in Table 4 went through selection, crossover and mutation stages.

Table 5. The chromosome and fitness of the second generation

Document	Chromosome	Fitness
Doc1	101011111100001111	0.700600
Doc2	111111110100000111	0.716735
..	..	..
Doc10	101011010001000111	0.567764
Average		0.643161

In evaluation stage, whether to continue evolution is decided. Since average fitness of chromosome of the second generation calculated in the third row of Table 5 is

0.64316, it doesn't fit in with conclusion condition of genetic algorithm. Accordingly, evolution to next generation continues.

Evolution continues repeating the above process until average fitness becomes 1. Table 6 demonstrates chromosome from the first generation to the last generation, the eighth, and average fitness of each generation.

Table 6. The chromosome evolution from the first generation to the last generation

Generation	Chromosome	Fitness	Average Fitness
1	doc1:101100000000100000 doc2:001000000000001001 .	0.277170 0.275670 .	0.517669
2	doc1:101011111100001111 doc2:111111110100000111 .	0.700600 0.716735 .	0.643161
3	doc1:101011110100001111 doc2:111111110100001111 .	0.774610 0.774650 .	0.684610
....	....	....	...
8	doc1:101011110100001111 doc2:101011110100001111 .. doc10:101011110100001111	1 1 .. 1	1.0000000

While evolution proceeds average fitness has increased, and in the eighth generation where average fitness becomes 1, evolution has been concluded. Association word that represents gene of 1 in chromosome of the eighth generation is adopted and association word that represents gene of 0 is removed. Accordingly, if association word that represents gene of 0 among game class association words in Table 1 is removed, game class of association word knowledge base is optimized.

4 Evaluation

In this paper, Apriori algorithm has been used to establish association word knowledge base and established knowledge base has been optimized through genetic algorithm. In order to evaluate it, Apriori algorithm has compared mutual information[15] that is established method to extract association word with Rocchio algorithm[8], and genetic algorithm has compared with word refining method where text filtering method[14] has been applied through TF·IDF. Word refining method through TF·IDF is to extract nouns after morphological analysis of document that users favor. Then, as for extracted nouns, TF·IDF is calculated through Equation (3). As a result of calculation, if TF·IDF of nouns that belong to association word of association word knowledge base is smaller than 1, the word is removed from association word knowledge base.

word frequency in tfidf$_{ik}$= document$_k$*log$_2$ {(total document number)/(number of document where words appear)}   (3)

In order to evaluate it, partition table[6] of classification result of each class is made as shown in Table 7.

Table 7. 2 X 2-partition table

Partition 1		Partition 1	
Partition 2		YES	NO
Partition	YES	a	b
2	NO	c	d

In Equation (4), P indicates accuracy and R indicates recall, and the larger Fmeasure the better classification. Beta indicates a relative weight for accuracy recall in Fmeasure measurement function. In this experiment, beta is 1.0.

$$F_{measure} = \frac{(\beta^2 +1)PR}{\beta^2 P + R} \qquad P = \frac{a}{a+b}100\% \qquad R = \frac{a}{a+c}100\% \qquad (4)$$

In case of beta=1.0, if Apriori algorithm is used, word classification performance by Fmeasure is 10.04% higher than when mutual information, and if Rocchio algorithm is used, it is 11.80% higher as shown in Fig. 3.

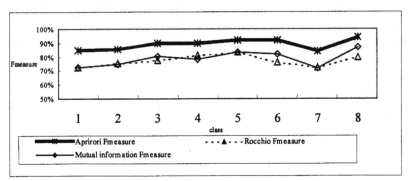

Fig. 3 Fmeasure of word classification

If it is beta=1.0 in Equation (4) as shown in Fig. 4, in refining performance of association word knowledge base by Fmeasure, genetic algorithm method generates 7.02% higher than when word filtering method using TF·IDF is used.

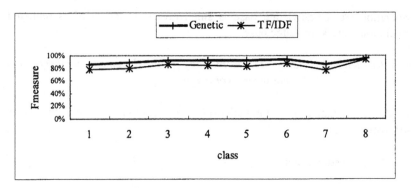

Fig. 4 Fmeasure of refining association word

5 Conclusion

In this paper, in order to establish knowledge base used in query expansion in knowledge based information retrieval system, web document related to computer has been collected and nouns have been extracted by class, and association word has been extracted through Apriori algorithm. Through application of genetic algorithm, association words that users do not favor have been excluded to establish optimized association word knowledge base by class. As for web document by class, association word extracted through Apriori algorithm designed in this paper, in word classification performance by F_measure measurement, has generated on average 5.46% higher than mutual information method and 7.26% higher than Rocchio algorithm method. In addition, genetic algorithm to refine association word knowledge base established by Apriori algorithm shows classification performance 7.02% higher than word filtering method that uses TF·IDF.

Reference

[1] R. Agrawal and R. Srikant, "Fast Algorithms for Mining Association Rules," Proceedings of the 20th VLDB Conference, Santiago, Chile, 1994.

[2] R. Agrawal and T. Imielinski and A. Swami, "Mining association rules between sets of items in large databases," Proceedings of the 1993 ACM SIGMOD Conference, Washington DC, USA, May 1993.

[3] P. Brown and P. Della and R. Mercer, "Class-based n-gram models of natural language," Computational Linguistics, 18(4), pp. 467-479, 1992.

[4] C. Clifton and R. Steinheiser, "Data Mining on Text," Proceedings of the Twenty-Second Annual International Computer Software & Applications Conference, 1998.

[5] M. Gondon, "Probabilistic and genetic algorithms for document retrieval," Communication of the ACM,31, pp. 1208-1218, 1988.

[6] V. Hatzivassiloglou and K. McKeown, "Towards the automatic identification of adjectival scales: Clustering adjectives according to meaning," Proceedings of the 31st Annual Meeting of the ACL, pp. 172-182, 1993.

[7] K. Hyun-Jin and P. Jay-Duke and J. Myung-Gil and P. Dong-In. "Clustering Korean Nouns Based On Syntactic Relations and Corpus Data," Proceedings of the LASTED International Conference Artificial Intelligence and Soft Computing, 1998.

[8] T. Joachims, "A Probabilistic Analysis of the Rocchio Algorithm with TFIDF for Text Categorization," Proceedings of 14th International Conference on Machine Learning, 1997.

[9] S. J. Ko and J. H. Lee, "Feature Selection using Association Word Ming for Classification," Proceedings of the DEXA, LNCS2113, 2001.

[10] H. IU and R. Setiono and H. Liu, "Effective Data Mining Using Neural Networks," Proceeding of the IEEE Trans. Knowledge and data engineering, V.8 N.6, pp. 962-969, 1996.

[11] G. Miller, "Wordnet:An on-line lexical database," International Journal of Lexicography. 3(4), pp. 235-244, 1990.

[12] K. Miyashita and K. Sycara, "Improving System Performance in Case Based Iterative Optimization through Knowledge Filtering," Proceedings of the International Joint Conference on Artificial Intelligence, 1995.

[13] T. Mitchell, *Maching Learning*, McGraw-Hill, pp. 249-273, 1997.

[14] D. W. Oard and G. Marchionini, "A Conceptual Framework for Text Filtering," Technical Report CAR-TR-830, Human Computer Interaction Laboratory, University of Maryland at College Park, 1996.

[15] C. Plaunt and B. A. Norgard, "An association based method for automatic indexing with a controlled vocabulary," Journal of the American Society for Information Science, 49, 888-902. 1998.

[16] P. C. Wong and P. Whitney and J. Thomas, "Visualizing Association Rules for Text Mining," Proceedings of the 1999 IEEE Symposium on Information Visualization, pp. 120-123, 1999.

[17] J. Xu and W. Bruce, "Query Expansion Local and Global Document Analysis," Proceedings of the 19th Annual International ACM SIGIR Conference on Research and Development in Information Retrieval, pp. 4-11, 1996.

Mining Temporal Patterns from Health Care Data[*]

Weiqiang Lin[1], Mehmet A. Orgun[1], and Graham J. Williams[2]

Department of Computing, Macquarie University Sydney, NSW 2109, Australia
CSIRO Mathematical and Information Sciences, Canberra, ACT 2601, Australia

Abstract: This paper describes temporal data mining techniques for extracting information from temporal health records consisting of a time series of elderly diabetic patients' tests. We propose a data mining procedure to analyse these time sequences in three steps to identify patterns from any longitudinal data set. The first step is a structure-based search using wavelets to find pattern structures. The second step employs a value-based search over the discovered patterns using the statistical distribution of data values. The third step combines the results from the first two steps to form a hybrid model. The hybrid model has the expressive power of both wavelet analysis and the statistical distribution of the values. Global patterns are therefore identified.

1 Introduction

Temporal data mining deals with the discovery of qualitative and quantitative patterns in temporal databases or in discrete-valued time series (DTS) datasets. Results to date on discovering periodic and similar patterns in discrete-valued time series datasets (e.g., [3]) have yet to lead to any well known general theory and general method of data analysis for discovering patterns from DTS.

In this paper we extend a framework introduced in [8,9] for discovering patterns from temporal health records by using wavelet analysis and regression. The approach employs three steps. The first step of the framework employs a distance measure and wavelet analysis to discover structural patterns (shapes). In the second step the degree of similarity and periodicity between the extracted patterns is measured based on the data value distribution models. The third step of the framework consists of a hybrid model for discovering global patterns based on results of the first two steps.

The paper is organised as follows. Section 2 discusses related work. Section 3 describes our Wavelet Feature Model (WFM). Section 4 briefly explains the background of the application, describes the application of the approach to a real-world dataset and discusses the results. The final section concludes the paper with a brief summary.

2 Related Work

The principle of general pattern mining from a dataset leads us to classify objectives in pattern searching into three categories: (1) Create representations in terms of algebraic systems with probabilistic superstructures intended for the representation and understanding of patterns in nature and science. (2) Analyse the regular structures from the perspective of mathematical theory. (3) Apply regular structures to particular applications and implement the structures by algorithms and code.

---

[*] Research supported in part by the Australian Research Council (ARC).

Y. Kambayashi, W. Winiwarter, M. Arikawa (Eds.): DaWaK 2002, LNCS 2454, pp. 222–231, 2002.
© Springer-Verlag Berlin Heidelberg 2002

In recent years various studies have only covered one or sometimes two of the above categories(e.g, [7] and [4]). Some studies have covered all the above three categories for searching patterns in data mining. For instance, Agrawal et al. [1] present a "shape definition language", called $\mathcal{SDL}$, for retrieving objects based on shapes contained in the histories associated with these objects. Das et al. [5] describe adaptive methods which are based on similar methods for finding rules and discovering local patterns and Baxter et al. [2] have considered three alternative feature vectors for representing variable-length patient health records.

In this paper we differentiate our approach in two ways. First, we use a statistical language to perform the search. Second, we divide the data sequence, or data vector sequence, into two groups: the structure based group and pure value based group.

In the structure-based grouping our techniques are a combination of the work of Agrawal at al. [1] and Baxter et al. [2]. With this grouping we use a distance measuring function on the structural wavelet's based sequences, similar to the work of Berger in [10]. Alternatively we could use a model-based clustering method on the state-space $\mathcal{S}$ (such as Snob as used in [2]) to find clusters but it does not facilitate the understanding of the pattern distribution within the dataset.

In the value-based grouping we apply statistical techniques such as a frequency distribution function to deal with the actual values in relation to their structural distribution. This is similar to the work of Das et al. [5] but it benefits from combining significant information of the two groups to gather information underlying the dataset.

3   Wavelet Feature-Based Pattern Mining

This section presents our temporal data mining model in searching and analysing patterns from a DTS using the wavelet feature-based regression models (WFMs). For an analysis of a real-world temporal dataset which may contain different kinds of patterns, such as complete and partial similar patterns and periodic patterns, we consider two groupings of the data sequences separately. These two groupings are: (1) structure-based grouping and, (2) pure value-based grouping. For structural pattern search we consider the data sequence as a finite-state structural vector sequence and apply a distance measure function in wavelet feature analysis. To discover pure value-based patterns we use data regression techniques on the data values. We then combine the results from both to obtain the final wavelet feature-based regression models (WFMs).

3.1   Definitions, Basic Models, and Properties

We first give a definition of DTS and then provide some definitions and notation to be used later.

Definition 1 *Suppose $\{\Omega, \Gamma, \Sigma\}$ is a probability space and T is a discrete-valued time index set. If for any $t \in T$, there exists a random variable $\xi_t(\omega)$ defined on $\{\Omega, \Gamma, \Sigma\}$, then the family of random variables $\{\xi_t(\omega), t \in T\}$ is called a **discrete-valued time series (DTS)**.*

We assume that for every successive pair of time points in the DTS $t_{i+1} - t_i = f(t)$ is a function (in most cases, $f(t) = $ constant). Let us now use the symbol $X(t_j)$ to denote the value of the series under study at the time instant t_j, $j = 1, 2, \ldots, \mathcal{N}$. For every successive three time points: t_{i-1}, t_i and t_{i+1}, the triple value of (X_{i-1}, X_i, X_{i+1}) has only nine distinct states (or nine local features), as enumerated in Figure 1, depending on whether the values increase, decrease or stay the same over the two time steps.

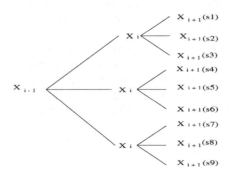

Fig. 1. $\mathcal{S} = \{s1, s2, s3, s4, s5, s6, s7, s8, s9\}$

Definition 2 *In this framework suppose S_s represents the same state as the previous state, S_u represents an increase over the previous state, and S_d represents a decrease over the previous state. Let $S = \{s1, s2, s3, s4, s5, s6, s7, s8, s9\} = \{(X_j, S_u, S_u), (X_j, S_u, S_s), (X_j, S_u, S_d), (X_j, S_s, S_u), (X_j, S_s, S_s), (X_j, S_s, S_d), (X_j, S_d, S_u), (X_j, S_d, S_s), (X_j, S_d, S_d)\}$. Then S is the **state-space**.*

Haar's Wavelet Function. We choose the simplest basis function of the wavelet system—the *Haar wavelet basis function*—in this paper. The Haar function was developed in 1910 [6][1] is given by:

$$\psi(x) = \begin{cases} 1 & \text{if } 0 \leq x < \frac{1}{2} \\ -1 & \text{if } \frac{1}{2} \leq x < 1 \\ 0 & \text{otherwise.} \end{cases} \quad (1)$$

If f is a function defined on the whole real line then for a suitably chosen function ψ we can expand f as:

$$f(t) = \sum_{j=-\infty}^{\infty} \sum_{k=-\infty}^{\infty} w_{jk} 2^{-j/2} \psi(2^{-j}t - k) \quad (2)$$

where the functions $\psi(2^{-j}t - k)$ are orthogonal to one another and w_{jk} is the discrete wavelet transform (DWT) defined as

$$w_{jk} = \int_{-\infty}^{\infty} f(t) 2^{-j/2} \psi(2^{-j}t - k) dt \quad (3)$$

where j and k are integers, j is a scale variable and k is a translation variable.

---

[1] Often called the *mother wavelet*

The Mahalanobis distance Function. In a distributional space (e.g., state space, probability space), two conditional distributions with similar covariance matrices and very different means are so well separated that the Bayes probability of error is small. In this paper, we use Mahalanobis distance functions which are provided by a class of positive semidefinite quadratic forms. Specifically, if $\mathbf{u} = (u_1, u_2, \cdots, u_p)$ and $\mathbf{v} = (v_1, v_2, \cdots, v_p)$ denote two p-dimensional observations of each different distance of patterns in the same distributional space on objects that are to be assigned to two of the g pre-specified groups, then, for measuring the Mahalanobis distance between $\mathbf{u}$ and $\mathbf{v}$ we can consider the function:

$$D^2(i) = (\bar{\mathbf{u}} - \bar{\mathbf{v}})^{\mathbf{T}} \sum\nolimits^{-1} (\bar{\mathbf{u}} - \bar{\mathbf{v}}) \tag{4}$$

where $\bar{\mathbf{u}} = \mathbf{E}\mathbf{u}$, $\bar{\mathbf{v}} = \mathbf{E}\mathbf{v}$ are means, and $\sum$ is a covariance matrix.

Local Linear Model. We consider the bivariate data (X_1, Y_1), ...,(X_n, Y_n), which forms an independent and identically distributed sample from a population (X, Y). For given pairs of data (X_i, Y_i), $i = 1, 2, \ldots, n$, we can regard the data as being generated from the model:

$$\mathbf{Y} = m(\mathbf{X}) + \sigma(\mathbf{X})\varepsilon \tag{5}$$

where $E(\varepsilon) = 0$, $Var(\varepsilon) = 1$, and X and ε are independent. For an unknown regression function m(x), applying a Taylor expansion of order p in a neighbourhood of $\mathbf{x}_0$ with its remainder ϑ_p,

$$m(\mathbf{x}) = \sum_{j=0}^{p} \frac{m^{(j)}(\mathbf{x}_0)}{j!} (\mathbf{x} - \mathbf{x}_0)^j + \vartheta_p \equiv \sum_{j=0}^{p} \beta_j (\mathbf{x} - \mathbf{x}_0)^j + \vartheta_p. \tag{6}$$

The first stage of methods for detecting the characteristics of those records is to use linear regression. We may assume the linear model is $\mathbf{Y} = \mathbf{X}\beta + \varepsilon$.

3.2   Mining Global Patterns from a Database

For any dataset we divide the dataset into two parts: the qualitative part and the quantitative part. The qualitative part is based on the above state space for structural pattern searching and the quantitative part is based on probability space for statistical pattern searching.

For qualitative pattern searching we first use multiresolution analysis (decomposition) with a Haar wavelet, then we apply the Mahalanobis distance function on the state-space $\mathcal{S}_j = \{s_{1j}, s_{2j}, \cdots, s_{mj}\}$ of $\mathcal{S}$. For quantitative pattern searching we only consider the structural relationship between the response variable $\mathbf{Y}$ and the vector of covariates $\mathbf{X} = (t, X_1, \ldots, X_n)^T$. By Taylor expansion we may fit a linear model as above and parameters can be estimated under LSE. The problem can then be formulated as the data distribution functional analysis of a discrete-valued time series.

We combine the above two kinds of pattern discovery to discover global information from a temporal dataset. For the structure group let the structural sequence $\{\mathcal{S}_t : t \in \mathbf{N}\}$ be data functional distribution sequence on the state-space $\{s_1, s_2, \ldots, s_N\}$. Then suppose the pure valued data sequence is a nonnegative random vector process $\{\mathbf{Y}_t; t \in \mathbf{N}\}$ such that, conditional on $S^{(T)} = \{\mathcal{S}_t : t = 1, \ldots, T\}$, the random vector variables $\{\mathbf{Y}_t : t = 1, \ldots, T\}$ are mutually independent.

4   An Application in Health Care Data

The dataset used in this study is Australian Medicare data. Medicare is the Australian Government's universal health care system covering all Australian citizens and residents. Each medical service performed by a medical practitioner is covered by the Medicare Benefits Scheme (MBS) and is recorded in the MBS database as a transaction. We present a case study on using our data mining techniques to analyse the medical service profiles of diabetes. This study complements a recent study of the time sequence dataset using a vector feature approach [2]. Similar to that study we use a subset of de-identified data (to protect privacy) based on Medicare transactions from Western Australia (WA) for the period 1994 to 1998.

There are three monitoring medical tests for controlling the conditions of the diabetic patients[2]: (1) Glycated hemoglobin measurements (Gl) provide information about the accumulated effect of glucose levels, (2) Ophthalmologic examinations (Op) are important in the early identification and of complications related to eye sight and (3) Cholesterol measurements via lipid studies (Ch) help identify possible complications relating to heart conditions.

Table 1. Types of services received by Patients and indicative guidelines.

Abbrev	Description	Guidelines
Gl	Quantitation of glycosylated hemoglobin.	2–4 times per year
Op	Ophthalmologic examination.	Every 1-2 years
Ch	Cholestorol measurement via lipid studies.	Every year

4.1   Experimental Results

The sample data includes 4916 elderly diabetic patients. We have only limited demographic information about each patient, such as age, gender and location. For each patient we also have the sequence of diabetes-related monitoring tests they have received over the time interval. We identified clusters in which patterns associated with nine states for diabetes patients were found.

We study each of the three tests separately to find out how a patient's treatment follows the guidelines. We also study the overall patterns which take all three tests into consideration. To this end we summarise all the events (the tests performed) into eight distinct types of events which are listed in Table 2.

Through this experiment we are interested in investigating the following issues which are of interest to medical experts with particular interest in changes to patterns of care in the management of Diabetes over time: Does there exist any temporal pattern P_t for all patients who have one, two, or three tests regularly? What features are there for those temporal patterns? and Does there exist any temporal subpattern in P_t or between patterns P_t's?

---

[2] The Health Insurance Commission of Australia http://www.hic.gov.au.

Table 2. Eight possible test combinations tests for patients

Test group	Description	Test group	Description
test 0	No test	test 4	Gl and Op
test 1	Gl only	test 5	Gl and Ch
test 2	Op only	test 6	Op and Ch
test 3	Ch only	test 7	Gl, Op and Ch

Modelling DTS. We assume a constant time gap for successive time points in a DTS: $t_{i+1} - t_i = c$ (constant). For mining temporal patterns from a real-world dataset we use the *time gap* between events of the same type as the time variable rather than the time gap between different events. An example patient record is given in Table 3.

Table 3. A patient test group transactional record illustrating the time gaps.

Test Group	Day of Test	Days since last same test
1	1	time gap = 1
1	191	time gap = 190
2	331	time gap = 1
7	487	time gap = 1
2	779	time gap = 448
1	894	time gap = 703
6	947	time gap = 1

From a DTS as in Table 3 we perform structural pattern searching on the state-space using the time gap as a variable for each test group. We may view the structural base as a set of vector sequences: $\mathbf{S}_{9 \times m} = \{\mathbf{S}_1, \cdots, \mathbf{S}_m\}$, where each $\mathbf{S}_i = (s1_i, s2_i, \cdots, s9_i)^T$ denotes the 9-dimensional observation on an object that is to be assigned to a prespecified group. Then the problem of structural pattern discovery for the sequence and each of its subsequence $\mathbf{S}_{ij} = \{si_1, si_2, \cdots, si_j : 1 \leq i \leq 9, 1 \leq j \leq m\}$ of $\mathbf{S}$ on the finite-state space can be formulated as a Haar's function with a Mahalanobis distance model.

We can also view the value-point process data as an N-dimensional data set[3]: $\mathbf{V} = \{\mathbf{V}_1, \cdots, \mathbf{V}_m\}$, where each $\mathbf{V}_i = (v1_i, v2_i, \cdots, vN_i)^T$, where the N is dependent on how many statistical values relate to the structural base pattern searching. Then the problem of value-point pattern discovery can be formulated as a stochastic distribution of the sequence and its subsequences $\mathbf{V}_j = \{v1_j, v2_j, \cdots, vN_j\}$ of a discrete-valued time series.

On structural pattern searching. We investigate the data structural base to test the naturalness of the similarity and periodicity on the Structural Base distribution. We consider seven test groups in the state-space for structural distribution: $\mathcal{S} = \{s1, s2, \ldots, s9\}$. For finding all levels of patterns (or clusters) we applied Haar's function (Equation 1) and the distance function (Equation 4) on a three-dimensional dataset. The first dimension

---

[3] According to their structural distribution model

is the test group, the second dimension is the time gap between each test group and the third dimension is the time gap within the same test group.

We have found an important result that there exist similar time gap frequency patterns between and/or within state one and state nine for all test groups. For example, the pattern of patients not taking any test is similar to the pattern of patients taking test group one and test group two with the time gap increasing (or, decreasing).

Other results include (1) there exist similar time gap frequency patterns between and/or within state two and state six for all test groups—the patients have not received adequate care according to the clinical guidelines and (2) there exist similar and periodic time gap frequency patterns between state three and state seven for all test groups—the patients have received adequate care according to the clinical guidelines.

In Figure 2, the x-axis represents natural integer sequence $\mathbf{N}$ and the y-axis represents the time gap for each state. Figure 2 explains some important facts: first that there exists the same time gap statistical distribution (e.g., the same tangent curve distribution) between the test group 1, test group 2, test group 3 and test group 5. It also explains visits to doctors are stationary in different time gaps for those four types of test groups. Second, there exists a hidden periodic distribution which corresponds to patterns on the same state with different distances, this means patients visit their doctors periodically and third there exist partial periodic patterns on and between some test group in state-space.

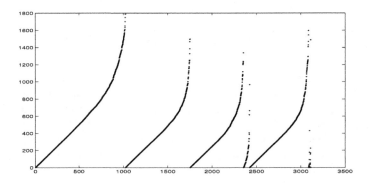

Fig. 2. Plot of the time gap within each test group for all 8 test groups in 1,875 business days.

On value-point pattern searching. We now illustrate our new method to analyse the value-point sequence of health temporal records for searching patterns. In these records, since each patient record length is different, we can only use their statistical value as variables in regression functions (e.g., frequency distribution functions). In the light of our structural base experiments, we have the series

$$Y_t = f_t^{testgroupi}(v_t) - f_t^{testgroupj}(v_t) \qquad (7)$$

where $f_t^{testgroupi}(v_t)$ is a frequency distribution function, its variable v_t is the time gap between the same state (e.g., $v_t = state\ k_{t_1} - state\ k_{t_2}$), in the same cluster. Then the observations can be modelled as a linear regression function,

$$Y_t = f_t^{testi}(v_t) - f_t^{testj}(v_t) + \varepsilon_t, \qquad t = 1, 2, \ldots, N \qquad (8)$$

and we also consider the $\varepsilon(t)$ as an auto-regression $AR(2)$ model

$$\varepsilon_{t'} = a\varepsilon_{t'-1} + b\varepsilon_{t'-2} + e_{t'} \qquad (9)$$

where a, b are constants dependent on the sample dataset, and $e_{t'}$ is a small variance constant which can be used to improve the predictive equation.

In Figure 3 the x-axis represents the frequency of time gaps between the same states and the y-axis represents the time gap between the same states. This confirms that: (1) there exists a Poisson distribution for each of test group 1 and test group 5—the period of medical treatment for test group 1 and test group 5 is stationary independent increment; (2) there exists the same patterns between two test groups with small distance shiftting—patients have received treatment for test group 1 or test group 5 by the guidelines.

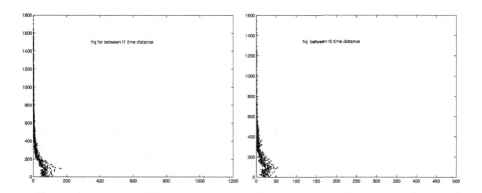

Fig. 3. Time distance frequency distribution of test group 1 and test group 5 are Poisson distributions.

Other results include (1) there exists an exponential distribution for test group 2. This means that the patient has a problem and is receiving treatment for the identification or control of the problem and (2) there exists a geometric distribution for test group 3. This means that patients have received regular treatment.

4.2   Mining Global Patterns

According to the above analysis, let $\{S_t : S_t \in \mathcal{S}, t \in \mathsf{N}\}$ be a structural process representing *state k* occurrence, and $\{V_t : t \in \mathsf{N}\}$ be the corresponding observed values, then we have the distribution of V_t conditional on S_t given by

$$\mathsf{P}(V_t = v|S_t = i) = p_{vi}^t \qquad (10)$$

For test group 1 and test group 5, $V_t^{testgroup1}$ and $V_t^{testgroup5}$ both have Poisson distribution with means $\lambda_i^{testgroup1}$ and $\lambda_i^{testgroup5}$. Two states satisfy

$$V_t^{testgroup1} = \alpha V_t^{testgroup5} + \theta_t \qquad (11)$$

Then the conditional mean of V_t and state-dependent probabilities given for all non-negative integers v_t will be:

$$\mu(t) = \sum_{i=1}^{m} \lambda_i W_t(t),$$

$$P_{v_t, statek} = e^{-\lambda_{i,v_t}} \frac{\lambda_{i,v_t}}{v_t!}$$

(12)

For test group 2, $V_t^{testgroup2}$ is an exponential distribution with parameters $\lambda_i^{testgroup2}$ and $\mu_i^{testgroup2}$. Then the conditional exponential distribution of $V_t^{testgroup2}$ and state-dependent probabilities given for all non-negative integers v_t will be

$$\mu(t) = \sum_{i=1}^{m} \lambda_i W_t(t),$$

$$P_{v_t, test2} = \begin{cases} \lambda_{(i,v_t)} e^{(-\lambda_{(i,v_t)}(v_t - \mu))} & v_t > \mu \\ 0 & v_t < \mu \end{cases}$$

(13)

For test group 3, $V_t^{testgroup3}$ is a geometric distribution with parameter $p_i^{testgroup3}$. Then the conditional geometric distribution of $V_t^{testgroup3}$ and state-dependent probabilities given for all non-negative integers v_t will be

$$\mu(t) = \sum_{i=1}^{m} \lambda_i W_t(t),$$

$$P_{v_t, testgroup3} = p_{i,v_t}^{statek}(1 - p_{i,v_t}^{statek})^{(v_t - 1)}$$

(14)

Test group 4, test group 6 and test group 7 are indepentent states. We use Haar function and local polynomial function for each of them to find their conditional distribution function $f_{testgroupk}(t)$. We found that there exist some similar patterns between each of their state but no patterns exist between each of their clusters of time gap, this means the patients have received number of treatments from test group k (k = 4, 6, 7) similar but for different time periods.

The main results from structural and value-point pattern searching are:

1. The behaviour of patients visiting doctors for diabetics is a Poisson distribution, having the same distribution of visits in the same period (e.g., within 7 days).
2. The distribution of tests between patients that more or less care is log-normal—the number of doctor visits is not symmetric around the mean, but extends considerably to the right (a pattern of less care)

Other results on the health dataset are as follows: There exist some full periodic patterns within and between states 1 and 5—the time gap between patients taking test 1, and the time gap between patients taking test 1 & test 3 are both stationary. There exist partial periodic patterns between states 1, 2, 3 and 5—the patients have sub-common problems such as eye problems (e.g., taking more eye tests, etc.). There exist similar patterns between states 1, 2, 3 and 5—there exists similar patterns of behaviour for patients visiting their doctors but for different tests.

5 Concluding Remarks

This paper has presented a new approach based on hybrid models to form new models of application of data mining. The rough decision for pattern discovery comes from the structural level that is a collection of predefined similar patterns. The clusters of similar patterns are computed in this level by the choice of distance measures. The point-value patterns are decided in the second level and the similarity and periodicity of a DTS are extracted. In the final level, we combine structural and value-point pattern searching into the wavelet's feature-based regression models (WFMs) to obtain a global pattern picture and understand the patterns in a dataset better. Another approach to find similar and periodic patterns has been reported(e.g., [8,9]); there the models used are based on hidden functional analysis.

References

1. Rakesh Agrawal, Giuseppe Psaila, Edward L. Wimmers, and Mohamed Zait. Querying shapes of histories. In *Proceedings of the 21st VLDB Conference*, September 1995.
2. Rohan A. Baxter, Graham J Williams, and Hongxing He. Feature selection for temporal health records. available from `Graham.Williams@cbr.dit.csiro.au`, APR. 2001.
3. C. Bettini. Mining temportal relationships with multiple granularities in time sequences. *IEEE Transactions on Data & Knowledge Engineering*, 1998.
4. G. Das, D.Gunopulos, and H. Mannila. Finding similar time seies. In *Principles of Knowledge Discovery and Data Mining'97*, 1997.
5. G. Das, K. Lin, H. Mannila, G. Renganathan, and P. Smyth. Rule discovery from time series. In *Proceedings of the international conference on KDD and Data Mining(KDD-98)*, 1998.
6. A. Haar. Zur theore der orthoganalen funktionen systeme. *Annals of Mathematics 69: 331–371*.
7. Cen Li and Gautam Biswas. Temporal pattern generation using hidden markov model based unsuperised classifcation. In *Proc. of IDA-99*, pages 245–256, 1999.
8. Wei Q. Lin, Mehmet A.Orgun, and Graham Williams. Temporal data mining using multilevel-local polynomial models. In *Proceedings of IDEAL-2000*, The Chinese University of Hongkong, Hong Kong, 2000.
9. Wei Q. Lin, Mehmet A.Orgun, and Graham Williams. Temporal data mining using local polynomial-hidden markov models. In *Proceedings of PAKDD-2001*, The University of Hongkong, Hong Kong, 2001.
10. S.Jajodia and S. Sripada O. Etzion, editor. *Temporal databases: Research and Practice*. Springer-Verlag, LNCS 1399, 1998.

Adding a Performance-Oriented Perspective to Data Warehouse Design

Pedro Bizarro and Henrique Madeira

DEI-FCTUC
University of Coimbra
3030 Coimbra - Portugal
[bizarro, henrique]@dei.uc.pt

Abstract. Data warehouse design is clearly dominated by the business perspective. Quite often, data warehouse administrators are lead to data models with little room for performance improvement. However, the increasing demands for interactive response time from the users make query performance one of the central problems of data warehousing today. In this paper we defend that data warehouse design must take into account both the business and the performance perspective from the beginning, and we propose the extension to typical design methodologies to include performance concerns in the early design steps. Specific analysis to predicted data warehouse usage profile and meta-data analysis are proposed as new inputs for improving the transition from logical to physical schema. The proposed approach is illustrated and discussed using the TPC-H performance benchmark and it is shown that significant performance improvement can be achieved without jeopardizing the business view required for data warehouse models.

1 Introduction

Data warehouses often grow to sizes of gigabytes or terabytes making query performance one of the most important issues in data warehousing. Performance bottlenecks have being tackled with better access methods, indexing structures, data reduction, parallelism, materialized views, and more. Although hardware and software power continuously increased, performance is still a central concern since the size of data is also continuously increasing.

Although it is possible to store the data warehouse in a multidimensional database server most of the data warehouses and OLAP applications store the data in a relational database. That is, the multidimensional model is implemented as one or more star schema formed by a large central fact table surrounded by several dimensional tables related to the fact table by foreign keys [1].

There are three different levels in a Data Warehouse (DW) development: conceptual, logical and physical. It is largely agreed that conceptual models should remain technology independent since their main goal is to capture the user intended needs. On the other end, going from the conceptual to the logical and physical schemes is almost always and semi-automated process. In this paper we argue that this path leads to sub-optimal physical schemes. Our view is that although the three

Y. Kambayashi, W. Winiwarter, M. Arikawa (Eds.): DaWaK 2002, LNCS 2454, pp. 232-244, 2002.

levels accomplish several degrees of independence, in the end the physical scheme is too much influenced by the conceptual model which will jeopardize performance.

In practice, current DW design methodologies are directed towards obtaining a model reflecting the real world business vision. Performance concerns are normally introduced very late in the design chain, as it is accepted that star schema represent a relatively optimized structure for a data warehouse. The designer attention is focused on the capture of the business model and the performance optimization is often considered an administrative task, something that will be tuned later on. In the end, the data warehouse designer is lead to a physical model in which there is almost no room for performance improvement. The DW administrator choices are reduced to the use of auxiliary data structures such as indexes, materialized views or statistics, which consume administration time, disk space and require constant maintenance.

In this paper we propose the extension of established DW design approaches [2] to include performance concerns in the early steps of the DW scheme design. This way, DW design takes into account both the business and the performance perspective from the beginning, and specific analysis to predicted DW usage profile and meta-data analysis is proposed to improve the transition from logical to physical schema.

The paper is organized as follows. Section 2 presents related work. Section 3 recalls current design methodologies and introduces our approach. In section 4 we present a motivating example and in section 5 we apply the design method to that example. Section 6 presents performance figures and section 7 concludes the paper.

2   Related Work

Improving performance has always been a central issue in decision support systems [3]. The race for performance has pushed improvements in many aspects of DW, ranging from classical database indexes and query optimization strategies to pre-computation of results in the form of materialized views and partitioning.

A number of indexing strategies have been proposed for data warehouses such as join indexes [4], bitmapped join indexes [5], and star joins [6] and most of these techniques are used in practice [6], [7], [5]. Although essential for the right tune of the database engine, the performance of index structures depends on many different parameters such as the number of stored rows, the cardinality of data space, block size of the system, bandwidth of disks and latency time, only to mention some [8].

The use of materialized views is probably the most effective way to accelerate specific queries in a data warehouse. Materialized views pre-compute and store (materialize) aggregates computed from the base data [9]. However, storing all possible aggregates causes storage space problems and needs constant attention from the database administrator.

Data reduction techniques have recently been proposed to provide fast approximate answers to OLAP queries [10]. The idea consists of building a small synopsis of the original data using sampling or histogram techniques. The size of the reduced data set is usually very small when compared to the original data set and the queries over the reduced data can be answered quite fast. However, the answers obtained from a reduced data set are only approximate and in most cases the error is large [11], which greatly limits the applicability of data reduction in the data warehouse context.

Many parallel databases systems have appeared both as research prototypes [12], [13], [14], [15] and as commercial products such as NonStop SQL fromTandem [16] or Oracle. However, even these "brute force" approaches have several difficulties when used in data warehouses such as the well-known problems of finding effective solutions for parallel data placement and parallel joins.

Recent work [17], [18] proposed the use of uniform data striping together with an approximate query answering to implement large data warehouses over an arbitrary number of computers, achieving nearly linear query speed up. Although very well adapted to data warehousing, these proposals still need massive parallel systems, which may be expensive and difficult to manage.

In spite of the numerous research directions to improve performance, the optimization of the data warehouse schema for performance has been largely forgotten. In [19] the use of vertical fragmentation techniques during the logical design of the data warehouse has been proposed, but the proposal of a design approach that takes into account both the business and the performance perspective in the definition of the data warehouse schema has not been proposed yet, to the best of our knowledge.

It is generally accepted that the star schema is the best compromise between the business view and performance view. We believe that usage profile and meta-data information can be used in early design stages to improve the data warehouse schema for performance and this is not contradictory with a data warehouse focused on the business view. This effort could lead to physical designs very far from the traditional star schema expected by most of the OLAP tools. However, the idea of having an intermediate layer to isolate queries from the physical details has already been proposed [20] and can also be used in our approach.

3 Data Warehouse Design: A Performance Perspective

Data warehouse design has three main sources of input: the business view, data from operational systems (typically OLTP systems), and a set of design rules [2]. The outcome is a model composed by several stars. Latter in the process, administrative optimizations are made, such as selecting and creating indexes and materialized views. These optimizations are manly influenced by the real usage of the DW. Figure 1 represents this design approach.

The star scheme is so popular manly because it is especially conceived for ad hoc queries. It is also assumed that there is no reason to presume that any given query is more relevant or frequent than any other query. Or at least, this does not influence greatly the design process. We argue that even in decision support with ad hoc queries it is possible to infer (during the analysis steps) some data that describes or reveals characteristics of future most frequent queries. Meta-data can also provide significant insight on how to further optimize the scheme. This information is essential to improve data warehouse schema for performance and this does not jeopardizes the business view desired for the data warehouse.

The design approach should then be changed to incorporate these additional input parameters in the design process as early as possible. Figure 2 shows the proposed data warehouse design approach.

The next sections describe the new design inputs "predicted usage profile" and "meta-data" and how they influence the DW design.

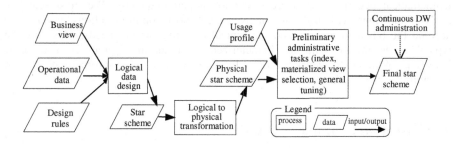

Fig. 1. Typical DW design approach

User's queries are largely unpredictable but only to a certain degree. The analysis method usually used to identify facts and dimensions in a business process can also help in the prediction of things such as:

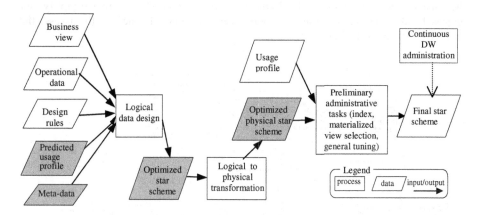

Fig. 2. Proposed DW design process

- that some facts are asked more frequently than others;
- that some dimension attributes are seldom used while others are constantly used;
- that some facts, or some dimension attributes are used together while some will almost never be used together;
- that some mathematical operations will be frequent while others will not;
- etc.

The key word is frequent. After all, the main goal in any optimization is to improve the frequent case. We cannot use probability numbers to classify the likelihood of some DW data being asked. But at least we can use relative classifications and say "x is more likely to happen than y" or "x is much more likely to happen than z" or "the probability of w happen is almost zero".

In general, what we want to know is which things (queries, restrictions, joins, mathematical operations, etc) are likely to happen frequently. We must schedule analysis meetings with users to uncover their most common actions, taking into account the business process and the typical decision support needs. This way the typical usage profile will be characterized to a certain degree, even if some knowledge is fuzzy. However, as we will see, even rough usage information can lead to significant performance improvement.

4 Motivation Example – TPC-H

The TPC Benchmark H (TPC-H) is a widely known decision support benchmark proposed by the Transaction Performance Processing Council [21]. Our idea is to illustrate the proposed approach using the business model of TPC-H. To do this we will redesign the original TPC-H scheme, preserving the business view but changing the scheme to take into account possible usage information and meta-data. Of course, the TPC-H "business" is not a real case (it is just a realistic example) but as we keep the business view and the TPC-H queries, this is a good way to exemplify our approach. At the same time, we will use the TPC-H queries to assess the improvements in performance.

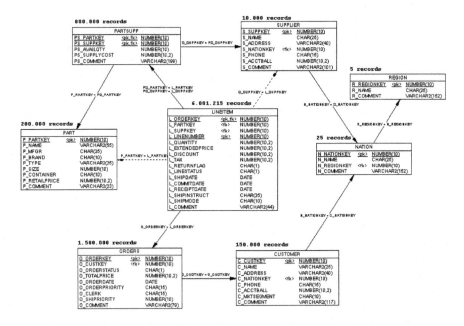

Fig. 3. TPC-H scheme

The TPC-H scheme consists in eight tables and their relations. Data can be scaled up to model businesses with different data sizes. The scheme and the number of rows for each table at scale 1 are presented in Figure 3.

The TPC-H represents a retail business. Customers order products, which can be bought from more than one supplier. Every customer and supplier is located in a nation, which in turn is in a geographic region. An order consists of a list of products sold to a customer. The list is stored in LINEITEM where every row holds information about one order line. There are several date fields both in LINEITEM and in ORDERS, which store information regarding the processing of an order (order date, ship date, commit date and receipt date). The central fact table in TPC-H is LINEITEM although PARSUPP can also be considered another fact table (in fact, TPC-H scheme is not a pure star scheme, as proposed by Kimball).

The dimensions are PART, SUPPLIER and ORDERS. There are two snowflakes, ORDERS→ CUSTOMER→ NATION→ REGION and SUPPLIER→ NATION→ REGION. Therefore, to find out in which region some LINEITEM has been sold it is necessary to read data from all the tables in the first snowflake.

5   Redesigning the Scheme towards Performance

5.1   Tuning TPC-H in the Kimball's Way

The TPC-H scheme is filled with real world idiosyncrasies and clearly there are improvements to be made. If one follows the guidelines of Kimball [1] the snowflakes must be removed since they lead to heavy run-time joins. A number of different schemes without the snowflakes or with smaller snowflakes can be devised. We show three of them in Figure 4, Figure 5 and Figure 6.

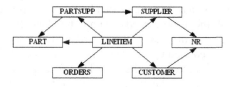

Fig. 4. TPC-H without snowflake from ORDERS to CUSTOMER

In Figures 4, 5, and 6, NR represents a join between NATION and REGION. Similarly CUSTMER_NR represents a join between CUSTOMER, NATION and REGION and finally SUPPLIER_NR represents a join between SUPPLIER, NATION and REGION.

The changes in these three schema are of two types: breaking snowflakes by transforming a snowflake table into a dimension (CUSTOMER in Figure 4 and Figure 5 and NR in Figure 5) and merging several tables into one bigger denormalized table (NR in Figure 4 and Figure 5, CUSTOMER_NR in Figure 6 and SUPPLIER_NR in Figure 6). It is possible to apply both techniques simultaneously.

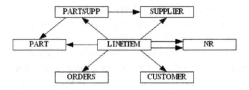

Fig. 5. TPC-H scheme without any snowflake

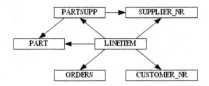

Fig. 6. TPC-H scheme with CUSTOMER and SUPPLIER highly denormalized

All these alternative schemes break the connection between ORDERS and CUSTOMER. CUSTOMER is now a dimension of its own, and therefore, any query fetching data from both LINEITEM and CUSTOMER will not need to read from ORDERS as before. The gains are considerable because ORDERS is a huge table.

5.2 Assumptions in TPC-H Analysis

Breaking snowflakes and denormalizing dimensions are traditional steps, as proposed by Kimball. By analyzing the model from the point of view of "predicted usage data" and "meta-data" we will show that the scheme can be further improved.

A thorough analysis of the users' needs cannot be done because TPC-H is a benchmark without real users. In what follows, we will consider that the TPC-H queries reflect closely the "predicted usage data". Therefore, we are assuming that the most common accessed structures in the 22 TPC-H queries (tables, columns, restrictions, operations, etc) are also the most common in the "predicted usage data".

5.3 Meta-data Analysis

Text attributes in a fact table (usually known as false facts), especially big strings, can degrade performance because they occupy too much space and normally are rarely used. In our example, TPC-H, the columns L_COMMENT, L_SHIPMODE and L_SHIPINSTRUCT are text attributes that occupy almost half the space in LINEITEM. However, the queries seldom read those attributes. Taking them out of LINEITEM will cause a slimmer fact table. That is especially good because almost every query reads the fact table. Similarly, O_COMMENT in ORDERS also occupies too much space and is rarely read. Removing O_COMMENT from ORDERS improves the overall performance since it is the second largest table both in size as in accesses.

Big dimensions represent a problem in a star scheme because they are slow to browse and to join with the fact table. With mini-dimensions [1] it is possible to break a big dimensions into smaller ones. However, having many dimensions implies many foreign keys in the fact table, which are very expensive due to the fact table size. Thus the reverse procedure may be applied to join (using Cartesian product) two smaller dimensions into a bigger, hopefully not to big, dimension. It is also common to denormalize (using joins) a snowflake into just one bigger table.

In Figure 5, there are two dimensions for NR representing the customer nation and region and the supplier nation and region. Having two dimensions forces LINEITEM to have two foreign keys (FK). One way to remove one FK is to make a new dimension representing the Cartesian join between NR and NR. This new dimension (lets call it NRNR) will hold every possible combination of customer nation and supplier nation. It is not a regular denormalization because there is no join condition.

NATION has 25 lines and REGION has 5, therefore, NR has 25 lines (because is a join). NRNR is the result of a Cartesian join of two tables (customer's NR and supplier's) each with 25 rows. It will have 25*25 = 625 rows. Having NRNR allows to remove one FK from LINEITEM while still having a small dimension with only 625 rows. Dimensions this size fit entirely in memory and represent no downside.

Note that conceptually, having NR and NR merged into a dimension represents a rupture from the business perspective because unrelated information is mixed.

5.4   Predicted Usage Data Analysis

5.4.1   Removing Less Used Facts

The analysis of the TPC-H queries reveals that the attributes L_SHIPINSTRUCT, L_SHIPMODE and L_COMMENT, in LINEITEM, are almost never read. Thus, we created a new table, LN_EXTRA, to hold them. Since LN_EXTRA must still be related with LINEITEM, it also needs to hold LINEITEM's primary key (PK) columns. The advantage of removing those three columns from LINEITEM is that queries reading it will find a slicker table. In this example, LINEITEM will be almost half its size after the removal of these columns. On the other hand, LN_EXTRA is a huge table with as many rows as LINEITEM. Queries reading LN_EXTRA fields will cause a join between LINEITEM and LN_EXTRA. However, the advantage surpasses the disadvantage because LINEITEM is queried every time where LN_EXTRA hardly is.

5.4.2   Frequently Accessed Dimensions

Due to the nature of the query patterns, some dimensions may also be hot spot places. If they are big it is especially important to tune them.

ORDERS is a huge table, which leads to slow joins and to slow queries. Furthermore ORDERS is frequently read. Small improvements in ORDERS will cause large or frequent gains. After analyzing the TPC-H queries, we noticed that by far, the most selected attribute in ORDERS is O_ORDERDATE. The field O_COMMENT is almost never selected, and O_TOTALPRICE, O_CLERK and

O_SHIPRIORITY are selected rarely. O_ORDERSTATUS and O_ORDER-PRIORITY appear frequently but not as much as O_ORDERDATE. Table 1 below shows the read frequencies of these columns and our changes to the scheme.

Table 1. Improvements due to ORDERS columns

Columns	Read frequency	Action and comments
O_ORDERDATE	Very frequent	Move to fact table
O_ORDERSTATUS, O_ORDERPRIORITY	Frequent	Move to NRNR; moving the hot spot from ORDERS to a smaller table
O_TOTALPRICE, O_CLERK, O_SHIPPRORITY	Rare	Leave in ORDERS
O_COMMENT	Very, very rare	Move to LN_EXTRA

O_ORDERDATE was changed to LINEITEM since it is usually read whenever the other date fields in LINEITEM are. Remember that O_COMMENT was changed to LN_EXTRA. Another change was moving O_ORDERSTATUS and O_ORDER-PRIORITY to NRNR. Since ORDERS cannot be directly related with nations and regions, another Cartesian join is needed. However, O_ORDERSTATUS has only 3 distinct values and O_ORDERPRIORITY has only 5 distinct values (meta-data information!). Thus, the new NRNR table will hold 625 * 3 * 5 = 9375 rows, which is still small. Thus the hot spot focus was moved to a much smaller table (ORDERS is more than 150 times bigger than NRNR having 1,500,000 rows).

5.4.3   Fields Accessed Together/Apart

The previous changes benefited from the fact that only the columns in the same read frequency are usually accessed together. If that was not the case, spreading ORDERS' columns all over the scheme would force run-time joins. For instance, with the new scheme, a query that reads both O_COMMENT, O_CLERK and O_ORDERSTATUS must join at run time LINEITEM, ORDERS, NRNR and LN_EXTRA. Therefore, the frequent access dimension analysis must be done together with the fields accessed together/apart analysis.

In the end, queries selecting O_ORDERDATE (and LINEITEM columns) will be faster than before because O_ORDERDATE is closer to where the other usually selected fields are. Queries to O_ORDERPRIORITY and O_ORDERSTATUS will also be faster because the NRNR dimension is very small and then joining it with LINEITEM is cheaper. Finally, queries to O_TOTALPRICE, O_CLERK and O_SHIPPRORITY will also be faster because ORDERS is now a much thinner table. Only the very few queries to O_COMMENT will be slower.

5.4.4   Store Common Reads, Calculate Uncommon Reads

Avoid run-time mathematical calculations if you can. If needed trade frequent run-time operations for less frequent run-time mathematical operations.

In the example, almost all queries calculate revenue at run-time using the formula: L_EXTENDEDPRICE * (1 - L_DISCOUNT). An obvious improvement is to store the value of revenue, let's call it L_REVENUE. The calculation will be done just once at load time. However, storing just L_REVENUE leads to the lost of information because it is not possible to determine the values of L_EXTENDEDPRICE and L_DISCOUNT. One better approach is to store not only L_REVENUE but L_EXTENDEDPRICE as well. This avoids the run-time calculation of L_REVENUE and still permits to compute the value of L_DISCOUNT

5.5   Optimized Star Scheme

Figure 7 presents our optimized scheme after all the changes mentioned so far.

Note that Figure 7 depicts a rather uncommon schema. Some dimension attributes are out of their natural place, spread over other tables (both over dimensions and fact tables). Artificial tables like LN_EXTRA were created only to lighten the burden on other more frequently accessed tables. Even stranger is NRNR, a new dimension holding information from customer's nation, customer's region, supplier's nation, supplier's region, and some order's information.

What is relevant is that Figure 7 scheme was a direct result of new design process, which accounts for predicted usage profile and meta-data information. We believe that current data warehouse design methodologies are unable to produce such performance driven scheme.

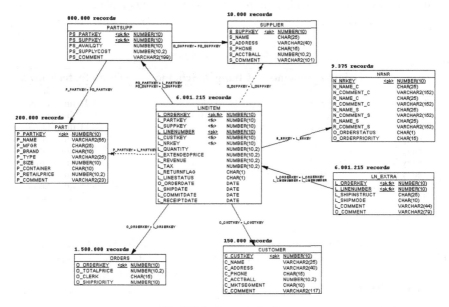

Fig. 7. The improved scheme

5.6   The Need of a Logical Level

The scheme of Figure 7 provides excellent performance results (see section 6). However, it models the business in a way that is not natural, at least from the end user's perspective. One way to present the right business view to the user, in spite of having a different scheme at the physical level, is to have a layer in between to insulate the physical from the conceptual scheme. This layer has been already proposed in the literature [20].

6   Results

To measure improvements in performance it is necessary to adapt the queries to the new scheme and compare their results to the ones obtained before the changes were made. Due to time restrictions, only some of the queries were tested. Their results are presented in Table 2.

All performance figures where taken in a Win2000 box with a 300 MHz clock and 320 Mbytes of RAM using Oracle 8i (8.1.6) server. To the fairness of experiments, all queries were optimized using indexes, hints, and statistics (statement ANALYZE). From all possible plans of each query and its scheme only the best execution plans were considered. This also proved another interesting result: it was much easier to optimize the queries with the new scheme than with the original one. The main reason was that the new scheme, which is simpler, yields less execution plans.

Table 2. Comparison of results

	Original Scheme	Changed Scheme	Times faster/slower
Query 1	204.1 s	264.2 s	1.29 times slower
Query 3	515.5 s	159.1 s	3.23 times faster
Query 4	398.3 s	61.6 s	6.47 times faster
Query 5	969.4 s	48.2 s	20.11 times faster
Query 6	78.9 s	49.6 s	1.59 times faster
Query 7	400.7 s	0.7 s	572.42 times faster
Query 8	239.9 s	47.7 s	5.03 times faster
Query 9	1661.2 s	1029.3 s	1.61 times faster
Query 10	471.1 s	257.9 s	1.86 times faster
Query 21	552.7 s	585.4 s	1.06 times slower

Regarding space, the main differences are due to LINEITEM, LN_EXTRA, ORDERS, NATION, REGION and NRNR. All the other tables and indexes are more or less the same in both schemes or its size is not relevant. Their space distribution is showed in Table 3.

Although the new scheme takes up more space, the hotspot part, the one with most of the reads, got 33% smaller.

Table 3. Differences in space

	Original Scheme	**Changed Scheme**
LINEITEM	757 Mb	550 Mb
ORDERS	169 Mb	60 Mb
NATION	≈ 0 Mb	--
REGION	≈ 0 Mb	--
NRNR	--	8
Hotspot Sub-Total	926 Mb	618 Mb
LN_EXTRA	--	920 Mb
Total	926 Mb	1538 Mb

7   Conclusions

DW performance is a major concern to end-users. However, performance considerations are typically introduced in the later stages of the DW design process. Almost every enhancement (new types of indexes, new types of joins, data reduction, sampling, real-time information, materialized views, histograms, statistics, query plan optimizations, etc) is applied after the physical scheme has been obtained.

We propose that data warehouse design must take into account both the business and the performance perspective from the early design steps. Specific analysis to predicted data warehouse usage profile and meta-data analysis are proposed as new inputs for improving the transition from logical to physical schema. Following this approach, the designer will face uncommon scheme options for performance optimization that do not directly portrait the business model, but still allow answering all queries. Some of these options break the fact or dimension frontiers. Examples are changing attributes from one table to another, splitting one big dimension into several smaller ones, merging several small dimensions into a bigger one, and placing in the same table attributes that are usually acceded together even if they belong to different entities. An intermediate software layer can used to allow schema optimization for performance without jeopardizing the business view required for data warehouse models at the end user level.

The TPC-H performance benchmark is used in the paper to illustrate and discuss the proposed approach. The execution of TPC-H queries in both the original and the optimized schema have shown that significant performance improvement can be achieved (up to 500 times).

References

1.   R. Kimball, "The Data Warehouse Toolkit", John Willey & Sons, Inc.; 1996.
2.   R. Kimball et. al, "The Data Warehouse Lifecycle Toolkit", Ralph Kimbal, Ed. J. Wiley & Sons, Inc, 1998
3.   E. F. Codd, S. B. Codd, C. T. Salley. "Beyond decision support". ComputerWorld, 27(30), July 1993.
4.   P. Valduriez. "Join Indices". ACM TODS, Vol 12, N° 2, pp 218-246; June 1987.
5.   P. O'Neil, D. Quass. "Improved Query Performance with Variant Indexes". SIGMOD 1997.

6.   "Star queries in Oracle8". Technical White Paper, Oracle, 1997. Available at http://technet.oracle.com/products/oracle8/htdocs/xsq4twp.htm, accessed in May 2001.

7.   T. Flanagan and E. Safdie. "Data Warehouse Technical Guide". White Paper, Sybase 1997.

8.   Marcus Jurgens and Hans-J. Lenz. "Tree Based Indexes vs. Bitmap Indexes: A Performance Study". Proceedings of the Int. Workshop DMDW'99, Heidelberg, Germany, 1999.

9.   S. Chauduri and U. Dayal. "An overview of data warehousing and OLAP technology". SIGMOD Record, 26(1):65-74, March 1997.

10. Joseph M. Hellerstein, "Online Processing Redux". Data Engineering Bulletin 20(3): 20-29 (1997).

11. P. Furtado and H. Madeira. "Analysis of Accuracy of Data Reduction Techniques". First International Conference, DaWaK'99, Florence, Italy, Springer-Verlag, pp.377-388.

12. H. Boral, W. Alexander, L. Clay, G. Copeland, S. Danforth, M. Franklin, B. Hart, M. Smith & P. Valduriez. "Prototyping Bubba, A highly parallel database system". IEEE Transactions on Knowledge and Data Engineering 2 (1990), 4-24.September 1990.

13. D. J. DeWitt et al.. "The Gamma Database Machine Project". IEEE Trans. Knowledge and Data Engineering, Vol. 2, N°1, March 1990, pp.44-62.

14. G. Graefe. "Query evaluation techniques for large databases". ACM Computing Surveys, 25(2):73-170, 1993.

15. Michael Stonebraker: "The Postgres DBMS". SIGMOD Conference 1990: 394.

16. Tandem Database Group. "NonStop SQL: A Distributed, High-Performance, High-Availability Implementation of SQL". HPTS 1987: 60-104.

17. J. Bernardino and H. Madeira, "Experimental Evaluation of a New Distributed Partitioning Technique for Data Warehouses", IDEAS'01, Int. Symp. on Database Engineering and Applications, Grenoble, France, July, 2001.

18. J. Bernardino, P. Furtado, and H. Madeira, "Approximate Query Answering Using Data Warehouse Striping", 3rd Int. Conf. on Data Warehousing and Knowledge Discovery, Dawak'01, Munich, Germany, 2001.

19. Matteo Golfarelli, Dario Maio, Stefano Rizzi, "Applying Vertical Fragmentation Techniques in Logical Design of Multidimensional Databases", 2nd International Conference on Data Warehousing and Knowledge Discovery, Dawak'00, Greenwich, United Kingdom, September 2000.

20. L. Cabibbo, R. Torlone: "The Design and Development of a Logical System for OLAP". DaWaK 2000: 1-10

21. The Transaction Processing Council. http://www.tpc.org.

Cost Modeling and Estimation for OLAP-XML Federations

Dennis Pedersen, Karsten Riis, and Torben Bach Pedersen

Department of Computer Science, Aalborg University
{dennisp,riis,tbp}@cs.auc.dk

Abstract. The ever-changing data requirements of today's dynamic businesses are not handled well by current OLAP systems. Physical integration of data into OLAP systems is a time-consuming process, making logical *federations* the better choice in many cases. The increasing use of XML suggests that the required data will often be available in XML format. Thus, federations of OLAP and XML databases will be very attractive in many situations. In an efficient implementation of OLAP-XML federations, cost-based optimization is a must, creating a need for an effective cost model for OLAP-XML federations.

In this paper we present a *cost model* for OLAP-XML federations, and outline techniques for *estimating* the cost model parameters in a federated OLAP-XML environment. The paper also outlines the cost models for the OLAP and XML components in the federation on which the federation cost model is built. The cost model has been used as the basis for effective cost-based query optimization in OLAP-XML federations. Experiments show that the cost model is precise enough to make a substantial difference in the query optimization process.

1   Introduction

OLAP systems [15] enable powerful decision support based on multidimensional analysis of large amounts of detail data. OLAP data are often organized in multidimensional *cubes* containing *measured values* that are characterized by a number of hierarchical *dimensions*. However, *dynamic data*, such as stock quotes or price lists, is not handled well in current OLAP systems, although being able to incorporate such frequently changing data in the decision making-process may sometimes be vital. Also, OLAP systems lack the necessary flexibility when faced with unanticipated or rapidly changing data *requirements*. These problems are due to the fact that physically integrating data can be a complex and time-consuming process requiring the cube to be rebuilt [15]. Thus, logical, rather than physical, integration is desirable, i.e. a *federated* database system [13] is called for. The increasing use of Extended Markup Language (XML), e.g. in B2B applications, suggests that the required external data will often be available in XML format. Also, most major DBMSs are now able to publish data as XML. Thus, it is desirable to access XML data from an OLAP system, i.e., OLAP-XML federations are needed. For the implementation of OLAP-XML federations to perform well, cost-based optimization is needed, creating a need for a cost model for OLAP-XML federations. However, existing cost models do not support such systems.

Y. Kambayashi, W. Winiwarter, M. Arikawa (Eds.): DaWaK 2002, LNCS 2454, pp. 245–254, 2002.

In this paper we present such a cost model for OLAP-XML federations, along with techniques for estimating cost model parameters in an OLAP-XML federation. We also present the cost models for the autonomous OLAP and XML components in the federation on which the federation cost model is based. The cost model has been used as the basis for effective cost-based query optimization in OLAP-XML federations, and experiments show that the cost model is powerful enough to make a substantial difference in the query optimization process.

To our knowledge, no general models exist for estimating the cost of an OLAP query (MOLAP or ROLAP). Shukla et al. [14] describe how to estimate the size of a multidimensional aggregate, but their focus is on estimating storage requirements rather than on the cost of OLAP operations. Also, we know of no cost models for XPath queries, the closest related work being on path expressions in object databases [7]. Detailed cost models have been investigated before for XML [5], relational components [2], federated and multidatabase systems [3,12,17], and heterogeneous systems [1,6]. However, since our focus is on OLAP and XML data sources only, we can make many assumptions that permit better estimates to be made. One previous paper [11] has considered federating OLAP and object data, but does not consider cost-based query optimization, let alone cost models. A common technique for acquiring cost information from federation components is *query probing* [16] where special *probing queries* are used to determine cost parameters. *Adaptive cost estimation* [4] is used to enhance the quality of cost information based on the actual evaluation costs of user queries.

We believe this paper to be the first to propose a cost model for OLAP-XML federation queries, along with techniques for estimating and maintaining the necessary statistics. Also, the cost models for the autonomous OLAP and XML components are believed to be novel.

The rest of the paper is organized as follows. Section 2 describes the basic concepts of OLAP-XML federations and the federation system architecture, and outlines the query optimization strategy. Sections 3 and 4 present the federation cost model and the cost models for the OLAP, XML, and temporary components. Section 5 outlines a performance study evaluating the cost model. Section 6 summarizes the paper and points to future work.

2   OLAP-XML Federation Concepts

This section briefly describes the concepts underlying the OLAP-XML federations that the cost model is aimed at. These concepts are described in detail in another paper [8]. The examples are based on a case study concerning B2B portals, where a cube tracks the cost and number of units for *purchases* made by customer companies. The cube has three dimensions: Electronic Component (EC), Time, and Supplier. External data is found in an XML document that tracks component, unit, and manufacturer information.

The OLAP data model is defined in terms of a multidimensional *cube* consisting of a *cube name*, *dimensions*, and a *fact table* with *measures*. Each dimension has a hierarchy of the *levels* which specify the possible levels of detail of the data. Dimensions are used to capture the possible ways of grouping data. A SQL-based OLAP query language, SQL_M, and a formal algebra has been defined.

XML specifies how documents can be structured using so-called *elements* that contains *attributes* with atomic values. Elements can be nested within and contain references to each other. For example, for the example described above, a "Manufacturer" element in the XML document contains the "MCode" attribute, and is nested within a "Component." XPath is a simple, but powerful language for navigating within XML documents. For example, the XPath expression "Manufacturer/@Mcode" selects the "MCode" attribute within the "Manufacturer" element.

The OLAP-XML federations are based on the concept of *links* which are relations linking dimension values in a cube to elements in an XML document, e.g., linking electronic components (ECs) in the cube to the relevant "Component" elements in the XML document. A *federation* consists of a cube, a collection of XML documents, and the links between the cube and the documents. The most fundamental operator in OLAP-XML federations is the *decoration* operator which basically attaches a new dimension to a cube based on values in linked XML elements. Based on this operator, we have defined an extension of SQL_M, called SQL_{XM}, which allows XPath queries to be added to SQL_M queries, allowing linked XML data to be used for decorating, selecting, and grouping fact data. For example, the SQL_{XM} query "SELECT SUM(Quantity),EC/Manufacturer/@MCode FROM Purchases GROUP BY EC/Manufacturer/@MCode" computes total purchase quantities grouped by the manufacturer's MCode which is found only in the XML document.

We now give an overview of the OLAP-XML federation system, the design considerations and optimization techniques as well as their use in the federation system. The overall architectural design of a prototype system supporting the SQL_{XM} query language contains two main component types, the OLAP component for storing cube data and the XML components for storing XML data. Additionally, three auxiliary components have been introduced to hold meta data, link data, and temporary data. SQL_{XM} queries are posed to the *Federation Manager*, which coordinates the execution of queries in the data components using several optimization techniques to improve query performance. A partial prototype implementation has been performed to allow us to make performance experiments. In the prototype, the OLAP component uses Microsoft Analysis Services and is queried with MDX and SQL. The XML component is based on Software AG's Tamino XML Database system, which provides an XPath-like interface. For the external temporary component, a single Oracle 8i system is used.

Since the primary bottleneck in the federation will usually be the moving of data from OLAP and XML components, our optimization efforts have focused on this issue. These efforts include both *rule based* and *cost based* optimization techniques, which are based on the transformation rules for the federation algebra. The optimization techniques are described in detail in another paper [9]. The *rule based* optimization uses the heuristic of pushing as much of the query evaluation towards the components as possible. The rule based optimization algorithm *partitions* a SQL_{XM} query tree, meaning that the SQL_{XM} operators are grouped into an OLAP part, an XML part, and a relational part. After partitioning the query tree, it has been identified to which levels the OLAP component can be aggregated and which selections can be performed in the OLAP component. Furthermore, the partitioned query tree has a structure that makes it easy to create component queries. The most important *cost based* optimization technique tries to tackle one of the fundamental problems with the idea of evaluating part of the query in a temporary component: If selections refer to levels not present in the result, too much data needs to be transferred to the temporary component. Our solution to this problem is to *inline* XML data values into OLAP predicates as literal data values. However, this is not always a good idea because, in general, a single query cannot be of arbitrary length. Hence, more than one query may have to be used. Whether or not XML data should be inlined into some OLAP query, is decided by comparing the estimated cost of the alternatives.

The use of cost based optimization requires the estimation of several cost parameters. One of the main arguments for federated systems is that components can still operate independently from the federation. However, this autonomy also means that little cost information will typically be available to the federation. Hence, providing a good general cost model is exceedingly difficult. In this context, it is especially true for XML components, because of the wide variety of underlying systems that may be found. Two general techniques have been used to deal with these problems: *Probing queries*, which are used to collect cost information from components, and *adaption*, which ensures that this cost information is updated when user queries are posed.

We now outline how the techniques discussed above are used in combination. When a federation query has been parsed, the system partitions the resulting SQL_{XM} query tree, splitting it into three parts: an OLAP query, a relational query, and a number of XML queries. The XML queries are immediately passed on to the Execution Engine, which determines for each query whether the result is obtainable from the cache. If this is not the case, it is sent to the Component Query Evaluator. The cost estimates are used by the Global Optimizer to pick a good inlining strategy. When the results of the component queries are available in the temporary component, the relational part of the SQL_{XM} query is evaluated.

3   Federation Cost Model

We now present a basic cost model for OLAP-XML federation queries, and then outline the optimization techniques that, in turn, leads to a refined cost model.

Basic Federation Cost Model: The cost model used in the following is based on time estimates and incorporates both I/O, CPU, and network costs. Because of the differences in data models and the degree of autonomy for the federation components, the cost is estimated differently for each component. Here, we only present the high-level cost model which expresses the total cost of evaluating a federation query. The details of how these costs are determined for each component are described later. The OLAP and XML components can be accessed in parallel if no XML data is used in the construction of OLAP queries. The case where XML data *is* used is discussed in the next section. The retrieval of component data is followed by computation of the final result in the temporary component. Hence, the total time for a federation query is the time for the slowest retrieval of data from the OLAP and XML components plus the time for producing the final result. This is expressed in this basic cost formula considering a single OLAP query and k XML queries:

$$Cost_{Basic} = \text{MAX}(t_{OLAP}, t_{XML,1}, \ldots, t_{XML,k}) + t_{Temp}$$

where t_{OLAP} is the total time it takes to evaluate the OLAP query, $t_{XML,i}$ is the total time it takes to evaluate the ith XML query, and t_{Temp} is the total time it takes to produce the final result from the intermediate results.

Refined Federation Cost Model: As discussed above, references to level expressions can be inlined in predicates thereby improving performance considerably in many cases. Better performance can be achieved when selection predicates refer to decorations of dimension values at a lower level than the level to which the cube is aggregated. If e.g. a predicate refers to decorations of dimension values at the bottom level of some dimension, large amounts of data must be transferred to the temporary component. Inlining level expressions may also be a good idea if it results in a more selective predicate.

Level expressions can be inlined compactly into some types of predicates [9]. Even though it is always possible to make this inlining [9], the resulting predicate may sometimes become very long. For predicates such as "EC/EC_Link/Manufacturer/MName = Supplier/Sup_Link/SName", where two level expressions are compared, this may be the case even for a moderate number of dimension values. However, as long as predicates do not compare level expressions to measure values the predicate length will never be more than quadratic in the number of dimension values. Furthermore, this is only the case when two level expressions are compared. For all other types of predicates the length is linear in the number of dimension values [9]. Thus, when predicates are relatively simple or the number of dimension values is small, this is indeed a practical solution. Very long predicates may degrade performance, e.g. because parsing the query will be slower. However, a more important practical problem that can prevent inlining, is the fact that almost all systems have an upper limit on the length of a query. For example, in many systems the maximum length of an SQL query is about 8000 characters. Certain techniques can reduce the length of a predicate. For instance, user defined sets of values (named sets) can be created in MDX and later used in predicates. However, the resulting predicate may still be too long for a single query and not all systems provide such facilities. A more general solution to the problem of very long predicates is to split a single predicate into several shorter predicates and evaluate these in a number of queries. We refer to these individual queries as *partial* queries, whereas the single query is called the *total* query.

Example 1. Consider the predicate "EC/Manufacturer/@MCode = Manufacturer(EC)". The decoration data for the level expression results in the following relationships between dimension and decoration values:

EC	Manufacturer/@MCode
EC1234	M31
EC1234	M33
EC1235	M32

Using this table, the predicate can be transformed to: "(Manufacturer(EC) IN (M31, M33) AND EC='EC1234') OR (Manufacturer(EC) IN (M32) AND EC='EC1235')". This predicate may be too long to actually be posed and can then be split into: "Manufac-turer(EC) IN (M31, M33) AND EC='EC1234' " and "Manufacturer(EC) IN (M32) AND EC='EC1235' ".

Of course, in general this approach entails a large overhead because of the extra queries. However, since the query result may sometimes be reduced by orders of mag-nitude when inlining level expressions, being able to do so can be essential in achieving acceptable performance. Because of the typically high cost of performing extra queries, the cost model must be revised to reflect this. The evaluation time of an OLAP query can be divided into three parts: A constant query overhead that does not depend on the particular query being evaluated, the time it takes to evaluate the query, and the time it takes to transfer data across the network, if necessary. The overhead is repeated for each query that is posed, while the transfer time can be assumed not to depend on the number of queries as the total amount of data transferred will be approximately the same whether a single query or many partial queries are posed. The query evaluation time will depend e.g. on the aggregation level and selectivity of any selections in a query. How these values are determined, is described in Section 4. The revised cost formula for k XML queries and a single total OLAP query that is split into n partial OLAP queries is presented in the following. The cost formula distinguishes between two types of XML query results: Those that have been inlined in some predicate and those that have not been inlined in any predicate. The estimated time it takes to retrieve these results is denoted by $t_{XML,Int}$ and $t_{XML,NotInt}$, respectively. In the formula let:

- $t^{MAX}_{XML,NotInt}$ be the maximum time it takes to evaluate some XML query for which the result is not inlined in any predicate,
- $t^{MAX}_{XML,Int}$ be the maximum time it takes to evaluate some XML query for which the result is inlined in some predicate,
- $t_{OLAP,OH}$ be the constant overhead of performing OLAP queries,
- $t^i_{OLAP,Eval}$ be the time it takes to evaluate the ith partial query,
- $t_{OLAP,Trans}$ be the time it takes to transfer the result of the total query (or, equiva-lently, the combined result of all partial queries).

Then the cost of a federation query is given by:

$$\text{MAX}(t^{MAX}_{XML,NotInt}, n \cdot t_{OLAP,OH} + \sum_{i=1}^{n} t^i_{OLAP,Eval} + t_{OLAP,Trans} + t^{MAX}_{XML,Int}) + t_{Temp}$$

Example 2. In Figure 1, four XML queries are used, of which XML_3 and XML_4 are inlined in the OLAP query. Hence, the OLAP query cannot be posed until the results of both of these are returned. The inlining makes the OLAP query too long and it is split into two partial queries. In parallel with this, the two other XML queries (XML_1 and XML_2) are processed. Thus, the final query to the temporary component, which combines the intermediate component results, cannot be issued until the slowest of the component queries has finished. In this case, the OLAP component finishes after XML_1 and XML_2, and thus, the temporary query must wait for it.

We made the assumption that the total evaluation time for a number of partial queries is close to the sum of the individual evaluation times. Note also that the number of inlining

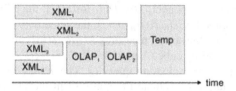

Fig. 1. Total Evaluation Times for the Component Queries for A Single Federation Query

combinations is exponential in the number of level expressions and that adding a level expression to the set of inlined expressions can both decrease and increase the overall cost. A discussion of these issues can be found in the full paper [10].

4   Component Cost Models

We now describe the models for the component costs that were used in the cost formulas in Section 3. This cost information is collected by the *Statistics Manager* and used by the cost evaluators. The amount of cost information available to the federation may vary between federation components. Du et al. [1] distinguish between three types of federation components: *Proprietary*, where all cost information is available to the federation, *Conforming*, where the component DBMS provides the basic cost statistics, but not full information about the cost functions used, and finally, *Non-Conforming*, where no cost information is available. A high degree of autonomy must be expected for XML components, while OLAP components may or may not provide access to cost information. Thus, we assume that the OLAP component is either conforming or non-conforming, while the XML components are non-conforming. The temporary component used by the federation is assumed to be a conforming component. For the temporary relational component we use a simplified variant of the cost model defined in [1].

OLAP Component Cost Model: The cost of an OLAP query is composed of a constant query overhead that does not depend on the particular query being evaluated, the time it takes to actually evaluate the query, and the time it takes to transfer data across the network if necessary:

$$t_{OLAP} = t_{OLAP,OH} + t_{OLAP,Eval} + t_{OLAP,Trans}$$

The statistical information that is needed to estimate these parameters, may be available from the OLAP component's meta data, in which case it is used directly. However, if such data is not available, we use probing queries to determine the statistical information and continuously update it by measuring the actual cost of all queries posed to the components. The probing queries are all relatively inexpensive and can be posed when the system load is low, and the overhead of adapting the cost information to the actual costs is insignificant. Hence, these methods introduce little overhead on the federated system.

The estimation of cost parameters is based on the following statistical information functions: $NetworkDataRate(C)$, the rate with which data can be transferred from cube C to the temporary component; $DiskDataRate(C)$, the rate with which data can be read from disk for cube C; $Selectivity(\theta, C)$, the selectivity of predicate θ evaluated on cube C; $FactSize(M)$, the size of measures M; $RollUpFraction(\mathcal{L}, C)$, the relative reduction in size when rolling cube C up to levels $\mathcal{L}$; $Size(C)$, the size of cube C; and $EvalTime(Q)$, the time for evaluating query Q. The $EvalTime(Q)$ function returns the estimated time it takes to evaluate the query Q in the OLAP component, taking *pre-aggregation* into account, please see the full paper [10] for details.

The estimation and maintenance of the OLAP cost parameters is performed using *probing queries* as the OLAP component is assumed to be non-conforming. The initial estimations are gradually adjusted based on the actual evaluation times using an *adaptive* approach. Due to space constraints, we cannot give the details here, they can be found in the full paper [10].

XML Component Cost Model: Estimating cost for XML components is exceedingly difficult because little or nothing can be assumed about the underlying data source, i.e. XML components are non-conforming. An XML data source may be a simple text file used with an XPath engine, a relational or OO database or a specialized XML database. The query optimization techniques used by these systems range from none at all to highly optimized. Optimizations are typically based on sophisticated indexing and cost analysis [5]. Hence, it is impossible, e.g., to estimate the amount of disk I/O required to evaluate a query, and consequently, only a rough cost estimate can be made. Providing a good cost model under these conditions is not the focus of this paper and hence, we describe only a simple cost model.

The cost model is primarily used to determine whether or not XML data should be inlined into OLAP queries. Hence, in general a pessimistic estimate is better than an optimistic, because the latter may cause XML data not to be inlined. This could result in a very long running OLAP query being accepted, simply because it is not estimated to take longer than the XML query. However, the actual cost will never be significantly larger than the false estimate. Making a pessimistic estimate will not cause this problem although it may sometimes increase the cost because XML data is retrieved before OLAP data instead of retrieving it concurrently. For that reason, conservative estimates are preferred in the model.

The model presented here is based on estimating the amount of data returned by a query, and assuming a constant data rate when retrieving data from the component. Similar to the cost formula for OLAP queries, we distinguish between the constant overhead of performing a query $t_{XML,OH}$ and the time it takes to actually process the query $t_{XML,Proc}$, see below. Only the latter depends on the size of the result.

$$t_{XML} = t_{XML,OH} + t_{XML,Proc}$$

In the following we describe how to estimate these two cost parameters given an XPath query. Although other more powerful languages may be used, the estimation technique can easily be changed to reflect this. For simplicity we consider only a subset of the XPath language where XPath expressions are on the form described in [9]. Because XML components are non-conforming, the estimates are based on posing probing queries to the XML component to retrieve the necessary statistics.

Estimation of the cost parameters $t_{XML,OH}$ and $t_{XML,Proc}$ is based on the statistical information described in the following. In the descriptions N is the name of a node, e.g. the element node "Supplier" or the attribute node "NoOfUnits", while E denotes the name of an element node. Let $path_{E_n}$ be a simple XPath expression on the form $/E_1/E_2/\ldots/E_n$, that specifies a single direct path from the root to a set of element nodes at some level n without applying any predicates. The statistical functions are as follows. $NodeSize(path_E)$:], the average size in bytes of the nodes pointed to by $path_E$; $Fanout(path_{E_n})$:], the average number of E_n elements pointed to by each of its parent elements E_{n-1}; $Selectivity(\theta)$:, the selectivity of predicate θ in its given context; $Cardinality(path_{E_n})$:], the total number of elements pointed to by $path_{E_n}$; $DataRate(x)$:] The average amount of data that can be retrieved from the XML document x per second;

Some of this information can be obtained directly if an XML Schema is available. In that case, information such as *NodeSize*, *Cardinality*, or *Fanout* is determined from the schema. DTDs can also be used to provide this information, but only if no repetition operators (i.e. the "*" and "+" operators) are used. However, if such meta data is not available, then the statistical information is obtained using probing queries that are based on the links defined for each XML document. Due to space constraints, we cannot give the details here, they can be found in the full paper [10].

5 Experimental Results

The primary purpose of any cost model is to be used in the query optimization process. Thus, the most relevant quality measure of a cost model is whether it can guide the query optimizer to perform the right choices, rather than how closely the model can predict the actual execution times. Following this reasoning, we have performed a series of experiments showing the effect of using the cost model in the optimization process. Because of space constraints, we only give a brief overview of the experiments, see the full paper [10] for details.

As described above, the cost model is not needed in the process of partitioning the queries, e.g., moving operations up and down the query tree, as the rule-based approach will always find the best solution. Thus, we illustrated the use of the cost model in the cost-based part of the optimization process, namely the choice of what XML data to *inline* in the OLAP queries. Three sets of experiments were performed: Without inlining, with the simple heuristic "always use inlining if the predicate is simple", and where the cost model is used to determine where to use inlining.

The results were that simple inlining is around 5 times faster than no inlining, but that cost-based inlining is 3 times faster than simple inlining and an amazing 15 times faster than no inlining. This result shows that the cost model is powerful enough to make a substantial difference in the query optimization process. Other experiments have shown that the federated OLAP-XML approach is only 30% slower than the integrated OLAP approach (which is very inflexible w.r.t. changing data), a surprising result that is largely due to the effectiveness of the query optimization process and the cost model.

6 Conclusion

Motivated by the need for efficient cost-based optimization in OLAP-XML federations, we have presented a cost model for OLAP-XML federations. Also, techniques for estimating cost model parameters in an OLAP-XML federation were outlined. The paper also briefly presented the cost models for the autonomous OLAP and XML components on which the federation cost model was based. Experiments showed that the cost model is powerful enough to make a substantial difference in the query optimization.

We believe this paper to be the first to propose a cost model for OLAP-XML federation queries, along with techniques for estimating and maintaining the necessary statistics for the cost models. Also, we believe the proposed cost models for the autonomous OLAP and XML components to be novel.

Future work will focus on how to provide better cost estimates when querying autonomous OLAP components and, in particular, autonomous XML components. For this purpose, extensive testing of commercial OLAP and XML database systems is needed. Also, better ways of obtaining cost parameters from the OLAP and XML components can probably be derived by an extensive examination of commercial systems.

References

1. W. Du, R. Krishnamurthy, and M.-C. Shan. Query Optimization in a Heterogeneous DBMS. In *Proceedings of the 18th VLDB Conference*, pp. 277–291, 1992.
2. R. Elmasri and S. B. Navathe. *Fundamentals of Database Systems*. Addison-Wesley, 2000.
3. G. Gardarin, F. Sha, and Z.-H. Tang. Calibrating the Query Optimizer Cost Model of IRO-DB, an Object-Oriented Federated Database System. In *Proceedings of the 22nd VLDB Conference*, pp. 378–389, 1996.
4. H. Lu, K.-L. Tan, and S. Dao. The Fittest Survives: An Adaptive Approach to Query Optimization. In *Proceedings of 21st VLDB Conference*, pp. 251–262, 1995.
5. J. McHugh and J. Widom. Query Optimization For XML. In *Proceedings of 25th VLDB Conference*, pp. 315–326, 1999.
6. H. Naacke, G. Gardarin, A. Tomasic. Leveraging Mediator Cost Models with Heterogeneous Data Sources. In *Proceedings of the 14th ICDE Conference*, pp. 351–360, 1998.
7. C. Ozkan, A. Dogac, and M. Altinel. A Cost Model for Path Expressions in Object-Oriented Queries. *Journal of Database Management* 7(3), 1996.
8. D. Pedersen, K. Riis, and T. B. Pedersen. XML-Extended OLAP Querying. To appear in *Proceedings of SSDBM*, 2002.
9. D. Pedersen, K. Riis, and T. B. Pedersen. Query Processing and Optimization for OLAP-XML Federations. *Submitted for publication*, 2002.
10. D. Pedersen, K. Riis, and T. B. Pedersen. Cost Modeling and Estimation for OLAP-XML Federations. *TR R02-5003, Department of Computer Science, Aalborg University*, 2002.
11. T. B. Pedersen, A. Shoshani, J. Gu, and C. S. Jensen. Extending OLAP Querying To External Object Databases. In *Proceedings of the 9th CIKM Conference*, pp. 405–413, 2000.
12. M. T. Roth et al. Cost models do matter: Providing cost information for diverse data sources in a federated system. In *Proceedings of 25th VLDB Conference*, pp. 599–610, 1999.
13. A. P. Sheth and J. A. Larson. Federated Database Systems for Managing Distributed, Heterogeneous, and Autonomous Databases. *ACM Computing Surveys*, 22(3):183–236, 1990.
14. A. Shukla et al. Storage Estimation for Multidimensional Aggregates in the Presence of Hierarchies. In *Proceedings of 22nd VLDB Conference*, pp. 522–531, 1996.
15. E. Thomsen. *OLAP Solutions: Building Multidimensional Information Systems*. Wiley, 1997.
16. Q. Zhu and P.-Å. Larson. Global Query Processing and Optimization in the CORDS Multidatabase System. In *Proceedings of the 9th PDCS Conference*, pp. 640–646, 1996.
17. Q. Zhu, Y. Sun, and S. Motheramgari. Developing Cost Models with Qualitative Variables for Dynamic Multidatabase Environments. In Proceedings of the 16th ICDE Conference, pp. 413–424, 2000.

Constraint-Free Join Processing on Hyperlinked Web Data

Sourav S. Bhowmick[1], Wee Keong Ng[1], Sanjay Madria[2], and Mukesh Mohania[3]

[1] School of Computer Engineering, Nanyang Technological University,
Singapore 639798
{assourav, awkng}@ntu.edu.sg
http://www.ntu.edu.sg/home/assourav
[2] Department of Computer Science,
University of Missouri-Rolla, Rolla
MO 65409
madrias@umr.edu
[3] IBM India Research Lab,
New Delhi 110016, India
mkmukesh@in.ibm.com

Abstract. In this paper, we introduce the concept of *web join* for *combining* hyperlinked Web data. A web join is one of the *web algebraic operator* in our *web warehousing* system called WHOWEDA (*WareHouse Of WEb DAta*). It can be used to gather useful, composite information from two *web tables*. Web join and *outer web join* (a derivative of web join) operations can be used to detect and represent changes to hyperlinked Web data. We discuss the syntax, semantics and algorithms of *web join* and *outer web join* operators. We also present how to detect and represent changes to hyperlinked Web data using these two operations.

1   Introduction

There has also been increasing research effort to extend the traditional concept of join to support non-traditional data, including temporal data, web data, and spatial objects. In the Web context, join operation in XML-QL [5] and Lorel [6] follows the traditional notion. In XML-QL, it is used to combine information collected from different portions of documents, which is necessary to merge information from multiple documents. It uses the same variable binding for character data in a tag element for causing a join between two data sources. Lorel uses an explicit equality predicate on character data to perform the join. In this paper, we introduce a novel technique for performing join operation on Web data, i.e., *web join*. As shall be seen, our approach differs in the sense that we perform join operation based on merging *identical* documents. Our join operation does not combine information from different portions of Web documents. Specifically, web join serves three important purposes: (1) Similar to its relational counterpart, web join can be used to gather useful, composite information from two *web tables*. (2) This information can be stored in a separate *web table* and can be

Y. Kambayashi, W. Winiwarter, M. Arikawa (Eds.): DaWaK 2002, LNCS 2454, pp. 255–264, 2002.

used for future queries. (3) Web join and *outer web join* (a derivative of web join) operations enable us to detect and represent changes to hyperlinked Web data [1].

Since our goal is to discuss join operation on Web data, we use as a starting point the WHOWEDA system, a web warehousing system for managing and manipulating relevant data extracted from the Web [2]. Informally, our web warehouse can be conceived as a collection of *web tables*. A set of *web tuples* and a set of *web schemas* [3] is called a web table. A web tuple is a directed graph consisting of a set of *nodes* and *links* and satisfy a *web schema*. Nodes and links contain content, metadata and structural information associated with web documents and hyperlinks among the web documents. To facilitate manipulation of Web data stored in web tables, we have defined a set of web algebraic operators (i.e., *global web coupling*, *web join*, *web select* etc.) [2].

Informally, web join is used to combine *identical* data residing in two web tables. In web join, web tuples from two web tables containing *joinable nodes* are *concatenated* into a single web tuple that can be materialized in a web table. A pair of nodes are *joinable* if they are *identical* in content and satisfy a set (possibly empty) of user-defined *join conditions*. We consider two nodes or Web documents identical when they have the same URL and last modification date. Observe that based on this definition of identity of Web documents, same documents stored in mirror sites having different URL are not considered identical. Also, nodes that represents Web documents which are formatted via CGI are not considered in this paper as their last modification dates are always updated when they are retrieved from the Web. By user-specified *join condition* we mean conditions enforced by the user on the selection of joinable nodes from the pool of identical nodes in the two web tables. These joinable nodes are subset of identical node pairs and hence may not reflect all possible pairs of identical nodes. Also, these conditions are optional. Consequently, a web join operation can be *constraint-driven* or *constraint-free* depending on the presence or absence of join conditions. In this paper, we focus our discussion on constraint-free web join operation.

Note that although we have introduced web join and outer web join in [1], our focus in that work was on change detection and representation. Hence, we did not discuss these two operators in detail. For instance, we did not present the algorithms for generating joined and outer joined web tables. In this paper, we address these issues.

2   Coupling Query

This section provides the foundation for our subsequent discussion on web join. Since we are interested in discussing join operation on Web data, we need to garner relevant data from the Web. This is performed in WHOWEDA by posing *coupling query* over the Web. We illustrate this with an example. Detailed discussion on the syntax and semantics of coupling query can be found in [4].

Assume that there is a Web site at `http://www.panacea.gov/` which provides information related to drugs used for various diseases. For instance, the struc-

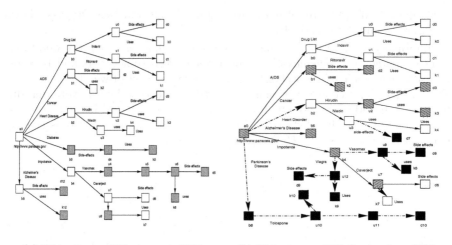

(a) Web site on 15th August, 2001.   (b) Web site on 15th September, 2001.

Fig. 1. Web site at http://www.panacea.gov/.

tures of the site as on 15th August, 2001 and 15th September, 2001 are shown in Figures 1(a) and 1(b) respectively. Note that the structure and content of a web site is dynamic and changes with time. The black boxes, patterned boxes and grey boxes in all figures (except Figure 4) in this paper depict addition of new documents, modification of existing documents and deletion of existing documents respectively. Furthermore, the dashed dotted arrows indicates addition, deletion or modification of hyperlinks.

Suppose on 15th August, 2001, a user wish to find out periodically (say every 30 days), information related to side effects and uses of drugs for various diseases. He/she may express his/her intention by formulating a coupling query [4] on 15th August, 2001 as shown below.

Let $G = \langle X_n, X_\ell, C, P, Q \rangle$ be a coupling query where $X_n = \{a, b, d, k\}$, $X_\ell = \{-\}$, $C \equiv k_1 \wedge k_2 \wedge k_3$ where $k_1 \equiv a\langle-\rangle b$, $k_2 \equiv b\langle-\{1,6\}\rangle d$, $k_3 \equiv b\langle-\{1,3\}\rangle k$ and $P = \{p_1, p_2, p_3, p_4\}$ where

$p_1(a) \equiv$ METADATA::a[url] EQUALS "*http://www[.]panacea[.]gov*"
$p_2(b) \equiv$ CONTENT::b[html.body.title] NON-ATTR_CONT
        ":BEGIN_STR: + *drug List* +:END_STR:"
$p_3(k) \equiv$ CONTENT::k[html.body.title] NON-ATTR_CONT
        ":BEGIN_WORD: + *uses* + :END_WORD:"
$p_4(d) \equiv$ CONTENT::d[html.body.title] NON-ATTR_CONT
        ":BEGIN_STR: + *side effects* + :END_STR: "

and $Q = \{q_1\}$ where $q_1(G) \equiv$ COUPLING_QUERY::G.polling_frequency EQUALS "*30 days*".

The above query will be polled every 30 days (i.e., 15th August, 2001, 15th September, 2001 etc. all at 10:00 PM). The results of the query (as on 15th August and 15th September) are a set of directed connected graph (also called

web tuples) and are materialized in web tables Drugs and New Drugs as shown
in Figures 2 and 3 respectively.

Informally, a web table W consists of the following: *name* of the web table,
a set of *simple web schemas* S [3] and a set of web tuples T bound by these
web schemas. Each simple web schema $S_i \in S$ binds a set of web tuples $T_i \subseteq T$.
The pair (S_i, T_i) is collectively called as *partition* (denoted by U). Note that due
to space constraints we do not discuss web schemas in detail here. The reader
may refer to [3] for detailed discussion. A web table can be realized as a set of
partitions, denoted as $\mathcal{U} = \{U_1, U_2, \ldots, U_n\}$.

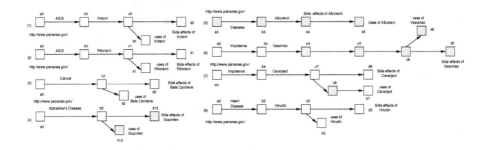

Fig. 2. Partial view of web tuples in "Drugs".

Formally, the two web tables Drugs and New Drugs can be represented
as follows. Let $W_d = \langle \text{Drugs}, \mathcal{U}_d \rangle$ be the web table Drugs where $\mathcal{U}_d = \{U_{d1}, U_{d2}, U_{d3}, U_{d4}, U_{d5}\}$ where (1) $U_{d1} = \langle S_{d1} = \langle X_{nd1}, X_{\ell d1}, C_{d1}, P_{d1}\rangle, T_{d1}\rangle$, $X_{nd1} = \{a, b, d, k, \#_1\}$,
$X_{\ell d1} = \{-_1, -_2, -_3, -_4\}$, $C_{d1} \equiv a\langle -_1\rangle b \wedge b\langle -_2\rangle\#_1 \wedge \#_1\langle -_3\rangle d \wedge \#_1\langle -_4\rangle k$, $P_{d1} = P$
and $T_{d1} = \{t_1, t_2, t_8\}$. (2) $U_{d2} = \langle S_{d2} = \langle X_{nd2}, X_{\ell d2}, C_{d2}, P_{d2}\rangle, T_{d2}\rangle$, $X_{nd2} = \{a, b, d, k\}$, $X_{\ell d2} = \{-_1, -_5, -_{13}\}$, $C_{d2} \equiv a\langle -_1\rangle b \wedge b\langle -_5\rangle d \wedge b\langle -_{13}\rangle k$, $P_{d2} = P$ and
$T_{d2} = \{t_3, t_4\}$. (3) $U_{d3} = \langle S_{d3} = \langle X_{nd3}, X_{\ell d3}, C_{d3}, P_{d3}\rangle, T_{d3}\rangle$, $X_{nd3} = \{a, b, d, k\}$,
$X_{\ell d3} = \{-_1, -_5, -_6\}$, $C_{d3} \equiv a\langle -_1\rangle b \wedge b\langle -_5\rangle d \wedge d\langle -_6\rangle k$, $P_{d3} = P$ and $T_{d3} = \{t_5\}$. (4)
$U_{d4} = \langle S_{d4} = \langle X_{nd4}, X_{\ell d4}, C_{d4}, P_{d4}\rangle, T_{4d}\rangle$, $X_{nd4} = \{a, b, d, k, \#_1, \#_2, \#_3\}$, $X_{\ell d4} = \{-_1, -_2, -_7, -_8, -_9, -_{10}\}$, $C_{d4} \equiv a\langle -_1\rangle b \wedge b\langle -_2\rangle\#_1 \wedge \#_1\langle -_7\rangle\#_2 \wedge \#_2\langle -_8\rangle\#_3 \wedge \#_3\langle -_9\rangle d \wedge \#_3\langle -_{10}\rangle k$, $P_{d4} = P$ and $T_{d4} = \{t_6\}$. (5) $U_{d5} = \langle S_{d5} = \langle X_{nd5}, X_{\ell d5}, C_{d5}, P_{d5}\rangle, T_{d5}\rangle$,
$X_{nd5} = \{a, b, d, k, \#_1, \#_4\}$, $X_{\ell d5} = \{-_1, -_2, -_3, -_{11}, -_{12}\}$, $C_{d5} \equiv a\langle -_1\rangle b \wedge b\langle -_2\rangle\#_1 \wedge \#_1\langle -_3\rangle d \wedge \#_1\langle -_{11}\rangle\#_4 \wedge \#_4\langle -_{12}\rangle k$, $P_{d5} = P$ and $T_{d5} = \{t_7\}$.

Similarly, let $W_{nd} = \langle \text{NewDrugs}, \mathcal{U}_{nd} \rangle$ be the web table New Drugs where
$\mathcal{U}_{nd} = \{U_{nd1}, U_{nd2}, U_{nd3}\}$ and (1) $U_{nd1} = \langle S_{nd1}, T_{nd1} \rangle$ where $S_{nd1} = S_{d1}$ and
$T_{nd1} = \{t_1, t_2, t_4, t_5, t_6, t_7, t_8\}$. (2) $U_{nd2} = \langle S_{nd2}, T_{nd2} \rangle$ where $S_{nd2} = S_{d2}$ and
$T_{nd2} = \{t_3\}$. (3) $U_{nd3} = \langle S_{nd3} = \langle X_{nd3}, X_{\ell d3}, C_{nd3}, P_{nd3}\rangle, T_{nd3}\rangle$, $X_{nd3} = \{a, b, d, k, \#_1, \#_2\}$, $X_{\ell nd3} = \{-_1, -_2, -_3, -_4, -_5\}$, $C_{nd3} \equiv a\langle -_1\rangle b \wedge b\langle -_2\rangle\#_1 \wedge \#_1\langle -_3\rangle\#_2 \wedge \#_2\langle -_4\rangle d \wedge \#_1\langle -_5\rangle k$, $P_{nd3} = P$ and $T_{nd3} = \{t_9\}$.

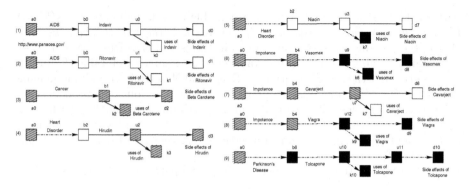

Fig. 3. Partial view of web tuples in "New Drugs".

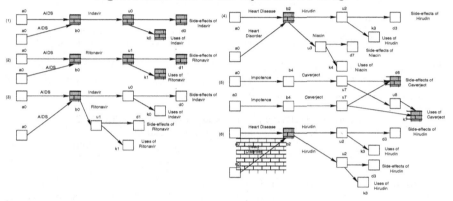

Fig. 4. Partial view of joined web table.

3   Web Join

The web join operator is used to combine two web tables by *joining* a web tuple of one table with a web tuple of other table whenever there exists joinable nodes. Let $t_a \in W_1$ and $t_b \in W_2$ be two web tuples. Then these tuples are joinable if there exist at-least one node in t_a which is joinable to a node in t_b. The joined web tuple contains the nodes from both the input web tuples. We materialize the joined web tuple in a separate web table. As one of the joinable node in each joinable node pair is superfluous, we remove one of them from the joined web tuple.

To perform web join on web tables W_1 and W_2, a pair of web tuples is selected, one from each web table, and all the pair of nodes are evaluated to determine if there exists joinable nodes. The process is repeated for all $|W_1| \times |W_2|$ pairs of web tuples. If there exists joinable nodes in a pair of web tuples then the web tables are joinable. We express web join between W_1 and W_2 as $W_{12} = W_1 \bowtie W_2$.

Example 1. Consider the web tables **Drugs** and **New Drugs**. These two web ta-bles are joinable since there exists joinable nodes (identical nodes) as shown by patterned boxes in Figure 4. The set of joinable node id pairs are $J = \{(b_0, b_0),$ $(b_2, b_2),\ (u_0, u_0),\ (u_1, u_1),\ (d_0, d_0),\ (d_1, d_1),\ (d_6, d_6),\ (k_0, k_0),\ (k_1, k_1),\ (k_7, k_7)\}$. Hence, the joinable node type identifiers in Drugs and New Drugs are $b, d, k, \#_1$. Performing a web join on these web tables creates a joined web table (Figure 4).

Observe that the set of partitions in Drugs and New Drugs containing joinable tuples are U_{d1}, U_{d5} and U_{nd1} respectively. Hence, the join operation between these two web tables will result in joining partitions U_{d1} and U_{d5} with U_{nd1}. Specifically, web tuples t_1, t_2 and t_8 in U_{d1} are joinable tuples with web tuples t_1, t_2, t_4 and t_5 in U_{nd1}. The joined web tuples are shown in Figure 4 (All tuples except the fifth one).

The set of partitions to represent these joined partitions are as follows:

1. $U_{wj1} = \langle S_{wj1}, T_{wj1} \rangle$ where $X_{nj1} = \{a, z, b, \#_1, k, d\}$, $X_{\ell j1} = \{^-1, ^-2, ^-3, ^-4, ^-6\}$, $C_{j1} \equiv z\langle^-6\rangle b \wedge b\langle^-2\rangle \#_1 \wedge \#_1\langle^-3\rangle d \wedge \#_1\langle^-4\rangle k \wedge a\langle^-1\rangle b$, $P_{j1} = P \cup \{p_7\}$ and $T_{wj1} = \{t_{j1}, t_{j2}\}$ where

$$p_7(z) \equiv \texttt{METADATA::z[url] EQUALS "http://www[.]panacea[.]gov/"}$$

2. $U_{wj2} = \langle S_{wj2}, T_{wj2} \rangle$ where $X_{nj2} = \{a, b, \#_1, \#_3, k, d, x, y, z\}$, $X_{\ell j2} = \{^-1, ^-2, ^-3, ^-4, ^-6, ^-7, ^-8, ^-9\}$, $C_{j2} \equiv a\langle^-1\rangle b \wedge b\langle^-2\rangle \#_1 \wedge \#_1\langle^-3\rangle d \wedge \#_1\langle^-4\rangle k \wedge z\langle^-6\rangle b \wedge b\langle^-9\rangle \#_3 \wedge \#_3\langle^-7\rangle x \wedge \#_3\langle^-8\rangle y$, $P_{j2} = P \cup \{p_7, p_8, p_9\}$ and $T_{wj2} = \{t_{j3}, t_{j4}, t_{j6}\}$ where

$$p_8(y) \equiv \texttt{CONTENT::y[html.body.title]NON-ATTR\_CONT}$$
$$\texttt{" :BEGIN\_WORD: + } uses \texttt{ + :END\_WORD:"}$$
$$p_9(x) \equiv \texttt{CONTENT::x[html.body.title] NON-ATTR\_CONT}$$
$$\texttt{":BEGIN\_STR: + } side\ effects \texttt{ + :END\_STR:"}$$

Similarly, the web tuple t_7 in U_{d5} is joinable with web tuple t_7 in U_{nd1}. The joined web tuple is shown in Figure 4 (fifth web tuple). The partition containing the joined web tuple is shown below:

1. $U_{wj3} = \langle S_{wj3}, T_{wj3} \rangle$ where $X_{nj3} = \{a, b, \#_1, \#_4, k, d, w, z\}$, $X_{\ell j3} = \{^-1, ^-2, ^-3, ^-4, ^-6, ^-7, ^-9, ^-11, ^-12\}$, $C_{j3} \equiv a\langle^-1\rangle b \wedge b\langle^-2\rangle \#_1 \wedge \#_1\langle^-3\rangle d \wedge \#_1\langle^-4\rangle k \wedge z\langle^-6\rangle w \wedge w\langle^-9\rangle \#_3 \wedge \#_3\langle^-7\rangle d \wedge \#_3\langle^-11\rangle \#_4 \wedge \#_4\langle^-12\rangle k$, $P_{j3} = P \cup \{p_9\}$ and $T_{wj3} = \{t_{j5}\}$ where

$$p_9(w) \equiv \texttt{CONTENT::w[html.body.title] NON-ATTR\_CONT}$$
$$\texttt{":BEGIN\_STR: + } drug\ List \texttt{ + :END\_STR:"}$$

The joined web table can be represented by the partition set $\mathcal{U}_j = \{U_{wj1}, U_{wj2}, U_{wj3}\}$. ∎

Algorithm: The algorithm of web join takes as input two web tables W_1 and W_2 and returns as output a joined web table W_j. The following steps are performed to generate the joined web table:

1. Retrieve sets of node ids (Each node in our web warehouse has a unique node id and a version id), denoted by N_1 and N_2, of all the nodes in W_1 and W_2.
2. Identify the set of joinable node ids and corresponding node type identifiers respectively in W_1 and W_2 (denoted by J and I). The algorithm for identifying joinable nodes is given in Figure 5.

```
Input: Set of node ids N₁ and N₂ of W₁ and W₂.
Output: Joinable node id set J, set of pairs of joinable node type identifiers I.

(1)    U = N₁ ∩ N₂;
(2)    for (i = 1 to |U|) {
(3)        v₁(i) = GetVersionId(U(i), W₁); /* Returns the version id of a
                                node having id U(i) in web table W₁ */
(4)        v₂(i) = GetVersionId(U(i), W₂);
(5)        if (v₁(i) = v₂(i)) {/* The nodes are joinable */
(6)            Insert U(i) in joinable node id set J;
(7)            Insert the identifiers (x_{a1}, x_{a2}) in I;
(8)        }
(9)        else
(10)           The nodes are not joinable;
(11)   }
(12)   return (J, I);
```

Fig. 5. Algorithm for computing joinable nodes.

```
Input: Web table name Z_j and web tables W₁ = ⟨Z₁, U₁⟩ and W₂ = ⟨Z₂, U₂⟩.
Output: Joined web table W_j = ⟨Z_j, U_j⟩.

(1)    N₁ = GetAllNodeIds(W₁); /* Returns a set of identifier of all the instances of nodes in W₁ */
(2)    N₂ = GetAllNodeIds(W₂);
(3)    (J, I) = ComputeJoinableNodeIds(N₁, N₂); /* Figure 5 */
(4)    U₁' = SelectJoinablePartition(W₁, J, left(I));
(5)    U₂' = SelectJoinablePartition(W₂, J, right(I));
(6)    if (U₁' = ∅ ∨ U₂' = ∅)
(7)        Return W_j = ⟨N_j, U_j⟩ where U_j = ∅;
(8)    else
(9)        U_j = GenerateJoinPartition(U₁', U₂');
(10)   Return W_j = ⟨N_j, U_j⟩;
```

Fig. 6. Algorithm of web join.

3. Identify the set of partitions $U_1' \subseteq U_1$ and $U_2' \subseteq U_2$ where each partition $U_i \in U_1'$ and $U_j \in U_2'$ contain web tuples with joinable nodes (Steps (4) and (5) in Figure 6). Note that I is a set of pairs of node type identifiers. That is $I = \{(l_{n1}, r_{n1}), (l_{n2}, r_{n2}), \ldots, (l_{nk}, r_{nk})\}$. We denote the sets of all left and right node type identifiers in I as $left(I)$ and $right(I)$ respectively.

4. Let T_i and T_j be the set of web tuples in U_i and U_j. Then, determine the possible pair of tuples in T_i and T_j which are joinable to one another. Let $T_i' \subseteq T_i$ and $T_j' \subseteq T_j$ denotes such a set of web tuples.

5. For each pair of tuples (t_k, t_r), $t_k \in T_i'$, $t_r \in T_j'$ generate the joined web tuple t_{kr} by joining these tuples over the joinable nodes. The issues involved in joining web tuples are encapsulated in this construct. Due to space constraints, we do not elaborate on it in this paper. For further details and algorithm of this construct please refer to [2].

6. Generate a joined schema S_{ij} from S_i and S_j to bind t_{kr}. Due to space constraints, we do not elaborate on the generation of joined schema in detail in this paper.

7. Create a partition $U_k = \langle S_{ij}, t_{kr} \rangle$.

8. Insert U_k in a partition collection U_{ij}'.

9. Repeat the above steps for all pair of web tuples in T_i' and T_j'.

10. The join construction process will generate a set joined partitions U_{ij} where the number of partitions $n \leq |T_i| \times |T_j|$. Each of these partitions bind a single joined web tuple. Hence, the number of partitions is equal to the number of joined web tuples generated during this process. The set of partitions may

```
Input: Web tables W₁ = ⟨Z₁, U₁⟩ and W₂ = ⟨Z₂, U₂⟩.
Output: Left or right outer web joined table Wₒ = ⟨Nₒ, Uₒ⟩.

(1)    N₁ = GetAllNodeIds(W₁);
(2)    N₂ = GetAllNodeIds(W₂);
(3)    J =ComputeJoinableNodeIds(N₁, N₂);/* Figure 5 */
(4)    if (left outer web join is to be performed) {
(5)        danglingNodeSet = N₁ - J;
(6)        Let temporary web table Wₜ = W₁;
(7)    }
(8)    else {
(9)        danglingNodeSet = N₂ - J;
(10)       Let temporary web table Wₜ = W₂;
(11)   }
(12)   for (r = 1 to |Uₜ|) {
(13)       Let Uᵣ = ⟨Sᵣ, Tᵣ⟩;
(14)       for (k = 1 to |Tᵣ|) {
(15)           Get tuple tₖ;
(16)           tupleNodeIdSet[k] = GetTupleNodeIds(tₖ);
(17)           if (tupleNodeIdSet[k] ∩ danglingNodeSet = tupleNodeIdSet[k])
(18)               Store tuple tₖ in Tₒᵣ;
(19)           else
(20)               tₖ is a joinable tuple;
(21)       }
(22)       if (Tₒᵣ ≠ ∅) {
(23)           Sₒᵣ = Sᵣ;
(24)           Insert Uₒᵣ = ⟨Sₒᵣ, Tₒᵣ⟩ in Uₒ;
(25)       }
(26)   }
(27)   return Wₒ = ⟨Nₒ, Uₒ⟩;
```

Fig. 7. Algorithm of outer web join.

share identical schemas if the set of joinable node type identifiers for some tuples are identical. Consequently, in this situation it is necessary to prune the partitions in order to combine the partitions having identical schemas into a single partition.

11. Repeat the above Steps (2) to (8) for each pair of partitions in U_1' and U_2'.

4   Outer Web Join

The web tuples that do not participate in the web join operation (dangling web tuples) are absent from the joined web table. In certain situations it is necessary to identify the dangling web tuples from one or both the input web tables. The outer web join operation enables us to identify them. Depending on whether the outer-joined web table must contain the non-participant web tuples from the first or second web tables, we define two kinds of outer web join: the *left-outer web join* and the *right-outer web join* respectively. Formally, given two web tables W_1 and W_2, the left-outer web join and right-outer web join on these two web tables are denoted by $W_1 =\bowtie W_2$ and $W_1 \bowtie= W_2$ respectively, where the symbols $=\bowtie$ and $\bowtie=$ corresponds to the different flavors of outer web join. The resultant web table W_o for a left-outer web join or right-outer web join will contain the dangling web tuples from W_1 or W_2 respectively. The algorithm for outer web join is given in Figure 7. Figures 8(a) and 8(b) are examples of left and right outer joined web tables created from Drugs and New Drugs.

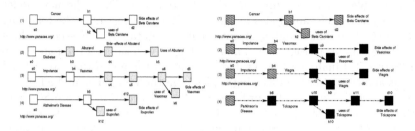

(a) Left outer web join.   (b) Right outer web join.

Fig. 8. Outer web join.

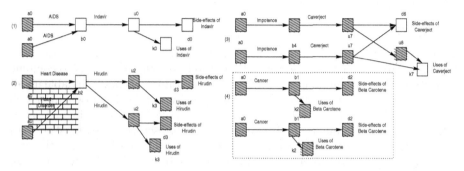

Fig. 9. Δ^M-web table.

5   Change Detection

In this section, we illustrate with an example how the web join and outer web join operations can be used to detect and represent *tuple level* changes in our web warehouse. A detailed discussions on in change detection is given in [1].

Consider the two web tables Drugs and New Drugs in Figures 2 and 3. We would like to find the various change operations that transform Drugs into New Drugs. Changes may include, insertion, deletion or update of nodes and links in Drugs. For each type of these changes, we create Δ^+, Δ^- and Δ^M web tables respectively to store these changes.

Figure 9 depicts the Δ^M-web table. The patterned boxes in this figure in each web tuple are the old and new version of the nodes. For example, the second web tuple in Figure 9 contains the old and new version of the nodes a_0, u_2, d_3 and k_3, along with the joinable node u_2 (content of u_2 has remained unchanged during the transition). Each web tuple shows how the set of modified nodes are related to one another and with the joinable nodes. Observe that the first four web tuples are extracted from the joined web table in Figure 4. The last web tuple (enclosed in a dotted box) is the result of the integration of two web tuples - one from the left outer joined web table in Figure 8(a) and another from the right outer joined table in Figure 8(b). The Δ^+-web table contains web tuples in which new nodes inserted into during 15th August, 2001 and 15th September, 2001. Similar to Δ^M-web table, each web tuple in Δ^+-web table shows how the new nodes are related to other relevant nodes in the web table. It consists of the following tuples from the web joined and right-outer joined web tables: The second, third and fourth web tuples in Figure 8(b) and the fourth web tuple of the joined web table in Figure 4. Finally, Δ^--web table contains all the nodes that are deleted from Drugs and consist of the following tuples from the web joined and left-outer joined web tables: The second, third and fourth web tuples in Figure 8(a) and the fifth web tuple in the joined web table in Figure 4 containing the deleted node u_8. Observe that we do not materialize the joined web tuples containing new or deleted nodes in Δ^+ and Δ^- web tables respectively. Instead, we extract the original web tuple containing these nodes from the joined web tuple and materialize them in Δ^+ and Δ^- web tables respectively.

6 Conclusions

In this paper, we have motivated the need for a join operation for the web data model and we have introduced the notion of web join that enable us to combine two web tables by combining web tuples from two tables whenever joinable nodes exist. We have shown how to construct the joined web table from two input web tables. Lastly, we have illustrated with an example how web join and outer web join operators can be used to detect and represent changes to Web data at the tuple level. Presently, we have implemented the first version of the web join operator and have interfaced it with other web operators. We will perform the experiments on real data (current implementation is done on synthetic web pages)to evaluate the efficiency of the operators once WHOWEDA is operational completely.

References

1. S. BHOWMICK, S. K. MADRIA, W.-K. NG, E.-P. LIM. Detecting and Representing Relevant Web Deltas Using Web Join. *Proceedings of the 20th International Conference on Distributed Computing Systems (ICDCS'00)* , Taiwan, 2000.
2. S. S. BHOWMICK. WHOM: A Data Model and Algebra for a Web Warehouse. *PhD Dissertation*, School of Computer Engineering, Nanyang Technological University, Singapore, 2001. Available at www.ntu.edu.sg/home/assourav/ .
3. S. S. BHOWMICK, W.-K. NG, S. K. MADRIA . Schemas for Web Data: A Reverse Engineering Approach. *Data and Knowledge Engineering Journal (DKE)*, 39(2), 2001.
4. S. S. BHOWMICK, W.-K. NG, S. K. MADRIA, E.-P. LIM . Anatomy of a Coupling Query in a Web Warehouse. *Internation Journal of Information and Software Technology*, Elsevier Science, 2002.
5. A. DEUTSCH, M. FERNANDEZ, D. FLORESCU, A. LEVY, D. SUCIU. A Query Language for XML. *Proceedings of the 8th World Wide Web Conference*, pp. 1155-1169, Toronto, Canada, May 1999.
6. R. GOLDMAN, J. MCHUGH, J. WIDOM. From Semistructured Data to XML: Migrating the Lore Data Model and Query Language. *Proceedings of WebDB '99*, pp. 25-30, Philadelphia, Pennsylvania, June 1999.

Focusing on Data Distribution in the WebD²W System[1]

Cristina Dutra de Aguiar Ciferri[1] and Fernando da Fonseca de Souza[2]

[1]Department of Informatics, State University of Maringá
Av. Colombo, 5790, CEP 87.020-900, Maringá, PR, Brazil
cdac@din.uem.br
[2] Department of Computer Science, Federal University of Pernambuco, CP 7851
CEP 50.732-970, Recife, PE, Brazil
fdfd@cin.ufpe.br

Abstract. The WebD²W system is a distributed client-server data warehousing environment, which is aimed not only at the data warehouse distribution, but also at the distributed access to these data using the Web technology as an infrastructure. In this paper, we introduce the WebD²W system, focusing on one of its main objectives: the data warehouse distribution. Such a system is presented in terms of its main components and their respective functionalities. The paper also describes the algorithm for fragmenting horizontally the warehouse data, which is used as a basis for the WebD²W system.

1 Introduction

In a data warehousing environment, operational data from autonomous, heterogeneous and distributed information sources are extracted, translated, cleaned, integrated and stored (materialized) into a single database, called as data warehouse. This data loading process is performed by the integration and maintenance component, which is also responsible for periodically refreshing the data warehouse to reflect updates of interest from the sources. On the other hand, the query and analysis component makes it possible for decision-making analysts both to access the previously stored data in the warehouse and to visualize and manipulate the obtained results [2].

Data in a warehouse are subject-oriented, integrated, non-volatile and historical, and are typically modeled multidimensionally. Furthermore, data in such a database are usually structured in crescent levels of aggregation (granularity). While the lower level contains detailed data consolidated from the operational environment, the higher level of the hierarchy stores highly aggregated data. Between these two levels there may exist several intermediate ones. Data stored in level n represent an aggregation from data stored in level $n-1$, and the lowest intermediate level uses data from the lower level as a basis for its aggregation.

In general, the warehouse data are stored in a centralized database. However, the distribution of such data introduces several advantages into a data warehousing envi-

---

[1] This research was partially supported by PICDT-CAPES/UEM program.

Y. Kambayashi, W. Winiwarter, M. Arikawa (Eds.): DaWaK 2002, LNCS 2454, pp. 265–274, 2002.

ronment. In [4], we have identified and analyzed these advantages. Recently, Moeller has also done a similar work [9]. The data warehouse distribution contributes to improving the OLAP (on-line analytical processing) query performance and to increasing the reliability and availability of the data warehousing environment. On the one hand, improving the query performance is essential since OLAP queries can access millions of records and perform a lot of scans, joins and aggregations. On the other hand, increasing the reliability and availability is important since these environments typically remain unavailable to users' queries during the data loading process. However, current data warehousing applications require 100% availability.

Besides, the distribution of the warehouse data also introduces another advantages into a data warehousing environment. First, the data warehouse distribution facilitates the decentralization of business functions, making it possible that information be located nearer to decision-making analysts and reducing problems related to remote users. Furthermore, the concept of distribution is inherent to the typical architecture of data warehousing environments, which may be composed of several data marts in addition to the main data warehouse. However, the distribution of the warehouse data as a step of the construction of data marts has been little explored so far. The data warehouse distribution can also serve as a basis for supporting data warehousing applications which best reflect the distributed nature of modern corporations. Finally, the distribution may be focused on as a solution for a novel requirement of nowadays data warehousing applications: support to a greater number of users.

The advantages mentioned above motivates not only the development of algorithms for distributing the warehouse data, but also the proposal of a distributed data warehousing environment aimed at facing several additional challenges introduced by such a distribution. Amongst these additional challenges, one may point out: (i) fragmentation, replication and allocation policies related to the distribution design must be based on particular characteristics of such environments, such as data organization in different levels of aggregation and data multidimensionality; (ii) methodologies aimed at maintaining the consistency of data warehousing environments must guarantee such a consistency both among data stored at a given site and among data stored redundantly and/or fragmented into two or more sites; (iii) OLAP query processing must also focus on the data warehouse distribution, in addition to the transparent reformulation of users' queries in terms of the most appropriate (detailed or correlated aggregated) data to answer them; and (iv) OLAP distributed query processing must minimize data transfer in the network.

Seeking to face such challenges, we are currently developing the WebD²W (Web Distributed Data Warehousing) system. WebD²W is a distributed client-server data warehousing environment, which is aimed not only at the data warehouse distribution, but also at the distributed access to these data using the Web technology as an infrastructure. The main objectives of the WebD²W system are: to increase the availability of the warehouse data, to increase the availability of access to such data, to maintain the *intra-site* and *inter-site* consistencies, to guarantee the fragmentation, replication and location transparencies in data manipulation, to improve the OLAP query performance and to support a great number of users.

In this paper, we introduce the WebD²W system, focusing on one of its main objectives: the data warehouse distribution. Such a system is presented in terms of its main components and their respective functionalities (section 3). Since the paper focuses on the data warehouse distribution in the WebD²W system and the Web is used by this system as an infrastructure, Web aspects are outside the scope of the paper (see [3] for details). In section 4, we describe the algorithm for fragmenting horizontally the warehouse data. The remaining sections of the paper are section 2, which briefly surveys related work, and section 5, which concludes the paper.

2 Related Work

Regarding data distribution, Datta *et al.* [6] have proposed a strategy for vertical partitioning of relational data warehouses based on star schema among a set of processors. Because this strategy is directed to parallel processing in multiprocessor architectures, the obtained vertical fragmentation may not be feasible to be applied to a distributed data warehousing environment. For instance, the processing of a query which requires the reconstruction of the fact table may incur high data traffic in the network. Munneke *et al.* [10] have introduced two multidimensional fragmentation strategies: slice and dice fragmentation and sever fragmentation. While the former is used to restrict the data being analyzed to subsets of those data, the latter fragments data by removing one or more numeric measures. However, such strategies are specified only analytically. No algorithms regarding how data should be partitioned are presented in [10]. The vertical fragmentation of multidimensional data implemented on relational database systems based on star schema has also been investigated by Golfarelli *et al.* [7]. According to the workload of the system, the proposed fragmentation may achieve two goals: partitioning the numeric measures of a view into two or more tables and unifying two or more views into a single table. Golfarelli *et al.*, though, do not foresee the location of the obtained fragments at several sites. The fragmentation algorithm offered by the Fragmentation/Replication Module of the distribution component of the WebD²W system aims at fragmenting the warehouse data horizontally (see section 4). This algorithm is based on the concept of derivation graph. Therefore, it can be applied to several business applications, and is independent from the implementation of multidimensional data in relational or specialized data structures.

3 The WebD^{2}W System

The WebD²W (Web Distributed Data Warehousing) system is a distributed data warehousing environment which focuses on data distribution considering two different perspectives. The first one refers to the distribution of the warehouse data, aiming at increasing the availability of such data. The second perspective is related to the distributed access to the distributed data warehouse, aiming both at increasing the availability of access to the distributed data and at guaranteeing the fragmentation, replication and location transparencies in data manipulation. Both increments, in the availability of data and in the availability of access, contribute to improving the OLAP query performance and to offering support to a larger number of users.

In this context, the architecture of the WebD²W system (Fig.1) supports two special components: distribution component and distributed environment query component. The former is responsible for the construction and maintenance of the distributed data warehouse from the global data warehouse (pre-existing centralized data warehouse). This component, therefore, creates the basis for the distributed environment. On the other hand, the distributed environment query component acts as a layer through which query and analysis tools (and indirectly end users) can access the distributed data warehouse transparently, as if there were only one centralized data warehouse.

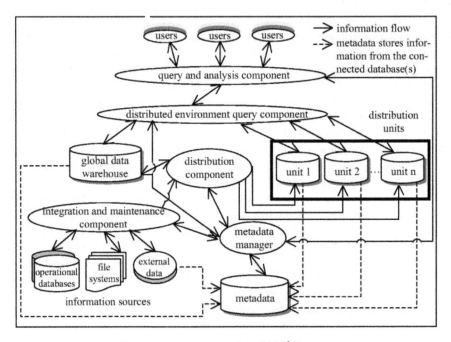

Fig. 1. The architecture of the WebD²W system

In the WebD²W system architecture, the distributed data warehouse consists of a collection of multiple, logically interrelated data warehouses distributed among several sites. More specifically, the distributed data warehouse is composed of the global data warehouse stored at a special site plus several distribution units. Each distribution unit refers to a specific portion of data of the global data warehouse stored at a particular site, including fragments of such data and possibly replicas of fragments located at other sites.

The functionalities of the remaining components of Fig.1 are summarized as follows. Information sources contain operational data according to different models and formats. Any information regarding the data warehousing environment is stored in the metadata repository and is manipulated by the metadata manager. The query and analysis component, for its turn, performs the functionalities mentioned in section 1. Finally, in the WebD^{2}W system the integration and maintenance component is aimed at both originating a set of updates to be applied to the distributed data and propagating such updates to the distribution component.

The presence of the global data warehouse in addition to the distribution units in the WebD^{2}W system architecture is justified by the following reasons: (i) the global data warehouse is the most up-to-date database of the system; (ii) the initial load of new distribution units besides the already existing ones or in replacement of the latter due to the specification of a new distribution design can be generated directly from the global data warehouse, without the need of reconstructing this consolidated database; (iii) according to the set of restrictions applied to the fragmentation process, the completeness of such a process may not be achieved; (iv) routines regarding the extraction, translation, cleaning and integration of data can be implemented through only a set of generic programs, allowing that the information flows in the WebD^{2}W system architecture remain from the information sources to the global data warehouse and from this one to the distribution units. This avoids overlap of efforts and any incompatibility related to the development of those routines; and (v) the global data warehouse is able to answer to any query of the managing level, minimizing data traffic in the network. The only restriction related to the presence of the global data warehouse refers to the volume of data stored in it. Should the storage space be a restrictive factor, one should perform a detailed investigation to identify aggregated datasets to materialize into the global data warehouse (e.g. [8, 11, 12]).

3.1 The Distribution Component

The two correlated functionalities of the distribution component are: (i) to distribute the data of the global data warehouse among several distribution units; and (ii) to maintain the consistency of such data. This component is composed of three main modules: the Design Module, the Fragmentation/Replication Module and the Maintenance Module.

The Design Module is aimed at identifying a set of criteria related to data fragmentation, replication and allocation processes to be followed. Based on such criteria, the distributed data warehouse designer is able to determine requirements to be applied to the fragmentation process and the needs for data replication, as well as allocation policies for the fragmented and possibly replicated data over the sites of the distributed environment. For instance, the requirements for the horizontal fragmentation process are the derivation graph which represents the global data warehouse, the cardinality of each graph vertex, the aggregation function, the dimension to be fragmented and the set of restrictions to be applied to the fragmented dimension.

On the other hand, the Fragmentation/Replication Module focuses on the initial load of the distribution units from the global data warehouse. Aiming at this objective, the Fragmentation/Replication Module offers a set of methodologies and algorithms which search the content of the global data warehouse, fragment its data according to the requirements identified by the distributed data warehouse designer and populate each distribution unit properly. During this process, all information regarding the distribution design is stored in the metadata repository. More specifically, the distribution design refers to information concerning data fragmentation, allocation and replication.

The Maintenance Module, for its turn, is responsible for maintaining the data consistency of the distributed data warehouse, considering both individually each particular site which stores portions of the distributed data warehouse (*intra-site* consistency) and all sites as a whole (*inter-site* consistency). While the *intra-site* consistency results from the ability to maintain the detailed and aggregated data stored at a given site consistent with each other, the *inter-site* consistency is achieved by maintaining the consistency of the fragmented and possibly replicated data stored at two or more sites. Intuitively, the maintenance process of the distributed data warehouse in the WebD^{2}W system begins with the detection of changes in data of interest from the information sources. The extraction, translation, cleansing and integration processes are then carried out by the integration and maintenance component. As a result of these processes, this component originates a set of updates to be applied to the data of the distributed data warehouse and propagates such updates to the Maintenance Module. Based on the information about the distribution design stored in the metadata repository, the Maintenance Module first maintains the global data warehouse according to the propagated set of updates and after that maintains asynchronously the distribution units which were affected by the updates. Updating the global data warehouse first introduces several advantages, which are similar to those ones discussed previously regarding the presence of such a database in addition to the distribution units.

3.2   The Distributed Environment Query Component

The distributed environment query component is responsible for guaranteeing the fragmentation, replication and location transparencies in the distributed data manipulation. Furthermore, this component is also aimed at taking advantage of the data localization for providing local access. The functionalities of the distributed environment query component are developed focusing on minimizing data transfer in the network [1].

Decision-making analysts access the WebD^{2}W system through the functionalities offered by the query and analysis component. The distributed environment query component then intercepts the users' queries submitted through the query and analysis component and manipulates them according to the information of the distribution design stored in the metadata repository.

For a given OLAP query submitted to the WebD^{2}W system via Intranet, the distributed environment query component verifies if the query can be answered from the warehouse data stored in the same site in which the query was posed. Should this condition be satisfied, the query is centrally processed there. The final result is sent to the query and analysis component, which formats and exhibits it to the decision-making analysts.

On the other hand, for a given OLAP query which does not satisfy the above condition or which is submitted to the WebD^{2}W system via Internet, the distributed environment query component is responsible for automatically: (i) redirect this query to the most appropriate site to answer it, so that the query can be centrally processed there; or (ii) break up this query into several subqueries, so that each one of these subqueries accesses different parts of the distributed data warehouse and is sent to and processed partially at the most appropriate site to answer it. In the WebD^{2}W system, we name the first functionality as redirecting of queries processed in a centralized way and the second one as management of queries processed in a distributed way. When a given query is centrally processed at a particular site (first functionality), the distributed environment query component is responsible for preparing the final result to the query and analysis component. Otherwise, when a given query is processed in a distributed way at several sites (second functionality), the distributed environment query component is also responsible for merging the partial results from the sites, besides preparing the final result to the query and analysis component.

4 Horizontal Fragmentation of the Data Warehouse

Before describing in section 4.2 the horizontal fragmentation algorithm used as a basis for the WebD2W system, we discuss in section 4.1 the concept of derivation graph. We make additional remarks about the algorithm in section 4.3.

4.1 Theoretical Basis

The horizontal fragmentation algorithm supported by the Fragmentation/Replication Module assumes that the global data warehouse is organized in different levels of aggregation. This particular manner of data organization is captured by the algorithm through a derivation graph, which is an appropriate diagram to represent the *lattice framework* [8, 11]. A derivation graph G is an oriented graph with a pair (V,E) of disjoint sets of vertices and edges, and two maps init: E→ V and ter: E→ V assigning to every edge e an initial vertex init(e) and a terminal vertex ter(e). The edge e is said to be directed from init(e) to ter(e). There are no loops or multiple edges. The set of vertices V(G) represents a set of *aggregations*, while the set of edges E(G) represents a set of *dependency relations* $\preceq$ between adjacent aggregations. Each graph vertex is an aggregation of numeric measures over the dimensions in that vertex. The $\preceq$ operator imposes a partial ordering on the aggregations; a view (or aggregation) v is dependent upon other view u (v $\preceq$ u) iff v can be determined using only the u results.

The derivation graph has two special vertices: one which can be used to derive any other view (the lower level of the aggregation hierarchy) and another one which can be calculated from any other view (the higher level of the hierarchy) and represents the completely aggregated view. We name the former as total derivation aggregation. Each graph vertex may have a set of ancestors and a set of descendants. For three aggregations v, w, and u $\in$ G: (i) ancestor(v) = {w | v $\preceq$ w}; (ii) descendants(v) = {w | w $\preceq$ v}; (iii) direct ancestors(v) = {w | v $\prec$ w, $\nexists$ u, v $\prec$ u, u $\prec$ w}; and (iv) direct descendants(v) = {w | w $\prec$ v, $\nexists$ u, w $\prec$ u, u $\prec$ v}. In these functions, v $\prec$ w means that v $\preceq$ w and v $\neq$ w.

4.2 The Horizontal Fragmentation Algorithm

The algorithm for fragmenting the warehouse data is based on the concepts of derivation graph, *propagation* of the fragmented dimension and respective restrictions to the graph vertices and *fragmentation* or *reconstruction* of aggregations. In addition to the derivation graph corresponding to the data warehouse to be fragmented, both the dimension to be used as a basis for the fragmentation process (fragmented dimension) and the restrictions to be applied to this process are also inputs for the Horizontal-Fragmentation algorithm. Other inputs are the function used for aggregating the numeric measures of the views and the cardinality of each graph vertex.

Given a derivation graph G corresponding to the global data warehouse, the algorithm produces k new derivation graphs $Gr_1,...,Gr_k$, according to the restrictions $r_1,...,r_k$ applied to the fragmented dimension d. The produced derivation graphs $Gr_1,...,Gr_k$ are semantically equivalent to G, since they represent the same dependencies among aggregations in relation to each combination of the same dimensions in G. However, such derivation graphs are respectively instantiated according to the restrictions $r_1,...,r_k$. More specifically, restrictions are boolean expressions of predicates. When applied to the dimension under fragmentation, they act as a filter for its instances.

The HorizontalFragmentation algorithm works as follows. For each vertex $v \in G$, starting from the total derivation aggregation (task 1), the algorithm verifies if v represents an aggregation over d. Should this condition be satisfied, v is *fragmented* according to $r_1,...,r_k$ and each one of the produced fragments f_i ($1 \le i \le k$) is associated to a derivation graph Gr_i (task 2). Otherwise (i.e., v does not represent an aggregation over d), the vertex $vr_i \in Gr_i$ ($1 \le i \le k$) related to v (i.e., vr_i and v aggregate the same dimensions) is *reconstructed*, using as a basis the fragments of direct ancestors of vr_i that are already present in Gr_i (task 3). Particularly, the *reconstruction* process uses the aggregation function and the cardinality inputs in its cost function. Each time a vertex of G is visited, the fragmented dimension and its respective restrictions are *propagated* to the direct descendents of this vertex (task 4). Finally, the algorithm creates k copies for each edge $e^j \in G$ ($1 \le j \le m$) (task 5). Each created edge e^j_i ($1 \le i \le k$) is associated with the respective derivation graph Gr_i, so that $E(Gr_i) = \{e^1_i, ..., e^m_i\}$. Such an edge creating process is done regarding the dependency relations between aggregations. Details concerning the HorizontalFragmentation algorithm and examples of the algorithm utilization can be found in [3].

In most real-life applications, dimensions consist of several attributes. The attributes of a dimension may have a relationship with other attributes of the same dimension through relationship hierarchies, which specify levels of aggregation and, consequently, granularity of data. Besides, there may be several relationship hierarchies in a same dimension, determining partial orders on the attributes that make up this dimension [8]. On the other hand, some attributes of a dimension are only descriptive attributes and therefore cannot be used in aggregations.

The horizontal fragmentation process of the derivation graph which represents the attributes of dimensions and their respective relationship hierarchies is similar to the one discussed above. Each graph vertex still represents an aggregation of numeric measures over the dimensions in that vertex, considering however the granularity of the attributes of the dimensions. Furthermore, in this case the restrictions must be logical compositions formed by predicates over the attributes of the fragmented dimension, according to the granularity of these attributes. In the horizontal fragmentation process of such derivation graphs, the granularity g of the attribute of the fragmented dimension d must be used to determine, amongst the graph vertices which represent an aggregation over d, which ones must be fragmented and which ones must be reconstructed. The reconstruction will be needed for the vertices whose granularity of the attribute of d is greater than g.

4.3 Additional Remarks

The HorizontalFragmentation algorithm can be applied in both situations: (i) when all aggregations that can be generated from the detailed data are stored in the warehouse and (ii) when not all aggregations are stored in such a database. A derivation graph represents only dependencies between adjacent aggregations, and not those in the transitive closure. However, for three aggregations v, w, and u of a derivation graph, if $v \prec w$ and $w \prec u$, we can argue that $v \prec u$. This means that the non-materialization of w still guarantees the properties of the derivation graph, and therefore the applicability of the HorizontalFragmentation algorithm.

A first optimization to the horizontal fragmentation process is related to reducing the dimensionality of some produced derivation graphs. Depending on the restrictions applied to the fragmentation process, the fragmented dimension of such graphs will have only a single value in its domain. Consequently, it may be removed. Another optimization refers to the identification of which aggregations of the produced derivation graphs should be materialized. Existing methodologies concerning this objective (e.g. [8, 11, 12]) might be used to assist this optimization.

5   Conclusions and Future Work

In this paper, we discussed the data warehouse distribution in the WebD^{2}W system. We first presented the architecture of such a system. We also described the algorithm for fragmenting the warehouse data horizontally, which is used as a basis for the WebD^{2}W.

In the current phase of the WebD^{2}W system development, we have identified in [4] a set of criteria related to the data fragmentation, replication and allocation processes. This set of criteria requires a detailed analysis of the data warehousing application in terms of the characteristics of: (i) its data organization in different levels of aggregation, including the volume of data of each level and the number of users which access each one of these levels; (ii) the static aspects of the multidimensional modeling of the application; (iii) the OLAP queries frequently submitted by the users' application; and (iv) the operation types supported by the environment.

A prototype implementing some functionalities of the distributed environment query component is described in [1]. Aiming at developing this prototype, we have identified a set of selectivity criteria to be used for determining which sites could answer to a given query. The following selectivity criteria were employed: the analysis of the users' queries to identify which data are required, the investigation of the sites to determine which data are stored in which *site*, the availability and the workload of the sites, the number of active connections in each site, the bandwidth of the communication channels and the processing capacity of each *site*. We have also determined in [1] a set of rules for assisting the tasks of redirecting of queries processed in a centralized way and management of queries processed in a distributed way. This set of rules was based on the aggregation level being searched, on the number of fragments being accessed and on the amount of data corresponding to the partial results to be transmitted in the network.

Finally, in [5] we have analyzed and compared so far existing methodologies aimed at maintaining the data warehouse consistency. We have also identified restrictions in the surveyed methodologies to a distributed data warehousing environment. Particularly, we have discussed the applicability of the surveyed methodologies for maintaining the *intra-site* consistency and have identified new costs which shall be considered by these methodologies in the *inter-site* consistency maintenance, besides highlighting the value of self-maintainable views in distributed data warehousing environments. In [5] we have also investigated and compared some methodologies for determining which aggregated datasets to materialize in the warehouse when it is not feasible to store all possible aggregations.

We are now developing the remaining functionalities of the Fragmentation/Replication Module of the distribution component of the WebD²W system. We are specifically addressing the proposal of an algorithm for the vertical fragmentation of the warehouse data. We plan to apply to the algorithm the same concepts employed in the HorizontalFragmentation algorithm: derivation graph, propagation of the fragmented dimension (and respective restrictions) and fragmentation or reconstruction of aggregations.

References

1. Ciferri, C.D.A., Ciferri, R.R., Souza, F.F.: A Replication/Fragmentation Architecture for Distributed Access to DW via Web. Proc. XXV CLEI Conference (1999) 139-150 (in Portuguese)
2. Chaudhuri, S., Dayal, U.: An Overview of Data Warehousing and OLAP Technology. SIGMOD Record, 26(1) (1997) 65-74
3. Ciferri, C.D.A., Souza, F.F.: The WebD²W System – Web Distributed Data Warehousing. Technical Report, DCS, UFPE, Brazil (2000) (in Portuguese)
4. Ciferri, C.D.A., Souza, F.F.: Distributing the Data Warehouse. Proc. XV SBBD Symposium (2000) 346-360 (in Portuguese)
5. Ciferri, C.D.A., Souza, F.F.: Materialized Views in Data Warehousing Environments. Proc. XX SCCC Conference (2000)
6. Datta, A., Moon, B., Thomas, H.: A Case for Parallelism in Data Warehousing and OLAP. Proc. 9th DEXA Workshop (1998) 226-231
7. Golfarelli, M., Maio, D., Rizzi, S.: Applying Vertical Fragmentation Techniques in Logical Design of Multidimensional Databases. Proc. 2nd DaWaK Conference (2000) 11-23
8. Harinarayan, V., Rajaraman, A., Ullman, J.D.: Implementing Data Cubes Efficiently. Proc. 1996 SIGMOD Conference (1996) 205-216
9. Moeller, R.A.: Distributed Data Warehousing using Web Technology. American Management Association, USA (2001)
10. Munneke, D., Wahlstrom, K., Mohania, M.: Fragmentation of Multidimensional Databases. Proc. 10th ADC Conference (1999) 153-164
11. Shukla, A., Deshpande, P.M., Naughton, J.F.: Materialized View Selection for Multidimensional Datasets. Proc. 24th VLDB Conference (1998) 488-499
12. Theodoratos, D., Bouzeghoub, M.: A General Framework for the View Selection Problem for Data Warehouse Design and Evolution. Proc. 3rd DOLAP Workshop (2000) 1-8

A Decathlon in Multidimensional Modeling: Open Issues and Some Solutions

W. Hümmer, W. Lehner, A. Bauer, L. Schlesinger

University of Erlangen-Nuremberg (Database Systems)
Martensstr. 3, Erlangen, D-91058, Germany
{huemmer,lehner,bauer,schlesinger}@immd6.informatik.uni-erlangen.de

Abstract. The concept of multidimensional modeling has proven extremely successful in the area of Online Analytical Processing (OLAP) as one of many applications running on top of a data warehouse installation. Although many different modeling techniques expressed in extended multidimensional data models were proposed in the recent past, we feel that many hot issues are not properly reflected. In this paper we address ten common problems reaching from defects within dimensional structures over multidimensional structures to new analytical requirements and more.

1 Introduction

A proper data model is the core of representing a part of the real world in the context of a database. The multidimensional data model ([43]) has proven extremely adequate for the explorative analysis of information stored in a data warehouse. Many variations of the multidimensional modeling idea were proposed in the recent past, extending the classical way of multidimensionally reflecting the world in different directions. However, no data model provides a comprehensive set of structural and operational tools necessary for a flexible and extensive analysis of information stored within a data warehouse system. After many years of research this paper provides a summary of open problems in the context of multidimensional modeling. From our point of view, these problems are of fundamental importance and need further investigation in the very near future, but we have to emphasize that the list of open problems surely is not complete.

The remainder of the paper identifies and discusses ten defects of current multidimensional data models. In identifying those defects we encourage the data warehousing community to develop adequate solutions to improve the service accomplished by a successful data warehousing infrastructure. In discussing the current state-of-the-art we are far from producing the ultimate solutions of these problems. However we want to pinpoint the single problems and produce a list following the same pattern every time.

The Surrounding Modeling Framework

The similarity to the design pattern approach by Gamma et al. ([11]) is not purely accidental. The goal is a modular data model extensible by plug-ins.

(0) To reflect a multidimensional application scenario properly, we need an extensible data model (i.e. a multidimensional meta model) to plug in certain modeling features, in the sense of modules, as needed.

Y. Kambayashi, W. Winiwarter, M. Arikawa (Eds.): DaWaK 2002, LNCS 2454, pp. 275–285, 2002.

Many application scenarios are well equipped with the idea of the simple multidimensional modeling. There are also many non-standard OLAP applications which would tremendously benefit from using OLAP technology. However, providing modeling techniques for every possible scenario does not seem like an adequate approach. Thus, the general concept is to provide a meta model from which application designers may instantiate a certain concrete multidimensional model with only the extensions they need for the actual scenario. This would help to develop and organize the modeling techniques in a very modular way. On the one hand, researchers are then able to provide new model extensions as simple plug-ins into the model. On the other hand, developers would have to demonstrate expertise only in those modules which they are really intending to use. Although many modeling proposals were made in the recent past, there is no well-known and widely accepted work providing a meta modeling framework. In proposing such a framework, the modular approach and the feature of extensibility of UML could be used as a guideline.

2   Ten Problems

The next ten sections deal with shortcomings of the multidimensional data model and sketches existing or possible solutions. We are focussing on dimensional, multidimensional aspects as well as meta information.

Problem: Unbalanced Hierarchies

(1) Complex applications modeled in an OLAP style require flexible classification structures. Current theory demands that every path from the generic top level node to any of the leaves has the same length. This is not always possible in practice.

Description: In general, two cases of unbalanced hierarchies are possible: an arbitrary subtree of the classification tree lacks an inner level in comparison to its siblings or it lacks the leaf level. In either case the result is an unbalanced hierarchy. Unbalanced hierarchies are not necessarily the result of a bad dimensional design. The real world may demand that kind of hierarchies; e.g. consider the product dimension of a bank or insurance company. Certain loan services are packaged and combined with other financial services, while the product of a simple savings account does not have any further subclassifications. The main problem of unbalanced hierarchies is that on a certain level of the classification tree the partitioning property is violated: it is not guaranteed that the sum of the sales figures for all nodes of a certain level really represents the total sum.

Discussion: The topic of unbalanced hierarchies is not treated in literature in detail ([22]). The simple approach is the introduction of dummy nodes: these are introduced where necessary to produce a regular, balanced hierarchy. This problem plays an important role also in some of the following problems. For example in the case of schema evolution (problem 10) aggregation over long periods of time has to deal with changing and thus unbalanced hierarchies. Further discussiuon of the topic also known as non-covering or heterogenous dimensions can be found in [15], [16], [33] and [42]

Problem: Irregular Hierarchies

(2) Another defect of the common classification hierarchy concept is that only pure
1:N-relationships between classification nodes of adjacent levels are allowed to
avoid irregularities in aggregations. Especially the product dimension demands to
drop this restriction, i.e. a general acyclic classification graph is needed.

Description: Nowadays we are surrounded by complex products that fulfil the functionality of several products. A mobile phone SL 45 is not a phone only, it also is a personal digital assistant (PDA) and an MP3 player. In a strict classification hierarchy it
can only be assigned to a single product family, e.g. to Mobile Phones. This 1:N-relationship is particularly important for aggregating along drill paths: only under this condition the sum of sales over all Articles is equal to the sum of sales over all Product Families (figure 1). In practice it might be interesting to also consider the SL 45 when calculating the sum of sales over PDAs or MP3 players. So it might be desirable to assign
it to all three product families (lower half of figure 1). This means to give up the 1:N
relationship in favour of a general N:M mapping which results in an acyclic classification graph for the dimension(s). However this approach causes a wrong result for the
sum over all product families because the phones sales fi gures go into the sum three
times instead of only once thus yielding 200,100 instead of 200,000, the correct result.

Discussion: Literature suggests two solutions
that both are not really satisfactory ([21], [20]).
The more general solution is to specify a distribution for the sales figures of the classification
node in question. For example the following
heuristic could be issued: 80% of all sales figures for the SL 45 are added to the Mobile
Phones category and 10% to each, PDA and
MP3 Players. Obviously this approach avoids
the different aggregation results on different
classification levels. However it only produces
estimated figures, its quality depending on the
quality of the distribution. The other solution is

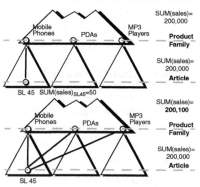

Fig. 1. 1:N Mapping vs. N:M Mapping

a special case of the distribution approach: the facts related to a multi-predecessor classification node are completely assigned to exactly one higher classification node
(100%). Further ideas are given in [34], [40], [42].

Problem: Detailed Feature Exploration

(3) The simple notion of a classification hierarchy is not capable of reflecting complex
dimensional information. Besides the hierarchical structure we demand an additional infrastructure to model complex features comprehensively describing simple
classification nodes.

Description: Consider a product dimension. Simple articles are grouped to product
groups, these in turn into product areas, families an so on. However, a single product
does exhibit a tremendous feature list, providing extra information with regard to color,

packaging type, delivery information and so on. If those features may be assigned to every product in a product dimension, the classical way of multidimensional modeling may look sufficient. However, if features are local to certain classes of products, extensions to the data model are necessary. For example the set of washing machines certainly exhibits a completely different set of properties as kitchen appliances do. But both are members of the same dimension. A second issue in annotating dimensional structures consists in the problem of detailing a dimensional structure beyond the leaf nodes of a dimensional hierarchy. Again, considering a product dimension, one may wish to expand each product regarding the single parts needed to construct this specific article. These parts may either appear as products themselves in the dimension or they may reflect sub-articles which are not part of the primary dimensional structure. Obviously, strong summarizability is not required with this technique. Instead, drilling sales figures beyond the atomic level may help the analyst to gain knowledge according to relationships to other product areas.

Discussion: Addressing the first problem in annotating dimensional structures with properties local to certain classification nodes was done in [23]. Unfortunately, this work misses a seamless integration with other wishful extensions. Work considering the second issue in splitting data beyond the leaf nodes of a classification tree must be seen as a variation of many other problems described. Since a single article is made of many parts or annotated with multiple features we consider this an N:M-relationship problem (problem 2). Moreover, if we require summarizability to a certain degree, dealing with de-aggregation is necessary to come up with a reasonable solution (problem 6).

Problem: Multidimensional Constraints

(4) While the hierarchical structure of a dimension exhibits strong functional dependencies between the single category attributes, the data cells of a multidimensional data cube are not subject of any constraints beyond a given data and summarizability type. We demand an additional multidimensional constraint mechanism focussing the sparsity, i.e. the existence or absence of explicit NULL-values.

Description: A multidimensional data cube usually exhibits a high degree of sparsity, because many possible combinations of dimensional elements do not show a corresponding data entry. In the same way the relational model types and limits NULL values the multidimensional model requires (a) an additional mechanism to type the non-existent data cell values according to their meaning and (b) a constraint mechanism to explicitly allow or prohibit the existence of data values for certain combinations. An example for different types of NULL values would be the case where a difference has to be made regarding data which is known to be delivered from external data sources but has not arrived yet and data which will never appear in the data cube.

Discussion: Regarding the first issue, we may extend the domain of all possible values of a measure by two constant values, NOT_KNOWN and NOT_EXISTENT following the classical NULL value theory from the relational world ([7]). While the first value denotes a not yet available but possible NULL value, the second value gives the user (and the system!) the hint that the corresponding data entry is currently not available and will never be accessible, because this combination does not make sense in the real world application. The second issue demands a way to declare multidimensional NULL constraints for sub-cubes defined over dimensional elements. In opposite to the relational model, a cell should be tagged ALWAYS_NULL to prevent any user data, NEVER_NULL to demand user data or ANY to keep the constraint unspecified. If a data cell tagged with ANY has no recorded value a NOT_KNOWN value takes place because a value may be inserted in the future. Moreover the system should have knowledge of these types so that they are excluded within an OLAP data cube and users are not permitted to explore, i.e. drill-down into those sub-cubes. Unfortunately no work in the area of multidimensional data models is aware of this problem and incorporates a solution seamlessly into the modeling framework.

Problem: Restricting Access to Multidimensional Information

(5) By integrating data from different data sources into a single data cube access restrictions must be introduced for the new (and often more valuable) information: in the static case, the data model should provide techniques to prevent certain user groups from accessing some areas of the data cube. In the dynamic case, user should not be able to gather "forbidden" data by inference applying tracker techniques.

Description: In using a data warehouse database users are suddenly able to retrieve combined and valuable information. Access mechanism compiled in the data model are required to grant access only to predefined areas of the data cube. Commercial products already restrict access to specific classification hierarchy nodes or provide only aggregated data or slices of the complete data cube. Besides these static problems, topics like inference - gathering new information from already known data - have to be considered.

Discussion: For solving the static access problem object privileges must be set up on a fine granularity, possibly on classification nodes or even on single data cells. To protect a data warehouse from inferring sensitive data we have to consider two ways to receive this sensitive data. First, there is *one-query-inference*, which generates the required information with one user query. Second, a user combines the results of multiple queries to receive the required data (audit based). This approach is called *multiple-query-inference*. Research work has been done in the area of scientific and statistical databases ([8]) but has to be adequately transferred to data warehousing. An example for a one-query-inference is to reduce the number of items of the result set by using parallel classifications, e.g. by characterizing products non-ambiguously with its feature values (problem 3). In [41] an indicator-based recognition algorithm is proposed which can be used for access control at runtime.

Problem: Missing Data

(6) While traditional analysis operators in data warehousing are defined on existing (raw) data, the application world is interested in operators to get information about areas where no data exist.

Description: Consider the following situation: Several industry companies are selling statistical data (parameterized by fact, granularity, and classification tree). Obviously, the price of data increases with the granularity and the coverage. If a customer periodically has to buy detailed data he has to spend a lot of money. The question for such a customer is as follows: Is it enough to get detailed data only every other period and esti-mate the data of the missing periods with the risk of missing some important deviations from what is normal? If the application is satisfied with such a strategy, the data model should be able to provide tools to estimate, i.e. substitute missing data cubes.

Discussion: One strategy to estimate missing data is to use interpolation between the known detailed data of two or more periods. The disadvantage of this idea is obvious: The missing data can only be computed retrospectively. Another technique might be *deaggregation*: Usually, the drill-down operator may be applied, only if detailed data is available. If the data does not exist then the deaggregation function splits aggregated values and generates detailed data according to a predefined pattern: If an equal distri-bution of the data is assumed then the deaggregation function divides the aggregated value by the number of the children of this node. A more complex strategy is the usage of a *distribution pattern*: If the distribution of the data in another period is known then the same distribution can be applied to the aggregated value of the current period. For example the percentage distribution of sold video recorders in Germany in January 2001 can be used to compute the distribution in January 2002. Furthermore, if data from the preceding months are known then the data of January 2002 can be estimated by trend exploration. Related work can be found in [3], [26].

Problem: Sequence Operations

(7) The classification nodes of a dimension reflect the idea of repetitive grouping to build a classification hierarchy. The ordering of classification nodes within a dimen-sion according to data values from inside of the data cube is not known yet.

Description: The need for sequence based analysis techniques is impressively shown by recent developments of SQL. Operators like OVER() with its ORDER BY or WINDOW-ING extensions enable the formulation of que-ries for cumulating sum or moving average values, whereby schema and fact data have to be considered in a different way. Although these operations are not yet fully standardized,

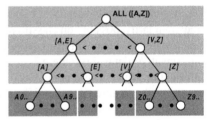

Fig. 2. Inheritance of a total order

the problems arising from sequence oriented queries in the relational area are well stud-ied and many concepts are published (e.g. [35]) or already implemented in commercial database systems or in OLAP-Tools. However, especially the implementations are quite proprietary and general concepts in the multidimensional data model are missing. The dimensional attributes of one dimension form a set which is characterized by having no order. A first level of ordering dimensional data is to rely on the domain of the elements. Time for example already exhibits a natural order. Persons may be sorted according to their name or additional features. A second level of ordering may be seen in relying on data from the data cube. For example, salesmen could be ordered according to their profit, whereat profit is a regular multidimensional fact. Finally the fact data itself could be ordered for some reason.

Discussion: If an order is defined on a specific level of the classification hierarchy, then the order of a classification level is inherited to all elements being on a lower level. Figure 2 illustrates the inheritance. A major problem are holes in one level: If holes exist, then it is impossible to classify new elements. Figure 2 illustrates the problem, if all elements of the interval [F;U] are not members of the classification hierarchy although the parent node is indicated by [A;Z]. Beside the ordering of the classification hierarchy it is also possible to order the fact data. While the order of the first one is given by the modeler and modifications affecting the order are rare, the fact data are updated quite often. Therefore, to order the elements after each update to support only a small number of operations makes no sense. Therefore, the fact data are ordered on demand. The basis is a classification tree, which is generated ad hoc, why we call this operation *ad hoc classification*. In the same way as [35] defines relational sequence operators for selection, projection or aggregation on sequences or for concatenating and shifting have to be defined in the multidimensional data model as well.

Problem: Progressive Query Answering

(8) While almost everything is said about cleaning, scrubbing and integrating data from multiple data sources into a single consistent data warehouse database, very little work has been performed discussing the problem of approximate answers.

Description: One of the major goals and biggest problems in data warehousing is to support real-time OLAP. In the last decade, several strategies like indexing ([30]), join optimization, or preaggregation ([13], [1]) were developed. However, running a query might still take a long time. The goal of query processing is always to produce 'exact results', which is worth to take a closer look at: Is it really important to get the exact result or is it sufficient to compute a quick result, which comes close to the exact result?

Discussion: The problem of fuzzy query answers is well known in the area of statistics ([26]), where sampling is one of the basic methods. This idea could be applied to data warehousing to get a first estimation of the result on existing data, e.g. only a fraction of the fact table is read, aggregated and the result extrapolated to get an appraised value of the exact one. The main advantage of this technique is that a fast preliminary result is computed and presented to the user in a first step, while the computation of the exact result can be executed in a traditional manner in a second step. The difference betweeen the approximated and the correct value depends on the sampling technique, which has to consider the distribution of the data. Another alternative is to compute the exact value of one partial sum and extrapolate the value to get an appraised value of the result which can also be dynamically refined. After computing the first partial sum, a second partial sum is computed, a new appraised value is generated and presented to the user. This proceeds until all partial sums are calculated which corresponds to the exact value. The main advantage of the sketched idea is that in each step the user gets an estimated value which is based on more exact partial sums. The incremental characteristic is called *online aggregation* which is introduced by [18] in the relational context. Recently [32] presented the idea of Iterative Data Cubes, which is a special kind of pre-aggregation for online aggregation by handling different dimensions independently.

Problem: Modeling Metadata Information

(9) To achieve the aim of data warehouse systems, the analysis of integrated data, meta data are essential in order to interpret the results and benefit from the expense of setting up a data warehouse. Proposals for standards of a common meta schema have been made but have not yet got accepted.

Description: If users cannot understand and interpret the results of OLAP queries, the acceptance and benefit of the whole data warehouse is suffering. An effective data consolidation can be realized only with support of well organized and structured meta data. To enable different systems to interact with each other a standardized API to process the meta data and a common conceptual schema or a data exchange format is required. A consistent exchange format not only enables the exchange of data directly between cooperating data warehouse systems but also may serve as a base to distribute multidimensional organized data over the web by a third party provider. If data can be interpreted, downloading and integrating data cubes in a local data warehouse would no longer be a vision.

Discussion: The common warehouse metamodel (CWM, [6]) has been set up by the OMG which includes in the meantime the Open Information Model (OIM, [31]). But it has not become that widely accepted and used as it is desirable. This is due to the lack of support for some applications. A common, standardized meta data framework has to be both flexible and detailed. An imprecise meta schema has no benefit and yields to desiderative utilization. On the other hand it has to be adaptable to a broad range of applications, otherwise it misses an effective support for these and usage is limited. A possible way to reach this aim is a plug-in mechanism to get a customizable meta schema. A comprehensive meta modeling has also to consider data exchange. An XML based encoding of multidimensional data with the purpose of data exchange is shown in [29]. Tightly connected to this topic is a query definition standard. A query formulated at one system must be transferred to another one, executed and the result passed back to origin warehouse. Some work has been done in this area ([27], [26]).

Problem: Schema Evolution

(10)The multidimensional schema may change in the course of time. Examples for modifications of the schema are the insertion of a new classification node or the deletion of a classification level. The schema has to reflect changes in the real world like introduction of new products or the modification of structure of the channels of distribution.

Description: In general one may distinguish between schema evolution and schema versioning. Schema evolution means that the data is adapted to the new structure and the old schema will be lost, whereas schema versioning retains the schemata for the according validity period. This enables evaluation of the data based on an arbitrary structure, the currently valid schema, the schema of a past point in time or the correlating schema of data creation. Schema evolution causes fewer problems as data is transformed into the new structure and afterwards query processing is just the same as in a regular data warehouse. Schema versioning requires more complex solutions.

Discussion: When storing data with its schema changes additional structures to represent the temporal aspects are necessary. One possibility is to introduce new attributes containing the time stamps for the begin and the end of the valid time. But the increased complexity of the storage schema entails an unsatisfying query performance. New concepts of query processing are necessary. Also preaggregation becomes more difficult as with schema historization another analysis dimension has to be considered. Furthermore multidimensional indices which support the evaluation of data according to different schemata are conceivable. At the user front end there is a lack of support by query languages and OLAP tools. For the relational interface e.g. TSQL, TSQL2 or TQUEL ([38]) have been developed. For further work see [16], [21].

3 Summary and Conclusion

This paper is meant to be a guide through still open problems of multidimensional modeling in data warehousing. The data warehouse is a well understood and well established technique in modern business. It reflects the core of OLAP, decision support, CRM, etc. We subject ourselves to the multidimensional data model because it enables us to efficiently follow predefined evaluation paths. Still there are several situations in real world business, that are not solved satisfyingly. The bottom line of this paper is that we have to accept that there will never be the one and only multidimensional data model. Instead we have to develop a catalogue of data warehouse patterns: whenever a problem arises the catalogue provides a detailed description of this problem and discusses the solutions at hand.

References

1   Baralis, E.; Paraboschi, S.; Teniente, E.: Materialized View Selection in a Multidimensional Database. VLDB '97, Athens, Greece, 1997
2   Brodsky, A.; Farkas, C.; Jajodia., S.: Secure databases: Constraints, inference channels, and monitoring disclosures. IEEE Trans. Knowledge and Data Engineering, 12(6):900–919, 2000.
3   Chaudhuri, S; Das, G., Narasayya, V.: A Robust, Optimization-Based Approach for Approximate Answering of Aggregate Queries. ACM SIGMOD, Santa Barbara, USA. 2001.
4   Chen, P. et al: Evaluating Aggregate Operation over Imprecise Data. IEEE Trans. on Knowledge and Data Engineering, 8(2):273-284, 1996.
5   Codd, E.F.: Codd, S.B.; Salley, C.T.: Providing OLAP (On-line Analytical Processing) to User Analysts: An IT Mandate, White Paper, Arbor Software Corporation, 1993
6   N.N.: Common Warehouse Metamodel specification. OMG (http://www.omg.org/cwm/)
7   Date, C.J.: An Introduction to Database Systems. 7th ed. Reading, Massachusettes, 2000
8   Denning, D.E.: Secure statistical databases with random sample queries. ACM Trans. on Database Systems, 5(3):291–315, 1980.
9   Dyreson, C. E.: Information Retrieval from an Incomplete Data Cube. VLDB'96, Bombay, 1996.
10 Gray, J.; Bosworth A.; Layman A.; Pirahesh, H.: Data Cube: A Relational Aggregation Operator Generalizing Group-By, Cross-Tab, and Sub-Total. ICDE'96, New Orleans, 1996

11 Gamma, E.; Helm, R.; Johnson, R.; Vlissides, J.: Design Patterns – Elements of Reusable Object-Oriented Software. Boston et al., 1994

12 Gupta, A.; Mumick, I.: Maintenance of Materialized Views: Problems, Techniques, and Applications. In: IEEE Data Engineering Bulletin, Special Issue on Materialized Views & Data Warehousing 18(1995)2

13 Harinarayan, V.; Rajaraman, A.; Ullman, J.D.: Implementing Data Cubes Efficiently. SIGMOD '96, Montreal, Canada, 1996

14 Hurtado, C.; Mendelzon, A.: Reasoning about Summarizability in Heterogeneous Multidimensional Schemas. ICDT'01, 2001.

15 Hurtado, C.; Mendelzon, A.: OLAP Dimension Constraints. PODS'02, Madison, 2002.

16 Hurtado, C.; Mendelzon, A.; Vaisman, A.: Maintaining data cubes under dimension updates. ICDE'99

17 Jagadish, H. V.; Lakshmanan, L. V. S.; Srivastava, D.: What can Hierarchies do for Data Warehouses? VLDB'99, Bombay, 1999.

18 Joseph M. Hellerstein, Peter J. Haas, Helen Wang: Online Aggregation. SIGMOD Conference 1997

19 N.N.: Hyperion Essbase OLAP Server, Hyperion Software Corporation, 1999 (http://www.hyperion.com/essbaseolap.cfm)

20 Inmon, W.H.: Building the Data Warehouse, New York, John Wiley & Sons, 1996

21 Kimball, R.: The Data Warehouse Toolkit, New York, John Wiley & Sons, 1996

22 Lehner, W., Albrecht, J., Wedekind, H.: Multidimensional Normal Forms. SSDBM'98, Capri, Italy, 1998

23 Lehner, W.; Ruf, T.; Teschke, M.: CROSS-DB: A Feature-extended multi-dimensional Data Model for Statistical and Scientific Databases. CIKM'96, Rockville (MD), U.S.A., 1996

24 Lenz, H.-J.; Shoshani, A: Summarizability in OLAP and Statistical Data Bases. SSDBM'97, Olympia

25 Malvestuto, F.M.; Moscarini, M.: Computational issues connected with the protection of sensitive statistics by auditing sum-queries. IEEE SSDM'98, 1998.

26 Mason, R.: Statistical Design and Analysis of Experiments: With Applications to Engineering and Science (Wiley Series in Probability and Mathematical Statistic), John Wiley & Sons, 1989

26 N.N.: OLAP Council API, MDAPI version 2.0 specification. OLAP Council (http://www.olapcouncil.org/research/apily.htm)

27 N.N.: The Multidimensional Expressions language (MDX). Microsoft Corporation (http://msdn.microsoft.com/library/default.asp?url=/library/en-us/olapdmad/agmdxbasics_04qg.asp)

28 N.N.: Microstrategy 6, MicroStrategy Inc., 1999, (http://www.microstrategy.com/Products/index.asp)

29 N.N.: XCube, 2002, (http://www.xcube-open.org)

30 O'Neil, P.: INFORMIX and Indexing Support for Data Warehouses. In: Database Programming and Design, v. 10, no. 2, February, 1997

31 N.N.: Open Information Model, Meta Data Coalition, (http://www.mdcinfo.com/)

32 Mirek Riedewald, Divyakant Agrawal, Amr El Abbadi: Flexible Data Cubes for Online Aggregation. ICDT'01, London, United Kingdom, 2001

33 Pedersen, T. B.; Jensen, C. S.; Dyreson, C. E.: Supporting Imprecision in Multidimensional Databases Using Granularities. SSDBM'99, 1999.

34 Pedersen, T. B.; Jensen, C. S.; Dyreson, C. E.: A foundation for capturing and querying complex multidimensional data. Information Systems, 26(5): 383-423, 2001.

35 Praveen Seshadri, Miron Livny, Raghu Ramakrishnan: The Design and Implementation of a Sequence Database System. VLDB'96, Mumbai (Bombay), India, 1996

36 Shoshani, A.: OLAP and Statistical Databases: Similarities and Differences, PODS'97, Tuscon, Arizona

37 Smith, J.M.; Smith, D.C.P.: Database Abstractions: Aggregation and Generalization, ACM Transactions on Database Systems 2(1977)2

38 Snodgrass, R. T. (Hrsg.): The TSQL2 Temporal Query Language. Kluwer Academic Publishing, Amsterdam, 1995

39 N.N.: ISO/IEC 9075: 1999, Informatik Technology – Database Languages – SQL, 1999

40 Song, I.; Rowan, B.; Medsker, C.; Ewen, E.: An Analysis of Many-to-Many Relationships Between Fact and Dimension Tables in Dimensional Modeling. DMDW'01, 2001.

41 Steger, J.; Günzel, H.; Bauer, A.: Identifying Security Holes in OLAP Applications. IFIP WG 11.3 Conference on Database Security, Schoorl, Netherlands, 2000

42 Tsois, A.; Karayiannidis, N.; Sellis, T.: MAC: Conceptual data modeling for OLAP. DMDW'01, 2001.

43 Vassiliadis, P.; Sellis, T.: A Survey of Logical Models for OLAP Databases. In: SIGMOD Record 28(1999)4

Modeling and Imputation of Large Incomplete Multidimensional Datasets

Xintao Wu[1] and Daniel Barbará[2]

[1] University of North Carolina at Charlotte,
xwu@Suncc.edu
[2] George Mason University,
dbarbara@gmu.edu

Abstract. The presence of missing or incomplete data is a commonplace in large real-word databases. In this paper, we study the problem of missing values which occur at the measure dimension of data cube. We propose a two-part mixture model, which combines the logistic model and loglinear model together, to predict and impute the missing values. The logistic model here is applied to predict missing positions while the loglinear model is applied to compute the estimation. Experimental results on real datasets and synthetic datasets are presented.

1 Introduction

The presence of missing or incomplete data is a commonplace occurrence in large real-world databases. Missing values occur for a variety of reasons, e.g., omissions in the data entry process, confusing questions in the data gathering process, sensor malfunction, and so on. Imputation missing data is critical for data warehousing, yet little has been done in the research field.

Consider a data cube [5][1] which summarizes sales data for a corporation, with dimensions "time of sale", "location of sale" and "product of sale." Some sales values for particular combinations of products, stores, and periods may be missing. Hence the analysis results based on the incomplete data may be not accurate. This paper presents a novel method to produce good estimators for missing values in a data cube.

The data in the cube is typically viewed as having multiple logical categorical attributes known as dimensions (i.e., store, product) with natural hierarchies defined on each dimension (the store can be grouped into city, state, region.) and one or more continuous attributes know as measures (i.e., sale). Typically, the measure in data cubes is non-negative and normally is a semicontinuous attribute which has a proportion of values equal to a single value (typically zero), and a positive continuous distribution among the remaining values. For example, the income or expenditures of economic surveys or sale values in superstores is

---

[1] The datacube is a widely used data model for On-Line Analytical Processing (OLAP). A datacube is a multidimensional data abstraction, where aggregated measures of the combinations of dimension values are kept.

Y. Kambayashi, W. Winiwarter, M. Arikawa (Eds.): DaWaK 2002, LNCS 2454, pp. 286–295, 2002.

a semicontinuous attribute instead as continuous attribute since these measures can often be zero for some combinations of dimension values.

In general, two assumptions about missing values are possible: 1) we know the positions of missing values by the combination of dimension values, but we do not know the measure values for those combinations; 2) we also know the positions of *structural zeros* which are known a-priori definitely to have a *null* value. Assumption 2) is easy to justify since usually stores know their products lists and send this information to the data warehouse. In the warehouse the structural zeros can be easily dealt with by using bitmaps that indicate their location. Therefore, for remaining of this paper, we only focus on the missing values of the semicontinuous measure.

The methods of handling missing data can be grouped into two broad classes. One is data deletion by ignoring the records with missing values during the analysis. Sometimes, ignoring a certain part of the data may result in the data being biased. Another is substitution by filling in the missing values with some values, e.g., the mean of the rest of the entries [10,6]. However, this simple approach failes to give good approximation.

Schafer and Olsen, in [16], review strategies for joint statistical modeling and multiple imputation of semicontinuous survey variables from statistics view. A two-part mixture of a normal distribution and a degenerate point mass is presented to model semicontinuous variables. In our paper, a different two-part mixture model of a multi-dimensional contingency table (modeled by loglinear) and a degenerate point mass due to missing values (modeled by logistic) will be studied for large incomplete data cube. The loglinear model can give a better description of association patterns among categorical dimensions such as product, store. In our previous work [3], we present a Quasi-Cube framework to do approximate query by partitioning the data cube into chunks and modeling the chunks by loglinear models. When the missing values occur in the underlying dataset, the range queries over Quasi-Cube will incur larger errors without properly imputing the missing values. The two-part mixture model is an extension of the previous work to deal with the missing values. In this paper, we will focus on how to impute the missing values and will not address again the issues about how to divide and model the chunks by loglinear model.

The rest of the paper is organized as follows. Section 2 presents the related work. In Section 3, we introduce the problems formally and present our technique in detail, including the description of two-part model for semicontinuous attribute, logistic model to describe the missing patterns, and loglinear model to predict the missing value. Section 4 presents the experimental results over real dataset and synthetic dataset. Finally Section 5 presents the conclusion and future work.

2   Related Work

The missing data are studied in statistics field and some popular approaches such as Mean substitution, Regression methods, Hot deck imputation, Expectation

Maximization (EM) approach, Multiple imputation etc. are well developed in statistical literature [14]. However those approaches deal with almost exclusively with parameter estimation rather than missing value prediction [10].

In RDBMS there has been some work that deals with null values when they represent innaplicability instead of missing values. Conditional tables were proposed in [9] to handle incomplete information in relational databases. The conditional table is an extension of a table with one more column containing logical formulas attached to the tuples of the relation. Materializing the conditional table usually leads to the creation of many tables. For the missing continuous attribute values, it is unknown how to apply conditional table techniques to estimate them. The authors of [2] developed a model that included probabilities associated with the values of the attributes to represent in a entities whose properties cannot be deterministically classified. The notion of missing probabilities is first introduced for partially specified probability distributions.

Rule induction techniques such as decision trees [12,13], decision tables [7, 6] are used to predict the value of missing attributes. The prediction is based on the value of the other attributes in that tuple. However, techniques based on rule induction models can only handle missing data for categorical attributes at a relatively high level of aggregation (which admit just a few values). To our best knowledge, we are not aware of any work that deals with missing values of semicontinuous attributes such as measures in data cube.

3   Our Method

In this section, we describe in detail how to impute missing semicontinuous attribute values in large data sets. Specifically, this involves the following two steps:

1. Identify the positions of non-zero values (and zero values) in the missing part of the dataset.
2. Estimate the non-zero missing values by using statistical models.

In this paper, we introduce a two-part model which combines logistic and loglinear components to impute the missing values. The logistic regression model [8,1] is applied here to identify which missing positions have zero or non-zero measure values. And then for those non-zero missing positions, the estimation values will be computed by loglinear models [1,3] which are constructed over known values in the dataset.

The two-part model is introduced in section 3.1. The algorithm to predict and estimate the missing value is given in section 3.2. Section 3.3 discusses in detail the issues about integrating this work to Quasi-Cubes to improve the accuracy of approximate range queries.

3.1   Two-Part Model for Semicontinuous Attribute

Given a fact table (or one chunk of table) with d-dimensions $\mathbf{X} = \{\mathbf{X}_1, \mathbf{X}_2, \cdots \mathbf{X}_d\}$ and one semicontinuous measure $\mathbf{Y}$, we assume each dimension has a set of bounded, totally ordered domains space[2].

We will suppose, as in Figure 1, that $\mathbf{Y}$ has non-zero values for tuple $1, \cdots, n_1$, and has sampling zero values for tuple $n_1 + 1, \cdots, n_2$. Missing value occurs in tuple $n_2 + 1, \cdots, n$ among which there are zero and non-zero values. The probabilities of missingness of $\mathbf{Y}$ may only depend on the attributes $\mathbf{X}_1, \cdots, \mathbf{X}_d$.

Equation 1 shows the two-part model where the semicontinuous attribute $\mathbf{Y}$ with data $y_1, \cdots, y_{n_2}$ are represented as one binary indicator $\mathbf{W}$ which takes the value 1 if $y_i \neq 0$ and 0 if $y_i = 0$, and one continuous attribute $\mathbf{Z}$ which is approximately poisson distributed by applying some monotonically increasing function (e.g. log or identity transformation function).

$$w_i = \begin{cases} 1 \text{ if } y_i \neq 0 \\ 0 \text{ if } y_i = 0 \end{cases}$$

$$z_i = \begin{cases} F(y_i) & \text{if } y_i \neq 0 \\ irrelevant & \text{if } y_i = 0 \end{cases} \tag{1}$$

TUPLE	DIMENSION			MEASURE		
	$\mathbf{X}_1$	$\mathbf{X}_2$	$\mathbf{X}_d$	$\mathbf{Y}$	$\mathbf{W}$	$\mathbf{Z}$
1	x_{11}	x_{21}	x_{d1}	42	1	42
2	x_{12}	x_{22}	x_{d2}	25	1	25
.				.		
n_1	x_{1n_1}	x_{2n_1}	x_{dn_1}	89	1	89
				0	0	U
n_2	x_{1n_2}	x_{2n_2}	x_{dn_2}	0	0	U
				M	?	?
n	x_{1n}	x_{2n}	x_{dn}	M	?	?

Fig. 1. Fact Table with missing values, U denotes Unavailable, M denotes Missing, ? denotes upon for prediction. The identity transformation is used to map $\mathbf{Y}$ to $\mathbf{Z}$ when $\mathbf{Y} \neq 0$.

The binary indicators $\mathbf{W}$ can only take the value 0 or 1 and is assumed as Bernoulli distribution with probability $P(w_i = 1) = \Pi(x_{11}, \cdots, x_{d1})$. The Maximum Likelihood estimates, $\hat{\Pi}$, then is computed by fitting the logistic over the known data. Based on $\hat{\Pi}$, the probability $\hat{P}_{i}$ of whether one missing value is non-zero can be computed by substituting $x_{1i}, \cdots, x_{di}$, where i is from $n_2 + 1, \cdots, n$.

---

[2] Without loss of generality and to keep the presentation simple, we assume in this paper that the actual attribute values are consecutive integer values from 0 to $\|\mathbf{X}_i\| - 1$ where $\|\mathbf{X}_i\|$ is ith-dimension attribute domain size. For the general case where the actual attribute values are not necessarily consecutive, we can map each actual attribute value to its rank.

3.2   Imputation Missing Values

In this section, we introduce imputation procedures for semicontinuous attributes with missing values. The imputation procedure for the missing values of semicontinuous attribute can be summarized as follows:

1. Fit the logistic regression model using known cases $1, \cdots, n_2$, saving the Maximum Likelihood estimate $\hat{\beta}$.
2. From the Bernoulli distribution with probability based on the estimated $\hat{\beta}$ coefficients (as shown in Equation 2), estimate w_i for each missing value.
3. Fit the loglinear model for $\mathbf{Y}$ using cases $1, \cdots, n_1$, saving the loglinear parameters.
4. Compute y_i from loglinear model if $w_i = 1$ for $i = n_2 + 1, \cdots, n$. Set $y_i = 0$ if $w_i = 0$.
5. Rebuild the loglinear model for $\mathbf{Y}$ using all cases $1, \cdots, n$, saving the loglinear parameters.

The goal of fitting logistic regression model is to find the best fitting and most parsimonious, yet reasonable model to describe the relationship between the response variable (measure occurance $\mathbf{W}$) and a subset of explanatory variables (dimensions $\mathbf{X}_i$). Equation 2 shows one example of the logistic model which includes all explainatory variables.

$$g(\mathbf{X}) = \beta_0 + \beta_1 \mathbf{X}_1 + \cdots + \beta_d \mathbf{X}_d$$
$$\Pi = \frac{e^{g(\mathbf{X})}}{1 + e^{g(\mathbf{X})}} \tag{2}$$

The maximum likelihood estimate value of $\hat{\beta}$ can not be computed directly for the expressions of likelihood equation are non-linear. The Newton-Raphson method [8] can solve the non-linear equations that determine the location at which a function is maximized.

It is typical that there are many independent attributes that could be included in the logistic model. The goal is to select those significant attributes that result in a parsimonious model that still explains data well. In this paper, we apply a heuristic strategy (forward selection and backward elimination) to select the attributes for logistic model. The idea is to check for the measure of statistical significance of the coefficient for the attributes, and either includes or excludes them on the basis of a fixed decision rule.

The estimate procedure for logistic model usually involves many iterations and needs many scans of raw data. It is formidable for large dataset. In our framework, we fit the logistic model over each chunk which is more likely fitted in memory.

To speedup the candidate dimensions selection for datasets with high dimensions, we may apply correlation analysis between each explaining attribute and response attribute or fisher discriminant index [17] to reduce the disk I/O.

3.3 Integrating Imputation to Quasi-Cube

The issues involved in integrating the imputation procedure to Quasi-Cube can be summarized as follows:

- Dividing the core cuboid into chunks. Each chunk is described as a structure which contains the following fields: *Chunk-number, Number-cells, Number-missing-cells, Number-Outliers, Level, State, Pointer-to-parent, Parameter-list, Cell-list, Outlier-list, Missing-Cell-list, Sum-Value, Max-Value* . Selecting chunks of the core cuboid that will be described by models (regions of the core cuboid that are sufficiently dense).
- For each chunk to be modeled by loglinear, computing the model parameters based on the known data contained in the chunk.
- Selecting chunks of the core cuboid that contains missing values.
- For each chunk containing missing values, computing the logistic parameters of logistic model based on the known data in the chunk. For each non-zero missing cell identified by the logistic model, computing the estimation using loglinear model.
- After imputation each chunk, recomputing the parameters of loglinear model over the new complete data and modifying the according values for chunk structure.
- Organizing the model parameters and retained cells to efficiently access them when processing range queries.

Note in this paper, we assume all the dimension attributes have no missing values. If the dimensions have occasional missing values, then a pair of regression models based on two-parts model may no longer suffice; the dimensions may need to be jointly modeled and perhaps imputed along with the semicontinuous measure. The general location model [15] can be applied for joint modeling and imputation of incomplete categorical and continuous attributes.

4 Empirical Evaluation

This paper targets modeling and imputation of missing semicontinuous attribute values in large multidimensional dataset. We first run the logistic fitting procedure over one real dataset which contains 86 dimensions. And then we show the two-part model helps improve the accuracy of approximate range queries when underlying data sets involve missing values.

4.1 COIL Challenge 2000 Dataset

The COIL Challenge 2000 [4] provides one real caravan insurance business dataset. The competition consists of two tasks: 1) Predict which customers are potentially interested in a caravan insurance policy; 2) Describe the actual or potential customers; and possibly explain why these customers buy a caravan policy. Information about customers consists of 86 attributes and includes product usage data and socio-demographic data derived from zip area codes. The training set consists 5822 descriptions of customers, including the information of whether or not they have a caravan insurance policy. A test dataset contains 4000 tuples which only the organizers know if they have a caravan insurance policy.

Note for this dataset, the unknown attribute (whether a customer will buy caravan insurance) is only a binary attribute as W in the two-part model, not semicontinuous attribute as Y. This experiment aims to show the performance of fitting by logistic model over datasets with a high number of dimensions. In our experiment, we first model the trainnig data set using our logistic model. We then look at the test data as missing value and predict the missing value based on logistic model.

$i-$th attribute	Name	Description	Significance Rank
47	PPERSAUT	Contribution car policies	1
68	APERSAUT	Number of car policies	2
43	MKOOPKLA	Purchasing power class	3
44	PWAPART	Contribution private third party insurance	4
59	PBRAND	Contribution fire policies	5
18	MOPLLAAG	Lower level education	6
65	AWAPART	Number of private third party insurance	7
42	MINKGEM	Average income	8
37	MINKM30	Income < 30K	9

Fig. 2. COIL significant attributes after univariate analysis

Figure 2 shows the most significant attributes after applying the univariate correlation analysis. Equation 3 shows the logistic equation after we do the forward selection and backward elimination.

$$g(\mathbf{X}) = -4.053 + 0.238X_{47} + 0.117X_{43} + 0.157X_{59} - 0.117X_{18}$$

$$\Pi = \frac{e^{g(\mathbf{X})}}{1 + e^{g(\mathbf{X})}} \qquad (3)$$

Intuitively, these predictors identify customers who have a car policies, high purchasing power class, fire policies, and not lower level education (-0.117). It is not surprising that these are the people who are most likely to have a caravan insurance. Our simple model (two scans of data) predicts 94 policy owners correctly out of 238 owners in the test data. For performance of a variety of other approaches, see [11].

4.2 Synthetic Dataset

We experimented with a synthetic dataset, mostly to determine the accuracy of our imputation approach when applied in Quasi-Cube. In this set, the core

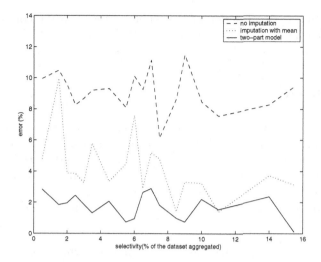

Fig. 4. Error of range queries over the synthetic dataset, computed from the approximate base cuboid compressed with relative error 0.4.

cuboid is 4-dimensional, with the four dimensions denoted by the letters A, B, C and D, with domains $80, 40, 20, 10$ respectively. The density distribution of the values is chosen to follow the following distributions: Normal with mean 20 and variance 400 (A and B), Normal with mean 15 and variance 25 (C), and Uniform with mean 10 (D). We also generate the cells values to follow Equation 4, where the factors are distributed as follows. Eff^A is distributed as U(10,40), similarly, Eff^B as U(10,20), Eff^C as U(1,100), Eff^D as U(40,80). We also generate two-factor effect Eff^{CD} as $N(20, 10^2)$. This leads to the loglinear model on Equation 5 being the best fit for the cells.

The datasets we generate contains $20,000$ cells among which 2500 cells are reassigned as zero to emulate the semicontinuous characteristic. We then randomly choose 2000 cells as missing values and the remaining $18,000$ as known values.

$$y_{ijkl} = 20 \times Eff^A_i \times Eff^B_j \times Eff^C_k \times Eff^D_l \times Eff^{CD}_{kl} \qquad (4)$$

$$l_{ijkl} = \log \hat{y}_{ijkl} = \gamma + \gamma^A_i + \gamma^B_j + \gamma^C_k + \gamma^D_l + \gamma^{CD}_{kl} \qquad (5)$$

Figure 4 shows the average error in the answers obtained by range queries as a function of the selectivity of the query (shown as a fraction of the number of cells in the core cuboid) over three Quasi-Cubes. Each Quasi-Cube are compressed by loglinear model with the same relative error 0.4. The first Quasi-Cube is constucted only over the known data by simply discarding the missing values. The second Quasi-Cube is constructed over the complete dataset where each missing cell is replaced by mean. The third Quasi-Cube is constructed over the complete dataset where each missing cell is estimated by two-part model. For each Quasi-Cube, we generate the same set of range queries with different selectivity (shown as a fraction of the number of cells in the core cuboid). As it can be seen from the results in Figure 4, the accruacy under two-part model exhibits the best accuracy.

5   Conclusions

In this paper, we have proposed a two-part model (logistic and loglinear) for modeling and imputing semicontinuous measures in large datasets. We have presented a heuristic strategy to speedup the process of getting the parsimonious logistic model. We have discussed how to combine this work into the Quasi-Cube framework to improve the accuracy of approximate range queries.

There are some aspects of this work that merit further research. Among them,

- We are trying to study the general location model when missing values occur at both measure attributes and dimension attributes. The general location model can be applied for joint modeling and imputation of incompletely categorical and continuous variables. We will study the pattern of missing values among continuous dimensions and their relationships to the categorical ones. The general location model will help answer *what if* questions, that is, estimate the measures of cells with domain values that have not occurred, but of which we are interested in studying for hypothetical scenarios. For example, *what if we were to sell this type of product in this store during this fall?* Assigning values to these cells produces answers to these kinds of questions.
- Sometimes, the aggregation value at higher level cuboids may be precisely available but detailed values at lower level are missing. For example, some stores are sometimes able to provide a total sale amount on a broad class of goods but can not break it down further into the narrow categories desired in the low level cuboid. In these cases, an imputation method must allocate the fixed total amount to the relevant subclasses. How to impute a group of interrelated semicontinuous attributes subject to an equality constraint placed on their sum becomes a very interesting research topic [16]. We will study the complex imputation procedures for this problem by looking at linear programming techniques.

References

1. A. Agresti. Categorical Data Analysis, Wiley Series in Probability and Mathematical Statistics, 1990.
2. D. Barbara, H. Garcia-Molina, and D. Porter. The management of probabilistic data, IEEE Transactions on Knowledge and Data Engineering. Vol. 4, no. 5, page 487-502, 1992.
3. D. Barbará, and X. Wu. Loglinear Based Quasi Cubes, Journal of Information and Intelligent System(JIIS),Vol 16(3), P255-276, Kluwer academic publishers.

4. COIL Challenge 2000: The Insurance Company(TIC) Benchmark.
   http://www.liacs.nl/p̄utten/library/cc2000

5. J. Gray, A. Bosworth, A. Layman, and H. Pirahesh. Data cube: A relational aggregation operator generalizing group-by, cross-tabs and sub-totals, In *Proceedings
   of the 12th International Conference on Data Engineering*, pages 152–159, 1996.

6. J.W. Grzymala-Busse, and M. Hu. A Comparison of Several Approaches to Missing Attribute Values in Data Mining. In *Proceedings of the second International
   Conference on Rough Sets and Current Trends in Computing*, RSCTC 2000.

7. J.W. Grzymala-Busse. On the unknown attribute values in functional dependencies, In *Proceedings of Methodologies for Intelligent Systems*, Lecture Notes in AI,
   542, page 368-377, 1991.

8. D.W. Hosmer, S. Lemeshow. Applied Logistic Regression, John Wiley and Sons,
   Inc. 1989.

9. T. Imielinski, and W. Lipski. Incomplete Information in Relational Databases,
   Journal of ACM, 31(4), page 761-791, 1984.

10. R.A. Little, and D.B. Rubin. Statistical analysis with missing data, New York,
    John Wiley and Sons, 1987.

11. P. van der Putten, M. van Someren. COIL Challenge 2000: The Insurance Company
    Case, Sentient Machine Research, Amsterdam, June 2000.

12. J.R. Quinlan. Induction of decision trees, Machine Learning, vol. 1, page 81-106,
    1986.

13. J.R. Quinlan. Unknown attribute values in induction, In *Proceedings of the Sixth
    International Machqine Learning Workshop*, page 164-168, 1989.

14. D. B. Rubin, Multiple Imputation for Nonresponse in Surveys, Wiley Series in
    Probability and Mathematical Statistics, 1987.

15. J. L. Schafer. Analysis of Incomplete Multivariate Data, Book number 72 in
    the Chapman and Hall series Monographs on Statistics and Applied Probability.
    London, Chapman and Hall,1997.

16. J. L. Schafer, and M. K. Olsen. Modeling and imputation of semicontinuous survey
    variables, In *Proceedings of Federal Committee on Statistical Methodology (FCSM)
    Reseach Conference*, Nov, 1999.

17. T.Y. Young, and T.W. Calvert. Classification, Estimation and Pattern Recogni-
    tion. Elsevier, 1974.

PartJoin: An Efficient Storage and Query Execution for Data Warehouses

Ladjel Bellatreche[1], Michel Schneider[2], Mukesh Mohania[3], and Bharat Bhargava[4]

[1] IMERIR, Perpignan, FRANCE
ladjel@imerir.com
[2] LIMOS, Blaise Pascal University 63177, Aubière, FRANCE
michel.schneider@isima.fr
[3] IBM India Research Lab, I.I.T., Delhi, INDIA
mkmukesh@in.ibm.com
[4] Computer Science Department, Purdue University, USA
bb@cs.purdue.edu

Abstract. The performance of OLAP queries can be improved drastically if the warehouse data is properly selected and indexed. The problems of selecting and materializing views and indexing data have been studied extensively in the data warehousing environment. On the other hand, data partitioning can also greatly increase the performance of queries. Data partitioning has advantage over data selection and indexing since the former one does not require additional storage requirement. In this paper, we show that it is beneficial to integrate the data partitioning and indexing (join indexes) techniques for improving the performance of data warehousing queries. We present a data warehouse *tuning strategy*, called *PartJoin*, that decomposes the fact and dimension tables of a star schema and then selects join indexes. This solution takes advantage of these two techniques, i.e., data partitioning and indexing. Finally, we present the results of an experimental evaluation that demonstrates the effectiveness of our strategy in reducing the query processing cost and providing an economical utilisation of the storage space.

1 Introduction

A data warehouse (DW) is an information base that stores a large volume of extracted and summarized data for OLAP and decision support systems [4]. These systems are characterized by complex ad-hoc queries (with many joins) over large data sets. Despite the complexity of queries, decision makers want those queries to be evaluated faster. Fast execution of queries and retrieval of data can be achieved if the the physical design of a DW is done properly. There are two major problems associated with the physical design of a DW, namely, the *selection of warehouse data (i.e., materialized views)* so that all the queries can be answered at the warehouse without accessing the data from underlying sources, and *indexing data* so that data can be retrieved faster. However, the solutions

Y. Kambayashi, W. Winiwarter, M. Arikawa (Eds.): DaWaK 2002, LNCS 2454, pp. 296–306, 2002.

of these two problems pose additional overheads of maintaining the warehouse data (materialized views) whenever the source data changes and storage cost for maintaining index tables. Given the large size of DWs, these costs are non-trivial. This prompts us to ask the following question: *is it possible to reduce the storage and maintenance cost requirements, without sacrificing the query execution efficiency obtained from indexing?*

We address this vital issue in our ongoing *PartJoin* project that combines data partitioning and join indexes in an intelligent manner so that one can reduce the storage cost and improve the query performance. We now briefly outline the status of this project. In [2], we have shown the utility of data partitioning and presented an algorithm for fragmenting a data warehouse modeled by a star schema. In [1], we have presented an indexing scheme called graph join indexes for speeding up the join operations in OLAP queries. These indexes are a generalization of star join indexes [7]. Later on, we figured out that conceptually a star join index or a horizontal fragment of a fact table can significantly improve the performance of queries (see the motivating example in section 2), but the utilization of indexes is constrained by a storage capacity and a maintenance cost. The use of partitioning does not require a storage capacity, but poses the problem of managing numerous partitions. Therefore, it appears very interesting to combine data partitioning and indexes in order to provide a better performance for queries and to minimize the storage and maintenance overheads.

In this paper, the terms fragmentation and partitioning are used interchangeably. We propose a new tuning strategy technique for efficiently executing queries while using space *economically*. Our approach exploits the similarities between join indexes and data partitioning. The crucial and the complex problem of this strategy lies in how it efficiently selects a *better partitioning schema* of a DW modeled by a relational schema and *appropriate join indexes* for a given set of queries. The main contributions of this paper are the following :
a) We have identified the similarities (in terms of performance point of view) between data partitioning and join indexes and the need for combining them to reduce the query processing, storage and maintenance costs.
b) We have proposed a tuning strategy called *PartJoin* for *fragmenting* a star schema under a threshold for the number of fact fragments that the warehouse administrator can manage them easily and then to *select* join indexes.
c) We have evaluated the *PartJoin* methodology using the APB benchmark [5].

To the best of our knowledge, the proposed work is the first article that addresses the problem of selecting a partitioning schema and join indexes in a DW under the fragmentation threshold constraint for the number of fact fragments and the storage constraint for indexes.

The rest of the paper is organized as follows. A motivating example is described in Section 2. Section 3 gives the architecture of our *PartJoin*, describes its components, presents an algorithm that decomposes a star schema. Section 4 outlines the results of our performance study. Section 5 concludes the paper.

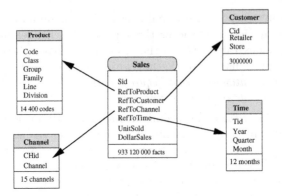

Fig. 1. An Example of a Star Schema (derived from APB-1)

2   A Motivating Example

In this section, we present an example to show how the data partitioning [2] can complement with the join indexes for improving the performance of OLAP queries in data warehousing environments [7]. We assume that the warehouse data is modeled based on a star schema. Figure 1 shows a star schema derived from APB-1 benchmark of OLAP council [5]. This schema consists of four dimension tables *Customer*, *Product*, *Time*, and *Channel* and one fact table *Sales*.

Suppose that the dimension table *Time* is horizontally partitioned using the attribute *Month* into 12 fragments $Time_1, ..., Time_{12}$[1], where each fragment $Time_i$ $(1 \le i \le 12)$ is defined as follows : $Time_i = \sigma_{T.Month="Month_i''}(Time)$. The fact table *Sales* can be partitioned based on the fragmentation schema of the dimension table *Time* into 12 fragments $Sales_1, ..., Sales_{12}$, where each fragment $Sales_i$ $(1 \le i \le 12)$ is defined as follows: $Sales_i = Sales \ltimes Time_i$, where $\ltimes$ represents the semi-join operation. This type of fragmentation is known as *derived horizontal fragmentation* [8]. The attribute *Month* is called the *partitioning attribute*[2]. A fragment of a fact table and a dimension table are called *fact fragment* and *dimension fragment*, respectively. The fragmentation of dimension and fact tables incurs the decomposition of star schema into set of sub star schemas.

Imagine a star join index between the fact table *Sales* and the dimension table *Time* that correlates the dimension tuples with the fact tuples that have the same value on the common dimensional attribute *Month*. A bitmap join index [7] on the month column in the *Sales* table can be built by using the month column in the *Time* table and the foreign key Time ID (Tid) in the *Sales* table. This representation is quite similar to a derived fragment of the *Sales* table. A star join index is a vertical fragment of a fact fragment and it contains only the foreign keys of the fact fragment.

---

[1] Our schema models one year sales activities

[2] We can have a fact fragment referring many attributes of several dimension tables.

Therefore, to execute queries, there can be two options: (1) *to partition* the warehouse so that each query can access fragments rather than whole tables, and (2) *to use join indexes* so that each query can access data that uses join indexes. To illustrate these options, let us consider the following query Q : SELECT Tid, Sum(UnitSold), Sum(DollarSales) FROM Sales S, Time T WHERE S.RefToTime = T.Tid AND T.Month = "June" GROUP BY Tid.

1. *With the partitioning option* : In this case, only one fact fragment (sub star schema) is accessed by the query Q. This option has two main advantages: (1) it reduces the query processing cost by eliminating 11 sub star schemas and (2) it does not require an extra storage cost.
2. *With the join indexes option* : Suppose we have a star join index I between the fact table *Sales* and the dimension table *Time* which refers to the sales done during June. It is defined as follows: $I = \pi_{Sid,Tid}(Sales \bowtie (\sigma_{Month="June"}(Time)))$. This index gives about the same performance as the partitioning option for reducing the cost of Q, but it needs to be stored, and updated when tuples are inserted or deleted in the underlying tables (*Sales* and *Time*).

Under these scenarios, we need to answer the following question : *for a given set of queries, which option should be used ?*

We consider three classes of queries when we are dealing with HP [2,6]: *best match queries, partial match queries*, and *worst match queries*

1. *Best match queries:* A query belonging to this type references all partitioning attributes, i.e., query selection predicates match with fragmentation predicates[3]. Ideally, a best match query accesses only one fact fragment (the above query is a good example of this class). For this type of queries, join indexes are not needed because we do not have any join operation and thus, the data partitioning may give equal or better performance than join indexes and without an additional storage cost.
2. *Partial match queries:* In this case, a query references a subset of the fragmentation attributes. Data partitioning may not very efficient for this type of queries, because we need to perform some join operations between fact and dimension fragments that can be costly. Therefore, the utilization of join indexes *may be suitable* to speed up these operations.
3. *Worst match queries:* In this type, a query does not contain any selection predicate, or it has some selection predicates defined on non fragmented attributes. By considering the partitioning option, we need to execute a query locally (on each sub star schema) and then assembly all local results by using the union operation. In this case, the data partitioning may perform badly and therefore the utilization of join indexes is recommended.

Our *PartJoin* tuning strategy gives to the DW administrator a *new option* to speed up his/her queries (best match, partial match and worst match) by combining the partitioning option (partitions the warehouse schema) and the join

---

[3] The fragmentation predicates are the predicates that are used in fragmentation process

index option (builds indexes on top of partitions). This new option guarantees query performance, a good utilization of the space storage and reduces the maintenance overhead.

3   The PartJoin Tuning Strategy

In this section, a formulation of the *PartJoin* problem and its architecture are described.

3.1   Formulation of PartJoin Problem

Given the following inputs, the *PartJoin* problem is formulated as follows:
Inputs: (1) A star schema $S : (F, D_1, ..., D_d)$, (2) a set of most frequently used OLAP queries $\{Q_1, ..., Q_l\}$ and their frequencies $\{f_1, ..., f_l\}$, (3) selectivity factors of simple and join predicates defined in the queries, (4) a storage capacity constraint C for join indexes, and (5) a fragmentation threshold W which represents the maximal number of fact fragments that the administrator can maintain.
Goal : The *PartJoin* problem consists in partitioning the star schema S into several sub star schemas $\{S_1, S_2, ..., S_N\}$ and in selecting join indexes on top of these sub schemas in order to minimize the processing cost of all queries. The selected indexes should be accommodated in C (storage capacity).

3.2   PartJoin Architecture

An architectural overview of the *PartJoin* system is shown in Figure 2. It has two main modules : *a partitioning module* and *an index selection module*.
The first one is responsible for fragmenting the warehouse schema and the second one for selecting the appropriate join indexes for partition(s) (sub star schema(s)). Our system works as follows:
The partitioning module identifies selection predicates used by the input queries. Using these predicates, it partitions first the dimension tables of the warehouse schema, and then the fact table using the derived fragmentation technique (see Section 2). If the data partitioning cannot satisfy all queries, the *index selection module* selects join indexes which respect storage constraint (C) to ensure that the performance of the rest of queries (those are not satisfied by partitioning module) is not deteriorated. Finally, we obtain a set of sub star schemas and join indexes that minimizes query processing and storage costs.
     To decompose the star schema S into a set of sub star schemas $\{S_1, S_2, ..., S_N\}$, the partitioning module starts by enumerating all the selection predicates used by the set of input queries. These predicates are classified based on their dimension tables (each dimension table has its own selection predicates). It takes into account only dimension tables having a non empty set of selection predicates. Therefore, it uses the COM-MIN procedure developed by Özsu et al. [8] to partition each dimension table. Once the dimension tables are partitioned, we then derive the horizontal fragments of the fact table.

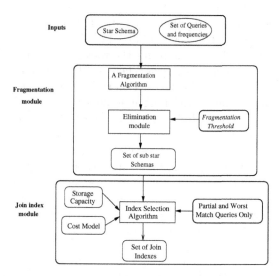

Fig. 2. The PartJoin architecture

To ensure query processing reduction of all queries, the join index module selects indexes after the partitioning process. When the warehouse is partitioned, the join index selection problem will be different than the join index selection in non partitioned warehouse. The main differences concern : The *number of queries* taken into consideration during the selection process, and *the warehouse schema* (with partitioning, we have N sub star schemas and not a single star schema. However, a sub star schema has the same characteristics as a whole star schema, thus we can apply any join index selection algorithm [1]).

Concerning the number of queries, we have previously mentioned that join indexes are not needed for best match queries. So, these queries will be removed from the initial set of queries Q and then a join index selection algorithm will take into account only queries that do not get benefit from the fragmentation process (worst match and partial match queries).

Figure 2 summarizes the main steps of the *PartJoin* tuning strategy.

3.3   Fragment Merging

Let g be the number of dimension tables participating in the fragmentation process. The number of fact fragments (N) generated by the partitioning algorithm is given by the following equation: $N = \prod_{i=1}^{g} L_i$, where L_i represents the number of fragments of the dimension table D_i. This number (N) can be very large. For example suppose we have the following partitioning schemas of dimension tables (cf. Figure 1: *Customer* is partitioned into 1440 fragments using the *store* attribute, *Time* into 12 fragments using the *month* attribute (we have one year of sales activities), *Product* into 50 fragments using the *family* attribute, *Channel* into 15 fragments using the channel attribute. This implies that the fact table will be decomposed into 12 960 000 (1440 * 12 * 50 * 15) fragments.

Consequently, it will be very hard for the warehouse administrator to install and maintain these fragments (sub star schemas). Thus it is important to reduce the number of fact fragments. This reduction is done by the *partition elimination* sub module, a part of the partitioning module (see Figure 2). To achieve this elimination, the warehouse administrator considers a fragmentation threshold denoted by W that represents the maximal number of fact fragments that he/she can maintain. By considering this threshold, the partitioning module task is to decompose the star schema S into N sub star schemas such that: $\mathbf{N \leq W}$.

Our goal is to reduce the number of fact fragments in order to satisfy the fragmentation threshold W. This reduction can be done by merging some fragments. The merging operation of two (or several) fragments is done by using the union operator of these fragments [8]. In this paper, this operation is done statically.

Since we have an important number of fact fragments, we should have a metric that identifies which fragments should be merged. Intuitively, a fact fragment is interesting if it reduces the cost of workload significantly. To compute the contribution of each fragment F_i ($1 \leq i \leq N$), we define the following metric: $Cont(F_i) = (||F|| - ||F_i||) \times \sum_{j=1}^{l} a_{ij} \times Freq(Q_j)$, where $||F||$ and $||F_i||$ represent the sizes of fact table and fact fragment F_i. The element a_{ij} ($1 \leq i \leq N, 1 \leq j \leq l$) can have a binary value (1 if the fragment F_i is accessed by the query Q_j, 0 otherwise). $Freq(Q_j)$ is the access frequency of the query Q_j. Recall that l is the number of queries in the workload. The merging operation is done as follows: each fragment F_i is assigned by a contribution $cont(F_i)$. We sort then these N fragments in a decrease order. We keep the $(W - 1)$ first fragments and we merge the rest into one fragment. By doing like this, the fragmentation threshold is satisfied.

After applying merging operations and satisfying the fragmentation threshold, the performance of certain queries may be affected. Therefore, the index module satisfies these queries.

4   Performance Evaluation of PartJoin Method

In this section, we present some performance results of *PartJoin* tuning method, that considers both query processing costs and storage requirements. The query processing cost is estimated in terms of the number of rows used during query execution. We then also compare the results of this method with *partitioning* and *join index* methods and the results show that *PartJoin* tuning strategy is better than these two methods for the best and partial match queries.

4.1   Experimental Setup

In our experiments, we use dataset from APB benchmark [5] (see Figure 1). The database size here refers to the size of the raw data, and thus does not include any overhead that may be added once the data is loaded. The number of rows of each table is given in Figure 1. In these experiments, the storage cost of a join index is estimated in terms of the number of rows in that index. The fact table is partitioned based on three dimension tables *Time*, *Product* and *Channel*, where each dimension table is fragmented as follows: *Time* into 12 fragments using the attribute Month, *Product* into 4 fragments using the attribute Family[4], *Channel* into 15 fragments using the attribute Channel. Therefore the fact table *Sales* is partitioned into 720 fragments ($W = 720$).

The fragmentation predicates are those referencing the attributes *Month*, *Family* or *Channel*. In all our experiments, we assume that the cardinality of fact fragments is uniform.

The workload used in our experiments is given in [3] (due to the space constraint).

4.2 Experimental Results

Evaluation of the three options. In first experiment, we compare the quality of solutions (in terms of query processing cost reduction) produced by (a) *partitioning option (PO)*, (b) *join index option (JIO)* and (c) *partjoin option (PJO)*. For JIO, we assume that a join index exists for each query.

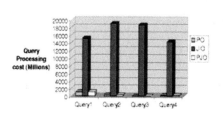

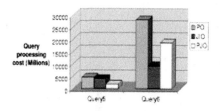

Fig. 3. Cost for best match queries

Fig. 4. Costs of partial and worst match queries

Figure 3 shows clearly that the partitioning option *outperform very well compared to join index option for best match queries* (queries 1 - 4, see [3]). Therefore, for this type of query, the PO is recommended. Note that for best match queries, the PO and PJO give the same performance, because for these type of queries, join indexes are not needed (see Section 2). For worst queries (query 6), the partitioning option performs badly compared to the join index and partjoin options (Figure 4). The utilization of join indexes improves the performance of worst match queries by at most 60% compare to the reduction obtained by PO. For the worst match queries, the join index option is recommended. We have also

---

[4] We suppose that products are grouped into four major families: child products, female products, male products, and mixed products.

observed that the partjoin option gives a better performance than other two options for partial match queries (query 5). Figure 4 shows that, the performance of partial match queries is improved by at most 50-55% compare the solution obtained by JIO and PO.

One of the interesting points that can be observed in Figure 3 is that when a query has selection predicates defined on all fragmented dimension tables, the *PartJoin* and partitioning options perform ideally.

Storage requirements of each option. To compute the storage requirements of each option, we suppose that indexes exist for each query (no storage constraint). We compute the storage cost for JIO by summing up the storage cost of each index used on evaluating the queries in the workload. For the PJO, we compute the size of join indexes selected by the index module.

In Figure 5, we observe that the partitioning option is much more efficient in terms of storage requirements (we can guarantee performance for free!), whereas the join index option requires a lot of space. The partjoin option is in between. By using the partjoin option, we save more at most 55% of space required for join indexes. Therefore the saved space can be used for other structures that need space (materialized views, indexes on single tables, etc.).

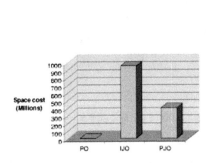
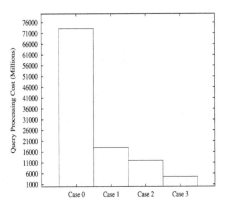

Fig. 5. Space requirements for each option

Fig. 6. The effect of fragmented dimension tables

The effect of number of fragmented dimension tables. In this experiments, we study the effect of the number of dimension tables participating on the fragmentation process. To do this, we will concentrate on the following cases: *Case 0:* all dimension tables are unpartitioned, in this case we consider the JIO, *Case 1:* only one dimension table is partitioned, for example, *Time* and the fact table *Sales* is fragmented based on that table, *Case 2:* two dimension tables are partitioned, for example, *Time* and *Product*. Therefore the fact table is partitioned based on fragmentation schemas of these two tables, and *Case 3 :* the three dimension tables *Time*, *Channel* and *Product* are partitioned and similarly, the fact table is fragmented based on these tables.

We evaluate our queries by considering each case and we compute the cost of executing all queries. From Figure 6, we observe that the number of partitioned dimension tables has a great impact on reducing the query processing cost. As we see, the PJO performance increases while the number of fragmented dimension tables increases.

5   Conclusion

In this paper we have introduced a new data warehouse tuning strategy called *PartJoin* which combines data partitioning and join indexes for executing efficiently a set of OLAP queries and for reducing the storage requirements significantly. *PartJoin* exploits the similarities between join indexes and data partitioning. Data partitioning avoids the use of join indexes and therefore guarantees an economical utilization of space. But with the data partitioning, the number of fact fragments can be very large and difficult to maintain. Therefore the proposed tuning strategy finds a compromise between the utilization of data partitioning and join indexes. To satisfy this compromise, we have developed a data partitioning algorithm for decomposing dimension tables and fact table that guarantees that the number of fact fragments are less than a threshold representing the maximal number of fragments that the data warehouse administrator can maintain. From our results, it appears that *PartJoin* method gives better performance than the partitioning option and the join index option for certain class of queries under the storage and data maintenance constraints.

We believe that our tuning method is directly applied to commercial databases with a little effort. PartJoin method does not presently take into account the maintenance cost. In the future work, we will extend our system in that direction by incorporating this cost on the merging process.

References

1. L. Bellatreche, K. Karlapalem, and Q. Li. Evaluation of indexing materialized views in data warehousing environments. *Proceedings of the International Conference on Data Warehousing and Knowledge Discovery (DAWAK'2000)*, pages 57–66, September 2000.
2. L. Bellatreche, K. Karlapalem, and M. Mohania. What can partitioning do for your data warehouses and data marts? *Proceedings of the International Database Engineering and Application Symposium (IDEAS'2000)*, pages 437–445, September 2000.
3. L. Bellatreche, M. Schneider, M. Mohania, and B. Bhargava. Partjoin: An efficient storage and query execution for data warehouses. *extended version, available at http://www.imerir.com/~ladjel*, January 2002.

4. S. Chaudhuri and V. Narasayya. An efficient cost-driven index selection tool for microsoft sql server. *Proceedings of the International Conference on Very Large Databases*, pages 146–155, August 1997.
5. OLAP Council. Apb-1 olap benchmark, release ii.
   http://www.olapcouncil.org/research/bmarkly.htm, 1998.
6. S. Guo, S. Wei, and M. A. Weiss. On satisfiability, equivalence, and implication problems involving conjunctive queries in database systems. *IEEE Transactions on Knowledge and Data Engineering*, 8(4):604–612, August 1996.
7. P. O'Neil and D. Quass. Improved query performance with variant indexes. *Proceedings of the ACM SIGMOD International Conference on Management of Data*, pages 38–49, May 1997.
8. M. T. Özsu and P. Valduriez. *Principles of Distributed Database Systems : Second Edition*. Prentice Hall, 1999.

A Transactional Approach to Parallel Data Warehouse Maintenance*

Bin Liu, Songting Chen, and Elke A. Rundensteiner

Department of Computer Science, Worcester Polytechnic Institute,
Worcester, MA 01609-2280, USA
{binliu, chenst, rundenst}@cs.wpi.edu

Abstract. Data Warehousing is becoming an increasingly important technology for information integration and data analysis. Given the dynamic nature of modern distributed environments, both source data and schema changes are likely to occur autonomously and even concurrently in different sources. We have thus developed a comprehensive solution approach, called TxnWrap, that successfully maintains the warehouse views under any type of concurrent source updates. In this work, we now overcome TxnWrap's restriction that the maintenance is processed one by one for each source update, since that limits the performance. To overcome this limitation, we exploit the transactional approach of TxnWrap to achieve parallel data warehouse maintenance. For this, we first identify the read/write conflicts among the different warehouse maintenance processes. We then propose a parallel maintenance scheduler (PMS) that generates legal schedules that resolve these conflicts. PMS has been implemented and incorporated into our TxnWrap system. The experimental results confirm that our parallel maintenance scheduler significantly improves the performance of data warehouse maintenance.

Keywords: Data Warehouse Maintenance, Parallel Maintenance, Concurrent, Data Update, Schema Change.

1 Introduction

Data Warehouse Environments. Data warehousing (DW) [5,10,8] is important for many applications, especially in large-scale environments composed of distributed information sources (ISs). A data warehouse management system (DWMS) is the management system that is responsible of maintaining the DW extent and schema upon changes of underlying ISs. In distributed environments, ISs are typically owned by different information providers and function independently. This implies that they will update their data or even their schema

---

* This work was supported in part by several grants from NSF, namely, the NSF NYI grant #IRI 97–96264, the NSF CISE Instrumentation grant #IRIS 97–29878, and the NSF grant #IIS 9988776.

Y. Kambayashi, W. Winiwarter, M. Arikawa (Eds.): DaWaK 2002, LNCS 2454, pp. 307–316, 2002.

without any concern for how these changes may affect the DW. When incremental maintaining these updates, the DWMS has to issue maintenance queries to ISs to calculate the changes to the DW. In such dynamic environments, the maintenance queries to ISs may return incorrect query results (due to concurrent data updates at the IS) or even may fail to complete (due to concurrent schema changes at the IS). We refer to these problems as **anomaly problem** [10].

Most work in the literature [1,10] addresses the problem only in data update environments. TxnWrap [3] is the first stable DW maintenance solution that supports maintenance of a DW even under concurrent data and schema changes. It introduces the concept of a DWMS-Transaction model [3] to formally capture the overall DW maintenance process as a transaction. Once cast in terms of transaction concepts, we then propose a multiversion timestamp-based concurrency control algorithm [2], called ShadowWrapper, to solve the anomaly problems in DW maintenance. However, like other solutions in the literature [1,3,4], TxnWrap applies a sequential approach towards maintaining concurrent updates. This limits its performance in a distributed environment where the maintenance of IS update endures the overhead of network delay and IO costs for each maintenance query.

Parallel Maintenance Scheduler. In this paper, we propose to develop a parallel maintenance scheduler that is capable of maintaining concurrent data and schema changes in parallel that significantly improves the performance of DW maintenance. For this, the transactional approach of TxnWrap naturally lends itself for achieving parallel DW maintenance. First, we characterise all potential conflicts among the data warehouse maintenance processes in terms of read/write of critical DWMS resources. Second, we design strategies to generate possible schedules that resolve these identified conflicts. We have implemented one parallel maintenance scheduler and incorporated it into the TxnWrap system at WPI [3,4]. Experimental studies show the performance benefits achievable by the parallel scheduler.

Outline. Section 2 introduces the basics of TxnWrap. In Section 3, we propose several enhancements to TxnWrap to enable us to move toward parallel scheduling. Several parallel scheduling algorithms are proposed in Section 4. Section 5 presents experimental studies for one of the schedulers. Section 6 discusses related work, while conclusions are presented in Section 7.

2   TxnWrap Revisited

The DW Maintenance Transaction Model. In a typical DW environment where one DW is built over several independent ISs, a complete DW maintenance process is composed of the following steps [3]:

- **IS_Update**: An IS update transaction at some IS_i is committed, denoted as "w$(IS_i)C_{IS}$" where w(IS_i) represents the write on IS_i, i is the index of the IS, and C_{IS} is the commit of this write.
- **Propagation**: The DWMS computes the effect to the DW caused by this update in order to maintain the DW, denoted as "$r(VD)r(IS_1)r(IS_2)\cdots r$

(IS_n)". Here VD represents the view definition in the DW and r(VD) stands for the operations that generate the maintenance queries for individual ISs based on the view definition. $r(IS_i)$ is a read over IS_i which represents the maintenance query to IS_i and its corresponding results to calculate the effect on the DW.

– **Refresh**: The result calculated in the propagation step finally is refreshed into the DW, denoted as "$w(DW)C_{DW}$", where w(DW) is to update the DW extent and C_{DW} is the commit of w(DW) to the DW.

TxnWrap introduces the concept of a global transaction, referred to as a **DWMS-Transaction**, to encapsulate the above three DW maintenance steps within the context of the overall data warehouse environment. A DWMS Transaction will be created only after C_{IS} of the corresponding IS update transaction has successfully been committed at the IS. The commit of the global DWMS-Transaction is right after the local commitment of the C_{DW} into the DW in the *Refresh* step.

A DWMS-Transaction is a conceptual rather than a real transaction model. It sits at a higher level above the DBMS transactions local to the IS or local to the DW. In the DWMS-Transaction model, there is no automatic rollback or abort mechanism, because the local IS transaction is out of the control of the DWMS and the committed IS updates must be propagated to the DW if we want the DW to stay consistent. So, for the brevity, we denote a DWMS-Transaction as "$w(IS_i)r(VD)r(IS_1)r(IS_2)\cdots r(IS_n)w(DW)$". Furthermore, we will refer to the *Propagation* and *Refresh* steps in one DWMS-Transaction ("$r(VD)r(IS_1)r(IS_2)\cdots r(IS_n)w\ (DW)$") as the DWMS-Transaction maintenance process, since these two steps correspond to the actual maintenance steps in the DWMS. Thus, we now can rephrase the DW anomaly problem as a concurrency control problem. The only conflict we must consider in the context of DWMS-Transactions is the 'read dirty data' conflict. That is, one operation in the *Propagation* phase may read some inconsistent query results written by the *IS_Update* phase of the maintenance process. See [3] for further details.

Concurrency Control Strategy in TxnWrap. It is well known that read/write conflicts of transactions can be dealt with by a locking or by a version-based strategy. Locking of source data is not feasible in our environment due to the autonomicity of data sources. Hence, TxnWrap designs a multiversion concurrency control algorithm [2] (called ShadowWrapper) to solve the anomaly problems in DW maintenance. In short, TxnWrap keeps versions of all updated tuples as well as the schema meta data in a dedicated IS wrapper. TxnWrap uses a globally unique identifier (*global id*) to label the version data in the wrapper related to the update and also to identify and track the corresponding DWMS-Transaction responsible for handling this IS update. To process a DWMS-Transaction, the DWMS manager generates maintenance queries for each source which are processed by extracting the appropriate version data from the wrapper instead of the IS. Integrated with the ShadowWrapper, the maintenance steps for each update in TxnWrap can now be characterized as $w(IS_i)w(Wrapper_i)r(VD)r(IS_1)r(IS_2)\cdots r(IS_n)w(DW)$. Here $w(Wrapper_i)$

generates the updated IS data as versioned data in the wrapper indexed by its *global id*, and $r(IS_i)$ $(1 \leq i \leq n)$ now refers to a read of the corresponding versioned data from the respective IS_i wrapper using the same *global id* rather than directly accessing the remote (non-versioned) IS_i.

Limitations of TxnWrap. Like other DW maintenance algorithms in the literature, TxnWrap [3] uses a serial processing model for the DW maintenance process. This restricts the system performance. Furthermore, in the propagation step of each DWMS-Transaction, the DWMS issues maintenance queries one by one to each IS_i and collects the results [1]. Thus only one IS is being utilized at a time in the maintenance propagation phase. In a distributed environment, the overhead of such remote queries is typically high involving both network delay and IO costs at respective IS_i. If we could interleave the execution of different DWMS-Transaction maintenance processes, we could reduce the total network delay, and possibly also keep all ISs busy. This way, the overall performance would improve.

3   Towards Flexible DWMS-Transaction Management

Using a *global id* in TxnWrap to track IS updates restricts the flexibility of scheduling DWMS-Transactions because it tightly binds the version management in the IS wrapper with the overall maintenance task of the DWMS server. Furthermore, the *global id* would have to be issued by a global id-server in the DWMS to assure its uniqueness in the overall data warehousing system. We relax this binding by introducing a *local id* for version management in the wrapper and a TxnID to manage DWMS-Transactions in the DWMS, as described below.

3.1   Version Management Using Local Identifier

We define a *local id* to be a timestamp that represents the time the update happened in the respective IS. Without loss of generality, we use an integer k (k ≥ 0) to represent the *local id*. Compared to the *global id*, two benefits can be gotten by using *local id* instead. First, the process of id generation can be done locally in each wrapper. Thus we no longer have to communicate with the DWMS during version management. Second, we have to assume a global FIFO in the overall DW system to use the *global id*, which is too restrictive for distributed environments. Using of *local id*s would relax this restriction of the global FIFO assumption. See [7] for further information.

Figures 1 and 2 illustrate the version management in the wrapper using *local id*s. As an example, the IS_1 wrapper in Figure 1 contains the data of relation R as well as the related meta information. The IS_2 wrapper stores the same for relation S. Two additional attributes #min and #max in the wrapper denote the life time of each tuple. #min denotes the beginning of the life of the tuple (by insertion) while #max denotes the end of the life of the tuple (by deletion). The value of #min and of #max of an updated tuple are set by the corresponding DWMS-Transaction using its local id. Assume in Figure 1, $DU_1 : Insert(3,5,5)$

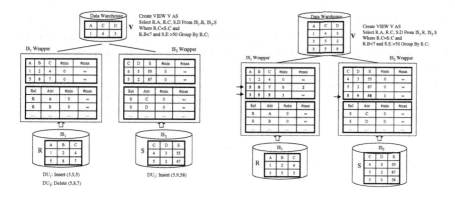

Fig. 1. Version Management (before Updates)

Fig. 2. Version Management (after Updates)

and $DU_2 : Delete(5, 8, 7)$ happened in IS_1. Then in the IS_1 Wrapper, one tuple (3,5,5) is inserted, which is depicted in Figure 2. Its [#min, #max] value is set to [1,∞]. This means that the life time of this tuple starts from the timestamp 1. Next, the tuple (5,8,7) is deleted. Its [#min, #max] value is thus changed from [0,∞] to [0,2]. This means that this tuple becomes invisible after timestamp 2. A similar process happens to the IS_2 Wrapper when $DU_1 : Insert(5, 9, 28)$ is committed in the IS_2. From a transaction point of view, the *local id* serves as the version write timestamp for the given IS update.

3.2   DWMS-Transaction Management Using TxnID

In the global DWMS environment, we still need identifiers to track each DWMS-Transaction, and to construct correct maintenance queries that access the appropriate versions of data in each wrapper. A TxnID τ is a vector timestamp, $\tau = [k_1 \ldots k_i \cdots k_n]$ with $\tau[i] = k_i$, that concatenates the current *local id* k_i of each IS_i (the largest *local id* that has been assigned thus far) when this TxnID is generated. n is the number of ISs and $0 \le i \le n$.

It's easy to see that though the local ids in each ISs may be the same, the TxnIDs are globally unique. From the view point of the DWMS, each entry of the TxnID vector records the current state of each IS on arrival of the IS update. As an example, assume three updates happened in the two ISs depicted in Figure 1, $IS_1:DU_1$, $IS_1:DU_2$ and $IS_2:DU_1$. Suppose they arrive at the DWMS in the following order, $IS_1:DU_1, IS_2:DU_1$, and $IS_1:DU_2$, then their TxnIDs will be [1,0], [1,1] and [2,1] respectively. We assume that the initial local ids are all 0 and no other updates happened before.

The TxnID serves a dual purpose: one is to uniquely identify each DWMS-Transaction in the global environment and the other is to record the underlying ISs' states in terms of timestamps when this update is reported to the DWMS. We know that the maintenance queries are all IS specific. Thus, it is now possible to identify the right versioned data in the wrapper with the help of its TxnID. For example, as in Figure 1, $IS_1:DU_1$ "Insert(3,5,5)" is reported to the DWMS first. Then we assign TxnID [1,0] to it. To maintain this update, we will issue a maintenance query "Q_1: Select S.C, S.D From S Where S.C=5 and S.E>50" to IS_2. Based on TxnID [1,0], we know that this maintenance query should see the timestamp 0 of IS_2. Thus we rewrite Q_1 into Q_1': "Select S.C, S.D From S Where S.C=5 and S.E>50 and (#min≤ 0 and #max > 0) ". Thus, even though another update $IS_2:DU_1$ has already happened, its effect can easily be excluded from Q_1' because of the timestamps recorded in its TxnID and the #min and #max values of each tuple in the wrapper.

4   Parallel Maintenance Scheduler

A direct extension of the serial scheduler is possible for achieving parallel maintenance in data update only environments. As we stated in Section 2, one data update DWMS-Transaction maintenance process can be represented as $r(VD)r(IS_1)r(IS_2)\cdots r(IS_n)w(DW)$. So, there will be no read block between DWMS-Transaction maintenance processes in TxnWrap because of its multi-version concurrency control strategy. Borrowing traditional concurrency control concepts [2], an aggressive scheduler is thus straightforward. That is, we can start the DWMS-Transaction maintenance processes for each data update almost at the same time as long as sufficient computational resources are available in the DWMS server because there are no read/write conflicts in the *Propagation* step of DWMS-Transactions.

4.1   Scheduling in a Mixed Data Update and Schema Change Environment

However, more issues must be dealt with if we take schema changes into consideration. First, we briefly review how schema changes are maintained [6,4]. There are three steps for maintaining a schema change:

- Determine which view in the DW is affected by the change. [r(VD)]
- Find the suitable replacement for schema elements removed from the view definition and rewrite the view definition in the DW if needed. [w(VD)]
- Calculate the delta changes in term of tuples to be added or to be deleted due to the replacement between the old and the new view definition and adapt the DW by committing these delta changes to the DW. [$r(VD)r(IS_1)r(IS_2)$ $\cdots r(IS_n)$]

As can be seen, the view definition (VD) of the DW represents a critical resource and the following sequence of operations occurs during schema change maintenance: r(VD)w(VD)r(VD). Thus, one schema change DWMS-Transaction maintenance process can be represented as **r(VD)w(VD)r(VD)**$r(IS_1)r(IS_2)$ $\cdots r(IS_n)$w(DW). That is, in case of scheduling mixed data updates and schema changes, we have to consider the potential r(VD)/w(VD) conflicts in these different transactions.

TxnID-Order-Driven Scheduler. In a DWMS-Transaction environment, we need to keep the assumption of FIFO for updates which come from the same information source, otherwise certain updates wouldn't be correctly maintained. For example, two updates "DU_1: Insert into A(1,2,3)" and "DU_2: Delete (1,2,3) from A" happened in the same IS in this order, we should maintain DU_1 before DU_2 in the DWMS. If not, it is possible that the maintenance result of DU_2 couldn't be refreshed in the DW because the corresponding tuple isn't in the DW yet. Thus, we can't reorder DWMS-Transactions randomly. Secondly, once we assign the corresponding TxnID (timestamps) to each update, more ordering restrictions need to be imposed. That is, we can't randomly reorder these DWMS-Transactions in the scheduler even if these updates come from different ISs, otherwise the maintenance result may also be inconsistent with the IS state. Due to space limitation, we ask the reader to refer [7] for detailed explanations.

Based on the above analysis, we propose the following TxnID-Order-Driven scheduler: 1. Start DWMS-Transaction maintenance processes based on their TxnID order. 2. Synchronize the w(VD) operations of schema change maintenance.

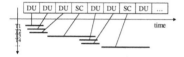
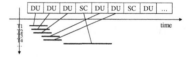

Fig. 3. Scheduling Example of TxnID-Order-Driven Algorithm

Fig. 4. Scheduling Example of Dynamic TxnID Scheduler

A sample execution plan is depicted in Figure 3. DU and SC each stand for their corresponding DWMS-Transaction maintenance process. For space limitations, the detailed control procedures of this scheduler are omitted [7].

The limitation of this algorithm is that once we assign the TxnIDs based on the arrival order of updates at the DWMS, we then have to keep this order in scheduling. That is, all the following data updates have to wait for the previous schema change to finish its view synchronization part. Below, we thus develop a dynamic scheduler that relaxes this ordering constraint.

Dynamic TxnID Scheduler. To have a more flexible scheduler, we first need to determine if it is possible to change the scheduling order of updates in the DWMS while still keeping the DW consistent in a mixed data update and schema change environment.

Observation 1 *The arrival order of updates at the DWMS doesn't affect the DW maintenance correctness as long as these updates come from different ISs.*

This observation gives us the hint that we should be able to exchange the scheduling order of updates in the DWMS that come from different ISs as long as we assign the corresponding TxnIDs dynamically. That is, if a schema change arrives, we can postpone its maintenance process, and go on maintaining the following data updates, as long as these data updates come from different ISs than the IS to which the schema change belongs to. This may give us some increased performance because less data updates would be waiting for scheduling. Figure 4 is an example of the Dynamic TxnID scheduler execution plan. Here, we assume that we generate a TxnID for each update only when we are ready to schedule it.

4.2   DW Commit and Consistency

Even if each individual update is being maintained correctly, the final DW state after committing these effects may still be inconsistent. This Variant DW Commit Order problem in a data update only environment has been addressed in [9]. We can apply this same commit control strategy to our mixed data update and schema change environments. However, the easiest control strategy is a strict commit order control. That is, only after we commit all the previous updates' effects, could we begin committing the current delta changes to the DW. If every DWMS-Transaction contains only one IS transaction, then this solution will achieve complete consistency.

5   Performance Studies

We implemented our parallel maintenance scheduler and incorporated it into the existing TxnWrap system [3]. We use Java thread to encapsulate the DWMS-Transaction maintenance process and correspondingly interleave the executions of these threads. Our experimental environment uses a local network and four machines (Pentium III PC with 256M memory, running Oracle 8.1.6.0 Server). We measure the total processing time for a set of updates.

We vary the number of threads and the number of schema changes (Figure 5). We set up six sources and one view defined as a join of three of them. These ISs are evenly distributed over three DB servers located on different machines. Each IS has two attributes and 10000 tuples. We use 100 concurrent data updates with different schema changes as our sample. The x-axis denotes the number of parallel threads in the system, with S denoting the serial scheduler, while the y-axis represents the total processing time.

If we only use one thread, then the total processing time is slightly higher than the serial one. This is due to the overhead of the parallel maintenance scheduler logic and thread management. Around thread number 5, the total processing time reaches its minimal. If we further increase the thread number, the processing time increases a little. There are two possible reasons. One is due to the extra overhead on the commit controller caused by an increase in updates waiting to be committed. The other is additional system overhead such as the maintenance queries processed by ISs are blocked by each other at every IS because the query capability of each IS is limited. The maximum percentage

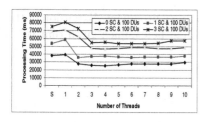
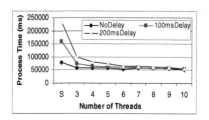

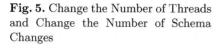

Fig. 5. Change the Number of Threads and Change the Number of Schema Changes

Fig. 6. Change the Network-Delay in each Maintenance Query

of performance improvement in this scenario is around 40%. We note that the CPU overhead can't be fully reduced by our multi-threading solution because we use a one-CPU DWMS server. The network delay in a local network environment is typical very small. The query processing time is also relatively small in our environments. Thus, an improvement linear in the thread number is not achieved.

From Figure 5, we also see that the total processing time increases if we add more schema changes because a schema change maintenance is much more time consuming than that of a data update. Furthermore, if we add more schema changes, the maximum improvement achieved by the scheduler will decrease because we can't fully maintain schema changes in parallel and all the subsequent data updates have to wait until the present schema change has finished its view synchronization.

In Figure 6, we measure the effect of changing the network delay in each maintenance query. We set up six ISs with each IS having 1000 tuples and use 100 concurrent data updates as sample. The performance changes from no network-delay to 100ms and then 200ms are listed. We see that the larger the network delay, the more performance improvement is being achieved. Clearly, we can fully make use of the network delay in the parallel scheduler.

6 Related Work

Maintaining materialized views under source updates in a data warehouse environment is one of the important issues of data warehousing [5]. In approaches that need to send maintenance queries down to the IS space, anomaly problems can arise. [10,1] introduced algorithms addressing these problems in data update only environments. TxnWrap [3] is the first transactional approach to handle the concurrency for both data and schema changes. TxnWrap encapsulates each maintenance process in a DWMS-Transaction and uses a multiversion concurrency control algorithm to guarantee a consistent view of data inside each DWMS-Transaction. PVM [9] addresses the problem of concurrent data update detection in a parallel execution mode and the variant DW commit order problem. However, PVM works in a data update only environment. Extension of this approach when considering schema changes would be complex given that it is a compensation based approach.

7 Conclusions

In this paper, we introduce a solution strategy that is able to maintain a data warehouse in parallel based on the DWMS-Transaction model. Several parallel scheduling algorithms are proposed and implemented based on TxnWrap system. The experimental results reveal that our parallel maintenance scheduler exhibits an excellent performance compared to sequential maintenance when maintaining a set of concurrent updates in a dynamic environment.

References

[1] D. Agrawal, A. E. Abbadi, A. Singh, and T. Yurek. Efficient View Maintenance at Data Warehouses. In *Proceedings of SIGMOD*, pages 417–427, 1997.

[2] P. A. Bernstein, V. Hadzilacos, and N. Goodman. *Concurrency Control and Recovery in Database System*. Addison-Wesley Pub., 1987.

[3] J. Chen and E. A. Rundensteiner. Txnwrap: A transactional approach to data warehouse maintenance. Technical Report WPI-CS-TR-00-26, Worcester Polytechnic Institute, November 2000.

[4] J. Chen, X. Zhang, S. Chen, K. Andreas, and E. A. Rundensteiner. DyDa:Data Warehouse Maintenance under Fully Concurrent Environments. In *Proceedings of SIGMOD Demo Session*, page 619, Santa Barbara, CA, May 2001.

[5] H. García-Molina, W. L., J. L. Wiener, and Y. Zhuge. Distributed and Parallel Computing Issues in Data Warehousing. In *Symposium on Principles of Distributed Computing*, page 7, 1998. Abstract.

[6] A. M. Lee, A. Nica, and E. A. Rundensteiner. The EVE Approach: View Synchronization in Dynamic Distributed Environments. *IEEE Transactions on Knowledge and Data Engineering (TKDE)*, 2001.

[7] B. Liu. Optimization Strategies for Data Warehouse Maintenance in Distributed Environments. Master's thesis, Worcester Polytechnic Institute, May 2002.

[8] K. Salem, K. S. Beyer, R. Cochrane, and B. G. Lindsay. How To Roll a Join: Asynchronous Incremental View Maintenance. In *Proceedings of SIGMOD*, pages 129–140, 2000.

[9] X. Zhang, E. A. Rundensteiner, and L. Ding. PVM: Parallel View Maintenance Under Concurrent Data Updates of Distributed Sources. In *Data Warehousing and Knowledge Discovery, Proceedings*, September, Munich, Germany 2001.

[10] Y. Zhuge, H. García-Molina, J. Hammer, and J. Widom. View Maintenance in a Warehousing Environment. In *Proceedings of SIGMOD*, pages 316–327, May 1995.

Striving towards Near Real-Time Data Integration for Data Warehouses

Robert M. Bruckner[1], Beate List[1], and Josef Schiefer[2]

[1]Institute of Software Technology
Vienna University of Technology
Favoritenstr. 9 / 188, A-1040 Vienna, Austria
{bruckner, list}@ifs.tuwien.ac.at
[2]IBM Watson Research Center
19 Skyline Drive
Hawthorne, NY 10532
josef.schiefer@us.ibm.com

Abstract. The amount of information available to large-scale enterprises is growing rapidly. While operational systems are designed to meet well-specified (short) response time requirements, the focus of data warehouses is generally the strategic analysis of business data integrated from heterogeneous source systems. The decision making process in traditional data warehouse environments is often delayed because data cannot be propagated from the source system to the data warehouse in time. A real-time data warehouse aims at decreasing the time it takes to make business decisions and tries to attain zero latency between the cause and effect of a business decision. In this paper we present an architecture of an ETL environment for real-time data warehouses, which supports a continual near real-time data propagation. The architecture takes full advantage of existing J2EE (Java 2 Platform, Enterprise Edition) technology and enables the implementation of a distributed, scalable, near real-time ETL environment. Instead of using vendor proprietary ETL (extraction, transformation, loading) solutions, which are often hard to scale and often do not support an optimization of allocated time frames for data extracts, we propose in our approach ETLets (spoken "et-lets") and Enterprise Java Beans (EJB) for the ETL processing tasks.

1. Introduction

The amount of information available to large-scale enterprises is growing rapidly. New information is being generated continuously by operational sources such as order processing, inventory control, and customer service systems. Organizations without instant information delivery capabilities will surrender their competitive advantage. In order to support efficient analysis and mining of such diverse, distributed information, a data warehouse (DWH) collects data from multiple, heterogeneous sources and stores integrated information in a central repository. Traditional DWHs need to be updated periodically to reflect source data updates. The observation of real-world events in operational source systems is characterized by a propagation delay. The update patterns (daily, weekly, etc.) for traditional data warehouses and the data integration process result in increased propagation delays.

While operational systems are among other things designed to meet well-specified (short) response time requirements, the focus of data warehouses is the strategic analysis of data integrated from heterogeneous systems [3]. Traditionally, there is no

Y. Kambayashi, W. Winiwarter, M. Arikawa (Eds.): DaWaK 2002, LNCS 2454, pp. 317-326, 2002.
© Springer-Verlag Berlin Heidelberg 2002

real-time connection between a DWH and its data sources, because the write-once read-many decision support characteristics would conflict with the continuous update workload of operational systems and result in poor reponse times.

Separated from operational systems, data warehouse and business intelligence applications are used for strategic planning and decision-making. As these applications have matured, it has become apparent that the information and analyses they provide are vital to tactical day-to-day decision-making, and many organizations can no longer operate their businesses effectively without them. Consequently, there is a trend towards integrating decision processing into the overall business process. The advent of e-business is also propelling this integration because organizations need to react much faster to changing business conditions in the e-business world [5].

The goal of a near real-time data warehouse (RTDWH, part of a so called *zero-latency DWH environment* [2]) is to allow organizations to deliver relevant information as fast as possible to knowledge workers or decision systems who rely on it to react in near real-time to new information captured by an organization's computer system. Therefore, it supports an immediate discovery of abnormal data conditions in a manner not supported by an OLTP system. Up till recently, *timeliness* requirements (the relative availability of data to support a given process within the time frame required to perform the process) were postponed to mid-term or long-term. While a total real-time enterprise DWH might still be the panacea, we will present an approach to enable DWHs to integrate particular data *"just-in-time"* to changing customer needs, supply chain demands, and financial concerns. As e-business erodes switching costs and brand loyalty, customers will consider instant service fulfillment and information access the primary relationship differentiator.

The remainder of this paper is organized as follows. In section 2, we discuss the contribution of this paper and related work. In section 3, we give an overview of requirements for real-time DWHs and discuss differences of operational data stores. In section 4 we discuss the ETL process of real-time DWHs and introduce a J2EE architecture for an ETL environment which supports a near real-time data propagation. Finally, we discuss our future work and give a conclusion in section 5.

2. Contribution and Related Work

The authors in [1] describe an approach which clearly separates the data warehouse refreshment process from its traditional handling as a view maintenance or bulk loading process. They provide a conceptual model of the process, which is treated as a composite workflow, but they do not describe how to efficiently propagate the data. Theodoratos and Bouzeghoub discuss in [11] data currency quality factors in data warehouses and propose a DWH design that takes these factors into account.

Temporal data warehouses address the issue of supporting temporal information efficiently in data warehousing systems [14]. Keeping them up-to-date is complex, because temporal views may need to be updated not only when source data is updated, but also as time progresses, and these two dimensions of change interact in subtle ways. In [13], the authors present efficient techniques (e.g. temporal view self-maintenance) for maintaining DWHs without disturbing source operations.

An important issue for near real-time data integration is the accommodation of delays, which has been investigated for (business) transactions in temporal active databases [8]. The conclusion is that temporal faithfulness for transactions has to be provided, which preserves the serialization order of a set of business transactions.

Although possibly lagging behind real-time, a system that behaves in a temporally faithful manner guarantees the expected serialization order.

In [12], the authors describe the ETL (extract-transform-load) tool ARKTOS, which is capable of modeling and executing practical ETL scenarios by providing explicit primitives for the capturing of common tasks (like data cleaning, scheduling, and data transformations) using a declarative language. ARKTOS offers graphical and declarative facilities for the definition of DWH transformations and tries to optimize the execution of complex sequences of transformation and cleansing tasks.

Our contribution in this paper is the characterization of RTDWHs, the identification of technologies that can support it, and the composition of these technologies in an overall architecture. We provide an in-depth discussion of using the J2EE platform for ETL environments of RTDWHs. The prerequisite for a RTDWH is a continual, near real-time data propagation. As a solution for this problem, we are proposing a J2EE architecture with ETL container and ETLets, which provide an efficient way of performing, controlling and monitoring the ETL processing tasks. To the best of our knowledge, there are no other approaches, which use container managed Java components for continual data propagating.

3. Real-Time Data Warehouse Requirements

A real-time data warehouse (RTDWH) aims at decreasing the time it takes to make the business decisions. In fact, there should be minimized latency between the cause and effect of a business decision. A real-time data warehouse enables analysis across corporate data sources and notifies the business of actionable recommendations, effectively closing the gap between business intelligence systems and the business processes. Business requirements may appear to be different across the various industries, but the underlying information requirements are similar – integrated, current, detailed, and immediately accessible.

Transforming a standard DWH using batch loading during update windows (where analytical access is not allowed) to an analytical environment providing current data involves various issues to be addressed in order to enable (near) real-time dissemination of new information across an organization. The business needs for this kind of analytical environment introduce a set of service level agreements that exceed what is typical of a traditional DWH. These service levels focus on three basic characteristics, which are described below.

- *Continuous data integration*, which enables (near) real-time capturing and loading from different operational sources.
- *Active decision engines* that can make recommendations or even (rule-driven) tactical decisions for routine, analytical decision tasks encountered [9, 10].
- *Highly available* analytical environments based on an analysis engine that is able to consistently generate and provide access to current business analyses at any time not restricted by loading windows typical for the common batch approach.

An in-depth discussion of these characteristics from the analytical viewpoint (in order to enable timely consistent analyses) is given in [2]. Near real-time integration for data warehouses does not minimize capturing and propagation delays of the operational source systems of an organization, which are responsible for capturing real world events. Data warehouses (in particular real-time DWHs) try to represent the history as accurately as possible (to enable tactical decision support). Therefore, late-arriving records are welcome because they make the information more complete.

However, those facts and dimension records are bothersome because they are difficult to integrate (e.g. when using surrogate keys for slowly changing dimensions).

The RTDWH provides access to an accurate, integrated, consolidated view of the organizations' information and helps to deliver near real-time information to its users. This requires efficient ETL (extract-transform-load) techniques enabling continuous data integration, which is the focus of this paper. Combining highly available systems with active decision engines allows near real-time information dissemination for DWHs. Cummulatively, this is the basis for *zero latency* analytical environments [2].

3.1. Continuous Data Integration

In e-business environments, information velocity is a key determinant of overall business growth capacity, or scalability. In an environment of growing volume, velocity increases as well. Greater volumes of data must be exchanged and moved in shorter time frames. For performing transactions faster and more efficient, operational systems are supported by business intelligence tools, which provide valuable information for decision makers. Real-time data warehouses help the operational systems deliver this information in near real-time.

ETL environments of RTDWHs must support the same processing layers as found in traditional data warehouse systems. Critical for RTDWHs is an end-to-end automation of the ETL processes. The ETL environment must be able to complete the data extracts and transformations in allocated time frames and it must meet the service-level requirements for the data warehouse users. Therefore, a continuous data integration environment facilitates better and faster decision making, resulting in streamlined operations, increased velocity in the business processes, improved customer relationships and enhanced e-business capabilities.

3.2. Real-Time DWH vs. Operational Data Stores

For handling real-time data propagations, companies often consider building an operational data store (ODS). An ODS bridges the information gap between operational systems and the traditional data warehouse. It contains data at the event detail level, coordinated across all relevant source systems and maintained in a current state. W.H. Inmon defines an ODS as an architectural construct, which is subject oriented, integrated, volatile, current valued, and contains detailed data [4].

But there are noteworthy differences between ODSs and RTDWHs. An ODS serves the needs of an operational environment while real-time data warehouses serve the needs of the informational community. The ODS and the RTDWH are identical when it comes to being *subject oriented* and *integrated*. There are no discernible differences between the two constructs with regard to those characteristics. However, when it comes to transaction support, volatility, currency of information, history and detail, the ODS and the real-time data warehouse differ significantly.

- **History of Data.** A data warehouse contains data that is rich in history. ODSs generally do not maintain a rich history of data, because they are used within operational environments and have strict requirements for the query response times. Consequently, an ODS is highly volatile in order to reflect the current status from operational sources.
- **Data Propagation.** For an ODS it is common that data records are updated. An ODS must stay in sync with the operational environments to be able to consistently operate within its environment. An ODS has predictable arrival rates for data and includes sync points or checkpoints for the loading process. RTDWH systems are generally read-only and track data changes by creating data snapshots. The absence

of frequent record-level update processing makes the load-and-access processing more efficient. Furthermore, RTDWHs have a higher variability of the size of the transactions and the variability of the rate at which the transaction arrive.

- **Transaction Support.**. Data in an ODS is subject to change every time one of its underlying details changes. An advantage of the ODS is that it is integrated and that is can support both decision support and operational transaction processing. An ODS often requires a physical organization which is optimal for the flexible update processing of data while the RTDWH system requires a physical organization which is optimal for the flexible access and analysis of data. RTDWH systems are not interwoven with operational environments and do not support operational transaction processing.

- **Aggregated Data.** The ODS contains data that is very detailed, while a RTDWH contains a lot of summary data. Data in the ODS can also be summarized, and a summarized value can be calculated. But, because the summarized value is subject to immediate change (ODSs are highly volatile), it has a short effective life. Summary data of a RTDWH is less dynamic, because aggregated values from history data are often not affected by new data.

A real-time DWH is not a replacement for an ODS. An ODS is an architectural construct for a decision support system where collective integrated operational data is stored. It can complement a RTDWH with the information needs for knowledge workers. The ODS contains very detailed current data and is designed to work in an operational environment.

4. ETL Environment for RTDWHs

We propose an architecture, which facilitates streamlining and accelerating the ETL process by moving data between the different layers without any intermediate file storage. We achieve this streamlining of the ETL process by using *ETLets* (explained in detail in section 4.1) and EJB components [17] for 1) extracting the data with high-speed J2EE connectors [15], 2) immediately parsing and converting the source data into the XML format, and 3) converting and assembling the data for the target format. This way, each layer of the ETL environment can process the source data and forward it to other layers for further processing. ETLets and EJB components are configurable Java components which perform the ETL processing tasks, such as data extraction, validation, transformation, or data assembly. They can be deployed on any Java application server and can be reused for several ETL processes.

Figure 1 shows the levels of a typical ETL process. Please note, that the processing steps for each layer may be executed in a distributed environment at different locations. The data propagation from the source system and the data movement within the ETL environment is managed in our approach by containers. We use containers, which ensure that the ETL components get instantiated for the processing and that the data is passed from one component to the next.

Because RTDWHs try to minimize the data latency and the time for propagating data from the source systems, the number of data extracts increases and the amount of data per data extract normally decreases. One of the most critical ETL processing tasks is an efficient data extraction. An ETL environment of a RTDWH must be able to establish high-performance connections to the source systems and optimize these connections. For instance, connections to databases or enterprise systems must be automatically pooled to optimize the resources and throughput times. In our approach, containers manage the connection pools to provide an efficient access to the data sources. Containers also create, destroy, and swap in and out of memory the ETL components to optimize the ETL processing in a structured and efficient way.

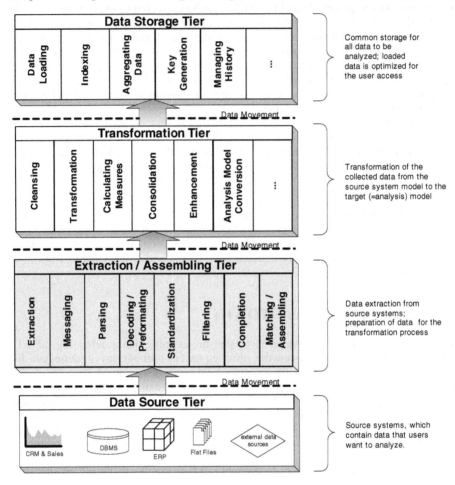

Fig. 1. ETL processing layers of a (near) real-time data warehouse

4.1 J2EE Architecture for RTDWHs

In this section we introduce a J2EE (Java 2 Platform, Enterprise Edition) architecture for an ETL environment of RTDWHs. Our architecture includes the familiar layers of a traditional data warehouse system, but also fulfills the requirements and characteristics of a RTDWH. For real-time data warehouses, a robust, scalable and high-performance data staging environment, which is able to handle a large number of near real-time data propagations from the source systems is essential.

We are proposing a J2EE environment for the extraction, transformation, and movement of the data, which fulfills these additional requirements. J2EE is a Java platform designed for the mainframe-scale computing typical of large enterprises. Sun Microsystems (together with industry partners such as IBM) designed J2EE to simplify application development in a thin client tiered environment and to decrease the need for programming and programmer training by creating standardized, reusable modular components and by enabling the tier to handle many aspects of programming automatically [16]. J2EE environments have a multi-tiered architecture, which provides natural access points for integration with existing and future systems and for the deployment of new sources systems and interfaces as needs arise. In J2EE environments, the container takes responsibility for system-level services (such as threading, resource management, transactions, security, persistence, and so on). This arrangement leaves the component developer with the simplified task of developing business functionality. It also allows the implementation details of the system services to be reconfigured without changing the component code, making components useful in a wide range of contexts. Instead of developing ETL scripts, which are hard to maintain, scale, and reuse, ETL developers are able to implement components for critical parts of the ETL process. In our approach, we extend this concept by adding new container services, which are useful for ETL developers. A *container service* is responsible for the monitoring of the data extracts and ensures that resources, workload and time-constraints are optimized. ETL developers are able to specify data propagation parameters (e.g. schedule and time constraints) in a deployment descriptor and the container will try to optimize these settings.

Most important for an ETL environment is the *integration tier* (in J2EE environments also called *enterprise information tier*). The J2EE integration tier contains data and services implemented by non-J2EE resources. Databases, legacy systems, ERP (Enterprise Resource Planning) and EAI (Enterprise Application Integration) systems, process schedulers, and other existing or purchased packages reside in the integration tier. The integration tier allows the designers of an ETL environment to choose efficient mechanisms and resources for the data propagation that is best suited for their needs, and still interoperate seamlessly with J2EE.

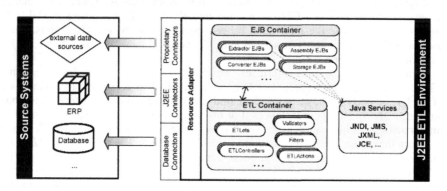

Fig. 2. J2EE ETL environment.

Figure 2 shows a J2EE ETL environment with resource adapters for the data extraction, which are available for the data propagation. Source systems for the ETL environment may require different types of access connectors. Note, that J2EE environments include a standard API for high-performance connectors. Many vendors of ERP or CRM systems (e.g. SAP, PeopleSoft) offer a J2EE connector interface for their systems. With our architecture, ETL developers can use existing high-performance connectors with a standard API without worrying about issues like physical data formats, performance or concurrency. ETL developers can implement reusable components, which run in a container that optimizes the processing, resources and data access. The J2EE platform includes synchronous and asynchronous communication mechanisms via J2EE connectors. Furthermore, the J2EE platform includes a standard API for accessing databases (JDBC) and for messaging (JMS) which enables the ETL developers to access queue-based source systems, which can propagate data via a messaging system.

An *ETL container* is a part of a Java application server that provides services for the execution and monitoring of ETL tasks. It manages the lifecycle of ETLets and provides default implementations for some of the interfaces shown in Figure 3. There are three possibilities to implement an ETL container: 1) implementing a new ETL container for an exiting Java application servers, or extending the EJB container of an Java application server with ETL functionality, 2) extending a Java-enable database management system that includes a Java virtual machine, or 3) writing an own Java application server for the ETL container. By choosing option 1 or 2, the existing functionality of a Java application server or a database management system can be reused and extended. Furthermore, the ETL processing performance can significantly benefit from the architecture and infrastructure of the Java application server or the database management system.

Like other Java-based components, ETLets are platform independent Java classes that are compiled to platform neutral bytecode that can be loaded dynamically into and run by a Java application server. ETLets interact with schedulers or ETL clients via a predefined interface of the ETL container. The ETL container supports filters and validators, which allow on-the-fly transformations and validations of data being processed. ETL filters can globally modify or adapt the data being processed. ETL validators are used to ensure data consistency and can be used to check business rules. Filters and validators are pluggable Java components that can be specified in the deployment descriptor for the ETL container. ETL controllers are Java classes that act as intermediaries between ETLets and the underlying ETL processing model. ETL controllers coordinate the ETL tasks by processing events with ETL actions, which use the EJB components (ExtractionBean, ConversionBean, AssemblyBean etc.) to perform the processing.

Figure 3 shows the Java interfaces, which are supported by the ETL container. ETLets of the same type share an ETLet context, which is accessible to all instances of an ETLet class and can be used to find out initialization parameters or to share attributes among all ETLet instances. For instance, the ETLet context can be used for implementing caching strategies. The *ETLetSession* interface is used by ETLets to maintain the business data for one run of the ETL process. The method *getETLData()* makes the extracted data accessible to all components used for the ETL process. The *ETLetConfig* interface provides information about the initialization parameters for the ETLet. The *ETLValidator* and *ETLFilter* interfaces must be implemented by validator and filter components, which can be used in several ETL processes by specifying them in the deployment descriptor. ETL developers can use the *ETLController* and *ETLAction* interfaces for implementing complex control logic for the ETL process. For simple ETL processes developers can simply implement the *runETL()* method of the ETLet. For more complex scenarios, developers can implement ETLActions to 1) encapsulate processing steps, 2) instantiate EJB components, and 3) to invoke methods from these EJB components. The ETLActions are invoked by an ETLController, which contains the centrally managed control logic.

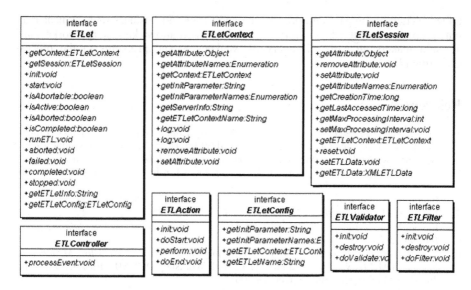

Fig. 3. Java interface supported by the ETL container.

The EJB container of the J2EE environment provides portable, scalable, available, and high-performance access to data and ETL processing. The Java application server manages the efficient access to instances of the EJB components regardless of whether the components are used locally or remotely. The environment automatically manages the implementation details of multithreading, persistence, security, transactions, and concurrent data extracts. ETL developers can implement EJBs for any type of processing of the source data.

5. Conclusion and Future Work

In this paper we investigated and characterized real-time data warehouses (RTDWH). We further examined technologies necessary to enable near real-time data integration, and described the composition of these technologies in an overall architecture. The ETL architecture uses *ETL container* and *ETLets*, which provide an efficient way of performing, controlling and monitoring the ETL processing tasks. The main advantages of ETLets are that they are lightweight Java components and that they allow a continuous ETL processing of the source data without using immediate file storage. Therefore ETLets are well suited for a near real-time data propagation. To our knowledge, we have seen no other approach, which uses container managed Java components for a continual and near real-time data propagating.

Presently, we use ETL controllers for managing complex ETL process. In our future work, we want to develop a model to formally describe and execute ETL processes. Besides managing the lifecycle of ETLets, we want to add a set of services including caching, concurrency, security, messaging, and transformation engines.

We want to use ETLets for propagating *workflow audit trail data* and related business data from various source systems. Workflows are typically executed on top of several business applications and are controlled by a workflow management system, which also tracks the execution. We want to give knowledge workers and decision makers an in-depth analysis of the executed business processes by providing valuable, process-oriented business metrics (cycle time, costs, quality, etc.) [6]. We utilize ETLets to prepare and process the audit trail and business data. A near real-time propagation of the data is very critical, because it allows knowledge workers and decision makers an early discovery of weaknesses and problems in the process execution [7].

References

1. Bouzeghoub, M., Fabret, F., Matulovic, M.: *Modeling Data Warehouse Refreshment Process as a Workflow Application.* Intl. Workshop DMDW'99, Heidelberg, Germany, June 1999.
2. Bruckner, R.M., Tjoa, A M.: *Capturing Delays and Valid Times in Data Warehouses – Towards Timely Consistent Analyses.* To appear: Journal of Intelligent Information Systems (JIIS), forthcoming, 2002.
3. Inmon, W.H.: *Building the Data Warehouse.* 2nd ed., J.Wiley & Sons, New York, 1996.
4. Inmon, W.H.: *Building the Operational Data Store.* 2nd ed., J.Wiley & Sons, NY, 1999.
5. Inmon, W.H., Terdeman, R.H., Norris-Montanari J., Meers, D.: *Data Warehousing for E-Business.* J.Wiley & Sons, New York, 2001.
6. List, B., Schiefer, J., Bruckner, R.M.: *Measuring Knowledge with Workflow Management Systems.* TAKMA Workshop, in Proc. of 12th Intl. Workshop DEXA'01, IEEE CS Press, pp. 467–471, Munich, Germany, September 2001.
7. Kueng, P., Wettstein, T., List, B.: *A Holistic Process Performance Analysis through a Performance Data Warehouse.* Proc. AMCIS 2001, Boston, USA, pp. 349–356, Aug. 2001.
8. Roddick, J.F., Schrefl, M.: *Towards an Accommodation of Delay in Temporal Active Databases.* Proc. of 11th ADC2000, IEEE CS Press, pp. 115–119, Canberra, Australia, 2000.
9. Schrefl, M., Thalhammer, T.: *On Making Data Warehouses Active.* Proc. of the 2nd Intl. Conf. DaWaK, Springer, LNCS 1874, pp. 34–46, London, UK, 2000.
10. Thalhammer, T., Schrefl, M., Mohania, M.: *Active Data Warehouses: Complementing OLAP with Analysis Rules.* Data & Knowledge Engineering, Vol. 39(3), pp. 241–269, 2001.
11. Theodoratos, D., Bouzeghoub, M.: *Data Currency Quality Factors in Data Warehouse Design.* Intl. Workshop DMDW'99, Heidelberg, Germany, June 1999.
12. Vassiliadis, P., Vagena, Z., Skiadopoulos, S., Karayannidis, N., Sellis, T.: *ARKTOS: towards the Modeling, Design, Control and Execution of ETL Processes.* Information Systems, Vol. 26(8), pp. 537–561, 2001.
13. Yang, J., Widom, J.: *Temporal View Self-Maintenance.* Proc. of the 7th Intl. Conf. EDBT2000, Springer, LNCS 1777, pp. 395–412, Konstanz, Germany, 2000.
14. Yang, J.: *Temporal Data Warehousing.* Ph.D. Thesis, Department of Computer Science, Stanford University, 2001.
15. Sun Microsystems, *J2EE Connector Specification 1.0*, 2001.
16. Sun Microsystems, *Designing Enterprise Applications with the Java 2 Platform, Enterprise Edition*, Second Edition, 2001.
17. Sun Microsystems, *Enterprise JavaBeans Specification*, Version 2.0, 2001.

Time-Interval Sampling for Improved Estimations in Data Warehouses

Pedro Furtado[1] and João Pedro Costa[2]

[1] Dep. Engenharia Informática, Universidade de Coimbra,
Polo II, Pinhal de Marrocos 3030 Coimbra, Portugal
`pnf@dei.uc.pt`
[2] Dep. Informática e de Sistemas, Instituto Superior de Engenharia de Coimbra
Quinta da Nora, Rua Pedro Nunes, 3030-119 Coimbra, Portugal
`jcosta@isec.pt`

Abstract. In large data warehouses it is possible to return very fast approximate answers to user queries using pre-computed sampling summaries well-fit for all types of exploration analysis. However, their usage is constrained by the fact that there must be a representative number of samples in grouping intervals to yield acceptable accuracy. In this paper we propose and evaluate a technique that deals with the representation issue by using time interval-biased stratified samples (TISS). The technique is able to deliver fast accurate analysis to the user by taking advantage of the importance of the time dimension in most user analysis. It is designed as a transparent middle layer, which analyzes and re-writes the query to use a summary instead of the base data warehouse. The estimations and error bounds returned using the technique are compared to those of traditional sampling summaries, to show that it achieves significant improvement in accuracy.

1 Introduction

Data warehousing plays an essential role in many decision-making processes. It allows an organization to evaluate and analyze enterprise data over time. The enormous amounts of data that must be processed in large data warehouses limits the time-to-answer, that the user can expect to get. The user will become frustrated for having to wait much longer than desired in any of the iterative steps of analysis and exploration.

This has motivated a lot of research on all kinds of structures, strategies and massively parallel systems to deliver faster answers to information-hungry ad-hoc users of such systems. There has been a considerable amount of work in developing statistical techniques for data reduction in large data warehouses. The major classes of techniques used are sampling, histograms and parametric modeling (see [3] for references).

Sampling summaries [4], [6] have proved to be extremely time effective while requiring only minor query rewriting and the combination of estimations with confi-

Y. Kambayashi, W. Winiwarter, M. Arikawa (Eds.): DaWaK 2002, LNCS 2454, pp. 327-337, 2002.

dence intervals [5], [6] gives the user the precise dimension of the accuracy of the result. However, there are important limitations with those summaries. Our focus is in one of the most important classes of OLAP queries – queries segmenting the data into groups and deriving some aggregate information for these groups (group-by queries), including analysis of temporal evolution patterns, forecasting based on past data and so on. The statistical nature of the estimation limits the usefulness of the estimation to groups that are represented by a sufficient number of samples. Typically, very aggregated queries have all groups well represented but, as the user drills down in more detailed exploration, the number of samples becomes a crucial issue and several groups may not exhibit acceptable accuracy. In those cases, the base DW data must be accessed to return the exact answer, giving rise to the time-to-answer problem.

We propose the use of time-interval stratified samples (TISS), a time-biased sampling strategy that produces summaries biased towards recency to minimize the representational issue by taking advantage of the fact that recent data is more relevant in most less-aggregated analysis. TISS makes a trade-off, with progressively slightly less exact representations of older periods in order to return accurate recent data. We show that in practice, this trade-off results in very good accuracy concerning at least the last two years without any significant impact in older data analysis. The technique does not require any modification to the existing system. As an add-on, it uses the data warehouse to build and refresh the summary and includes a transparent middle layer that analyzes and rewrites the query to use the summary. In this paper we propose TISS and discuss all major issues, including the re-writing middle-layer and TISS lifecycle management. We conduct experiments on TPC-H [10] to show the advantage of using TISS by comparing the results obtained.

2 Related Work

Approximate query answering strategies have deserved some additional attention recently, as researchers seek the best approach to return fast approximate answers to queries that require extensive scanning and joining in large data warehouses [1], [2], [5], [6]. Online aggregation [6] proposes a framework for approximate answers of aggregation queries, in which the base data is scanned in random order at query time and the approximate answer is continuously updated as the scan proceeds. A graphical display depicts the answer and a confidence interval as the scan proceeds, so that the user may stop the process at any time. The Approximate Query Answering (AQUA) system [4] provides approximate answers using small, pre-computed synopses of the underlying base data. The system provides probabilistic error/confidence bounds on the answer [2]. Finally, Matias [7], [8] proposed and studied approximate data structures for providing faster (approximate) answers to data structure queries.

The samples representation problem is considered an important issue, which has been the main driver of important recent work. Join Synopsis [2] are proposed to minimize the problem of poor quality approximations in the estimates of the output of multi-way joins. Congressional samples [1] propose a general framework for pre-computed, hybrid uniform and biased sampling summaries. It tries to guarantee a minimal representation of samples for pre-defined groups. One of the difficulties faced by this strategy is the enormous number of combinations of group-by patterns in star queries of typical OLAP ad-hoc environments. The technique proposed in this paper is compatible and can be used together with both join synopsis and congressional samples to further improve the accuracy by taking the best possible advantage of the time dimension and the importance of recency in most data analysis.

3 The Time-Interval Stratified Sampling Strategy (TISS)

The TISS technique presented in this paper is implemented on a summary warehouse context (TISS-SW). The SW comprises one or more summaries able to return fast approximate answers to many queries. When the summaries cannot return accurate estimations, the base data must be accessed instead, thereby loosing the performance advantage of accessing the small summary. When possible and desired, the estimation returns a confidence interval of the result. The SW includes a middle layer, which does the necessary query rewrite operations to use the SW instead of the DW when possible. Additionally, summaries can also be used in a personal computer offline (without access to the base data warehouse). In this case, queries that cannot be answered by the summary will have to be postponed until the user is back online, but he is still able to do extensive analysis without the base data. This is the basic approach that is followed in many systems such as AQUA [4] and it is also followed in TISS-SW.

The rest of this section presents TISS, discussing the rationale and formulas for traditional and TISS sampling strategies and the major issues of TISS-SW summary.

3.1 Traditional Sampling

The time dimension is one of the most relevant dimensions in any data warehouse (expressed as an explicit TIME entity or in date/time recording attributes as in TPC-H). Businesses revolve around time and the most recent data is also the most important when the past performance is analyzed or the future forecasted. It might be important to analyze the evolution of sales in the last two years to plan the best strategies for the future. It will probably be important to analyze sales by brand and down to some individual products or by product type. A lot more predicates can be incorporated in an iterative analysis. In fact, successive aggregation group-by queries are being made, with the ever-present time dimension. These queries can be posed against sampling summaries with minor query rewrites, which are based on the following suppositions:

- Summaries based on samples are very effective because they return very fast estimations, allowing the user to go through iterative exploration steps efficiently
- For each individual group that is represented by a reasonably large number of samples, the estimated value can be very close to the real value
- Confidence intervals are returned together with the estimations

The estimation procedure from a uniform random sampling summary is reasonably simple. Let N be the number of values aggregated within a group when the query is ran against the base data and n the number of samples aggregated within the equivalent group when the query is ran against the sampling summary. The estimations returned for the most frequent aggregation operators are computed as,

$$AVERAGE_{estimated} = AVERAGE_{sample\_set} \tag{1}$$

$$COUNT_{estimated} = COUNT_{sample\_set} \times \frac{N}{n} \tag{2}$$

$$SUM_{estimated} = SUM_{sample\_set} \times \frac{N}{n} = AVERAGE_{sample\_set} \times N \tag{3}$$

$$MAX_{estimated} = MAX_{sample\_set} \qquad MIN_{estimated} = MIN_{sample\_set} \tag{4}$$

In this paper we have already pointed out the major limitation of these estimation procedures as the representational problem: the inability to estimate many group-by results for lack of samples. The importance of having as many samples as possible in these estimation procedures cannot be overemphasized because the aggregation of the sample set will be more reliable, but also because N, the real number of values within each specific group (a COUNT on the base data), is not known in most real situations. This quantity is estimated by replacing N/n in formulas (2) and (3) by the inverse of the "sampling percentage". The extrapolation and the aggregation of the sample set are of crucial importance to the accuracy of the estimation, as both terms in the product contribute to the error. If there are a sufficiently large number of samples in a group, both the aggregate of the samples and the extrapolation will become more accurate and the overall estimation error will be significantly reduced. A similar rationale applies to confidence intervals, which can be derived using either CLT (Central Limit Theorem), Hoeffding or Chebyshev formulas [2]. It is easy to see in table 1, that the number of samples (|S|) is very important for tighter confidence intervals.

Table 1. 90% confidence intervals for AVG

Method	Formula
Central Limit Theorem	1.65 * σ(S) / sqrt(|S|)
Chebyshev (estimated σ(R))	3.16 * σ(S) / sqrt(|S|)
Hoeffding	1.22 * (MAX-MIN) /sqrt(|S|)

The previous discussion and our experimental data show that the representational issue is indeed an important factor for the applicability of summaries in many analyses. The time-interval stratified sampling strategy (TISS) proposed in this paper aims to minimize the representational problem by implementing a time-biased sampling strategy to take the best possible advantage of the time dimension and the importance of recency in most data analysis. It is based on the following assumptions:

- In many user analyses, recent detail is far more relevant then older detail. The user will be concerned with the evolution of some parameter and occasionally analyze some more detailed measures for specific categories, focusing in the most recent in-

formation and frequently even forecasting to the future based on recent performance

- Older data is still relevant in ad-hoc queries but is usually accessed in more aggregated fashion, in which case the representational problem is much less severe

3.2 Time-Interval Stratified Sampling

TISS warehouse (TISS-SW) has a set of time-intervals (strata), which are filled using
a stratified sampling approach. The number of intervals, length and sampling percentage (SP) for each interval are configurable. The most recent stratum (most recent
quarter in table 2b) is the best-represented period, while the last interval, containing
the oldest data, has the smallest SP. As a result, although the summary in table 2b has
an overall sampling percentage of 3%, the most recent data, has an SP of 25%, resulting in very accurate estimations in this time frame. The last (most recent) two years
are also much better represented than the corresponding 3% uniform sample summary.
These sampling percentages are achieved in the expense of older data. However, the
corresponding sampling of those older intervals (2% and 1% in the figure) are still
acceptable when compared with the 3% USS summary and the premise that the older
data is mostly useful in more aggregated analysis.

Table 2. Generic Strata and SP (a) and a possible scenario for a 3% TISS-SW summary (b)

Strata	Percentage (SP)	Period	Percentage (SP)
P1	SP1	Last 3 Months	25.00%
P2	SP2	Last 12 - 4 Months	8.00%
P3	SP3	Last 24 - 13 Months	5.00%
...	...	Last 48 - 25 Months	2.00%
Pn	SPn	Before 49 Months	1.05%

It is easy to see how values should be estimated in TISS. When all the values of a
group fall into one stratum (e.g. when sales are being analyzed by quarter), the formulas (1) to (4) return the final results. Otherwise, the formulas for COUNT (2) and
SUM (3) are still valid within each stratum of TISS-SW, yielding, for each group Gi
and stratum Sj, the quantities COUNTGiSj and SUMGiSj. From those, the aggregation results for each group can be determined as,

$$COUNT_{Gi} = \sum_{j=1}^{n} COUNT_{GiSj} \qquad (5)$$

$$SUM_{Gi} = \sum_{j=1}^{n} SUM_{GiSj} \qquad (6)$$

$$AVG_{Gi} = SUM_{Gi}/COUNT_{Gi} \qquad (7)$$

$$MAX_{Gi} = MAX_{j}(MAX_{GiSj}) \qquad MIN_{Gi} = MIN_{j}(MIN_{GiSjt}) \qquad (8)$$

In practice, the previous formulas are easily implemented through query rewriting, with minor changes to the basic query, requiring the sampling percentage values to be kept in the summary warehouse for each summary and accessed whenever required.

3.3 TISS-SW Structure and Query Processing

The only major difference of TISS-SW relative to the data warehouse schema is an additional item, which identifies the sampling percentage (SP) for each time interval (the SP column). The correspondence between time intervals (or strata) and SP values can be stored as an additional column in the fact table or in the time dimension.

TISS includes a transparent middle layer, which is responsible for query analysis and re-writing to optionally use a summary instead of the data warehouse. The rewritten query uses the SP column and requires only minor modifications as shown below,

Normal query: Rewritten query:

```
SELECT count(*),sum(sales),        SELECT sum(1/SP),sum(sales/SP),
average(sales) , ...                sum(sales/SP)/sum(1/SP), ...
FROM  SalesFact, Time, ...          FROM SW_SalesFact, SW_Time, ...
WHERE joins and restrictions        WHERE joins and restrictions
GROUP BY group conditions           GROUP BY group conditions
```

TISS middle layer is configurable in what concerns the information that should be returned about the amount of error in the estimations. This includes the type and value of the confidence interval(s) to be returned (calculus: none, Hoeffdings, Chebyshev, CLT; values: 80%, 90%, 95%, 99%, ...; type: absolute or relative confidence interval).

4 Managing the Lifecycle of TISS

After the TISS-SW structure is created, important decisions need to be taken regarding the number, width (time interval or period P) and sampling percentage (SP) of time intervals (strata). Those definitions are of utmost importance, because they should be chosen so that the best advantage can be taken from the summary to provide the most accurate analysis. The choices depend heavily on the business being modeled and the typical analysis that are required.

After constructed, TISS-SW follows the same lifecycle steps of a normal data warehouse (DW). In a DW, an initial load is made to populate the structure with data from the operational schema. Afterwards, the DW must be "periodically refreshed" with new data. As a summary of the DW, TISS-SW will be loaded in a subsequent step, from the data that was already loaded into the DW, without delaying or interfere with the loading of DW. The initial TISS-SW loading can easily be achieved through a series of sampling and loading steps. Each stratum i must be filled with a fraction $SP_i\%$ of the data from the corresponding time interval P_i of the DW using an efficient random sampling algorithm [11] over the data in P_i, with the number of samples determined by $SP_i\%$.

In order to make the structure queriable and similar to the actual data warehouse, it is also necessary to populate each TISS-SW dimension. Copying each tuple of the DW dimensions that is pointed by the foreign keys of TISS-SW facts does this.

After each periodic load, the DW gets an additional set of data corresponding to the newly loaded data. The first TISS-SW stratum is then loaded with samples from this data that was just loaded into the DW. As a consequence of the new, most recent time subinterval that was inserted into this stratum, the equal sized eldest time subinterval of the same stratum expires and must be shifted (aged) to the next stratum. This process is repeated for the other strata in a cascading effect called aging. Each shift requires the data to be sampled to adjust from one SP to the SP of the following stratum. For instance, if stratum i and i+1 have SP=25% and 12.5% respectively, only 50% of the data to be shifted from stratum i is inserted into stratum i+1.

5   Evaluating the Efficiency and Accuracy of TISS

In this section, we present the results of an experimental evaluation of the TISS system, conducted on a Intel Pentium III 750 MHz CPU with 20 GB IDE hard disk and 256 MB of RAM, running Windows 2000 professional with an Oracle 8i (8.1.7) DBMS. Using data from TPC-H benchmark (scale factor 0.3=300MB) and typical queries that perform aggregations and joins, processing a large number of rows of the fact table and returning group results (e.g. queries Q1, Q5 or Q6) we show the effectiveness of a 3% TISS summary in providing speedup and highly accurate answers presenting comparisons with the actual correct answer and with a 3% uniform sampling summary (USS). Comparing both the actual error and the confidence intervals, which are the actual measure of the error that the user gets, assesses the accuracy.

5.1   Speedup of TISS

In this section we analyze the speedup of TISS to show that is advantageous to use the summary instead of the DW data whenever feasible. Table 3 shows the execution times. To obtain reliable results, each time value was computed as the average obtained in 10 runs and excluding the highest and lowest times. Additionally, the results come with a 90% confidence interval. The results show that TISS achieved a speedup between 11.38 and 29,80 for this query set and workload. Query Q5 takes much longer, because it involves a number of costly joins between distinct tables.

Table 3. TISS and DW query response time (in seconds) (TPC-H scale factor 0.3)

Scale Factor 0.3	DW Time	TISS Time	%Time Needed	X times Faster
Query 1	20.60 ± 0.07	0.69 ± 0.10	3.36%	29.80
Query 5	152.37 ± 0.28	13.39 ± 0.14	8.79%	11.38
Query 6	20.74 ± 0.16	0.70 ± 0.01	3.39%	29.47

The results show a significant speedup, even though the workload in the experiment is reasonably small. The expected speedup of a 3% summary could be about 1/0.03= 33.3 times if a multitude of factors and optimizations affecting the query processing in database engines is not taken into account.

5.2   Accuracy of TISS

In this section, we analyze the accuracy of TISS by comparing the errors observed in typical queries with those of the USS strategy. In this section, we analyze the accuracy of TISS. We compare the actual answer of running the query Qa on the full TPC-H database (DW) against the approximate answers obtained from TISS and USS. Qa computes aggregate quantities per brand and a defined time period (e.g. month), with an optional time constraint specifying time intervals (e.g. last two years),

```
SELECT    p_brand,to_char(l_shipdate,'yyyy-mm'), count(*),
avg(l_quantity), sum(l_quantity), max(l_quantity)
FROM      lineitem, part     WHERE  l_partkey=p_partkey
AND       to_char(l_shipdate,'yyyy')>= '1997'
GROUP BY p_brand, to_char(l_shipdate,'yyyy-mm')
```

Figure 1 compares the AVG (1a) and SUM (1b) estimation errors of TISS and USS using Qa aggregated per brand and month for the last two years. The results show that cumulative error distribution of SUM estimations is less accurate than the estimations of AVG, because SUM requires an estimator for the AVG and an extrapolation. TISS displays much better accuracy than USS for both AVG and SUM. For instance, we can see that 55% of the AVG answers returned by TISS have an error inferior to 5%, against only 36% of the answers of USS. Additionally, USS returns 25% of answers with error greater than 25%, whereas TISS returns only 9% of answers in that range.

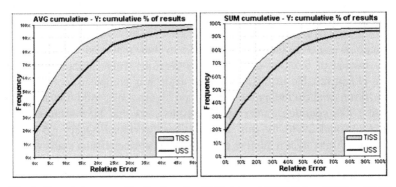

Fig. 1. Cumulative error distributions for AVG (a) and SUM (b) on TISS and USS

Table 4 compares the accuracy of TISS and USS using average aggregation errors over all groups. TISS is significantly better than USS for all time intervals within the last two years. Even though TISS decreases the sampling percentage as time ages, the accuracy is still much better than USS for all strata having higher sampling percentages than USS. Additionally, yearly aggregates (last column) highlight the fact that TISS results are almost as accurate as USS when more aggregated queries are posed against older strata, as expected. The results also show that SUM and COUNT present larger estimation errors than AVG or MAX, especially for USS. For instance, USS estimations of monthly brand SUMs over the last three months had an error of 63,8%, whereas the equivalent TISS estimations had a much smaller error (16,2%).

Table 4. Average group aggregation errors for distinct time intervals

Average Aggre- gate Error	Aggregate by month						Aggregate by Year	
	Last 3 months		Last 1 year		Last 2 years		All Years	
	TISS	USS	TISS	USS	TISS	USS	TISS	USS
AVG	9.2%	29.4%	8.7%	19.1%	10.8%	17.5%	5.6%	4.9%
SUM	16.2%	63.8%	19.1%	40.4%	22.0%	35.6%	12.7%	9.2%
MAX	4.5%	26.7%	3.8%	14.9%	5.1%	12.7%	1.0%	0.4%

Confidence intervals are very important, as they are the only information the user receives concerning the magnitude of the error. Figure 2 compares the AVG 90% confidence level for the Central Limit Theorem confidence intervals of TISS with those of USS using a cumulative distribution for the group results from query Qa aggregating per brand and month for the last two years. TISS intervals are much stricter than those of USS, as can be seen from the results. For instance, 90% of TISS confidence intervals for the SUM have a magnitude of less than 40% relative to the result, against only 25% of the answers of USS.

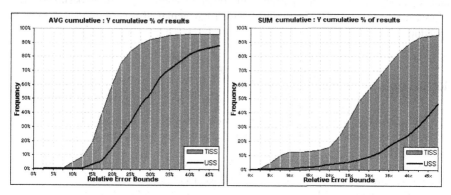

Fig. 2. Cumulative error bound distributions for AVG (a) and SUM (b) on TISS and USS

In Table 5 we show average values of the Central Limit Theorem confidence intervals over all the group results considering distinct time intervals, once more proving that TISS achieves very impressive results.

Table 5. Average group aggregation error bounds for distinct time intervals

Average Aggregate Bound Error	Aggregate by month					
	Last 3 months		Last 1 year		Last 2 years	
	TISS	USS	TISS	USS	TISS	USS
AVG	15.8%	39.1%	15.4%	32.4%	18.0%	30.8%
SUM	19.0%	62.4%	18.5%	45.3%	22.0%	41.8%
COUNT	20.5%	59.6%	19.8%	39.9%	22.4%	35.8%

6   Conclusions

This paper describes the time-interval stratified sampling (TISS) for fast, highly accurate approximate query answers. Traditional sampling summaries, though very fast and accurate when aggregating large data sets, are limited in accuracy of more detailed exploration steps. TISS explores the possibility to achieve more accurate estimations by biasing samples towards recency, allowing accurate focused analysis using well-represented recent data, without degrading estimations from older data significantly.

We develop formulas for the computation of approximate answers from the time-stratified samples. We describe the summary structure (TISS-SW), the query processing middle layer of TISS, and show how it processes user queries to return approximate answers together with confidence intervals derived from the stratified set of samples. We show how TISS-SW manages the summary warehouse lifecycle (loading and aging). We conduct experiments with the TPC-H benchmark to assess the speedup and accuracy of TISS, comparing with other strategies. These experiments have shown the relevance of the technique, which has achieved a very good accuracy and speedup.

References

1. Acharaya, Gibbons, Poosala. "Congressional Samples for Approximate Answering of Group-By Queries", ACM_SIGMOD Intl. Conference Management Data (Jun. 2000), 487-498
2. Acharaya, Gibbons, Poosala, Ramaswamy. "Join synopses for approximate query answering", ACM_SIGMOD Intl. Conference Management Data (Jun. 1999), 275-286
3. Barbara, DuMouchel, Faloutsos, Haas et al. Data Reduction Report. Bulletin of the TCDE (1997), 20(4): 3–45
4. Gibbons, Matias. New sampling-based summary statistics for improving approximate query answers. ACM SIGMOD Int. Conference on Management of Data (Jun1998), 331–342
5. P. J. Haas. Large-sample and deterministic confidence intervals for online aggregation. In Proc. 9th Int. Conference on Scientific and Statistical Database Management (Aug. 1997)

6. J.M. Hellerstein, P.J. Haas, and H.J. Wang. "Online aggregation", ACM SIGMOD Int. Conference on Management of Data (May 1997), 171-182

7. Yossi Matias, Jeffrey Scott Vitter, Wen-Chun Ni. Dynamic Generation of Discrete Random Variates. In Proc. 4th ACM-SIAM Symp. On Discrete Algorithms (Jan. 1993), 361-370,.

8. Yossi Matias, Jeffrey Scott Vitter, Neal E. Young. Approximate Data Structures with Applications. In Proc. 5th ACM-SIAM Symp. On Discrete Algorithms (Jan. 1994), 187-194

9. C.-E. Sarndal, B. Swensson, and J. Wretman. Model Assisted Survey Sampling. Springer-Verlag, New York (1992)

10. TPC Benchmark H, Transaction Processing Council (June 1999)

11. J.S. Vitter, Random sampling with a reservoir. ACM Transactions on Mathematical Software (1985) 11(1):37-57

Author Index

Lecture Notes in Computer Science

For information about Vols. 1–2358
please contact your bookseller or Springer-Verlag